WITHDRAWN

ILLINOIS CENTRAL COLLEGE
JN234 1980.B44
STACKS
The government of the United Kingdo

A12900 349478

JN
234   BELOFF
1980   The government of the United
.B44   Kingdom.

Illinois Central College
Learning Resources Center

The Government of The United Kingdom

COMPARATIVE MODERN GOVERNMENTS

General Editor: Max Beloff

Gladstone Professor of Government and Public Administration,
University of Oxford

Further Titles to Be Announced

The Government of The United Kingdom

POLITICAL AUTHORITY IN A CHANGING SOCIETY

MAX BELOFF

*Former Gladstone Professor of Government and
Public Administration in the University of Oxford*

GILLIAN PEELE

Fellow and Tutor in Politics, Lady Margaret Hall, Oxford

W · W · NORTON & COMPANY
NEW YORK · LONDON

I. C. C. LIBRARY   67237

W. W. Norton & Company, Inc., 500 Fifth Avenue, New York, N.Y. 10110
W. W. Norton & Company Ltd., 25 New Street Square, London EC4A 3NT

Copyright © 1980 by Max Beloff and Gillian Peele

Library of Congress Cataloging in Publication Data
Beloff, Max, 1913–
  The government of The United Kingdom.

  (Comparative modern governments series)
  Bibliography: p.
  Includes index.
  1. Great Britain—Politics and government—1964—
I. Peele, Gillian, 1949– joint author. II. Title.
JN234.1980.B44   320.441   80-12773
ISBN 0-393-01344-8
ISBN 0-393-95135-9 (pbk).

1 2 3 4 5 6 7 8 9 0

Contents

Acknowledgements

In the course of writing this book we have been helped and encouraged by many friends, colleagues and students. We particularly wish to thank Michael Attwell, Eric Barendt, Michael Beloff, Sandra Burman, David Butler, Mary Brown, Sheila Chaplin, David Cockroft, Andrew Durand, S.E. Finer, John Francis, Ruth Goldman, Robert Hoveman, Nevil Johnson, Catherine Jones, Ann Kennedy, Peter Mandelson, Geoffrey Marshall, Walter Merricks, Evan Luard, Leslie Pickering, John Pemberton, Michael Pinto-Duschinsky, Jane Ridley, Richard Rose, Roger Rosewell, Mary Skinner, Leslie Seidle, Lord Scarman, Gabrielle Stoy and Michael Wheeler-Booth.

Several organizations helped us by answering our queries and providing information about their work. In particular we should like to thank the Communist Party, the Conservative and Unionist Party, the Labour Party, the Liberal Party and the Scottish National Party. MIND and The Runnymede Trust also assisted our researches.

We thank Professor R.M. Jackson and the Cambridge University Press for permission to reproduce tables from *The Machinery of Justice in England*, and David Butler and Anne Sloman and The Macmillan Press, Ltd for permission to reproduce from *British Political Facts* the table of British general election results,.1900–79. We also gratefully acknowledge permission from the comptroller of Her Majesty's Stationery Office to reproduce a map.

Our thanks are due to the Librarians of All Souls College and Lady Margaret Hall, Oxford, and of the University College at Buckingham for their general assistance. A special debt of gratitude is owed to the staff of Nuffield College Library.

Mrs Margaret Croft skilfully prepared the index and Paula Iley showed exemplary patience in her editorial capacity.

THE UNITED KINGDOM OF
GREAT BRITAIN AND
NORTHERN IRELAND

Introduction

The aim of this book is to introduce the reader to the basic outlines of the United Kingdom's system of government and to
draw attention to some of the changes that have occurred in
the country's politics in recent years. The British system of
representative government has been accorded by students of
politics a significance which extends far beyond the relatively
small land-area known as the British Isles. Many of the basic
features of British constitutional practice were exported to
Commonwealth countries where they have been modified to
suit the political conditions of such societies as those of Australia,
Canada and New Zealand. The 'Westminster model' has therefore been as often studied as a prototype of other political systems as it has been examined in terms of its implications for the
conduct of British politics. The United Kingdom's governmental structure has also attracted interest because of the way
the system has combined historical continuity in the state – epi-
tomized in the institution of monarchy – with radical changes
in the basis of political authority. And in the refined set of
programmes designated after 1945 by the title of the 'welfare
state', the United Kingdom offered an early example of extensive governmental intervention in the field of social policy.

All these reasons for studying the government and politics
of the United Kingdom remain valid. However, the emphasis
of a book written at the end of the 1970s is bound to be very
different from one written, say, in the 1950s. The importance
of Britain's contribution towards the political development of
the old Commonwealth has been overshadowed both by the

failure of the 'Westminster model' to take root in much of Asia and Africa, and by the United Kingdom's increasing concern with her European associates. From a position where British practice could be confidently held up as a standard for other countries to follow, the United Kingdom has moved to a situation in which it is recognized that the practices of other countries with very different political traditions will affect British political behaviour. Complacency about the ability of British institutions to adapt to the demands of a mass democracy is bound to be more difficult after two decades which have seen the subjection of a range of British political institutions to critical, if inconclusive, scrutiny, and the growth of disillusionment in the electorate about the ability of British government in general (and the two major parties in particular) to cope with the variety and seriousness of the problems facing the country. Disillusionment and uncertainty have also affected the operations of the welfare state as the conflicting criteria in the various fields of social policy have become apparent, and as constraints on public expenditure have applied their own logic to a system whose fundamental values were always imprecisely articulated.

The past two decades of British political history can thus in some ways be seen as a period in which the United Kingdom's complacency about the adequacy of its political arrangements was undermined and in which there took place an erosion of the consensus about the scope of the state's activities and the appropriate administrative machinery for these activities. These decades were also significant because they saw other changes in British society – changes which have already begun to have political repercussions, although their full impact has undoubtedly not been felt as yet.

The first such change has been in the composition of British society. The United Kingdom had generally been considered a relatively homogeneous society. The late nineteenth and early twentieth centuries had seen a short-lived but concentrated degree of Jewish immigration into the United Kingdom; the special situation of Ireland has meant that there has been free movement of labour from Ireland into Britain, even after the major part of Ireland became a separate and independent state outside the Commonwealth in 1949. What distinguished the

2

1950s and 1960s was the influx of first West Indian, and then Asian, immigrants to the United Kingdom. The abandonment of the policy of free entry to Britain for Commonwealth citizens was the result of the political reaction to this immigration – immigration which was heavily concentrated in a few urban areas of the country. By the middle of 1977, when immigration other than that of dependents of immigrants already settled here had virtually ceased, it was apparent that the United Kingdom had acquired a substantial 'New Commonwealth' population distinguishable from the rest of society by colour, by culture and in some cases by language. Estimates as to their number varied, but the mid-year estimate of one reliable body reckoned that there were in 1977 some 1,771,000 residents of New Commonwealth or Pakistani origin – a figure which at the end of 1977 would have represented approximately 3.2% of the total population of 55,900,000.[1]

The highly visible transformation of some areas of the United Kingdom into multi-racial communities had a number of further consequences. Race became an issue in political debate and a factor in the electoral strategies of both major parties. Legislation establishing machinery to prevent discrimination and attempting to create racial harmony was passed, and was revised as circumstances seemed to warrant more drastic action. Local authorities and a variety of public agencies – who frequently discovered it necessary to provide information about their services in Hindi and Urdu – found themselves confronted with novel problems as the concentration of immigrants put pressures on such facilities as schools, health services and housing.

The second change which affected British political debate in the 1970s was the return of unemployment as part of the economic and social scene. Full employment had been the principal goal of Keynesian economic policy in the 1940s and 1950s; indeed, in 1951 only 0.2 million Britons were unemployed – a fact which in many respects stimulated mass immigration to the country from parts of the Commonwealth where employment prospects were less good. By the middle of 1971, however, that number had risen to 0.7 million and in the middle of 1977 it was 1.5 million.

In addition to unemployment, Britain, in common with

other industrial societies, experienced a high level of inflation. The result was increased trade-union militancy as some workers tried by means of industrial action to preserve or improve their standards of living while others reacted to the narrowing of differentials which was the result of policies embarked on by government in order to handle inflation. The trade-union movement had grown in size during the 1960s and 1970s, and from a figure of 9.5 million members in 1951 had expanded to well over 12 million in 1978. That growth was in large part attributable to the expansion of trade unionism among the so-called 'white-collar sector'; indeed, one of the most marked features of industrial relations over this period was the spread of direct action as a method of resolving disputes from the traditionally militant manual workers to what had previously been thought of as non-militant professional groups in such occupations as teaching and nursing.

The coincidence of high unemployment and a high rate of inflation which characterized the 1970s did more than diminish the electorate's faith in the competence of governments. It also suggested that the Keynesian economic analysis which had guided policy since the Second World War was itself inadequate. According to Keynesian doctrines, unemployment was the result of inadequate demand for the products of industry and could be countered by a policy of stimulating the economy through the injection of purchasing power by public expenditure finances through budget deficits. If the pressure on the economy was so high that prices began to move upwards, this inflation, it was thought, could in turn be checked by higher taxation and a consequent budget surplus. In other words Keynesian doctrine proclaimed that fiscal management alone would enable a government to iron out the fluctuations of the trade cycle.

Why this policy had suddenly failed to work was differently interpreted by different schools of economic thought. Monetarists held that inflation was the real enemy and itself a cause of unemployment, so that they advocated a strict control of the money supply through restraint on public expenditure and limits on the creation of the new money needed to finance it. Others believed that the Keynesian analysis had made insufficient allowance for the strength of trade-union pressure for rises in money incomes and placed their faith in incomes policies, whether using statutory or voluntary means. A third school of thought attributed some of Britain's problems in pursuing Keynesian policies to the country's general commitment to free trade and its particular commitment to the Common Market, and proposed a return to a highly protective system within which national economic planning could be pursued. Governments themselves seemed too weak to keep to any one line of policy, and indeed the erosion of a consensus among economists meant that the Treasury itself was deeply divided about the advice which it should give to ministers. The state of the economy had come to be regarded as being the determining factor in the electorate's verdict on a government but it was increasingly unclear how far either major party could be identified with a coherent economic strategy or to what extent the economy itself would be affected by political decisions.

If the economy and its management continued to provide politicians with major difficulties during the 1960s and 1970s, the situation in terms of living standards for the mass of the British population was undoubtedly brighter at the end of the 1970s than it had been in the 1950s. The real personal disposable income per head in 1951 was just over half what it was by 1975, although the figure had fallen slightly by 1978. The vast majority of British families in 1978 possessed a car, a washing machine and a refrigerator. Almost all households (96%) had a television set and over 50% had a telephone and/or central heating. Life expectations had risen dramatically for men and for women, who were now moving into the workforce in increasing numbers, and the educational opportunities available were significantly more numerous at the end of the 1970s than they had been at the beginning of the 1950s. In 1951 only 2% of the relevant age group were at a university; by 1977 the figure was 5.7%, and the numbers in all forms of higher education, including those who in other countries such as the United States would be reckoned as at university, had risen from 130,000 in 1951 to 524,000 in 1977.

By the late 1970s the United Kingdom had also become a more tolerant and liberal society than it had been previously. The laws affecting divorce, homosexuality and abortion had all been reformed in a direction more appropriate to a society where there was decreasing religious observance and only a limited moral consensus.

Yet the Britain which was by the end of the 1970s so obviously improved in terms of affluence and tolerance was also a society in which crime was more prevalent and violence a much more common aspect of the country's life. The prison population in 1951 had been 24,000; in 1977 it had more than doubled to 49,000. Indictable offences recorded by the police in England and Wales alone had increased five times from 550,000 in 1951 to 2,637,000 in 1977. And the number of people found guilty of violence against the person had increased almost ten times in England and Wales from 4,000 to 1951 to 39,000 in 1977. In one part of the country – Northern Ireland – law and order had so broken down by the 1970s that terrorism, sectarian murder and arson had become almost a part of daily life.

Thus if British society had obviously changed by the end of the 1970s the trends were by no means welcome in all respects and the politicians, like the electorate, seemed powerless to explain, much less to control, them. Opinion polls revealed scepticism about the problem-solving capacities of government – scepticism which went far deeper even than the already mentioned intractable problem of the economy. One typical poll taken at the beginning of 1977 revealed that 6% of the adults in Great Britain thought that the existing parties were capable of solving the economic and political problems facing Britain; 31% thought that they were 'quite capable' of solving them; 26% thought that the parties were 'not at all capable'; and a further 37% thought that they were 'not very capable' of doing so. Such political disenchantment was greatest among the 18–24-year-old age group, where only 31% thought the parties either quite or very capable of solving the country's problems and a full 69% pronounced them not very or not at all capable.[2] There was a similar lack of faith in the value of Parliament, with only 27% of a total sample surveyed in 1977 recording a belief that Parliament represented their personal interests either very well or quite well, as against 73% who thought that Parliament represented their interests not very or not at all well.[3]

The doubts expressed about the competence of Parliament also affected trust in the executive branch of government. There was in particular a strong reaction against the increasing centralization of the country; demands for a greater say in decision making at a regional level took on a nationalist flavour in Scotland and Wales, although how much this movement was the result of generalized economic and political dissatisfaction rather than localized claims was difficult to say. Certainly before the general election of 1979 some commentators believed that the unity of the United Kingdom was in danger, while others saw a greater threat to the power of national government from encroachments made upon it by supra-national institutions, especially the authorities of the European Communities.

The events of the early months of 1979 did something to limit wider speculation. After a winter of industrial unrest and referendums on devolution that showed only a half-hearted response to the idea in Scotland and considerable hostility to it in Wales, the minor parties joined together to vote with the Conservatives on a motion of no confidence in Mr Callaghan's Labour Government. The motion of no confidence was carried by one vote, and for the first time since 1924 an administration was effectively turned out of office by a vote of the House of Commons. The fact that the Government's defeat was due to a combination of minor parties voting against it had been anticipated by Mr Callaghan in the debate itself; never before, he suggested, had turkeys voted for an early Christmas.

The ensuing general election produced an overall Conservative majority of forty-three. But in many ways the election results kept open questions which they might have been expected to resolve. Thus although both the Scottish National Party and Plaid Cymru fell back, the Liberal share of the vote and the number of seats obtained by the Party were only marginally down on the peak 1974 figure. The two-party system, while it had recovered to some extent, had not unambiguously ousted third-party competitors. Moreover, the Conservative Party victory – achieved by a massive swing of 5.2 % – was built on two unexpected and disturbing developments. The first was a marked divergence between voting patterns in the north of England and the south. A line roughly drawn along the River Trent seemed in the eyes of many observers to divide the mainland into two nations. In the south, which registered heavy swings to the Conservatives, the predominant issues seemed to be those of taxation and industrial unrest. In the north, where the movement towards the Conservatives was much less marked, the primary issue of the election appeared to be unemployment, and fear of the loss of work took precedence over demands for tax cuts. The second feature which seemed to emerge from an early analysis of the election results was that the groups which had swung most heavily towards the Conservatives were not those naturally wedded to the Party. Skilled manual workers, trade unionists and new voters all appeared to have fuelled the Conservative revival. On one level this development might be taken to indicate that by 1979 the erosion of the ties between social stratification and partisan identification which was so commented on in respect to the late 1960s and 1970s had progressed even further. On another level it suggested that the basis of the Conservative vote was an unusual coalition of potentially volatile voters whose support might be withdrawn as swiftly as it had been given. The superficial reestablishment of a pattern of two-party politics could not therefore be taken as evidence that the rumblings beneath the surface of British politics in the 1970s could after 1979 safely be ignored.

It is against this background of uncertainty about the future of British institutions and policies that our discussions of some of the more familiar themes of British government should be set. We realize that at times our interpretation will be a controversial one, but we have tried to ensure that the suggestions about further reading for each chapter will be a guide to the range of opinions available on each topic. At the very least we hope that the reader will feel at the end of the book that the complexities of British government have been made a little more comprehensible, and that he will be able to identify some of the intriguing questions which confront the British citizen as much as the student of political science about the character of the United Kingdom's government in the 1980s.

1   The Constitution

The 1960s and 1970s saw political developments in the United
Kingdom which caused many of the traditional interpretations
of the country's system of government to seem in need of revision. Few developments as forcefully underlined the degree
of change which had come over the governmental structure as
did the reappearance upon the United Kingdom's political
agenda of fundamental constitutional issues. Some of the state's
most basic features – the traditional electoral and party systems,
role of Parliament and position of the House of Lords, and even
the unitary character of the constitution – have thus been called
into question in a way which is difficult to reconcile with the
normal assumption that in the United Kingdom change is
gradual and evolutionary rather than radical and abrupt. It
is important not to exaggerate the impact or extent of these
developments, because clearly there remains a substantial element of continuity in the system of government; but there is
now some justification for the belief that the United Kingdom
is witnessing a period of constitutional transition in which the
balance of the constitution is shifting and new institutional patterns are emerging. If it is still too early to assess the precise
extent of these changes, it is possible to identify the points in
the system which have produced tension and the constitutional
relationships which are under strain. The reader must then
judge for himself whether these tensions cumulatively confirm
our view that important aspects of the constitutional system
are in the process of transformation or whether in fact the
older structure will be able to integrate and accommodate

the changes of the last decade and a half into a harmonious whole.

One of the problems of discussing the British constitution arises from the difficulty of defining what is meant by the concept of a 'constitution' in a country where there is no readily available central constitutional text. Of course, even in countries where there is a constitutional text and perhaps a bill of rights as well as specialized constitutional courts – for example the Supreme Court of the United States or the German Federal Republic's *Bundesverfassungsgericht* – it will sometimes prove difficult to distinguish with perfect precision constitutional issues from ordinary political questions. In the United Kingdom, however, the absence of any basic constitutional document containing the ground rules of political life and the lack of any constitutional court or council to enforce them have produced a noticeable political vacuum when serious and fundamental disputes arise; these deficiencies have meant that the vocabulary of British political debate is not characterized by constitutional concepts and ideas with fairly firm and familiar meanings.

The absence of a distinct constitutional text and a body of constitutional rules with their own institutions to enforce them often in the past led observers to remark that the British had no constitution. Such a mistake, however, confuses the constitution with what is usually only one of its sources. Any constitution can be defined as the sum of those norms or values which prescribe the nature of relationships between the several institutions of authority in a state – for example between central and local government or between the executive and the legislature – and also between public authorities and the individual. In other words, a country's constitution is the whole body of rules which govern and shape the distribution of authority within the political system. The rules may be derived from a number of different sources – from a written constitutional text, from a declaration of independence, from statutes, from judicial decisions and from political habit or practice. What will vary from country to country will be the balance between those elements as sources for constitutional values and doctrines.

In the United Kingdom – and this is what makes the country's constitution appear amorphous – the least formal source of constitutional norms, political practice, has, at least until very recently, proved a particularly fertile source of constitutional values. Constitutional rules, values or norms derived from political habit or traditional ways of doing things are known as 'conventions' to distinguish them from constitutional rules derived from statutes or from judicial pronouncements. The courts could and did apply constitutional rules derived from formal legal sources; they would not apply conventions. Hence there was no legal sanction against a politician who deviated from a convention; indeed, the occasional deviation in the light of changing circumstances was generally thought to be desirable, and the flexibility which the British constitution therefore exhibited was counted by its supporters as one of its most admirable features. Thus, for example, as government became increasingly dependent upon political support in Parliament rather than upon royal favour, it became conventional for the monarch to choose as Prime Minister an individual whose ability to command that support was clearly demonstrable. In the twentieth century – with the extension of the franchise and the reduction in the power of the non-elective upper chamber, the House of Lords – it is by convention that the monarch chooses as Prime Minister the leader of the majority party in the House of Commons.

The importance of conventions in the British constitution should not, however, be allowed to obscure the fact that statutes and judicial pronouncements are also important sources of constitutional rules and values as in other constitutions. A number of the most basic questions of British institutional practice are now in fact governed by statute so that, for example, anyone who wishes to know what formal powers the House of Lords has in relation to the House of Commons must start by referring to the Parliament Acts of 1911 and 1949. It will be necessary thereafter to investigate what unwritten rules govern the use of those powers – in what circumstances, for instance, the Lords will in practice challenge a decision of the Commons – but the initial framework is now statutory.

Sometimes doubts about the force or meaning of a convention, or a deliberate political challenge to one, will result in legislation to settle the point. Thus although it had been assumed for many years prior to the Parliament Act of 1911 that the House of Lords should defer in matters of finance to the House of Commons, in 1909 the convention was challenged when the House of Lords threw out the Government's budget. That challenge in turn led to a political crisis and a statutory definition of the powers of the upper House. In the same way, there are occasions on which challenges to conventions may lead to court actions and judicial resolution of disputes. However, it should be borne in mind that in such cases the court will not be applying a convention as such but will perhaps be developing its own common-law rules to cover the issue. One such event occurred in 1975 when the convention governing the publication of ministerial memoirs and Cabinet documents was breached by the publishers of the diaries of a former Cabinet minister, Richard Crossman, and the High Court claimed the power to control such publications where necessary, although it did not in that case act to prevent publication.[1]

Judicial pronouncements and the rules of common law are of especial importance in the area of civil liberties. The absence of a comprehensive bill of rights defining the safeguards which the citizen may invoke against the state has meant that civil liberties such as freedom of speech and freedom of political association are dependent on statutes and judicial interpretation of them. The role of the courts in this area illustrates the traditional position of the judges in the British political system. In the seventeenth century it seemed possible at one point that common-law doctrines would be applied so that the judges could review or restrict parliamentary statutes which did not conform to their interpretation of 'right reason';[2] yet by the end of the eighteenth century the supremacy of parliamentary legislation and the absence of any power to review legislation were established and by the middle of the nineteenth century the doctrine of parliamentary sovereignty had become judicial orthodoxy.[3] Although, as will be seen throughout this book, there are now important reasons why the traditional doctrine of parliamentary supremacy needs to be subjected to scrutiny, the courts have in general been reluctant to articulate broad statements of individual rights which would be protected judicially in all circumstances. They have certainly shied away from pronouncements which would suggest any ambition on their part to develop a power to review legislation such as, for example, the US Supreme Court developed after 1803.[4] Even when individual judges have been at their most creative and innovatory in developing legal protection for citizens – as some have been in the past decade and a half – judicial intervention has usually been carefully justified by reference to the court's wish to give effect to the true purpose of a statute, or the judges have appealed to values which Parliament is assumed to share even if it has not explicitly acknowledged them in an individual statute. Ultimately, therefore, many of the judicial remedies and protections which the citizen is afforded at law are available only where Parliament has not explicitly limited them and where the attitudes prevailing among the judiciary encourage them to use their powers to defend the individual's interests.

The realization that civil liberties could not be fully guaranteed, combined with the legal uncertainty surrounding a large number of traditional areas, such as freedom of speech and political association, in the 1970s, led to a demand in some quarters for the incorporation into the British system of a formal declaration of individual rights.[5] The serious consideration afforded to the suggestion that the circumstances of British politics now required the introduction of a bill of rights to give formal protection to individuals and minorities against the majority is perhaps the most eloquent evidence of the extent to which the United Kingdom's traditional constitutional habits and values have altered in recent years. Formerly it would have been almost universally assumed that British citizens had no need of formal legal protection since there was sufficient general agreement about the principles which ought to limit state action. Previously a Parliament which enjoyed the support of the majority of the population and where government and opposition could expect to alternate in power had been regarded as a sufficient safeguard for democracy and liberty; devices such as bills of rights would, it was commonly assumed, only hand additional power to a non-elected judiciary and impede the ability of Parliament to make laws in the interests of society as a whole. Now, however, in the eyes of many commentators, the consensus of values in which all politicians acknowledge the existence of restraints upon their powers, and on which a large number of the constitutional rules depend, has broken down. The complex web of common attitudes and beliefs which enabled British democracy to work with very few formal statements of powers, rights and obligations no longer appears to bind either the political elite or the electorate at large.

The erosion of this implicit common understanding was reflected in an increased ideological tension between the two major parties. In part the sharpened doctrinal conflict at the national level of politics can be traced to the leftwards shift within the Labour Party, which quickened noticeably when Labour went into opposition in 1970. This movement of opinion within the Labour Party was paralleled by a growth in ideological divisions and factions within the Conservative Party, although the change was less marked than in the Labour ranks and the trade unions. The development of this heightened partisan tension was constitutionally significant because it revealed the extent to which many of the orthodox practices of British political life require an atmosphere of muted controversy for their successful operation. The stability which had for so long seemed a characteristic of the United Kingdom's political arrangements was in truth based on the fragile understanding between the two major parties that neither of them when in power would alter the country's most important political institutions or use the power of the state in ways which could not command the support of a cross-section of the population. The internal dynamics of the two major parties in the period after 1970 seems at the very least to have put that understanding in jeopardy and, some would argue, to have destroyed it altogether.

The two major parties are of course central to any account of the British constitution because in normal times they can expect to control the legislation which Parliament enacts and to set their style on the conduct of politics. Yet the 1970s have been distinguished by the trend among the British electorate to desert the two major parties, either by not voting at all or by supporting minor parties. This development culminated in February 1974 in a Parliament where no single party had an overall majority – a situation not greatly changed by the October election – and the normal verities of British parliamentary practice no longer applied. This unusual development in turn called into question how far the United Kingdom would return to its former electoral habits and how far parliamentarians would abandon new-found opportunities of influencing the outcome of legislation. Above all, the electorate's desertion of the two major parties suggested that the political homogeneity which had once buttressed the country's institutions had been replaced by a degree of social and political diversity which was not finding expression through the two-party system. In these circumstances it was quite possible that until the diverse elements were able to find adequate expression the whole constitutional order would lack legitimacy for a part of the population and that the country would experience governmental instability.

It is against this background of mounting concern about the continued efficient operation of the delicate and integrated mechanism of the constitution that the specific areas of constitutional tension in this period must be analysed. Six such areas of tension can be identified, but it must be remembered that changes in one ostensibly discrete area of the constitution can very easily have repercussions on the political system as a whole.

Parliamentary Sovereignty and the Challenge of Europe

The first and perhaps the most significant problem which has been created in Britain's constitutional arrangements arises from the success of Britain's application to join the European Communities. From 1972 when the United Kingdom signed the Treaty of Rome and related agreements and Parliament passed the European Communities Act incorporating the provisions of these Treaties into British law, Britain has been a full member of a community of nine nations pledged to an increasing amount of economic and political integration. The implications of British membership of the European Communities have not as yet been fully appreciated; some of them are further discussed in Chapter 13. But one aspect of British accession to the Communities is clear enough: the doctrine of parliamentary sovereignty, which has traditionally been seen as one of the distinguishing features of the United Kingdom's constitution, now stands in need of substantial modification.

The traditional doctrine of parliamentary sovereignty has normally been expressed in two propositions – first, that under the British constitution Parliament has the 'right to make or unmake any law whatever', as Dicey's definition put it; and secondly, that 'no person or body' will be recognized as 'having a right to override or set aside the legislation of Parliament'.[6] The proposition that Parliament may legislate as it pleases has generally been understood by British politicians and by British courts, if not always by British academics, to mean that no Parliament can bind its successors. A bill of rights, for example, while it might prevail against legislation in force at the time it was enacted, and while it might provide a fertile source of values to which politicians and judges alike could appeal in argument, could not offer much protection against subsequent legislation which either deliberately or inadvertently violated its provisions. Nor could it be guaranteed against direct repeal.

The obstacles to entrenching legislation in the British constitutional system – of giving particularly important laws special protection against repeal or amendment – seem difficult to overcome. Some authorities, it is true, argue that although Parliament cannot bind itself and its successors with regard to the substance of legislation, it can do so with respect to the manner and form of legislation. Thus, for example, Parliament could enact that in future all bills in the United Kingdom affecting the freedom of speech should be subject to a special procedure before they could be passed into law, such as approval by a two-thirds majority of the House of Commons or approval by referendum. Nevertheless, while Parliament – or either House – could choose to follow certain conventions in its treatment of important classes of bills, unless there is a radical change of attitude by the judiciary it is equally free to depart from those conventions at any time: the courts will not look beyond the bare fact of an Act's existence on the Parliament roll nor inquire into its legislative history to determine whether certain procedures have been followed.

There have been several attempts to challenge this aspect of the British constitution in the courts, but in general such assaults on the doctrine have proved unsuccessful. Even where a later Act has not explicitly repealed the provisions of an earlier piece of legislation, the courts have given effect to the later amendment: an Act of 1919 dealing with the provisions for compensation for property acquired by public authorities included the phrase 'so far as inconsistent with this act [other statutory] provisions shall not have effect', but it was held to have been superseded by an Act of 1925 which did make different provisions.[7] However, in the two Scottish cases – *MacCormick* v. *Lord Advocate* (1953) and *Gibson* v. *Lord Advocate* (1975) – the question of whether the Scottish courts would be bound to give effect to legislation which was in breach of the Treaty of Union of 1706 which united the English and Scottish Parliaments, was left open; indeed, in *MacCormick*'s case doubt was expressed by Lord Cooper on whether the doctrine of parliamentary supremacy really applied in Scotland: 'The principle of the unlimited sovereignty of Parliament', he said, 'is a distinctively English principle which has no counterpart in Scottish constitutional law.' Yet neither of the plaintiffs succeeded in their cases and most legal authorities think it unlikely that Scottish courts would, except perhaps in an extreme case such as an attempt to disestablish the Presbyterian Church or to abolish the Scottish legal system, strike down an Act of Parliament as incompatible with the Treaty of Union.[8]

The second proposition entailed in the doctrine of parliamentary sovereignty – that no body or person can set aside or override parliamentary legislation – does not imply merely that the courts cannot disregard or review legislation when it is not in conformity with their interpretation of the constitution. It also implies that they cannot invalidate an Act of Parliament when it is in conflict either with the general principles of international law or with some specific Treaty to which the United Kingdom is a party.

The change which occurred as a result of British entry into the European Communities was that as a condition of membership British courts must now give effect to legislation emanating from the Communities, and where there is a conflict between European legislation and parliamentary legislation European law has priority. The European Communities Act of 1972 defines the rules of statutory interpretation in such a case of conflict: where there is a dispute about the validity, effect or interpretation of the European Treaties or of secondary legislation made under them, the matter is to be treated by the British judges as a question of law. Such a conflict cannot therefore be avoided on the grounds that it is politically contentious or involves matters which are not justiciable. If this kind of conflict should reach the House of Lords there must – under article 177 of the Treaty of Rome – be a reference to the Court of Justice of the European Communities, which has the task of harmonizing law within the European Communities; such a reference for the European court's opinion may also be made if a lower court in the judicial hierarchy wants guidance in order to be able to resolve a legal dispute with a European element.

This development has a significance which Lord Denning, the Master of the Rolls, the senior appellate judge, recognized during a suit designed to prevent British entry into the Communities precisely because it would fetter parliamentary sovereignty. Although his remarks were not necessary for the decision and therefore not binding on other courts, Lord Denning said he believed that if Britain entered the European Communities the United Kingdom would be taking 'a step that is irreversible'. The sovereignty of these islands,' he declared, 'will thenceforth be limited.'[9] Certainly legal theory traditionally taught that one Parliament could not bind another; but this was now out of harmony with constitutional and political reality. Despite a later evaluation of the European Treaties as 'equal in force to any statute' rather than superior to them, Lord Denning has continued to draw attention to the significance of European law in limiting the autonomy of the British legal system.[10]

The limitations on parliamentary sovereignty which are implicit in the European Communities Act and the European Treaties to which that Act gives effect are of course only likely to be powerful sources of constitutional change if Britain remains in the Communities and if those Communities continue to operate decisively. If they were to lose their sense of common purpose then the demonstrable results of British membership would be few, although of course the theoretical significance would remain.

The Rule of Law and the Challenge of Violence

A second area where traditional constitutional premises came under attack in the period between 1964 and 1979 was that of the rule of law. This doctrine entails the linked ideas of equality before the law and procedural fairness. The desire to improve the mechanisms whereby substantive and procedural fairness can be applied to conflicts between public authorities and individuals has resulted in the establishment of a set of new institutions – a Parliamentary Commissioner, the Local Commissioners for Administration, a Health Service Commissioner and a Council on Tribunals – as well as a renewed determination by judges to develop and apply the fundamental principles of administrative law. Such improvements have given fuller meaning to the principle that the law, whether in statutory form or not, should apply with equal force to individuals, groups and public authorities. What has given cause for concern, however, has been the increase in the number of groups which have found the parliamentary process inadequate for their needs and resorted instead to direct action to achieve their ends.

The most obvious arena in which direct action and violence displaced orthodox political action was Northern Ireland. The reappearance of terrorism there after forty years of relative tranquillity was followed by an extension of the Irish Republican Army's bombing campaign to the mainland of the United Kingdom, which culminated in November 1974 in a series of explosions in Birmingham, where 21 people were killed and 162 injured. Admittedly this number was small compared with the figures in Ulster itself where 415 people had been killed between 1972 and 1975,[11] but it brought home to the British population the extent to which regular government had broken down in Northern Ireland, as well as the need for more effective security measures against internal terrorism. The immediate result of the Birmingham bombings was a Prevention of Terrorism (Temporary Provisions) Act which Parliament passed in its entirety within a week of the bombings and which it renewed in later years. This legislation made it a criminal offence to belong to the IRA or to aid its cause and strengthened the powers of the police in matters such as the length of time suspects could be held for questioning.

The terrorism of the IRA in the years after 1971 was complemented by a growing determination on the part of Ulster's Protestant population to resist policies which in their view undermined their hegemony in the Province and threatened its links with the rest of the United Kingdom. The suspension of Northern Ireland's system of devolved government in 1972 and the reintroduction of direct rule from Westminster was effected in the hope that such a move would increase respect for the law; by replacing Stormont, Ulster's regional Parliament, the British Government had hoped to remove a sectional Parliament which lacked legitimacy in the eyes of the Province's Roman Catholic population. Once the instruments of the Protestant domination of Northern Ireland had been destroyed the Government in London assumed that it could build a new governmental structure which this time would have the support of both the Roman Catholic and Protestant sections of the Ulster community. Unfortunately it has become increasingly obvious that Westminster's legislation lacks legitimacy for both the majority Protestant and the minority Catholic portions of the Ulster population. The complex constitutional solution of 1973 – which attempted to create political institutions in which power was shared between the two religious communities – could command no real support in Northern Ireland when it was brought into operation. That constitutional settlement was destroyed as a result of a fourteen-day general strike by the Protestant Ulster Workers' Council, which used its control of the power stations and other essential services to bring to a halt normal life in the Province.

The success of the Ulster Workers' Council strike illustrated Westminster's impotence in the face of powerful organizations which preferred the techniques of direct action and intimidation to the electoral process. It also demonstrated the difficulty of rebuilding support for constitutional values and democratic methods of resolving disputes in a situation where large sections of the population have accepted resort to direct action as legitimate. Perhaps it is not surprising that no political solution to the Northern Irish problem has emerged since 1974, although the experience of the ill-fated constitution of 1973 has made it likely that only arrangements which are the product of negotiations between the Ulster parties themselves will be tried again.

It could be argued that the violence and the erosion of the rule of law and its accompanying values in Northern Ireland reflected the peculiarities of the Irish problem and had no implications for British politics as a whole. Yet challenges to the rule of law were not confined to groups concerned with Northern Ireland; indeed, direct action appears to have become so much a feature of the country's way of life that it has almost ceased to cause concern or condemnation except where the level of violence is high – as in the series of clashes between rival political demonstrations which became a feature of British politics in the 1960s and 1970s – or where the police make tactical errors in their attempts to control such demonstrations themselves. Even the Young Liberals endorsed direct action at one point, as a method of preventing juggernauts from entering the United Kingdom and as a way of stopping South African sporting teams from touring the country.

The clearest example of a challenge to the principle of the rule of law occurred when the trade-union movement decided that it would use its strength to prevent the Industrial Relations Act of 1971 – which introduced comprehensive regulation of trade-union powers – from becoming effective. The trade unions' denial of the legitimacy of this piece of legislation appeared at times to amount to a general refusal to acknowledge Parliament's right to legislate in the field of industrial relations without first securing the consent of the unions themselves. Certainly the history of trade unionism in the United Kingdom has always been marked by a suspicion of the judiciary and the legal machinery; an attempt to introduce detailed legal regulation in an area which had hitherto been immune from legal intervention was bound to arouse trade-union opposition. What was remarkable, however, was the support which the trade unions' sabotage campaign received both inside and outside Parliament, and the way in which appeals to respect existing parliamentary legislation were overridden by claims that the unions were under no obligation to obey laws which conflicted with their view of their members' interests. Ultimately the trade unions won their battle by persuading the Labour Party to commit itself to repeal of the legislation; when a minority Labour Government replaced the Heath Government in 1974, a series of measures tailored to trade-union demands were quickly passed and the legislation of 1971 repealed.

The Industrial Relations Act of 1971 was not the first attempt by a government to change the framework of industrial relations in the United Kingdom. In 1969 the Labour Government attempted to introduce legislation to regulate industrial disputes, but such was the reaction to those proposals that a Cabinet commitment to legislation had to be withdrawn. The Conservatives' difficulties with the unions between 1970 and 1974 were compounded by the fact that while they were seeking to implement legislation introducing new machinery to settle industrial disputes they were also trying to secure trade-union cooperation for their incomes policy. These two issues undoubtedly dominated the relationship between the Government and the unions from 1970 to 1974, but other features of industrial relations, especially at shop-floor level, were also of constitutional significance. It became increasingly apparent after the miners' strike of 1972 that violence and intimidation might arise from an industrial dispute and that traditional assumptions about picketing needed to be re-examined.

The increase in the amount of violence occasioned during strikes was influenced by two developments which seriously worried many trade-union leaders as well as the police. The first was the cultivation of a technique of mass picketing whereby large numbers of people – many of them unnecessary to the task of persuading workers to strike – would stand outside a factory to demonstrate solidarity with the strikers. The second was the exploitation of industrial disputes by extremist organizations such as the (Trotskyist) Workers' Revolutionary Party.[12] With these developments it was hardly surprising that confrontations with the police should occur and that arrests and criminal charges arising out of industrial disputes should become more frequent. Yet such was the hostility towards the apparatus of the law in some sections of the trade-union movement that even clear examples of intimidation and violence towards fellow workers were not condemned. One such case occurred at Shrewsbury where the convicted pickets were regarded as martyrs because their assaults on fellow workers earned them prison sentences.

The general confusion about what the role of law should be in the field of industrial relations and the successful resistance to parliamentary legislation by the trade unions undoubtedly contributed to the decline in respect for both the courts and the authority of the Government. But it also highlighted the failure of British constitutional practice to accommodate the corporate strength of the unions. The decision to call a general election in February 1974 posed the question, 'Who rules the country – the unions or the Government?' in stark terms. But, as the electorate's indecisive response revealed, the question was infinitely easier to ask than to answer. Certainly there is a conflict between the authority derived from the democratic process and the electoral system, and power which comes from the simple ability to interrupt essential services. Yet as governments rely more and more on the trade unions to frame and execute their policies in such areas as those covered by the Manpower Services Commission and the Health and Safety Commission (see Chapter 3), and as society becomes increasingly composed of large numbers of organized groups, each with their own claims to influence the machinery of the state, individualistic assumptions which run through such doctrines as the rule of law seem harder and harder to fit with the facts of life. The peculiar importance attached to the trade-union movement in this period and the attempt to associate it, as well as the management side of industry through the Confederation of British Industry, with the policy-making process led some observers to attach the label 'corporatism' to the politics of the United Kingdom. Such a label seems somewhat out of place given the (proven) inability of governments to control the groups concerned and indeed of groups to control their own members, but that it should have been applied at all indicates the degree to which British politics and government have ceased to fit a model in which authority is ultimately dependent on parliamentary elections, and in which society is assumed to consist of a number of individuals of equal legal status.

The Unitary State and the Challenge of Nationalism

The third major constitutional challenge of the 1970s arose from the growth in electoral support for the Scottish National Party and, to a lesser extent, for Plaid Cymru in Wales. By-elections during the 1966–70 period had indicated a degree of support for these parties which was unusual given the normal domination of Scotland by the two main parties and of Wales by the Labour Party. The establishment of a Royal Commission on the Constitution in 1969 was a response to these develop-ments; it reflected the extent to which dissatisfaction with the operation of British political institutions had increased in the 1960s. Given the amorphous nature of the constitution, it was not entirely surprising that the Royal Commission did not reach unanimity about the scope of its inquiry; its report in 1973 was overtaken by the results of the general elections of 1974, which gave the Scottish National Party and Plaid Cymru sufficient parliamentary seats to persuade the Government that new arrangements had to be devised for the government of Scotland and Wales.

The proposals for devolution contained in the Scotland Act of 1978 and the Wales Act of 1978 represented a fundamental questioning of the arrangements for governing the United Kingdom, and a recognition that the country as a whole con-tained distinct geographic and national areas which needed separate political treatment. Indeed in some respects the Acts, if implemented, would have transformed the United Kingdom into a quasi-federal state: the law-making powers which West-minster had exercised on all subjects for Scotland would have been replaced by a system in which power was shared between an Assembly in Edinburgh and Parliament at Westminster, and the question of where powers might constitutionally be exer-cised would have been determined by a neutral body – the Judicial Committee of the Privy Council – and not by the superior legislature. Where the proposed system would have differed from a wholly federal one would have been in the absence of any uniform pattern in the division of powers between the component parts of the United Kingdom. Unlike the situation in the United States for example, where certain powers are exercised by the federal government and others by the states individually, the United Kingdom after devolution would have had a different distribution of powers in Scotland – where the Assembly would have been able to legislate directly – from that in Wales, where the Assembly would have had power to make only secondary legislation within the broad framework of policies established at Westminster. Northern Ireland would have been different again: the Province enjoyed substantial legislative autonomy between 1921 and 1972 on the lines envisaged for Scotland in the Devolution Act, but the use of that autonomy in the interests of the Protestant section of Ulster's population resulted, as has been seen, in the abrogation of the system. England would presumably have continued to be governed as before from Westminster, as Northern Ireland would have been while direct rule remained.

The other major difference between the Government's devolution proposals and a federal system lay in the financial arrangements between the several parts of the United Kingdom. The devolved units were not to have their own taxing powers or to be able to determine the overall expenditure on services within their areas. Together with the inequalities of powers between the several parts of the United Kingdom this failure to devolve financial control would have created a degree of instability in the proposed arrangements which would have meant that all British constitutional arrangements would have been called into question for some years to come.

However, the Scotland Act of 1978 and the Wales Act of 1978 were not to become operative unless they had been confirmed by a referendum in each area, and in neither country was the necessary majority obtained. The use of the referendum on the question of devolution confirmed suspicions that its earlier use in 1975 to determine whether the United Kingdom should remain a member of the European Communities had not been a once-for-all event. The need for that referendum then arose because of the Labour Party's internal divisions over the issue. These divisions could not be overcome by the normal convention of Cabinet government whereby minorities simply have to abide by the decision of the majority or resign. The issue cut too deeply into the Labour Party for such a settlement to be possible, and so it was decided to transfer responsibility for the decision directly to the voters. However, the experiment has constitutional implications of a serious nature; it is significant that not merely did the Labour Government use it over two issues but the Conservative leader announced her interest in the device for use on a much wider range of issues, including industrial relations.

The Referendum and the Challenge to Parliamentary Government

The most serious attempt to introduce a national referendum in an earlier period of British history was that made by the Conservative Opposition during the interlocking crises over the powers of the House of Lords and the issue of Home Rule for Ireland in 1910. It had been suggested that a Home Rule Bill which had twice been rejected by the House of Lords should be put to the electorate for its verdict. However, the proposal found no favour with the Liberal Government of the day, which preferred to reach its goal by restricting the powers of the upper House. Nor did the proposal for a referendum on protection, which was frequently mooted between 1906 and 1931, meet with much approval among parliamentary leaders.

The circumstances of the 1975 referendum were very different. Although an unsuccessful attempt had been made by the previous Labour Government to gain admission to the European Communities – following an earlier unsuccessful application by Harold Macmillan's Government in 1961 – a Treaty of Accession by which Britain joined the Communities was secured by Edward Heath's Government. A bill to incorporate its provisions into British law was passed in 1972, although on its second reading it was approved by 309 votes to 301, a reduction in the Government's normal majority which reflected the internal divisions in all parties on the question. In the Parliamentary Labour Party, however, there was by then a majority opposed to British membership, although at its highest levels there were some passionate pro-Europeans.

The divisions over Europe within the Labour ranks made it difficult to devise a common policy for the election manifesto of February 1974, but Labour eventually fought the election on a policy of re-negotiating the terms of entry and of offering the British public a clear choice on the principle of membership.

It was not entirely clear from the Labour manifesto whether this choice was to be exercised in the traditional manner or whether a referendum would be held. Whatever the success of the re-negotiation, however, it became evident that a Labour Government would be divided, so that the option of a referendum became all the more appealing. Thus the referendum was not merely a device to allow the normal rules of cabinet responsibility to be suspended but also an aid in the immediate problem of party management; it was, as James Callaghan is reported to have remarked in the Shadow Cabinet, a 'rubber dinghy' into which all the senior Labour figures could climb to survive the rough seas of Labour's internal politics.[13]

Similar considerations of party unity caused the referendum provisions to be written into the devolution legislation. The Government was not entirely in control of the devolution bills as they proceeded through Parliament, because it did not have an overall majority in the House of Commons. Back-bench amendments accounted for a provision that at least 40% of the electorate of each country – and not a simple majority of those voting – had to vote 'yes' for the provisions of the devolution Acts to become operative. While this provision made the task of the pro-devolutionists more difficult, it did not resolve the status of such referendums. Moreover there was no provision for any referendum to be held in England, even though it could be argued that any movement towards federalizing the United Kingdom would have as much of an impact on England as on Scotland and Wales.

Although it seems that referendums are well on the way to becoming an accepted part of the constitution, no clear rules governing their operation have had time to develop. No referendum is possible without the passage of legislation through Parliament so it could be said that to that extent the introduction of the referendum is not detracting from parliamentary government. On the other hand, referendums on major constitutional issues are a way of bypassing Parliament as much as of overcoming internal party difficulties; they could very easily lead to a conflict between the authority of the people expressed in the referendum choice and the authority of the people's representatives in the House of Commons.

The constitutional impact of the referendum on Europe

would have been much greater had the vote gone against membership of the Communities. The Government would then in theory have been committed to introducing legislation to take the United Kingdom out of the Communities; ministers who deplored such a course could have resigned, but individual MPs might have felt bound to follow the referendum verdict rather than their own consciences. The traditional Burkean theory has been that MPs exercise their own judgement on issues and are not delegates either of their electors or their constituency parties. This theory has already begun to wear a little thin in the Labour Party where the doctrine of the mandate – which binds Labour MPs to proposals contained in the party manifesto – plays a much larger role than in other parties; it is unclear how it could survive a change in the constitution to allow frequent use of the referendum.

The possibility of a clash between individual MPs' preferences and the verdict of their constituents makes the arrangements for counting a referendum vote a somewhat sensitive subject. In the European referendum it was suggested that because a simple 'yes' or 'no' vote was required the whole country should be treated as a single constituency. Such a course would have met the objection to counting by parliamentary constituencies, that individual MPs who knew the way their constituents voted could suffer reprisals if they thereafter defied their wishes in a parliamentary vote. On the other hand, the coincidence of the European issue with the pressure for devolution made Scottish and Welsh nationalists anxious to have a form of voting which would enable differences in sentiment between the component parts of the country to emerge. The ultimate decision was a compromise which allowed the votes to be counted on the basis of units of local administration, the counties, thereby concealing in all but two cases the views of individual parliamentary constituencies while revealing geographic divisions. As it happened there was noticeable conformity both between the component parts of the United Kingdom and among the English regions; though Scotland, Wales and Northern Ireland were rather less enthusiastic than England about membership.

One final constitutional implication of the referendum device is that its introduction may have provided the United Kingdom

Table 1
*The Results of the 1975 European Referendum: Turnout and 'Yes' Vote
by Area*

	Turnout	'Yes' Vote
England	64.6%	68.7%
Scotland	61.7%	58.4%
Wales	66.7%	64.8%
Northern Ireland	47.4%	52.1%

with a political way of entrenching legislation. A government
which has persuaded the electorate to support a measure at a
referendum in addition to persuading Parliament to accept it
may feel that an incoming government of a different political
colour would hesitate to repeal the Act without at least putting
it to the population again.

The Cabinet and the Challenge of Open Government

The introduction of the referendum device into British constitutional practice was one sign of the strains to which the
orthodox theory of Cabinet government was being submitted
in the 1970s. There were, however, other indications during
this period that the norms governing the behaviour of the
Cabinet had altered to accommodate the distinctive features
of Labour government.

The classic doctrine of collective responsibility which lies at
the heart of the British understanding of Cabinet government
can be interpreted in a variety of ways. In essence, however,
it means that once a majority has decided an issue in Cabinet
those in the minority must accept that decision and indeed
defend it as the decision of the Cabinet as a whole if necessary.
In theory, whatever the internal divisions of the Cabinet, its
members should both be reticent to reveal disagreements and
contribute to the impression of Cabinet unity given to Parliament and the electorate.

Between 1945 and 1964, however, it became increasingly
common to find the supporters of a minority position inside the
Cabinet identified in the press. Sometimes this was the result

of a so-called 'unattributable leak' to the press; sometimes it was sheer guesswork on the part of journalists who knew an individual Cabinet minister's likely position on an issue. But after Labour returned to power in 1964 the number and extent of these leaks increased; the press was able to draw conclusions about disunity within the Cabinet from the participation by some Cabinet ministers in extra-parliamentary Labour Party activities even where the tone of those activities was distinctly hostile to the Labour Government.

As long as the relationship between the Labour leadership in Parliament and the extra-parliamentary Party remained a broadly harmonious one and the instances of disagreement within the Cabinet relatively trivial, this trend towards a more open style of Cabinet government did not perhaps matter unduly. In the latter years of the Wilson Government of 1966–70, however, harmony was replaced by acute conflict as the Labour Government wrestled with economic problems and attempted to reform the conduct of industrial relations. In those circumstances it was perhaps natural that critics of government policy within the Cabinet should publicize their opposition to measures unpopular with the Party outside Parliament and use any positions they held on the National Executive Committee – the controlling organ of the Party in the country between the annual Conferences – to dissociate themselves from the Cabinet position.

Harold Wilson has commented on the difficulty of managing a Cabinet in which some members also held office in the NEC and consequently had a dual loyalty. Constant reminders were necessary that Cabinet ministers should not become too closely identified with National Executive Committee policies and in 1969 – the time of heightened tension over the Government's *In Place of Strife* proposals for regulating the trade unions – a formal statement about the meaning of collective responsibility was actually read to the Cabinet.[14] Again in 1974 when there was disagreement between the NEC and the Labour Cabinet over aspects of foreign policy, the Prime Minister had to write to three Cabinet ministers who had expressed disagreement with government policy to warn them that they were bound by the doctrine. Finally in 1976 Harold Wilson had to introduce a rule that no minister who was chairman of an NEC subcommittee could undertake press briefings on its behalf if it meant announcing policies which in any way deviated from those of the Government.

The referendum on British membership of the European Communities necessitated the temporary suspension of the rules of collective responsibility so that cabinet members opposed to membership could campaign for a 'no' vote, although the official government position was to recommend the public to vote 'yes'. The justification for this decision was that normal constitutional conventions could not apply in such unusual circumstances. Yet the expectation that life would return to normal once the referendum had been held turned out to be false: the patterns of political behaviour which had been developing throughout the 1960s and 1970s proved hard to break, and there were several well publicized incidents of cabinet disharmony both on European issues – such as direct elections to the European Assembly – and on economic policy. The Government's decision to adopt a formal pact with the Liberal Party in April 1977 in order to maintain a parliamentary majority was also criticized from within the Cabinet and the resultant divisions made public.

The need to relax the conventions of collective responsibility to accommodate anti-European sentiment within the Cabinet, and the pressures from the left within the Labour Party on economic strategy, arose because of the character of the Labour Party itself. It is a party with strong ideological divisions and factions which must be balanced inside the Cabinet; it is also a party with a strong tradition of internal democracy. Inevitably, therefore, the management of a Labour Cabinet will prove more difficult than the management of a Conservative one; in addition defeated factions will take advantage of the Party's power structure to redress their defeat at other levels of the Party. When Labour first became a party of government it was anxious to obtain constitutional respectability, and therefore the norms of Cabinet government were an effective brake on party faction. Now, however, its own internal structure has begun to alter the values and norms of Cabinet government to accommodate the Party's heterogeneity. At one level that change is reflected in the adoption by Labour Cabinets of procedural and formal rules, such as those governing when matters settled in committee may be reopened in full Cabinet; at another level it is reflected in a much greater degree of openness and tolerance of dissent than Conservative Cabinets have hitherto permitted.

The trend towards a more flexible interpretation of the doctrine of collective responsibility may thus be stemmed when there are Conservative Cabinets, and indeed Mrs Thatcher indicated at an early stage of her administration that there would be little room within her Cabinet for prolonged debate or disharmony. On the other hand, the movement towards greater openness to the press and public in government generally may prove difficult to reverse.

Parliament and the Challenge of Minority Government

The pressures which the internal dynamics of the Labour Party placed upon the traditional practice of Cabinet government may thus have accelerated the progress of British government towards a more open and less secretive manner of conducting its affairs. Open government and fuller information about the processes of decision making were also advanced by the doubts and ambiguities surrounding the role of Parliament in the system. The major themes of debate have been the adequacy of Parliament as a legislative body and the maximum possible effectiveness of its techniques of administrative scrutiny.

In the 1960s doubts were cast on the relevance of the House of Commons' contribution to scrutinizing government as well as on its legislative efficiency. Such scepticism led to a series of experiments with the procedures of the House, most notably the expansion of select committee activity. This remedy for the alleged weaknesses of Parliament was devised on the assumption that what made Parliament ineffectual and purposeless as a body was that through party discipline the Government was able to exert a considerable degree of control over its proceedings. If, it was argued, select committees could become a useful forum of activity in their own right, and if party factors could play a reduced role there, the individual back-bench MP might again be able to make a contribution to policy and to legislation. As will be seen, however, the select-committee experiment has in many ways also been obstructed by party factors, and the whole parliamentary reform movement has lost direction.

What is constitutionally significant about the parliamentary reform experiments, however, is that as a result of select-committee assertiveness after 1966 many of the conventions restricting parliamentary questioning of civil servants on policy matters were eased. The general fiction of ministerial responsibility, which had erected a barrier between MPs and the internal decision-making processes of central-government departments, was also modified to allow greater appreciation of the advice which civil servants give to ministers and of the grounds on which civil servants themselves take action. Of particular importance here has been the work of the Parliamentary Commissioner for Administration, whose creation symbolized Parliament's recognition that it could no longer scrutinize the complex workings of government without the aid of a specialized staff. The result is that much more is now known about who is really responsible for particular decisions; also, Parliament can acquire much more information about the operations of an individual department. The constitutional problem raised is that once officials are exposed to public and parliamentary examination some of the assumptions about an apolitical civil service equally acceptable to governments of all parties will have to be modified: the more that is known about civil servants' views and contributions to a debate the harder it becomes to assume their neutrality.

The years between the February 1974 general election and May 1979 were highly unusual as far as the organization of Parliament was concerned. The steep rise in the Liberal Party vote, the defection of the Ulster Unionists from the Conservative Party with which they had long been associated, and the growth of support for nationalist parties in Scotland and Wales contributed to the rise in the number of minor parties represented in the House of Commons. In fact from February to October in 1974 the Government had no overall majority, and although the general election of October gave the Labour Party an overall majority of three, by-election defeats soon destroyed that majority. The combination of uncertain government majorities and a large number of minor-party representatives meant that for the duration of those Parliaments the Government was unsure of being able to pass legislation through the House. Thus not only did we see a Government lose a second-reading debate – the stage at which the principles of a bill are endorsed by Parliament – for the first time since the Second World War; there have also been major amendments of government legislation on a number of issues, including devolution.

The absence of an overall majority led the Labour Government in 1977 to negotiate formal arrangements with the Liberal Party – a development which, although short-lived, gave the United Kingdom a taste of the style of coalition bargaining which might be expected if electoral reform wére ever introduced. But setting aside the concrete experience of the Lib–Lab pact and the substantive amendments to legislation which Parliament was able to achieve between 1974 and 1979, the key question of constitutional significance remains to be answered: what will the impact of those years be on legislators' attitudes and the amenability of MPs to party discipline? Various studies have documented a slight tendency for dissent to grow within the major parliamentary parties since 1970, although of course by comparison with the individualism of American legislative parties British parties are extremely cohesive. There is the distinct possibility that MPs, having experienced a modest increase in their influence over the Government, will be less than enthusiastic about returning to the role of 'lobby fodder'.[15]

Dissatisfaction with Parliament's role as a legislative body and as a check on government was supplemented in the period after 1974 by a pronounced growth in the movement for electoral reform.

It was perhaps natural that the results of the two general elections of 1974 should focus attention on the British electoral system with its simple formula – the first-past-the-post principle – of distributing seats. For from the point of view of the smaller parties, and especially the Liberals, the system is unfair: they achieve a very much smaller proportion of parliamentary seats than the share of the total vote appears to entitle them to. A change to some form of proportional representation, it could be argued, would produce a more just system of representation and a House of Commons which more accurately reflected public opinion.

The criticisms levelled against the 'rough justice' of the British electoral system were in many respects familiar because the case for electoral reform had been part of the Liberals' platform for many years. What was novel in the situation after 1974 was that the electoral system in the eyes of many commentators became identified as the single most important cause of a wide range of political weaknesses in Britain, especially the structure of party competition. From a limited case for improving the mechanics of representation, the argument for electoral reform was extended into a comprehensive critique of the British style of politics. This argument linked the electoral system to what was dubbed the 'adversary' style of politics; it traced the cause of the discontinuities of British policy and the growth of electoral apathy to the current nature of the two major parties.[16]

The Labour and Conservative Parties each felt obliged when in opposition to attack the policies of the Government, whatever their merits. In developing alternative policies the opposition would be guided by party activists whose perceptions reflected neither electoral opinion as a whole nor the reality of the problems with which they were confronted. The policies framed by a party in opposition would be included in its general-election manifesto and in the event of a return to power the party would seek to implement them. Reality and moderation might, however, intervene at this stage and the policies might be adjusted to accommodate the experience of government. Indeed frequently the new governing party would find itself being pushed by events towards the policies of the former Government which it had attacked while in opposition. Yet by this stage the former government party, now in opposition, would have begun its own process of policy reappraisal and would certainly want to differentiate itself from the Government. Consequently its policies in opposition would be likely to produce further disruption if it were again returned to power.

On this analysis the party system, and particularly the proclivity of incoming governments to reverse the work of their predecessors, created a climate of instability in which investors and citizens alike could have no faith in the future. Electoral

35

reform, it was argued, by broadening the political contest and making coalitions more likely, would break the syndrome of two-party alternation and create the conditions for a political system in which all parties could search for agreed solutions to problems.

The importance of this argument was not that it found favour inside the major parties themselves, for it manifestly did not. Its constitutional significance was that it reflected a changing attitude to British politics and an erosion of the United Kingdom's constitutional complacency. A generation ago most observers would have identified the electoral and the two-party systems as important contributors to an ordered structure of Cabinet government, stable representative democracy and policies which harmonized with the moderation of the electorate. Now for many observers – though not of course for all – the electoral and party systems are the joint villains in a scenario of increasingly extremist policies, economic decline and electoral alienation.

The difficulty of predicting the impact of this questioning is that as long as the two major parties conceive the present system to be in their common interest, it is unlikely that there will be any concessions made to the electoral reformers' case. In the short term therefore no outward change seems likely. The long-term development of the British constitution, however, will to a large extent depend on the assessment of why British political parties – which are fundamental to the workings of British government – no longer contribute towards consensus and stability. It may be that a more heterogeneous society will inevitably have its cultural, ethnic and political values reflected in the parties themselves and that therefore the parties can no longer contribute to the stability and moderation of the system in the way that they were once alleged to do. On the other hand it could be that the parties themselves no longer adequately represent the society which it is their function to link to the formal institutions of government, in which case government at the national level could become dangerously divorced from the mass of the British population. The latter interpretation would mean that ways of altering the party system and opening it up to public participation would have to be found if alienation were not to be a permanent feature of British government.

The former analysis, however, would suggest that the comfortable model of stable government operating on the basis of consensus must be abandoned finally, and that political scientists and citizens alike must accustom themselves to a United Kingdom in which there are fundamental and continuing divisions over the goals of public policy and over the institutions responsible for reaching them.

2 The Functions of Government in the British Welfare State

The pattern of a country's political institutions will in large part reflect the functions which that society expects government to perform. Inevitably, the range and character of those functions will change from one generation to another as new problems are identified or as existing problems come to be seen as suitable subjects for governmental treatment. The flexible nature of Britain's constitutional and administrative arrangements makes it possible for government to intervene swiftly when an emergency occurs and to respond to new demands in the manner which seems most convenient at the time. In some cases additional governmental responsibilities will be tackled by creating new agencies to deal with them; in other cases it will seem more appropriate to expand existing institutions. The continual re-definition of the tasks of government means that the structure of central departments and the allocation of responsibilities between them has proved extremely fluid and the description of the United Kingdom's executive arrangements is correspondingly difficult. The description that follows is essentially that of the position before the change of government in 1979.

The changes which one might expect in any governmental structure as a result of social developments have been multiplied in recent decades in the United Kingdom by a preoccupation on the part of successive governments with reorganizing the distribution of responsibilities within the political system. This perpetual mutation – which has affected local authorities and regional administrative agencies as well as central departments – has been inspired by no clear principles, so that there is frequently no yardstick against which to measure the success of any changes.

At the same time ingrained administrative habits can prove resistant to permanent change. Although both world wars left permanent legacies to the structure of government, the striking thing was the degree to which, after the emergency was over, the former administrative patterns reasserted themselves. By the end of 1922 Britain was governed very much as she had been in 1914; by 1950 the differences from the position in 1939 were fewer than the similarities. It is therefore more accurate to regard wartime experience as a catalyst of existing trends than as the main source of innovation in governmental practice. It is difficult to believe that some kind of Cabinet secretariat would not have evolved sooner or later as government's responsibilities became more varied and as the informality of the pre-1914 Cabinet proceedings became less and less appropriate. Nor could government for long have avoided assuming some responsibility for the development of applied science and technology along the lines indicated by the establishment of the Committee of Council (the Privy Council) for Scientific and Industrial Research in 1915 and of the new Department of Scientific and Industrial Research in the following year.

The dismantling of economic controls after both world wars also reminds one that the line of development has never been a straightforward one from less government to greater intervention, or from an individualist and *laissez-faire* approach to some kind of collectivism. Such aspects of modern government as intervention in the economy and public provision for the relief of poverty are not innovations of the present century. While it is true that the structure of British government today is in many respects a very different thing from that presided over by Gladstone or Disraeli, it reproduces in some sectors the attitudes of an earlier age.

The novel elements in the welfare state are to be found in its methods rather than its objectives. Improvements in communications have made possible a degree of centralization impossible to contemplate in earlier periods; what previously had to be done locally can now be performed by central government.

Even those services which are still administered on a local basis are largely – and even increasingly – centrally inspired, directed and financed.

Uneven historical development and the preference of politicians for improvisation make it impossible to set out in any logical order the wide variety of functions performed by British government in the 1970s apart from its classic responsibilities for national defence, law and order, and the administration of justice. An additional difficulty in describing the British administrative structure is that while some functions are the responsibility of the central departments, others have been allocated to the Scottish, Welsh and Northern Ireland Offices. For the purposes of the present chapter, England's administrative arrangements will be taken as the norm.

Before proceeding to describe the way in which functions are distributed between the various agencies of government, one must remind oneself of the huge scale of governmental operations. According to some reckonings, the public sector of the economy accounted by the mid-1970s for more than a tenth of the national product and nearly a fifth of total fixed investment. Some estimates would put the share of government in spending at about 60% of GNP as against about 45% in the mid-1950s. Much of the growth of the civil bureaucracy is recent. The number of non-industrial civil servants in departments other than the Post Office increased from about 250,000 in the late 1950s to about 434,000 in 1976. By this time there were about five million people directly employed by central or local government and about another two million in the nationalized industries.

One reason for this growth is that once a government assumes a particular function it rarely abandons it, although it may change the agency through which it acts. For example, the Post Office was one of the oldest government departments: the first Postmaster General was appointed in 1667. The Post Office, which has been a public corporation since 1969, now deals with both mail and telecommunications and acts as an agency for a variety of government departments, dealing with the payment of pensions for the Department of Health and Social Security, the issuing of passport forms for the Foreign and Commonwealth Office, and so on. It also provides the link between the Department of National Savings and the public, and offers its own banking facilities. But the position of Postmaster General has disappeared; its successor in 1969, the new Minister of Posts and Telecommunications, lasted only until 1974 when this Ministry was absorbed into the Department of Industry.

One way of classifying governmental functions would be to separate those directly run by central departments and headed by ministers responsible to Parliament from those delegated to the organs of local government that Parliament has created. But quite apart from the system of interdependence of central and local government there are now also regional agencies of various kinds; these are essentially emanations of central government and have no directly elected element. There are in addition a number of *ad hoc* or special purposes authorities – regional and area health authorities and regional water authorities, for instance – and these further complicate the picture.

Particularly important from the constitutional point of view are the arrangements made for dealing centrally with certain functions for which organization on the departmental model and the direct responsibility of ministers are thought inappropriate. Thus while the principles of taxation policy have always been a matter for ministers responsible to Parliament, the collection of taxes from individuals has been shielded from direct ministerial intervention through the operations of the quasi-autonomous Boards of Inland Revenue and of Customs and Excise. Some of the more recently created institutions have similar aims, for instance the University Grants Committee established in 1919 was intended to act as an independent buffer between the Government as paymaster and the universities as the recipients of funds. Its formation was regarded as a guarantee of the universities' continued 'academic freedom', though its value in this respect has diminished since 1964 when responsibility for the UGC was transferred from the Treasury to the Department of Education (which had then to be renamed the Department of Education and Science) with the consequent danger that the universities would be subordinated to the Government's general educational policies.

In very general terms, the institutions of the British state which we have to describe have developed to administer seven distinct categories of governmental action. However, these categories overlap in practice and separate functions of government are not necessarily or invariably the responsibility of distinct departments.

The earliest positive functions of government were those of external defence and the maintenance of law and order, including the provision of courts for handling both civil and criminal cases. The machinery of justice and of law enforcement will be outlined in a subsequent chapter; together they form part of the overlapping responsibilities of the Lord Chancellor, the Home Secretary and the Law Officers of the Crown – the Attorney and Solicitor General.

The second and perhaps the most ambiguous category of governmental responsibility is that of taxation combined with the overall control of credit. It is ambiguous because taxation is used to further several objectives: there is the basic one of providing revenue for supporting all the other aspects of government, including, of course, such fundamental responsibilities as defence and law and order; also, taxation has increasingly become the instrument through which, in deference to egalitarian principles, some resources are shifted from one sector of the population to another; and in addition it is regarded as a means of influencing the general economic climate, as is the control of credit. A national budget is thus an instrument of economic as well as fiscal policy.

The third area of governmental activity – and it is the increasing sophistication and scale of operations here which has caused the label 'welfare state' to be applied to the form of government enjoyed in the United Kingdom – is that of services provided by the Government, whether in cash, as with pensions, or in kind, as with education. The basis of this provision has varied over the twentieth century, and some services may be supported out of taxation while others are financed by compulsory insurance.

The fourth area is that of direct state intervention to protect by law certain categories of persons such as those employed in mines, in factories or at sea; women and children at work; and tenants or consumers. Such a principle was well established by the end of the nineteenth century, but it has been expanded during the twentieth century. Recent legislation against discrimination on the basis of race or sex might be regarded as extending the state's powers in this area; so too could legislation intended to redress the alleged weaknesses in the bargaining powers of various groups such as trade unionists.

The fifth field of activity has been created by the Government's entry into the economic arena as the owner and manager of particular branches of industry. In Britain this is a relatively recent development which has occurred largely in deference to the view that natural monopolies – for example railways – should not be privately owned. It was in the 1945–50 period that the extension of this kind of public ownership took place. More recently individual firms have been taken into government ownership in an attempt to prevent them from closing down and so adding to unemployment. In addition there is the idea, exemplified in the establishment of the National Enterprise Board in 1975, that the state should acquire shares in industrial undertakings without proceeding to the nationalization of the whole industry. For this development a longstanding precedent existed in the shape of British Petroleum where the Government had long been a 51% shareholder.

The sixth area of activity is that of economic controls short of public ownership – in other words government intervention in such matters as prices and incomes, whether by legislation or by use of other powers to enforce mere exhortation. The Government's power to award contracts to private industry, for instance, became a matter of controversy when used to promote an allegedly voluntary incomes policy. In addition to the controls affecting the entire workforce or particular branches of production, there are ways in which the Government can intervene – through the assignment of subsidies or other privileges – to ensure that the location of particular enterprises suits its economic, or even its electoral, requirements.

The seventh area is the hardest to define. It consists of all those functions of government which can be related to long-term ideas about the development of the country's human and physical resources. These functions are difficult to disentangle from the more immediate concerns to which they are likely to be sacrificed. The debate about energy resources has been a conspicuous example: a balance has to be struck between current demands, future needs, natural amenities, and – in the case of nuclear energy – questions of safety. Land-use planning, a major function of local government since the Town and Country Planning Act of 1947, has become an even more tangled issue. Should one give priority to people's preference for low-density housing over the need to preserve agricultural land? How does agriculture fare in the scale of importance compared with motorways and airports? There is no easy way of balancing against each other economic and amenity issues. Where population is concerned, the state has long exercised powers over immigration and at times over emigration as well. The unusual scale of immigration in recent decades has highlighted this aspect of policy and the agencies responsible for its implementation. Attempts by fiscal and other means to influence the rate of reproduction are yet another feature of modern government.

The word 'planning' which occurs in so many contexts in modern government is thus an ambiguous one. Effective planning depends upon the ability to forecast successfully developments in a variety of overlapping fields, many of them outside national control; because this has so far proved an impossible task, the planning related to it has lost much of its credibility. Demographic projections have been particularly misleading. The Department of the Environment, created in 1970, which could be thought to have a special responsibility for the country's natural resources, suggests by its title a more ambitious frame of reference than its actual performance has justified. It remains little more than a loosely co-ordinated collection of a variety of functions under a single ministerial head, all of them previously performed somewhere else in the governmental machine, and has indeed shed one of its most important original areas of responsibility, namely transport.

Defence

The organization of the country's defence forces has responded to changes in the international situation and in technology. By the present century, the two professional services – the army and the navy – had become wholly national in their recruitment, training and deployment. There were at one time in addition various reserve services intended largely for home defence, reflecting in their locally based organization the traditional duties of citizens to be equipped for an emergency. In the First World War demands for much larger forces led to general conscription. After 1919 the old system of voluntary recruitment was restored with the significant addition, after much debate, of an independent air force. Conscription reappeared on the eve of the Second World War and was maintained as 'national service' for a number of years after the ending of hostilities; by 1962, however, Britain's armed forces were again composed wholly of volunteers.

In recent years the three dominant features of the defence picture have been the decline in the proportion of the national budget going to defence, about 8.9% in 1978 as against 11.9% in 1975; the greater cohesion between the armed services shown by their sharing of some common facilities; and the declining importance attached to reserve forces, with the consequent erosion of the local elements in the system. Arrangements for civil defence, which in the immediately pre- and post-war years were of some local importance, lapsed in 1968.

The modern Ministry of Defence is headed by a Secretary of State whose position incorporates the duties of three historic offices – the First Lord of the Admiralty, the Secretary of State for War and the Secretary of State for Air. Its junior ministers and array of boards and committees are organized partially on a functional and partially on a service basis; its staffing is partly military and partly civilian. With the disappearance of most of the overseas responsibilities of the defence forces, the suggestion sometimes made by the services that force levels could be fixed irrespective of considerations of foreign policy has been abandoned and the need for close consultation between the Ministry of Defence and the Foreign and Commonwealth Office is now taken for granted. Another development has been that the Ministry has become deeply involved in the problems of Northern Ireland because of the unusual assumption by the army of responsibilities for domestic peacekeeping, and this in turn will bring the Ministry of Defence into contact with domestic departments concerned with Northern Ireland. As a purchaser of increasingly sophisticated equipment, the Ministry of Defence is also closely involved with important aspects of industry and with the promotion of scientific and technological research.

Finally, one may add that the professional character of the armed forces does not mean that their members are as remote from society in general as in earlier times. It is no longer the case that officers have passed through a wholly segregated educational system or spent most of their professional life overseas. Nowadays they have much more often passed through universities, and the opportunity for training in skilled trades has become one of the principal incentives towards joining the forces in the lower ranks. Decisions about their pay and conditions now have to take into account general incomes policies.

Taxation, Finance and the Economy

In Britain as in all modern states, nearly all the money required for government expenditure is derived from taxation, or from loans secured on the product of future taxation. Most taxation is levied by central government. A part of it which is raised by local authorities, a property tax known colloquially as 'rates', will be discussed in the chapter on local government, as well as that important part of public expenditure which consists of subsidies to local authorities.

The principal financial department of the British Government is the Treasury, which deals both with the provision of funds and with the control of their expenditure. A major function of the Treasury, particularly following the changes in organization after the First World War, involved personnel matters in government, although with the most senior appointments this must always be a direct concern of the Prime Minister. In 1968, this aspect of the Treasury's activities was separated from the Treasury, and a new Civil Service Department was created with the Prime Minister as its nominal head but with another senior minister – such as the Lord Privy Seal, a minister without portfolio, during Mr Callaghan's premiership – responsible for day-to-day administration. Its Permanent Secretary, rather than the Permanent Secretary to the Treasury, then became the Head of the Home Civil Service. At the time of writing, after a decade's experience, it is still unclear whether this arrangement will survive.[1] One school of thought takes the view that personnel matters in the public service are so intimately connected with questions of public expenditure that a departmental separation of responsibilities for the two aspects is illogical, and causes difficulties in controlling the growth of the Civil Service. The Treasury incidentally continues to fulfil another role in relation to the Civil Service by being the department from which a number of the senior personnel in other departments are drawn. This fact has obvious policy implications in that many Permanent Secretaries in the spending departments are likely to have been imbued with the Treasury outlook.

The Chancellor of the Exchequer is the minister responsible for the structure of the national system of taxation and for changes both in the nature of the taxes levied and in their level. Historically, changes in either were presented to Parliament in an annual budget in the spring when the fiscal year begins; this was the climax of the parliamentary year. The British budget was thus concerned only with ways and means for raising money, and not with expenditure. Proposals for expenditure were dealt with earlier in the parliamentary year as 'estimates'. A great deal of secrecy attaches to the budget procedure; even the Chancellor's colleagues are only informed of his proposals immediately before their presentation to the House. The ostensible purpose of this secrecy is to avoid the possibility of financial speculation; the disadvantage is that it inhibits full consultation with interests likely to be affected and a proper scrutiny of new proposals.

In recent years, however, there have been some important changes, though these have to some extent had opposite effects. On the one hand, most public expenditure is supposed to be planned on a 'rolling' five-year basis; this means that government commitments should in theory be known well in advance, thus limiting the Chancellor's freedom of action. On the other hand, the economic vicissitudes that the country has been undergoing, and the attempts to correct its undesirable features by fiscal means over and above the regulative powers of the Chancellor, have meant a growing number of summer or autumn budgets in addition to the annual regular spring budgets. The more frequent budgets become, the less is the mystique attached to them, and the less, perhaps, their importance compared with all the other means of intervention in the economy that modern governments possess. In addition to taxation, large-scale borrowing to meet current outgoings – in the past mainly a feature of wartime finance – has become normal practice. In a period of acute inflation, this involves winning and retaining the confidence of the international monetary institutions and the governments they represent; an important part of the Chancellor's task is therefore now a diplomatic one.

The section of the Treasury that deals with policy is small. The detailed working out of tax proposals and the responsibility for their implementation are in the hands of two other departments – the Board of Inland Revenue and the Board of Customs and Excise which, as has been seen, stand in a quasi-autonomous relationship to the Chancellor. The organization of the Board of Inland Revenue is perforce largely a localized one; this situation stems from the practice of earlier periods, when it was necessary to rely on groups of local notables to assess and collect taxes due to the Crown.

Although the Treasury decides what proportion of the public outgoings are to be met by borrowing rather than taxation, the raising of loans and their management are again something entrusted to other bodies. Savings by the population at large and their investment in different forms of government stock are a matter for the Department of National Savings which in 1969 took over the former functions of the Post Office in this area. The day-to-day management of the national debt and government intervention in matters affecting the international money market are the responsibility of the Bank of England, which has been the principal agent of the state in these fields since its foundation as a private institution in 1694. The Bank of England's nationalization in 1946 did not conspicuously diminish its independence in representing the moneyed community to the Treasury, or detract from its role and standing among foreign and international monetary and financial institutions.

In recent years the Bank has been drawn further into the Whitehall network; the gulf between its outlook and that of the Treasury may have diminished with more of the Bank's directing personnel having an academic rather than a banking background. Even so, it is largely staffed by men who have made their way in the banking world, entering it often directly after leaving school, in contrast to the university graduates who dominate the Treasury. The Governor of the Bank occupies a special position. Appointed for a five-year period, his tenure is unaffected by political changes. On the other hand, unlike a Permanent Secretary or other senior civil servants, he claims the right to make his views known, through speeches to the public as well as to ministers in private. As he sees the world from a rather different point of view from that of ministers or Treasury civil servants, the Governor's pronouncements may not always accord with those of the Government's own spokesmen, particularly at times when there is disagreement over economic policy – a possibility which has come in for criticism.

Historically the main work of the Treasury itself was the control of public expenditure; a variety of constitutional rules and conventions made its consent necessary for any projected expenditure by departments. This consent was also required for all legislative proposals involving expenditure. More recently, under the influence of Keynesian economic thinking, this primary function has been supplemented – or some would think even superseded – by a wider concern. The Treasury now believes that it can influence the economic climate as a whole by 'managing' demand.

The role of the Treasury has been enhanced by the growing importance of government as an employer and spender: its own industrial activities now obviously do much to determine the general state of the economy. The other factor that gives particular importance to central economic management is the extreme significance to Britain of foreign trade and overseas investments. Despite the continued importance of invisible exports – shipping, banking, insurance, consultancy work, higher education and training – Britain still depends upon her exports of manufactures to pay for a high proportion of her food and raw materials. The position in this respect has not been static: domestic agricultural production has increased; the share of foodstuffs in the total import bill has been falling; so too has the share of raw materials, with the substitution of synthetic for natural products; and the rapid growth of North Sea oil production is now diminishing Britain's dependence upon imported oil. On the other hand, there has been a tendency recently for the import of manufactured and semi-manufactured goods to increase with any upward turn in the economy. This development has led to pressure for protection of home industries to cope with mounting unemployment. Most worrying of all has been Britain's declining share of the world's export markets, from 18.2% in 1958 and 13.8% in 1965 to 8.7% in 1976 and 9.3% in 1977. The balance of payments and the stability of the currency have therefore been an understandable preoccupation of all post-war governments.

It is not surprising that it is in the economic field that changes in the machinery of government have been most conspicuous. To some extent these developments reflect differences in the theoretical perception of the economic problems, and to some extent the divergent philosophies of the two main parties. Administrative arrangements for ordered and detailed forms of government intervention in the economy may turn out to be less important than the ability of senior ministers to respond swiftly to the signs of an economic squall. Rapid improvisations rather than systematic treatment have also been characteristic of attempts to curb the growth in public expenditure. Whether these attempts have taken the form of new machinery for Treasury or parliamentary control, or of formal reviews of significant aspects of public expenditure, notably defence, they have usually been superseded by measures taken rapidly and under pressure to meet a particular financial crisis. (By the late 1970s 'cash limits', the setting of annual ceilings on specific areas of expenditure, were the favourite nostrum.) It could be argued that the successive innovations which have taken place in the administrative structure were largely ways of escaping from a head-on confrontation with problems that no government felt strong enough to solve; their chief result was to dissipate the energies of senior civil servants, and to some extent of ministers, on the mere mechanics of organization, when they would perhaps have been better devoted to examining the substantive issues involved.

In the early 1960s, even before the advent of the Labour Government of 1964, there were moves towards a greater degree of intervention in the economy. The National Economic Development Office and Council (NEDDY) were set up in 1961, to bring about tripartite discussion between government, the employers and the unions about the handling of problems of the domestic economy. The incoming Labour Government in 1964, influenced to some extent perhaps by the French example of 'indicative planning', divided up ministerial functions in a new way. A Department of Economic Affairs was set up to handle the long-term planning of the economy, while short-term responsibilities in the economic sphere remained with the Treasury. A new Ministry of Technology was created to give government assistance in the modernization of British industry. In 1965 a National Board for Prices and Incomes was added to the system in the hope that a non-political and presumably impartial body of this kind would help to restrain inflationary wage settlements and avoidable price increases. As a further complication, it was decided to treat as a separate issue the highly varied effects of economic developments on different regions, and in particular the uneven geographical spread of unemployment. Questions of regional policy and the types of government intervention required to make it effective were left to the Board of Trade. In April 1968 the major responsibility for incomes policy, which was of increasing importance in overall government strategy, was vested in the Ministry of Labour; this was renamed the Department of Employment and Productivity.

The economic difficulties of the latter years of the Labour Government of 1966–70 forced ministers to devote more attention to the monetary and fiscal aspects of policy and produced a reaction against the earlier confidence in long-term economic planning. In October 1969 the Department of Economic Affairs, already much weakened, was abolished; its general economic responsibilities reverted to the Treasury, and its direct relationships with particular industries were transferred to the Ministry of Technology.

The Conservative Government that came into office in 1970 was at least as convinced as its predecessor of the importance of devising a correct administrative framework for making and executing government economic policy. Its initial steps were greatly influenced by an ideological preference for minimal intervention and its consequent hostility to a formal incomes policy. The National Board for Prices and Incomes, which had played a lesser role in the latter years of the Labour Government, was abolished. The Department of Employment and Productivity was renamed yet again and became simply the Department of Employment, with the accent on its conciliatory functions in industrial disputes. The Ministry of Technology was merged with the Board of Trade to form one of the new super-departments, the Department of Trade and Industry.

The course of economic events, and particularly the rate of inflation, forced the Government back towards an incomes policy. Ideally it would have looked to cooperation with the unions to bring about a voluntary restraint in wage claims. But relations with the unions had been soured by the Industrial Relations Act of 1971 and by union resistance to the two organs set up under its provisions, the Industrial Relations Commission and the Industrial Relations Court. The Government therefore gave itself statutory control over prices and incomes by the Counter-Inflation Act of 1973, setting up two new bodies, a Pay Board and a Price Commission.

The defiance of the incomes policy by the miners and the Government's defeat in the general election of February 1974 brought into power a Labour Government hostile to the idea of a compulsory incomes policy and pledged to abolish the industrial relations legislation to which the trade unions objected. Repeal was achieved in full only after the election of October 1974 gave the Government an overall majority: the machinery set up under the Industrial Relations Act and the Counter-Inflation Act, except for the Prices Commission, was abolished. The formal link between government and labour remained the Department of Employment; however, two important aspects of its work were hived off to semi-autonomous bodies – the Manpower Services Commission, responsible for employment services and industrial training, and the Advisory Conciliation and Arbitration Service, which was supposed to advance the cause of trade-union recognition and to handle strikes and other forms of industrial strife.

When this Government in turn embarked upon an incomes policy influenced by the concept of the 'social wage' as an addition to money wages – in other words improved welfare benefits and facilities – it did not back it up with compulsory powers but relied on general agreement with the TUC, which was obtained for its earlier phases. Any sanctions available arose from the dependence of individual employers upon various forms of government patronage and assistance. At the same time, prices remained under statutory control and the Prices Commission an important weapon in the government armoury. The Prices Commission was abolished by the new Conservative Government in May 1979.

The Department of Trade and Industry did not long remain as originally created. The Conservative Government had already removed all aspects of energy policy from it to the newly established Department of Energy. The Labour Government of 1974 now also separated off the Department of Trade, which was to be largely concerned with the international field, and a Department of Prices and Consumer Protection, which in addition took over some of the powers formerly exercised by the Ministry of Agriculture, Fisheries and Food. The latter – along with the Department of Energy – and the Ministry of Transport are the survivors of the old system, where ministries had specific aspects of the economy under their care.

The Ministry of Agriculture's survival must be attributed in part to the political weight of the agricultural community, which persists despite its relatively small size. By 1973 agriculture accounted for only 1.7% of the unemployed workforce as against 3.4% in Belgium, 6.4% in West Germany, 10.8% in France and 15.1% in Italy.

It is not possible to say whether this process of change in the organization of economic departments has ended, but at present the situation is that responsibility for the management of the public sector of the economy is divided, on an industry-by-industry basis, between several different departments and ministers. Some sectors, such as civil aviation, are even outside the departmental framework altogether. (A Civil Aviation Authority was set up in 1971.) These arrangements represent the repudiation of an alternative scheme, which retains some support, and by which all the nationalized industries would be grouped under a single minister. The responsibilities of such a comprehensive ministry would then correspond to the way the House of Commons has scrutinized the nationalized industries through a single select committee.

To see the matter solely in the light of departments and

ministers is itself an oversimplification. The legislation of 1975 and 1976, and the close political cooperation of the trade-union movement and the Labour Government for the period of the so-called 'social contract', gave trade unions new opportunities for influence. In the years 1974–9 many basic decisions in the field of public policy were the fruit of negotiations with organized labour – and to a lesser extent with organized business through the CBI – rather than the result of independent governmental strategy. While this was especially true of such general questions as prices and incomes policy, other policies were of course still conceived within the governmental machine itself or attributable to individual ministers and their party commitments. The major economic departments must, however, be regarded – even under a Conservative Government where the ties with organized labour are obviously less close and the ties with business not precisely comparable – as focal points in a continual process of bargaining with outside interests rather than as instruments of the state applying policy determined solely by the Cabinet.

An alternative view of the Government's role in the economy emphasizes the importance of planning and of ensuring the correct future distribution of real resources as the key to growth. This belief was enshrined, as has been seen, in the creation in 1964 of the Department of Economic Affairs to take over long-term aspects of the Treasury's work, although it has been argued that the Prime Minister's real motive was the more political one of fostering a creative tension between his two possible rivals for the party leadership, the one as Chancellor of the Exchequer (James Callaghan) and the other as First Secretary and head of the new Department, George Brown. The Department of Economic Affairs, its 'national plan' and the concept of long-term planning as a whole did not survive the strains that culminated in the devaluation of 1967. However, the National Economic Development Council earlier referred to has survived through various reorganizations and changes of government emphasis to play a respectable if not major role in exploring some aspects of the economy and acting as a sounding board for governments.

The nationalized industries occupy a particularly ambiguous position in the governmental structure. The favoured model for their organization has been the 'Morrisonian' one, named after Herbert Morrison, a leading figure in the 1945 Labour Government. This means that nationalized industries are not run directly by government departments but organized in a quasi-autonomous fashion under their own boards whose members are nominated by the minister. It was hoped that this form of organization would combine the principle of public ownership with the flexibility of commercial concerns. In fact the industries concerned have been unable to meet the different demands made upon them – by the public for high-quality services and low prices; by their workers for better wages and conditions; and by government as it pursues its own economic and social objectives. They have been expected to recruit the best managerial talent, but have been restrained from paying the high salaries needed to attract it by governments afraid of back-bench criticism. Above all, the chairmen of the boards have encountered great difficulties in their relations with ministers: their wish to follow policies suggested by economic criteria has conflicted with the wishes of ministers who have had to take party and even constituency considerations into account.

Education, Social Services and Information

The governmental provision of social services is carried out mainly by two very large departments – Health and Social Security, brought together in 1968, and Education and Science. These have serious problems of internal organization because of the variety of services they provide, and there is some overlap between them. They are also confronted with three sets of problems.

First, both departments deal largely with matters which are the direct responsibility of local rather than of central government: local authorities, either individually or through their associations, are involved in the making as well as the execution of policy. The problem is complicated by the fact that at any given time many local authorities will not be under the control of the party in power at Westminster, and yet the main political parties may hold radically different views on some issues. In extreme cases a consensus may be unattainable and government may compel recalcitrant local authorities to fall into line. Secondly, both departments are large-scale employers of labour either directly or indirectly through the local authorities. The trade unions into which the workforce is organized are therefore able to use industrial action not merely in pursuit of higher remuneration or better conditions for their members but also to promote their own views of what the departments' general policy should be. Finally, unlike the nationalized industries which are expected to follow pricing policies enabling them to 'break even taking one year with another', the DHSS and the DES, which supply mainly free or heavily subsidized services, have no economic criteria for deciding upon the distribution of the resources at their command.

The British system of state education is organized on a dual basis. Primary schools, most secondary schools, teacher training colleges – now mainly affiliated to universities or polytechnics – colleges of further education, adult education and polytechnics are the responsibility of the larger local authorities; however, the Department of Education and Science determines a large amount of policy and subsidizes expenditure out of central funds. Part of the school system and some of the training colleges are connected with religious denominations, although they depend for finance largely upon public funds. The forty-five universities – the two ancient English foundations, Oxford and Cambridge; the ancient Scottish ones; the nineteenth- and early twentieth-century, largely civic, foundations; the so-called 'red-brick' universities; the more recent 'plate-glass' institutions; the former colleges of advanced technology subsequently granted university status, and the Open University are financed overwhelmingly from central funds, and all except the Open University through the University Grants Committee.

The division in higher education between the locally controlled and financed polytechnics and the universities which is known as the binary system has been the subject of a good deal of controversy. The spokesmen for the polytechnics claim that they receive a less generous apportionment of funds than the universities and are discriminated against by the Research Councils through which most government money for research is channelled. It is possible that the boundary between the two types of institution is not yet finally settled; some would like to see it disappear. Controversy is heightened by the fact that higher education and further education are no longer the most rapidly expanding parts of the educational system. Between 1961 and 1970 the amount spent on universities went up from 10.8% to 14.2% of the total educational budget while the proportion spent on schools declined from 65.6% to 56.7%. During the 1970s, however, the priorities changed and there were persistent pressures for economy upon the higher education sector. In comparison with its western European neighbours, Britain provides a system of higher education notable for the lavishness of its provision of physical facilities for students, for a high ratio of staff to students, and also for its system of grants – subject to a parental means test – for all students who succeed in obtaining a place in higher education. This means that quite apart from the direct financing of the universities by the UGC, students themselves are normally beneficiaries of public funds in the form of fees and living expenses.

There have been deep controversies over the organization of secondary education within the state system in which legislation, its interpretation by the Department of Education and Science and the wishes of individual local authorities have all been involved. As the system stood after the important Education Act of 1944 British education was characterized by the existence of two major groups of schools whose intake was determined on a selective, and hence primarily academic, basis – the state-funded grammar schools, which were one of the local authorities' responsibilities, and the direct-grant schools, which were partly fee-paying but had some free places directly subsidized by the central government. The direction of change, however, has been towards eliminating the grammar schools and basing all local-authority schools on the neighbourhood comprehensive pattern, similar to the American high-school model. The direct-grant schools have been obliged to choose between entering the state system, which involved abandoning selection by ability, or becoming fully independent. Wherever possible they have opted for the latter course.

In the past grammar schools have provided the opportunity for children of working-class or lower middle-class parentage to go on to university or professional training. In 1970 both the outgoing and the incoming Prime Ministers were the product

57

of such schools. The disappearance of such opportunities – for many comprehensive schools cannot, or even may not wish to, provide them – could combine with the survival and expansion of the private sector to create significant effects quite contrary to those intended by the social egalitarians who were the protagonists of the change. There is a depth of conviction in the arguments over education policy which explains why it plays so much more of a part in politics in Britain than it does for instance in the United States, and why a new Education Act was one of the first pieces of legislation introduced by the incoming Conservative Government of 1979.

The organization of the health services suggests both similarities with and differences from education. In the field of health as in education, the state originally stepped in to fill the gaps in private provision but has gradually become the major provider. In both education and health fields an important private sector remains in being, though there is pressure within the Labour Party to have it abolished. However, because of the existence of private beds in National Health Service hospitals, which were being phased out by the Labour Government of 1974–9, and because practitioners within the national system can also engage in private practice, the two sectors are more closely involved with each other in health than is true in education. In conflicts over policy and remuneration the medical profession is better organized than the teaching profession, and in a better position to secure its interests – partly because its skills are more readily internationally marketable. The education and health systems do share a genuine uncertainty about the respective roles of central and local government, though in the Health Service it is central government that has increasingly had the upper hand.

Local authorities are mainly confined to responsibility for measures such as enforcing standards of hygiene and for the medical aspects of personal welfare services. The National Health Service, which was established in 1948, comes directly under the authority of the Secretary of State. His powers are exercised through 14 regional health authorities, which control 90 area health authorities in England and 12 area health authorities in Wales; there are 15 health boards in Scotland which have been under the jurisdiction of the Scottish Office. The health areas normally delegate powers to health districts, which usually contain a district hospital. The boards are mainly composed of unpaid part-time members, mostly nominees of the Secretary of State, the rest local-government representatives. The system is thus both centralized and bureaucratic. Concern about the welfare of individual patients under this system led to the establishment in 1973 of the appointment of a Health Service Commissioner or ombudsman with powers similar to those of the Parliamentary Commissioner for Administration; in addition direct application could be made to him by the public, without the intervention of a Member of Parliament. The two offices, together with the theoretically separate appointments of Health Service Commissioners for Wales and Scotland, are combined in the same individual.

There are some points at which the health and education services overlap. There has to be close cooperation between the National Health Service – which provides for the medical inspection of schoolchildren – and the education authorities, and between the National Health Service which is responsible for the management of the teaching hospitals and the universities which provide the teaching given in them and which are represented on the area authorities.

To the Secretary of State for the Social Services falls the governmental function of the payment of cash benefits to individuals. The system of social security includes national insurance against sickness, unemployment and widowhood, and for retirement; insurance against industrial injuries; family allowances and income benefits; and the supplementary benefits available to families or persons in need, together with war pensions.

Although administrative convenience now dictates the handling of all these schemes within a single departmental framework, their historical roots and contemporary policy goals are by no means identical. Part of the system has developed from the assumption by the Tudor state of the responsibility for relieving distress, which followed the religious and social upheaval of the Reformation; part is the outcome of early twentieth-century ideas – largely inspired by the German model – for compensating through insurance for the vicissitudes befalling the individual worker in an industrial society; and part arises from the state's acceptance of particular responsibilities for those who have served it, whether in a civilian or a military capacity.

However, the total expenditure on such services and the manner in which it is raised and disbursed remain matters of political controversy. Family allowances, for instance, may be regarded as an instrument of population policy rather than as a palliative for poverty. Benefits awarded subject to a means test have always been criticized as humiliating to the recipient. In the area of pensions, the transition from flat-rate to earnings-related benefits after retirement has anti-egalitarian implications. There is also the problem of the conflict between the general provisions for old age made by the state and the particular provisions made for government servants, especially now that the latter are calculated to take inflation into account. Some aspects of such provisions may affect people's readiness to change their employers, or even their occupations. Furthermore, there may be a clash between a governmental priority given to economic growth, which calls for a highly mobile population and fluid social structure, and an existing system of social security which is conducive to the maintenance of a rigid status quo.

The Department of the Environment has to grapple with similar conflicts of policy. Local-authority housing may encourage people to stay within a particular local-government area so that their turn for council accommodation may come along. The problems inherent in the different approaches to land-use planning – economic and environmental – have already been noted. The problems of industrial waste and pollution bring the Government into another area where the application of economic criteria may be challenged and where a local community's interest may conflict with that of an individual enterprise, or with the national interest.[4] The siting and regulation of nuclear installations highlighted in the Windscale inquiry of 1978 are an example.[5]

The diverse activities of government, with more specifically economic governmental functions, demand an ever larger apparatus of statistics and an increasing sophistication in their interpretation. The Central Statistical Office, which is directly attached to the Cabinet Office, is now the agent of most statistical inquiries; the importance of its own interpretation of economic trends as a factor in government policy has been stressed by some observers of the Whitehall scene. If long-term planning is to be successful, future demands for manpower and physical resources will require study in greater depth; for instance, attempts to match provisions for places in higher and further education with employment opportunities demand calculations about the future shape of the economy, and these have hitherto been extremely unreliable.

From at least the time of the First World War, the need to be internationally competitive has obliged British governments to encourage research in all the sciences and to allot an increasing amount of expenditure for this purpose. Advice on non-departmental research is now given by the five Research Councils, which are composed of specialists in the relevant disciplines – the Science Research Council, the Agricultural Research Council, the Medical Research Council, the Natural Environment Research Council and the Social Science Research Council. Government-financed research may be undertaken at establishments directly under their authority or, by contract, at universities and other independent institutions.

The steep rise in the research budget and the claim that the aims of some publicly funded research were too remote from the nation's requirements led in 1972 to an investigation by Lord Rothschild, the head of the Central Policy Review Staff. Many of his proposals were accepted by the Government and implemented: the budgets of three of the Councils – Agricultural Research, Medical Research and Natural Environmental Research – were cut, and the money was made available to government departments so that they could contract directly with outside bodies for research projects tailored to their own needs. There was nevertheless some criticism of the Rothschild Report on the grounds that it misconceived the nature of the research process and that the customer–contractor formula was inappropriate. These criticisms have some foundation since it is felt that departments are bound to think in a short-term or 'tactical' framework in contrast to the 'strategic' thinking of the Research Councils. Universities have undoubtedly suffered as a result of cuts in the funds that were formerly obtainable from the Research Councils.[6]

One problem that has caused controversy in the United States is the possibility of conflict between government funding of research and academic freedom. Can government control the publication of the results of such research? This question is particularly acute where defence matters are involved. In Britain, however, such research, which is done not only for itself but for its spin-off effects, is undertaken not in universities but in governmental establishments. The most powerful government scientist of recent times, Lord Zuckerman, was both Chief Scientific Adviser to the Secretary of State for Defence, and Chief Scientific Adviser to the Government, with offices in both the Ministry of Defence and the Cabinet Office. After his retirement the two posts were divided, and since 1976 the latter has remained unfilled.

In the field of the humanities and fine arts, government patronage is both more restricted than in the scientific field and in many respects more recent. The British Academy, a private body, acts as a research council for the humanities. National museums and libraries and the care of historical buildings and archaeological sites are important governmental responsibilities. Subsidies to music, theatre and the plastic arts are given, if not very lavishly by some standards, through the medium of the Arts Council established in 1946. These activities were until 1979 co-ordinated at the ministerial level by a Minister of State in the Department of Education and Science, colloquially known as the 'Minister for the Arts'. Under the new Conservative Government responsibility for the Arts was transferred to the Chancellor of the Duchy of Lancaster and Leader of the House of Commons, Mr Norman St John-Stevas.

The predominance of central government in this area is noticeable in the comparison of Britain with some other countries – Germany for instance – where municipal patronage is much more conspicuous. British local authorities, although empowered to spend money to promote the arts, have so far done little in this direction. On the other hand, the system of public libraries, which is very highly developed, is organized locally, although there is a central mechanism for inter-library loans. Some progress has been made by some local authorities in developing libraries as centres for musical and dramatic activities.

An important feature of modern government is the need to make its activities known to the general public and to those particularly affected by individual policies. The Stationery Office publishes the mass of formal government documentation, as well as the principal series of historical records. The Central Office of Information brings out the more popular presentations of different aspects of government's work under the direction of the relevant departments.

The two functions of information and promotion of the arts and sciences are linked in the British Broadcasting Corporation, one of the earliest public corporations. Although its role in television is shared with commercial television – which is under the supervision of the Independent Broadcasting Authority – the peculiar stamp on broadcasting given by the original BBC monopoly has not vanished. Television is available to government for presenting information, and its role in presenting party politics depends upon agreements reached between the parties; its more general function as an opinion former is always likely to be a subject of debate. Whether television and especially the BBC should reflect opinion objectively or lead it in moral, social or artistic matters; whether in presenting a current controversy it should give equal importance to the authorities and to those challenging them; and whether entertainment values should remain supreme – all these questions are likely to remain unsettled. In comparison with France where broadcasting is similarly a state function but where it is much more closely controlled, Britain does give a much greater weight to broadcasting in both the political and the general cultural field. What is remarkable is that democracy, in the sense of government through elected persons, plays no role in either the Arts Council, the BBC, or the IBA. As in many other public bodies patronage determines senior posts, though there is a career structure for the employees.

As we shall see in the concluding chapter of this book, the handling of the domestic tasks of British government has been powerfully affected by the growth of international institutions, and will be even more powerfully affected if the European Economic Communities develop beyond their original functions. Meanwhile the traditional British apparatus for dealing with foreign states and international institutions remains in being. The fact that traditional diplomacy has had to be supplemented by a great deal of economic or technical expertise has meant that the primacy of the Foreign and Commonwealth Office and of the Diplomatic Service has been repeatedly challenged. Much multilateral and conference diplomacy has for a long time required the participation of officials from departments other than the F C O and often of their ministerial chiefs.

A report by the Central Policy Review Staff in August 1977 recommended radical changes in the Diplomatic Service including the establishment of a 'foreign policy group' within a unified Civil Service.[7] But the prospect of inter-departmental co-ordination on bilateral matters through a committee within the Cabinet Office rather than through the Foreign and Commonwealth Office; the likelihood that uncertain authority would remain to the Heads of Posts overseas; and the widespread criticism of the C P R S's study of information work, cultural work and the roles of the B B C and British Council, secured for the report as a whole so hostile a reception in Whitehall and Westminster alike that only on minor points were its recommendations accepted.[8]

Despite financial stringencies, which fall particularly heavily on the technical side of broadcasting, the promotion of Britain's image abroad has been quite effectively managed. Some of this work is done by the F C O itself, often employing the Central Office of Information as its agent. Non-political tasks such as English language teaching and cultural exchanges fall to the British Council, a semi-autonomous body maintained mainly from public funds; this collaborates with the F C O on the basis of accepted conventions. The external services of the B B C are the only agency through which British opinions, official and unofficial, can be made known to peoples whose governments are hostile to their dissemination. Because all such broadcasting, even simply the presentation of news, has a definite political purpose, F C O control is perforce tighter than it is over the British Council.

Not all areas of governmental activity fall neatly within the responsibilities of particular departments. An example is the vexed question of immigration controls: here the Home Office is the department responsible for administering the relevant legislation, but the impact of its procedures is felt more acutely by the FCO, and the controls have to be administered at overseas posts for which the FCO is responsible. As will be seen in the next chapter, it is in such areas of overlapping responsibilities that the machinery of co-ordination is especially important.

3 The Executive

The growth in the number of functions discharged by government would perhaps have been sufficient by itself to create an imbalance of power between the executive and the individual and between the executive and legislature. In addition, however, the British executive has inherited powers and a degree of autonomy which reflect the fact that the origins of the British state are monarchical rather than republican and that in consequence some of the features of royal absolutism have been retained in the constitutional arrangements of a mass democracy. Thus for example although the vast majority of the legislative authorizations which ministers and departments require to carry out the routine tasks of government are derived from statutes which must in turn have been passed by Parliament, the executive exercises some of its functions by powers known as prerogative powers. These powers enable it to sign treaties without recourse to prior parliamentary approval and to reduce punishments imposed by the courts. The prerogative of mercy, which derives from the theory that the monarch is the fount of all justice in the United Kingdom, is less significant now than when the death penalty existed. However, it can still be significant when long-term prison sentences are at issue, and needs no legislative endorsement – although the personal responsibility of the Home Secretary, who exercises the prerogative on the monarch's behalf, is in part mitigated by the existence of a specialized parole board to advise him on whether to release dangerous offenders.

The fact that foreign affairs, including the making of treaties, was originally the personal preserve of the monarch has meant that a British government, although it might feel constrained to offer opportunities to Parliament to discuss an international development, has considerable freedom of action in this field. The fundamental constitutional change which occurred when the United Kingdom joined the European Communities was achieved by the executive's signature of the relevant European Treaties. Admittedly parliamentary legislation was required to make the Treaties part of British law, but the formal accession to the Communities could be achieved by the executive alone.

The form of the executive in modern Britain, as well as its powers, reflects the monarchical origins of the British system of government. By the executive in Britain we generally mean both the Cabinet – the senior part of a ministry formed from the majority party in the House of Commons – and the civil servants or officials acting under its direction. The Cabinet has developed from that group of the monarch's intimate advisers who came to constitute the Privy Council. It was only in the eighteenth century that the outlines of a modern Cabinet emerged, but it is important to note that at that time the authority of the executive was still derived from the sovereign, and the continuation of a government more dependent on the sovereign's good will than on being able to command parliamentary support. Only in the nineteenth century did the Crown lose the power to choose who should become Prime Minister and to veto ministers who were personally objectionable to the sovereign.

The Privy Council has survived as the formal machinery through which the monarch exercises her prerogative powers when necessary. Although membership of the Privy Council is extensive, comprising all past and present cabinet ministers and a number of other public figures to a total of about three hundred in all, its working character is that of a small number of ministers who are called together to witness the signature by the monarch of some formal document, such as the declaration of a state of emergency under the provisions of the Emergency Powers Acts of 1920 and 1964. There are also standing and *ad hoc* committees of the Privy Council which the monarch does not attend and which carry out specific functions in various fields. The Privy Council Office is under the supervision of the

Lord President of the Council, but his formal responsibilities are not onerous; his post is available, along with the ancient offices of Lord Privy Seal, Chancellor of the Duchy of Lancaster and Paymaster General, for the Prime Minister to confer upon ministers to whom he wishes to entrust special non-departmental duties.

The Cabinet will have a number of these so-called 'sinecure offices', but most of its membership will be composed of the heads of the major departments. The Cabinet, presided over by the Prime Minister, both makes policy and supervises its implementation. Lesser ministers outside the Cabinet and civil servants also have this dual function. Even civil servants far removed from the central policy-making apparatus may affect policy if their contacts with members of the general public suggest the need for change. The domestic departments will differ greatly amongst themselves because they have different responsibilities, different clienteles and distinct traditions. Their internal organization will also be affected by whether or not their function is one administered directly by the department. Some functions, such as social security and employment, are the responsibility of central-government departments which have their own local offices. Other functions, such as education and housing, are not exercised directly by central government and involve a complex set of relationships with local authorities and other bodies such as new town corporations. The variety of regional and local structure is in striking contrast to those continental systems of which France is the exemplar. In France the Prefect represents at the local level the general political interests of the government of the day. In the British system, there are simply the separate outposts of the government departments, whose work is co-ordinated only at the summit.

Prime Minister and Cabinet

Although a discussion of British government will frequently start with a description of the Prime Minister and Cabinet as the formal apex of the decision-making procedure, the environment in which they operate must constantly be borne in mind.

It would be easy but too simple to see British administration as a machine and to treat the Cabinet as the central power-house to which one transmission belt carries information and from which another expedites instructions. In reality, however, there are a number of other sources of influence and information which affect the way in which problems are analysed and decisions implemented. The machinery of the governing party, the contacts which ministers have with pressure-group leaders in the industrial, commercial and professional worlds, the regular experience of ministers in Parliament and even information obtained from the press and television – all these will provide alternative sources of information and keep ministers aware of attitudes which exist outside the departments.

It might be thought that, with such a range of contacts and sources of information, the system would function with great success because it would appear to possess built-in safeguards against error. Yet even with increasingly sophisticated data available to it, the recent record of British government suggests that there are weaknesses in the system itself which constrain the policy-making process and limit the achievements of governments. Policy failures are not of course unique to contemporary British politics; however, a combination of raised expectations that government can solve national problems with a general decline in the country's self-confidence in the economic sphere has perhaps made such mistakes less acceptable than in the past.

Broadly speaking, two main culprits have been identified in the attempt to explain the mistakes made by governments over the post-war period. One is the modern British party system. Governments, it is argued, may feel tied to a doctrinal view expressed in a party manifesto and feel obliged to implement it, despite the later discovery of factors ignored or underestimated by party zealots when the commitment was initially made. Certainly both major parties have been victims of this situation.[1] Edward Heath's Government was pledged to sacrificing industry's 'lame ducks', but had to intervene to prevent Rolls-Royce and Upper Clyde Shipbuilders from going under for reasons connected with the employment position and international prestige. Both Labour and Conservative governments have been forced to adopt incomes policies, although adherence to the principles of free collective bargaining or monetarism has caused hostility to such policies in the respective parties.

A second major explanation of policy failures points to the crucial role of the civil service. It is not simply that Labour politicians and commentators will always be tempted to blame an 'elitist' civil service for impeding socialist policies, or that a Conservative administration will allege that civil servants have a vested interest in preserving collectivism; it is rather that, whatever the external sources of information available to ministers themselves, officials can frequently become insulated from the outside world. If departmental policy coincides with the sympathies of a government, it is all too easy to neglect advice from other quarters. For example, many people who were directly concerned with the problem of juvenile delinquency foretold the consequences of the Children and Young Persons Act of 1969. This Act removed most of the powers of the juvenile courts and attempted to place the full responsibility for the care of young offenders upon the social services. Had it been possible at the same time to expand greatly the provision of social workers, it is arguable that this policy might have been successful, but it was clear to most people that the funding for such an expansion would not be forthcoming, as indeed proved to be the case. An Act intended to diminish juvenile crime has thus in the eyes of many magistrates contributed to its increase as a result of the 'Whitehall knows best' mentality.

In addition to these two potential sources of error there are also features of the Cabinet system itself which may weaken the quality of decision making. If the Cabinet is viewed as the institution with responsibility for major policy decisions, one might expect that the questions which would come up to the Cabinet for resolution would be the most significant ones, and especially those decisions having implications for the rest of government policy. Yet the reality is by no means as logical as that. Apart from parliamentary business, the only issues which seem to be regularly discussed as a matter of course by the Cabinet are those concerned with foreign affairs and defence; in relation to many other issues the Cabinet is simply an agency for ratifying decisions taken elsewhere – in Cabinet committees, in direct bilateral negotiations with the Treasury or in inter-departmental committees.

An important feature of the British system of government is the network of committees at all levels. Of especial importance is the structure of committees which underpins the full Cabinet. In order to preserve at least the fiction of full Cabinet responsibility, it is a convention that the names and membership of most Cabinet committees are not revealed. Cabinet ministers themselves may not always know the structure and personnel of every Cabinet committee in existence during a Parliament, and of course the Prime Minister can establish new cabinet committees to cope with special problems. Thus in 1978, for example, Cabinet committees were established to draft white papers on the reform of the official secrets legislation and on broadcasting. Even standing committees of the Cabinet can be changed at will. However, at least one standing committee of the Cabinet – the one which organizes the legislative programme – appears to have become a permanent feature of the structure, and it will normally contain those members of the Cabinet concerned with the strategic aspects of getting legislation through Parliament. In July 1978, for example, it was understood to include the Leader of the House of Commons, the Attorney General, the Lord Advocate, the Chief Whip and the Government's Chief Whip in the House of Lords. Committees set up to deal with issues which have suddenly erupted, such as the question of Northern Ireland, may appear temporary at first but then acquire permanence as a problem becomes part of the regular concern of the administration. Conversely, *ad hoc* committees established in response to an emergency which dies down may quickly cease to have any purpose, so that the structure of an administration's Cabinet committees may well contain a number of moribund ones. Thus the real significance of individual standing and *ad hoc* committees of the Cabinet can probably be known only by the Prime Minister.

The need to associate the Cabinet as a whole with decisions which may have been taken by only some of its members and not comprehensively discussed in full Cabinet derives from the nature of Cabinet government itself. Collective responsibility in the British system demands that a decision taken by government must be defended by all the members of the Cabinet, regardless of whether those members as individuals were initially in favour of it. The divisions inside the Labour Party have in recent years caused this doctrine to be interpreted rather more flexibly, but in essence collective responsibility requires a minister to resign from the administration if he cannot support the final decision of the Cabinet on an issue. Yet it would obviously be a mistake to assume from this formal doctrine that all the Cabinet's individual members are equally significant in the decision-making process. The special position of the Prime Minister is clear and will be discussed in more detail later; but on many matters the Chancellor of the Exchequer is also at an advantage in relation to his Cabinet colleagues. The Treasury remains a law unto itself in the Whitehall hierarchy, and its superior position has in the past occasioned attempts to reduce its influence by redistributing its functions. Yet its role remains crucial to the whole strategy of an administration – although it is a curious feature of British government that the budget, which embodies the decisions most relevant to that strategy, is not revealed to the Cabinet as a whole until it is much too late for any changes in the budget to be suggested.

The leadership which the Prime Minister exercises within the Cabinet is of great significance because it enables the system of collective Cabinet government – which could prove unwieldy – to function smoothly. It is not necessary here to rehearse the academic arguments about the relative powers of the Prime Minister and the Cabinet, nor to see the relationship in the stark terms employed by some contributors to that debate.[2] The interests of a Prime Minister and his Cabinet are usually the same, and in any serious conflict a Prime Minister could not follow policies which he could not persuade a majority of his Cabinet colleagues to back. Undoubtedly he has the power to delay matters and to shape the form in which they come to Cabinet, and he certainly has superior opportunities to control the debate within Cabinet; but he is unlikely to want to exploit such advantages unless he feels that there is also a substantial body of opinion in Cabinet on his side.

The Prime Minister's position will normally stem from his or her leadership of the political party which has won a majority of seats at a general election. The fact that the Prime Minister will be the leader of the largest party in the House of Commons thus confers authority on him or her in Parliament – although the amount of time which modern Prime Ministers can devote to the House of Commons has declined since Baldwin's day, despite the prominence of Prime Minister's Question Time and the occasional set speech on the floor of the House. Moreover since 1942 the office of Leader of the House of Commons has been separated from the partnership, as it was also, temporarily, during the Lloyd George coalition of 1916–22.

The authority conferred on the Prime Minister as leader of his party in the country varies between the two major parties. In particular the autonomy of a Conservative leader is generally greater than that of a Labour leader both because of the different traditions of the parties and because, in tangible terms, the Conservative Party leader has greater control over the making and breaking of political reputations than his or her Labour opposite number. To become a Conservative minister it is necessary to attract the attention of the leader, and usually an apprenticeship will be served while the Party is in opposition. When the Labour Party is in opposition, however, the Parliamentary Labour Party as a whole elects the central core of the Shadow Cabinet, so that the leader has to work with colleagues who may not be his personal choice. Moreover there is much more scope in the Labour Party to build up a reputation by cultivating its extra-parliamentary elements. Thus although a Labour Prime Minister, like his Tory counterpart, is constitutionally free to decide who shall hold what office in his administration, he operates under some additional constraints and cannot count on personal loyalty to the same extent.

One important advantage which a Prime Minister does have over ordinary members of the Cabinet is that he or she has control over the central machinery of government, including the Cabinet Secretariat. The Cabinet Secretariat was established when Lloyd George became Prime Minister at the end of 1916. Its first head, Maurice Hankey, drew on the experience of the Committee of Imperial Defence – in abeyance during wartime – which had itself largely functioned through subcommittees. Initially the Secretariat was regarded with some suspicion as an innovation calculated to enhance Lloyd George's personal power, but it was not dismantled after Lloyd George lost office in 1922. Today the Cabinet Secretariat consists mainly of officials temporarily seconded from the individual departments

– a practice which means that they remain sensitive to trends within the departments and to the various departments' relationships with each other.

As has been seen, an important part of the daily work of the Cabinet is carried out through Cabinet committees. The Prime Minister not only decides on the membership of the Government and the Cabinet as a whole but also on what Cabinet committees shall be created and who shall serve on them, including who shall chair each committee. This ability to control the structure of the Cabinet committee system can be significant if a Prime Minister expects policy differences within his Cabinet on specific issues, or even if he wishes to minimize the general role played by an individual or group within his government. However, such manipulation is best done with subtlety if it is not to prove counter-productive. The Prime Minister also controls the actual agenda of Cabinet meetings, and the conclusions of Cabinet discussions are recorded under his direction. Although the Cabinet Secretariat is to a very large extent the Prime Minister's instrument rather than the instrument of the Cabinet as a whole, there have in recent years been signs that the private office of the Prime Minister, partly staffed from outside the civil service, is coming to play a greater role. However, there is nothing corresponding either in scope or scale to either the personal White House staff or the Executive Office of the American President.

The conventions which govern the operation of Cabinet government are usually sufficiently flexible to allow for each Prime Minister to adapt his Cabinet's practices to the personalities and politics of his particular colleagues. On a trivial level this is reflected in such minor rules as whether or not smoking is allowed; on a more important level it may be reflected in quite different procedural habits between different administrations. The Prime Minister determines how to conduct Cabinet deliberations and decides whether he can assume consensus or should take a formal vote. The formal vote – which may have become more frequent under recent Labour administrations – does of course entail the risk of identifying the minority, and Prime Ministers will often prefer to avoid a course which might lead to open revolt or resignations. The Prime Minister can decide on what terms he will allow matters decided in a Cabinet committee to be reopened in full Cabinet. Harold Wilson, for example, operated the convention that issues settled in Cabinet committee could only be raised in full Cabinet with the consent of the committee's chairman or of the Prime Minister; such a rule would give the Prime Minister substantial power: as he determines the composition of these committees, he can thereby isolate opposition. Edward Heath, on the other hand, appears not to have needed such a rule – presumably because his Cabinet was more homogeneous in outlook than that of Harold Wilson.[3] The desirability of avoiding confrontation in full Cabinet acts as a powerful incentive to ministers and the Prime Minister to iron out inter-departmental, political and personal differences in committee. If a dispute is serious enough of course the most rigid convention will not contain it, but matters rarely reach that level of conflict.

Apart from the Prime Minister's prestige and powers of persuasion he has at his service a vast amount of patronage. A high proportion of MPs of a governing party will be able to look for office or promotion. The history of the figures here is significant. Before 1970 the total number of ministers had reached 100. The Heath Government cut down the size of the Cabinet and reduced the size of the administration as a whole. However, the subsequent growth of the Cabinet was accompanied by a rise in the total number of ministers: in July 1978 there were 113 members of the ministry, of whom 97 were in the House of Commons. Unpaid parliamentary private secretaries may be regarded as part of the government team because they are subjected to the principle of collective responsibility in their voting behaviour in the House of Commons. And, although chosen by a minister, it is to the Prime Minister that they look for further promotion. These figures are large compared with the size of ministries in other parliamentary systems. In a British House of Commons of 635 members, which is quite evenly balanced between government and opposition, about one third of the members on the government side are part of the 'pay-roll vote'. The proportion would be still higher if parliamentary private secretaries were included. At the peak of the eighteenth-century system – generally regarded as one marked by extensive patronage – about 200 members in a House of Commons of 558 members held government appointments, of whom less than 40 might be regarded as the equivalent of modern ministers.

The interconnections between different areas of government policy and the difficulties created by the series of changes in the departments have drawn attention in recent years to the need for stronger agencies of central control and better co-ordination of executive activity. This need has been reflected in proposals for reforming the existing instruments of co-ordination – the Treasury, the Cabinet Office including the Central Policy Review Staff, and the Civil Service Department. There is also growing support for the idea of a specialized Prime Minister's department. However, the administrative upheavals of the last decade perhaps suggest that too much of the time of experienced civil servants has been spent on the mechanics of reorganization at the expense of policy. Only the future historian will know whether Prime Ministers were opposed or supported by their civil servants in making such frequent changes; these have taken place on a scale previously known only in wartime.

One variation in the administrative arrangements of the executive has been the size of Cabinets. Each Prime Minister has tried at the beginning of his ministry to create a Cabinet of manageable size, but personal and political factors have usually eroded these good intentions. There must be enough members to man the principal committees of the Cabinet and sufficient posts to provide suitable billets for all the leading party members. Each Prime Minister has found it easier to augment than to diminish the size of his Cabinet. In the last decade Cabinet membership has fluctuated between seventeen and twenty-three. Mrs Thatcher began with twenty-two, having merged the independent Department of Prices and Consumer Protection with the Department of Trade.

Whatever machinery is created to facilitate its business, and although in a body of the Cabinet's size an informal hierarchy of some kind is bound to develop, the Cabinet itself remains the decisive element. The published lists of ministers give the order of precedence among them determined by the Prime Minister, but whether an inner Cabinet of some kind develops in addition is wholly a matter for him to decide. Formal indications of the existence of an inner Cabinet, such as Harold Wilson's 1968 announcement of the establishment of a Parliamentary Committee, are unusual, and that particular experiment did not survive long. After Harold Wilson resumed office in 1974, a new form of 'inner Cabinet' consisting of the head of the social services departments and the Prime Minister was created, with a view to improving the overall co-ordination of the services offered by government and their administration and expenditure.

Peculiar features of the Prime Minister's personal position may be unique to Britain. There does of course exist in the modern world a tendency towards the personalization of power and the cult of personality – a tendency for which the mass media must at least to some extent be responsible. Summit meetings called to solve international problems confer further authority upon their participants, whether they are Presidents or mere Prime Ministers. Yet perhaps the trend is not as recent as is sometimes suggested. Much of what is said about the British Prime Minister's position can be shown to have nineteenth-century antecedents. When Disraeli brought 'peace with honour' back from Berlin in 1878 could it be said that the Prime Minister did not control foreign policy? At the time of Gladstone's Midlothian campaign could it be said that the electorate was not being asked to make a basic choice between two candidates for the post of Prime Minister, or that their respective parties were not thought of in terms of the contenders' personalities?

Cabinet government has survived with many of its fundamental features unaltered because it has proved flexible in changing circumstances. The Lloyd George and Churchill war Cabinets were so different in size, composition and methods of conducting business from peacetime Cabinets – for example in the frequency of their meetings, the number of outsiders present and the style of leadership exercised by the two premiers – that they would hardly seem cast in the same mould. Yet their authority rested upon the same constitutional understanding as that of the peacetime Cabinets. When peace returned the essentials of the former system were restored, although in Lloyd George's peacetime administration the Cabinet was strengthened by the retention of the Cabinet Secretariat.

The Departments

There are no clear doctrines governing the appropriate scope of a single department or the correct distribution of functions between departments. No attempt at an overall view of this problem has been made since the Haldane Committee reported in 1918.[4] That Committee, like all other efforts at resolving this question, was influenced by contemporary controversies over particular issues. The guiding principle of the Haldane Report was that government work should be organized according to the service rendered rather than the clients served; thus it was felt that all questions of health, whether adults or children were concerned, should be the responsibility of a single ministry. On the whole this principle has been followed in British government, but never with complete consistency. As services have multiplied a needy person or family might require attention from a number of different government agencies. Critics have frequently urged reorganization of departments on the basis of a more family-centred approach so that all a family's social-policy needs would be handled by a single department. Such an approach was supported by the Seebohm Committee on the Social Services and the Redcliffe-Maud Commission on Local Government. However, it has been implemented only to a very limited extent and voluntary agencies such as the National Council on the Social Services and the Citizens' Advice Bureaus have also tried to meet the problems caused by the continuing dispersion of responsibilities between governmental agencies and departments.

As far as the organization of departments is concerned, governments have found three ways of dealing with the accretion of new functions. The first was that adopted by Winston Churchill between 1951 and 1953. The theory was that a number of government departments could each be headed by non-Cabinet ministers under the supervision of a non-departmental minister or 'overlord', who would represent them in Cabinet. This system may have owed something to Churchill's wartime experience. It could also have been influenced by the ideas of the former minister Leo Amery who had argued for a small Cabinet of ministers largely free from departmental duties and therefore theoretically able to spend more time on considerations of general policy. The experiment did not, however, last long; its abolition was largely the result of parliamentary difficulties, because MPs resented the blurring of the delineation of responsibility.

The second method of accommodating additional governmental functions has in the past been to exclude some departmental heads from membership of the Cabinet. They would be summoned to Cabinet meetings only if their own departments were directly involved in a matter on the agenda. Today this device is rare, because so much business cuts across departments and adequate discussion demands that every interest is represented at Cabinet level. The Ministry of Overseas Development was made a separate department and its head given Cabinet status in the 1974 Wilson Government; however, it had been taken into the Foreign and Commonwealth Office, with only a junior minister at its head, in the Heath Government of 1970. In a re-shuffle of the Wilson Government, the Ministry was reabsorbed into the FCO; at first it was apparently intended that its new head, Reginald Prentice, should be outside the Cabinet in which he had hitherto sat as Secretary of State for Education and Science, but as a result of pressure from his colleagues, he was ultimately allowed to retain his Cabinet status. Under Mr Callaghan, Overseas Development again became a separate department with a new non-Cabinet head. In the Conservative Government of 1979 Overseas Development was again absorbed into the FCO.

The final method of avoiding the proliferation of departments has been to amalgamate existing departments with larger ones – sometimes known as 'super-departments'. However, this notion conceals two different processes of amalgamation. First, the new unit could really be thought of as a single department, and the ministries of which it is composed can lose their former identities. Such a process was envisaged when the Ministry of Defence was created in 1964: the political heads of the services – army, admiralty and air force – were demoted by stages to the rank of Under-Secretary. The second, alternative process was illustrated in the creation by the Heath administration of the Department of Trade and Industry and the Department of the Environment. Here the former departments were allowed to retain their identity and each retained a non-Cabinet minister

at its head. However, the super-departments presented difficulties of their own: the Department of Trade and Industry
began breaking up into its component parts even before the
end of the Heath administration, and the Department of the
Environment did not survive intact under the incoming Labour
Government. The title of 'super-department' might be thought
more appropriate for departments with more than one Cabinet
minister each; in 1978 this was the case with the Treasury and
the Department of Health and Social Security but not the FCO.[5]
The Foreign and Commonwealth Office, which had enjoyed
that privilege more than once in the past, had by 1978 only one
minister in the Cabinet. In 1979, however, when a peer, Lord
Carrington, was appointed Foreign and Commonwealth Secretary, another Cabinet minister, the Lord Privy Seal, was allotted
to the Foreign Office to be its spokesman in the Commons.

With few exceptions, senior ministers are now styled 'Secretaries of State'. Originally there was only one Secretary of
State; this history means that any Secretary of State can if
necessary formally act on behalf of any other. The proliferation
of Secretaries of State has also helped to limit the access of parliamentary committees to government papers, for there has
been a convention since the nineteenth century that papers
emanating from a department headed by a Secretary of State
could only be requested if Parliament itself presented a formal
address to the sovereign.[6]

Apart from the law officers, who are in a special position,
there are now three tiers of junior ministerial posts. The first
is that officially styled 'Ministers not in the Cabinet'. In July
1978 there were in this category 25 'Ministers of State' as well
as the Financial Secretary to the Treasury and the Parliamentary Secretary to the Treasury, who is the Chief Whip of the
government party. It is this tier that has grown most in recent
years: in Attlee's Government there were only 4 or 5 ministers
not in the Cabinet. The second tier consists of Under-Secretaries of State, of whom there were 30 in July 1978, and at
the bottom there are the Parliamentary Secretaries, of whom
there were then only 4.

Ministers of State and other junior ministers may either
share in the general work of their department or be allotted
specific areas of responsibility. At a time when changes in the

machinery of government were less frequent – broadly speaking before the Second World War – parliamentary action was required to transfer functions from one ministry to another. However, this process was simplified by the Ministers of the Crown (Transfer of Functions) Act of 1946, and since then parliamentary interest in such questions has declined, except where burning political issues or personal rivalries are involved. This means that reorganizations can proceed relatively easily. The consequent fluctuations are reflected in the figures: there were 25 departments in 1965–6; 19 in 1970; and only 15 in 1971. By 1976 the number was up again to 20.

It could be argued that the disadvantages of constant change are offset by the advantages of political and administrative flexibility. For instance, when it was decided to transfer the personnel functions of the Treasury to the newly created Civil Service Department the Prime Minister was made the political head of the new Department and so it was possible to maintain his involvement with major personnel issues. Another Cabinet minister with only a sinecure office, such as the Lord Privy Seal or the Lord President of the Council, was able to handle the daily business of the Department. Similarly, when a senior minister was needed to negotiate the details of British entry into the European Communities, the Chancellor of the Duchy of Lancaster was given a place in the Foreign and Commonwealth Office, and then transferred to the Cabinet Office when the inter-departmental as opposed to the purely diplomatic aspects of the negotiations became uppermost. In 1972, with the development of the crisis in Northern Ireland and the reintroduction of direct rule from Westminster, a new Department for Northern Ireland was created with its own Secretary of State. New ministries can also be established to deal with finite pieces of work such as the temporary Ministry of Aviation Supply which existed from 1970 to 1971. In 1974 the Lord President of the Council was given a Minister of State and a Parliamentary Secretary in the Privy Council Office to deal with the plans for devolution.

Pressures for further change are perhaps endemic in the system – and of course no one can predict when a crisis in some hitherto quiescent area of government may require administrative changes. Sometimes, however, even where there appears to be a case for reform there are reasons for not interfering with existing arrangements. Thus the case for a ministry of justice is resisted, on the grounds that the responsibilities for manning the courts and for law reform, for prosecutions and civil suits on behalf of government and for the police ought to remain divided between the Lord Chancellor's Office, the law officers and the Home Secretary for the sake of liberty and impartiality. Even with the present threefold division there is some tension between the Attorney General's role as an adviser to government on the legal aspects of its policies, and his role as an initiator of legal proceedings in matters where the public interest is involved and where he is supposed to exercise an independent judgement.

The creation of super-departments added a further complication to the already difficult issues presented by the convention of ministerial responsibility. It remains constitutional doctrine that the collective responsibility of the Cabinet for policy does not impair the individual responsibility of ministers for the work of their departments. The burden of steering bills through Parliament and its committees must still fall on ministers or their juniors because civil servants, while at hand for consultation, cannot participate in debate. If opposition develops it is the minister who must personally satisfy the critics, and yet the actual text of a bill is often expressed in obscure language on the basis of departmental instructions, and may involve technical legal considerations beyond the lay politician's scope. However, it is only in the most formal sense that a minister can be held responsible for decisions within his department taken in his name. The size of departments precludes his knowledge of more than a fraction of the routine business transacted by it. Even if a department's decision is ultimately admitted to have been wrong, it would now be considered quixotic for a minister to think of resigning. Were major flaws in the organization of a department to be revealed, the minister would most probably be retained until he could be inconspicuously removed during some general re-shuffle.

The main reason for this relative immunity of ministers from parliamentary control is the solidarity of Cabinets and the cohesiveness of parties. Even if it can be demonstrated that a questioned decision is a minister's own, it will be difficult to press home the attack against him. The appointment of a Parliamentary Commissioner has not made much difference to this aspect of the system: if the Commissioner's inquiries reveal a degree of personal responsibility on the minister's part the Government may simply reject his findings.

In a super-department the element of fiction in the constitutional doctrine of ministerial responsibility is further increased because ultimate responsibility rests with the head of the department, the Secretary of State. Parliament will therefore not readily accept a defence of the department's actions from the junior minister, even when he is the effective head of the relevant section of the super-department where the decision was taken and when the Secretary of State is patently extremely remote from the area concerned. This is also a powerful argument against the 'overlord' system or any other device for separating matters of high policy from routine decisions. It is also one reason for the Government's reluctance to publish either the terms of reference or the membership of Cabinet committees. It is generally in the Prime Minister's interest for there to be no identifiable intermediate groups between the Cabinet as a whole and individual ministers. Clearly there are pressures in the other direction, however, and his reluctance to reveal the mechanics of Cabinet decision making would have to change if the recent suggestion of the Select Committee on the Parliamentary Commissioner for Administration were to be accepted and the PCA given access to Cabinet papers, or Cabinet documents were regularly leaked to select committees.[7]

Non-departmental Government Agencies

The traditional picture of British central government as a series of departments manned by permanent civil servants and headed by responsible ministers has never altogether corresponded to reality. As has been seen, there have always been a number of boards, commissions or councils with nominated membership and with staff who may not necessarily be civil servants. Such bodies may exercise advisory, executive or even policy-making functions; the relationship with the minister most closely connected with their subject area can vary enormously.[8] Such bodies have multiplied in recent years, but it is not only the degree of patronage which they provide which has focused attention upon them; it is also that such bodies are not subject to even the minimal amount of control which Parliament can exercise over departments.[9] The acronym 'quango' – quasi-autonomous national governmental organization – has been used to describe them although some of these bodies are regional or local rather than national in operation. In a national budget as vast as the United Kingdom's, the expenditure on quangos cannot bulk very large, though the extravagance that has been detected is an argument for tighter control. The question of patronage in their recruitment will be dealt with in a later chapter; what is of interest here is the substantive role which these bodies play in British government.

Certainly, it is difficult to bring them all within a single classification. In 1976 the Civil Service Department listed 295 national and local bodies with full- or part-time membership, but this excluded those bodies where, although members were unpaid, expenses might be claimed. The list was compiled at a time when the number of quangos was increasing: it was estimated that between 1974 and 1978, 42 new quangos were created, of which only 5 had purely advisory functions. Another method of classification is to take bodies whose staffing is subject to ministerial control, which means that at least half their income is derived from public funds. In 1978 such bodies numbered 171. If disqualification from membership of the House of Commons is taken as the criterion, in 1975 there were, excluding the courts, 45 bodies whose membership was disqualified from sitting in the Commons. This number rose to 107 in 1978.

Their origins vary. Of major importance are the boards of the nationalized industries, which were created on terms specified in the individual statutes nationalizing particular industries. Others are the result of secondary or delegated legislation which authorizes a minister to create agencies for functions prescribed in the parent Act – area health authorities and water authorities, development corporations, marketing boards, industrial training boards and wages councils, for example. A Royal Charter or Warrant has been used in the past to set up Royal Commissions and the Research Councils. Advisory councils and similar groups – which are normally unsalaried but whose members may receive fees as well as expenses – can be established by ministerial fiat, although parliamentary sanction used to be thought necessary if a body was intended to be permanent. Even such active bodies as the Metrication Board, the National Consumer Council and the Energy Commission have no legislative sanction, though the first two have figured in white papers. (The Metrication Board was mentioned in a white paper for the first time a full three years after its creation.) White papers, despite appearances to the contrary given their use to impose incomes policies, are simply documents expressing a government's intentions and have no legal force.

The variety of organizations spawned by government could also be classified on the basis of their types of activity. There are the familiar regulatory bodies, governing areas of commercial activity, for instance, the Civil Aviation Authority. Some bodies exist to distribute public money: the University Grants Committee, the Arts Council and several sporting bodies are obvious examples. However, other spending bodies also finance themselves by levies and fees.

The local bodies tend to detract from the system of local self-government which, as will be seen in a later chapter, has been held to be an especially noteworthy characteristic of the British polity. In England alone there are 9 regional water authorities, which levy water and sewerage rates at their own discretion; 8 regional economic planning councils; 9 port or harbour authorities; 14 regional health authorities; and 90 area health authorities. Some nationalized industries also have a regional organization; thus there are 12 area electricity boards. In addition, attached to each nationalized industry are a number of consultative councils and users' bodies designed to represent the consumers of the monopoly services which the nationalized industries provide.

Finally there are quangos which combine the promotion of social goals with quasi-judicial functions – the Commission for Racial Equality and the Equal Opportunities Commission, for example. Such a proliferation of agencies, for which ministerial responsibility is at best ambiguous, complicates both the operation and the description of the policy-making process. There is a permanent feedback from them to the departments, and to some extent they also make policy themselves.

The public corporations, which run by far the larger part of the public sector of the economy, raise complex questions for government organization. Their structure and their relationship with ministers and Parliament manifest the doctrine that bodies which have a commercial role ought not to be organized like government departments or run by civil servants. Their boards, it was thought, ought to behave like the boards of private companies except that their economic target is not the ideal of maximizing profit but merely that of achieving a balance of profit and loss over a period of years. They may have, for social reasons, to provide some services that are unprofitable – railways in rural Scotland and Wales for example – but this is a matter for which the sponsoring minister rather than the board is supposed to take responsibility. He is given specific powers concerning capital expenditure and borrowing, and can issue a formal directive to the board if it is unwilling to take his advice.

It had been assumed originally that ministerial intervention would be rare and confined to matters of general policy, while matters of day-to-day management would be left to the boards and their officers. Parliament, too, is debarred from asking questions about the detailed running of the public corporations. However, experience has cast serious doubts on the practicability of this approach: the minister cannot limit himself simply to such matters as capital investment and uneconomic services. The important role played in the economy by the prices of products or services offered by the nationalized industries makes it impossible for governments worried about inflation to refrain from intervening – and the monopolistic position of these industries increases the pressure for such intervention. An even more significant factor is that employees in these industries make up a large part of the total workforce, and the success of any form of incomes policy will therefore depend on the wage settlements in the public sector. Not only does this situation produce inter-departmental strife, as ministers primarily concerned with industrial peace clash with those primarily seeking to control inflation; it can also cause ministers to intervene in the policies of the corporations in order to maintain employment, even where purely economic criteria would suggest a reduction in the labour force.

All the principal public corporations have failed for much of the time to meet the demands that they should be run on ordinary commercial lines and balance their budgets. Huge losses that have to be met from the public purse, by taxation or by borrowing, have become normal; the idea that such enterprises could be shielded from political pressures in a way not possible for central-government departments has proved illusory.

In the late 1960s there was a fashionable idea that central-government departments could usefully 'hive off' certain functions – usually ones with limited political implications – into distinct units which could be separately accountable for their activities. Experience with the public corporations may have discouraged this development. The position of ministers in relation to public corporations has been an uneasy one; for it appears that ministers have exercised less authority over the boards of public corporations than the language of the original nationalization statutes might suggest. Ministers have been unwilling to incur the odium associated with issuing formal directives, and have tried to achieve their aims by bargaining with the boards in a manner that blurs the ultimate responsibility for policy. Their only important sanction, that of refusing money for investment purposes, is a blunt weapon. To use persuasion effectively, a minister must know the business from the inside; that means that he and his department must duplicate work already done by the boards in amassing the necessary information.

Another difficulty is that ministers cannot easily use their authority to nominate members of the boards in order to influence policy. The opportunity to nominate chairmen largely depends upon the accidents of retirement or death, while some other board members will be required to have specialist knowledge of the industry. Thus the area of recruitment is limited. It is difficult to dismiss a board member or a chairman without risking the accusation of political bias or of manipulation of the nationalized industries as part of a spoils system. The result is a built-in tension between chairmen of these boards who are mainly conscious of economic criteria and their sponsoring ministers who are alive to social and political considerations. It is therefore not surprising that in the 1970s a number of chairmen of nationalized industries left them for the private sector.

If ministers find themselves frustrated in their dealings with the nationalized industries, Parliament is in an equally ambiguous situation. The Select Committee on Nationalized Industries could probably operate more effectively only if more information on day-to-day matters were made available to it, and yet the provision of detailed information would be an added burden on management and a brake on commercial efficiency.

Ministers and Civil Servants

It has been seen that one of the reasons for experimenting with the public corporation was that it was not felt desirable to reproduce in commercial enterprises the structural features of a government department. Of especial importance among those features was the relationship between ministers and their civil servants.

Ministers are not normally expected to be specialists in the subject matter of their departments and the high turnover of ministers would itself preclude familiarity with the policies and problems involved. The political skills which a minister is supposed to contribute are allegedly independent of the subject matter with which he has to deal, so he relies heavily on his civil servants for advice on policy matters. To be effective he must therefore become acquainted as quickly as possible with the outlines of the department's responsibilities and the principal personalities within it.[10]

The suitability of the present higher Civil Service to the conditions of modern Britain will be examined in a later chapter; however, it is undoubtedly the case that the traditional conventions of ministerial responsibility give it great power. It was perhaps inevitable that as this power became more obvious there should be attempts to penetrate the veil of official anonymity, and in fact the questioning of civil servants on matters with a policy content by parliamentary select committees has become much more frequent. Similarly tribunals and other instruments of public inquiry, as well as the Parliamentary

Commissioner for Administration, have also become readier to name individual civil servants or to reveal circumstances which make identification not too difficult. The power of the Civil Service is inevitably reinforced by the frequent re-shuffles of departmental ministers: without continuity in a department's political leadership, the department can develop its own attitude or tradition, and this may prove difficult for the incoming minister to accommodate or make his own. Because of this the case has been made for a ministerial *cabinet* within each department – on the continental model – which would allow a minister to appoint a body of advisers and assistants from outside as well as inside government service. Such a body would be distinct from the present private office of a minister, which is a small group of promising young civil servants selected from within his department. In fact the French *cabinet*, the prototype of this idea, consists of civil servants from different branches of government; it has been cogently argued that what British ministers need is not so much outsiders but a group of civil servants from other departments who can help them function effectively in Cabinet committees, in full Cabinet and inside the department itself. This suggestion draws attention to the fact that the Civil Service is not monolithic: each department develops its own perspectives, which may nevertheless have to be transcended if new policy initiatives are to be successful.

The suggestion that British ministers should have *cabinets* on the continental model would entail major changes in administrative practice. Such a development would in particular affect the position of the Permanent Secretary in each department, who is in many ways the central non-political figure in British administration. For it is the Permanent Secretary, appointed when a vacancy occurs by the Prime Minister himself in consultation with the Head of the Home Civil Service, who is both the intermediary through whom a department's views are made known to the minister, and the individual responsible for ensuring that the minister's policy is carried into effect.

Objections to the introduction of a *cabinet* system are partly attributable to the natural reluctance of civil servants to downgrade the post of Permanent Secretary, which currently represents the summit of the ambitions of members of a highly self-conscious professional body. In addition, there is the objection that departments are not to be treated as self-sufficient empires, even if they do develop their own distinct characteristics. Much work has to be done through inter-departmental committees; although the proliferation of such committees was one of the reasons for creating super-departments, the increase in the size of departments has not much altered this aspect of government. Responsibility for manning such committees at the official level must rest with the regular departmental machine. Much can be done by informal consultation between private offices but, if chaos is to be avoided, regular procedures and formal record keeping are essential; there is no safe way in which the departmental hierarchy can be bypassed. This is also true of departmental consultation with the Treasury, which all departments undertake on a regular basis.

The Machinery of Co-ordination

In the inter-war years the Prime Minister, as First Lord of the Treasury, had as his principal advisers the Permanent Secretary, who was also Head of the Civil Service, and the Secretary to the Cabinet, who was also at the time secretary to the revived Committee of Imperial Defence, so that co-ordination was to some extent achieved by these two powerful civil servants. The Foreign Office remained somewhat apart from the general governmental machine and maintained its separate procedures for recruitment and promotion. It was the policy consequences of this separation which caused Neville Chamberlain during his premiership to obtain Sir Horace Wilson as a personal adviser on secondment from the Treasury.

In the post-war period a number of changes occurred: the Committee of Imperial Defence was not revived; the Cabinet Office took on wider co-ordinating functions; and the Treasury acquired new responsibilities and hence more contact with other departments as more interventionist and positive economic policies were adopted. For a time the position of Permanent Secretary of the Treasury was divided into two posts, with one of the holders also acting as Secretary to the Cabinet and the other as Head of the Home Civil Service. When, following the Fulton Committee recommendations on the Home Civil Service in 1968, a separate Civil Service Department was established and its Permanent Secretary became Head of the Home Civil Service, he became the Prime Minister's adviser on both personnel matters and the machinery of government. The Treasury then had only one Permanent Secretary combining responsibility for financial and economic matters. However, as has been seen, for a short stage in 1964–6 the short- and long-term aspects of economic management had been divorced, and a specialized department – the Department of Economic Affairs – had attempted to exercise responsibilities for long-term planning and growth, as opposed to financial control in the short term. While the Prime Minister remains formally the head of the Treasury, the Permanent Secretary's ministerial chief is in fact the Chancellor of the Exchequer.

The Secretary to the Cabinet, now once more an office held on its own, emerged from these changes with even more influence on the Prime Minister regarding the substance of policy and the co-ordination of the whole governmental machine. The personal position of the Secretary to the Cabinet should however be distinguished from the Secretariat over which he presides. The Secretariat is responsible for framing and circulating the minutes of the Cabinet and its committees. It can therefore exert (subject to the Prime Minister's authority) considerable influence by its choice of the wording of Cabinet conclusions should they be left unclear by the discussions. When Cabinets are divided, and verbal compromises are necessary to maintain the appearance of unity, this role can be extremely important. There is also a tendency for the Secretary to the Cabinet – whose tenure of the post may outlast several administrations – to regard himself as the custodian of the collective Cabinet conscience. Such would appear to be the rationale of allowing him to act as the arbiter of what it is proper for ministers to publish in their memoirs or of what documents the Parliamentary Commissioner for Administration may see.

The co-ordinating role of the Cabinet Office was strengthened in October 1970 by the creation of a new unit within it – a body which was originally styled the 'central capability unit' but which has come to be known as the Central Policy Review Staff or, more colloquially, the 'think tank'.[11] The creation of the Central Policy Review Staff was announced in a white paper about the new Conservative administration's projected measures to improve the management of government business.[12] It was explained that the new instrument was to be at the service of all ministers, to enable them to 'work out the implications of their basic strategy in terms of policies in specific areas' and to 'establish relative priorities to be given to different sectors of their programme as a whole'. It was ostensibly intended to fill the gap created by the alleged inability of ministers to know enough about policies of other departments to be able to make a valuable contribution to collective decision making. Now they would have a new source of information. It was, however, clear that the inquiries the CPRS would be asked to undertake would be decided largely by the Prime Minister; indeed, the new CPRS was in some quarters regarded as the nucleus of a Prime Minister's department. It was also clear from the recruitment of the original CPRS – mainly from economists and people with business experience – that the emphasis would be on cost-benefit analysis of long-term programmes and individual projects.

In its early years the CPRS enjoyed considerable advantages. It had a distinguished initial membership of about sixteen; it made free use of outside expertise; its first chairman, Lord Rothschild, was eminent both as a scientist and as a man of affairs. He understood the need to combine long-term inquiries with a consideration where necessary of short- and medium-term issues, so that his team never felt totally detached from the activities of government itself. When the CPRS was thought to be in the Prime Minister's confidence, departments had every incentive to assist in its work, much of which consisted of writing briefs on major policy issues that might come before the Cabinet and that could be updated, if necessary, when they did. Subjects in which the 'think tank' took an interest included energy policy, the ship-building industry, the computer industry, government research and development, nuclear reactor policy, population, race relations, and worker participation. The most striking innovation of the earlier period of the CPRS's existence was the introduction of six-monthly briefings to Cabinet and to junior ministers. In addition, on some occasions when there were strong departmental disagreements the CPRS was asked to arbitrate. It was hoped that the CPRS, because it was within the Cabinet Office but not of it, could sense what problems were likely to arise and could be prepared for them.

Perhaps the CPRS had lost some of its initial glamour even before the fall of the Heath Government. Lord Rothschild himself ran into trouble when he gave his personal views on the state of the nation in a public speech which earned a rebuke from the Prime Minister – a rebuke which raised the question of how far temporary advisers and units of the CPRS kind are covered by the civil-service conventions of political neutrality and anonymity. Moreover, growing concern with the immediate economic and industrial situation detracted from interest in long-term issues.

Under the Labour Government the CPRS became even more firmly embedded in the Cabinet Office system and its head, Sir Kenneth Berrill – whose experience was basically that of a Treasury official – did not have the political reputation to play the kind of independent role that Lord Rothschild had done. The repudiation by the Government of most of the CPRS report on overseas representation, which examined Britain's role in the world, including the position of the British Council and the BBC World Service further diminished its reputation. Neither Harold Wilson nor James Callaghan shared Edward Heath's interest in long-term planning, and preferred the advice of their newly strengthened private offices, where party considerations could be given greater weight. While the CPRS may survive as a useful instrument for undertaking confidential examinations of problems which cut across departmental boundaries, its creation may in the long run simply have added to the centralizing impetus of the Cabinet Office.

4   Parliament

In the 1975 referendum on whether the United Kingdom should remain a member of the European Communities, one argument of the anti-Europeans was that membership involved a diminution of the sovereignty of Parliament, which they regarded as the distinctive element in the British political system.[1] Yet it was clear that Parliament itself was not, except in the most formal sense, fulfilling the role which the opponents of membership assigned to it.

Until the 1970s electoral participation had been high and the proceedings of Parliament had commanded much attention; but after 1970 both these indices of Parliament's importance in the country showed a marked decline. Between 1974 and 1979, despite the drama inherent in a 'hung' Parliament – a Parliament in which government has no overall majority – there was little evidence of a recovery. The reluctant acquiescence of a majority of MPs in an experiment with radio broadcasting of parliamentary proceedings suggested that they were apprehensive about the impact this would have on their reputation. The available opinion-poll data on the electorate's perceptions of politicians following the experiment did indeed seem to confirm the MPs' initial fears. Criticisms of the quality of British politicians and of the 'adversarial' style of British politics were linked with criticisms of the party system and led during this period to demands for electoral reform which would break the rigid hold of the two major parties over parliamentary and political life.

It is also, however, the role of Parliament itself that has been questioned. What is Parliament meant to contribute to the British system of government and how far is it properly equipped for its tasks? Since the 1960s there has been a full decade of procedural reform of various kinds along lines put forward by the academic members of the Study of Parliament Group and by some of the younger MPs of the 1966 Labour intake. But it is not clear that these reforms have done what it was hoped they would do.[2] For those who made so much of preserving parliamentary sovereignty in the debate about accession to the European Communities, these reforms, which were largely intended to strengthen Parliament's ability to oversee and control the executive, were not of great importance. Most of them did not mean by the sovereignty of Parliament an active role for all the 635 members of the House of Commons in the political affairs of the nation; they had in mind the ability of the executive to secure the enactment of its legislation by virtue of its majority in the House of Commons, however slim that majority might be and regardless of whether it reflected a majority of votes for the governing party in the country. From their point of view, the more opportunities MPs had to play an active role in the legislative process or to scrutinize the operations of the executive, the less satisfactory the situation, since such participation could only reduce government's ability to change society through legislative and administrative action. The desire for more rapid and unhampered action in the cause of radical change inevitably came most sharply into conflict with the wish for a more positive function for MPs in the Labour Party, where the demand for legislative intervention was greatest. Indeed ever since the 1930s there has been a strand in Labour thinking which favours confining Parliament to the enactment of enabling legislation, which would leave the executive free to fill in the details to an even greater extent than has now become the case.

The importance attached to macro-economic management, and the fact that modern governments are usually judged by their ability.to deal with such issues as unemployment, inflation and the balance of payments, have further weakened the role of Parliament. The more governments are forced to pre-empt policy decisions by bargains with organized labour and capital and with other governments or international organizations, the less room there will be for Parliament to play a significant role. The most vivid illustration of this occurred when the budget was presented to Parliament in April 1976. Important changes in taxation were left undecided pending the outcome of negotiations between the Government and the Trades Union Congress on the next phase of incomes policy. Furthermore Parliament cannot play any effective role in the framing of financial policy before a budget is presented to it, for the convention persists that even the Cabinet is not informed of the contents of a budget until a few hours before it is made public. Measures that cannot be safely imparted to the Chancellor's senior Cabinet colleagues must *a fortiori* be withheld from the opposition and even from a government's own back-benchers. The hopes entertained in the 1960s that the annual white paper giving a 'forward look' at the Government's thinking on public expenditure would give an opportunity for effective debate proved without foundation. Not only do MPs not have the economic expertise or information to participate in financial policy making, but they also show by the distribution of their time and energies that they are well aware of their own limitations.

To some extent the generalizations about Parliament's role in the British system have had to be adjusted to accommodate the experience of a Government which between 1974 and 1979 had at first only the narrowest of majorities and, after 1976, was dependent upon minority parties for the passage of its legislation. In these circumstances it was possible for minority parties, who were stronger than at any time since 1931, to align with the Conservative Opposition and the occasional Labour rebel to secure changes in the texts of measures, or even the total abandonment of bills. In standing committee the task of government was yet more difficult since it no longer commanded an automatic majority there, and even with the support of minor-party representatives it was vulnerable to absenteeism. From a situation in which the executive might expect the passage of its full legislative programme in virtually unaltered form, the Government had therefore to adjust to one in which neither the principles nor the details of bills were immune from parliamentary amendment.

A quick glance at the legislative record of the Labour

Government of 1974–9 may indicate the extent of the change. In 1975–6 five bills failed to pass through the House of Commons. One bill – for the nationalization of the aircraft- and ship-building industries – was passed only after very substantial amendment. It had been found that this could not be treated as an ordinary bill since it affected some private interests differently from others; it was in consequence a 'hybrid' bill – part public and part private – and would have to go through a special and time-consuming procedure which might lead to its being lost altogether. The Government therefore chose to drop the parts of the bill that had been challenged. In 1976–7, eight bills out of fifty failed to complete their passage.[3] In the 1977–8 session, the legislative programme was more limited but the Government failed to carry the commencement order necessary to make operative an Act dealing with dock labour which had been promised to the Transport and General Workers' Union. The difficulties of the Government extended even to questions of finance. In both 1977 and 1978, the Liberals helped to force through major changes in the Government's tax proposals. If a situation developed in which minor parties were again to have this strategic role in the House of Commons and overall majorities for government were no longer the norm, much that has been said about Parliament by commentators in recent years would need revision. In the light of the election in 1979 of a House of Commons where the Government had a majority of forty-three over all other parties, it is perhaps more useful to concentrate on the practice of Parliament in normal circumstances.

Parliament needs to adapt itself to the new demands made by the changing nature of modern government, while preserving for ministers and back-benchers alike the substance of the roles that they regard as important – roles conditioned by the almost unbroken development of Parliament over some seven hundred years. In contrast to the parliaments of other European countries which had to be created afresh after medieval estates had withered away under powerful dynastic absolutisms, the British Parliament is a direct survival of the English parliaments of the Middle Ages. All three of Parliament's earliest functions – judicial, legislative and financial – are still evident in its composition and procedure, though the judicial role of the

House of Lords is completely separate from its position as the second chamber. Parliament's legislative activity originated in the need for the medieval monarch to associate the great feudal lords and other representatives of the propertied classes with the process of law making. The monarch also required that the representatives of the tax-paying groups should assent to the levying of taxes. The need for taxation arose whenever some emergency – principally war – made it impossible for the monarch to meet his expenses out of the revenues from his own lands. From this function of supply came Parliament's demands for the redress of grievances. Eventually it became accepted that ministers must be able to command the confidence of the House of Commons, which became exclusively powerful in all matters of finance.

The composition of the two Houses of Parliament also reflects their medieval origins. In the House of Lords the principle of hereditary membership survives from the period when social, and hence political, power lay with the holders of great estates and titles; their attendance in person at Westminster was but one among many public duties. The presence of representatives of the established Church of England – the twenty-six archbishops and bishops – and of no other religious body reflects the country's earlier religious unity. The hereditary principle now commands diminishing support. The work of the House of Lords has in recent times been left increasingly to newly created peers who have come to it very often after experience in the House of Commons. By the Life Peerages Act of 1958, it became possible to create peers without their titles passing to their heirs and this widened the choice of Prime Ministers, in whose gift peerages lie, and of opposition leaders, who occasionally make nominations. By now, newly created life peerages do not do much more than balance losses through deaths. A significant element of the working House of Lords now consists of life peers, and they of course are especially significant for Labour Party representation in the House of Lords.

Since 1963 it has been possible for someone inheriting a peerage to disclaim it for his lifetime and remain a commoner. Moreover, since 1964 no new hereditary peerages have been created. It now seems very unlikely that either party would add to their number. The attempt by the Government in 1968 to take the process of reform one stage further and turn the House of Lords into a wholly nominated body reflecting the balance of party strength in the House of Commons failed – not because of any affection for the existing situation but because the more rational the composition of the House of Lords, the easier it would be for the Lords to exercise their powers with popular support.[4] The increased use of the powers of the House of Lords in the very special political circumstances of 1976–8 strengthened the support within the Labour Party for a unicameral Parliament, and by the end of 1978 abolition of the House of Lords had become official Labour Party policy, though this was watered down to the abolition of the Lords' delay and veto powers in the manifesto for the 1979 election. In contrast the idea of an elective upper House, free from the taint of the hereditary principle, seemed an increasingly attractive one to Conservatives.

The present composition of the House of Lords is clear enough. In January 1979 there were 809 hereditary peers, 321 life peers including the law lords, and 26 bishops. In 1977 143 peers formally applied for leave of absence, but many hereditary peers never put in more than the occasional appearance. On the other hand many life peers regard attendance as an obligation and both Labour and Liberal peerages are created with the actual work of the House of Lords in mind. Since 1957 the attendance of all peers has been stimulated by a daily attendance allowance and travelling expenses. While in the mid-1950s the average daily attendance in the House of Lords was below 100, it now stands at about 280. In July 1979 there were 3 peers in the Cabinet – including the Lord Chancellor – and 10 other peers held junior office.

Among those who take an active part in the work of the House of Lords, over 400 take the Conservative whip. About 150 take the Labour whip and about 40 the Liberal whip. In contrast to the situation in the House of Commons, non-party members or 'cross-benchers' form a recognized group and currently number about 90. Important issues can, however, still bring out the so-called 'backwoodsmen', who are overwhelmingly Conservative in sympathy; over 500 peers voted in the major divisions on the European Communities Bill.

The superior political position of the House of Commons

was established in the nineteenth century by convention, but it now rests upon two statutes – the Parliament Acts of 1911 and 1949. While the House of Lords has no powers over finance, it can delay other legislation by up to thirteen months. A bill rejected by the House of Lords can be carried by the House of Commons alone only if it is reintroduced in a new session of Parliament; this means that a Labour government may find it difficult to carry through a measure introduced in the last session of a Parliament.

The House of Lords' power to amend bills and thus to force the House of Commons to spend time debating its amendments was obviously a more serious problem for the Government between 1976 and 1979 because of the lack of a clear majority in the House of Commons. How far the House of Lords will use its power depends upon the tactical sense of the Conservative leadership. Conservative leaders are generally anxious to avoid a direct confrontation between the House of Lords and the House of Commons, especially when this could be exploited electorally. On occasion, however, the House of Lords will make its point firmly. Thus for example in 1969 it drastically amended a bill to redistribute a limited number of constituencies because it believed that the Government ought to have implemented the recommendations of the Boundary Commissioners in full. The Government had to withdraw its bill and, although the comprehensive recommendations were not introduced at that time, the House of Lords had succeeded in giving publicity to an issue which was widely seen as a piece of government gerrymandering. (The fact that this particular question related to the composition of the House of Commons made the Lords' intervention the more remarkable.) In 1974–5 the Government failed to secure the passage of a Trade Unions and Labour Relations Amendment Bill after the House of Lords had inserted a form of words guaranteeing newspaper editors against some of the bill's closed-shop provisions. The bill was, however reintroduced during the 1976–7 session when an amendment to deal with the position of editors was inserted in the House of Lords but rejected by the House of Commons. The House of Lords did not insist further and the Bill received the royal assent without recourse to the Parliament Act of 1949, which would have secured its passage by the Commons alone.[5]

In constitutional matters and questions affecting the basic rights of the citizen the House of Lords claims a special right to be heard. This was shown in its handling of the bills to establish devolved Assemblies for Scotland and for Wales in the 1977–8 session. In the event the number of issues which the Conservatives were willing to press was very small and the bills reached the statute book by the end of the session.

Like the House of Lords, the House of Commons reflects its medieval origins, though again rather remotely, because representation in the Middle Ages was felt to be of communities rather than of individuals. The communities were the counties and boroughs, which were also the principal units of local administration and justice. Representation of the universities began in the early seventeenth century and lasted until 1950; this was non-territorial since graduates could vote for their university's representative regardless of where they resided. Today the representative system is wholly territorial and based on the single-member constituency. In addition, as will be seen in the next chapter, although some effort is still made to ensure a relationship between parliamentary constituencies and local-government areas, even this is proving hard to maintain. Except perhaps in remote rural areas, it is natural that there should be some erosion of territorial loyalties: increased mobility in work and leisure makes it likely that the ties of occupation and social class will be greater than those of locality.

Furthermore the role of political parties has the effect of diminishing the importance of local issues and concentrating attention on national ones. The overriding role of political parties in the electoral system was for a long time not recognized formally. It was not until 1969 that a parliamentary candidate's party allegiance was allowed to appear on the ballot paper. Now that a start has been made with financing parties out of public funds – for their parliamentary functions – it may be assumed that the role of party organization will be more frequently acknowledged in law. Certainly, many of the discussions about the existing electoral system as a whole now revolve around whether changes will advance the cause of one or other party rather than whether the system is fair to individuals or localities.

Support for the present electoral system comes primarily from those who regard the principal function of the House of Commons as that of sustaining a ministry in office. The historic distinction between the executive and the legislature – which was never complete – came to an end in the eighteenth century with the emergence of the Cabinet as the effective executive. Before the middle of the nineteenth century, responsible government – the dependence of the Cabinet upon a majority of the House of Commons rather than upon the favour of the monarch – was fully established. In the middle of the nineteenth century, Cabinet government existed in the context of a party system in the House of Commons of a fairly fluid kind. Groups had to come together if a government were to be formed with sufficient backing; it was possible to regard the House of Commons as actually choosing the government. After 1868 the advent of modern mass parties and the discipline which their existence imposed upon their supporters in Parliament meant that the result of an election itself directly determined the complexion of the ensuing government.

Since the second Reform Act of 1867 it has been normal for a government defeated at the polls to resign without waiting for Parliament to meet. But this practice is only unquestioned when the new House of Commons has a clear majority for another party. Stanley Baldwin met Parliament in 1923 because although he had no overall majority he was still the leader of the largest single party in the House of Commons; and Edward Heath hesitated before resigning following the election of February 1974 in order to explore the possibility of remaining as Prime Minister in a coalition government. A single Parliament would not be expected to sustain successive governments of different parties: if, as happened in 1931, there were an internal shift leading to a new government, an election would be expected to follow.

Experience between 1976 and 1979 showed that it is for government itself to decide when its majority must be considered as lost. So long as the Callaghan Government could rely on the Liberal Party's support in any vote of confidence, it was prepared to accept a number of defeats which might have prompted another government to dissolve Parliament. In other words the vital votes, other than those of no confidence, are those government chooses to regard as such; then the possibility of calling a second vote normally allows any intra-party rebellions to be contained by permitting the rebels to return to the party fold on the crucial question of confidence after voting against the leadership on the substantive issue.

The basic framework of parliamentary debate takes the form of a dialogue, not between the executive and the legislature, but between government and the major opposition party. Where government and opposition differ so greatly that continuity of policy is difficult, the dialogue has been designated, as has been seen, 'adversary politics'.[6] The distinction between government and opposition is certainly all-pervasive in the organization of parliamentary proceedings: a government is able to exert control over the parliamentary timetable as well as the domestic concerns of Parliament such as the salaries of MPs and the services available to them.

In normal times the domination of the executive rests upon the ability of the Cabinet always to command the votes of its nominal supporters. The main areas of serious controversy and the main focus for the exercise of leadership skills are within the ruling party itself. This generalization is more evidently true when Labour is in power because the Labour Party is a more factional and internally democratic party than the Conservative Party, though the 1970–4 Parliament witnessed a considerable degree of intra-party dissent among Conservatives. Even majority governments may have to abandon legislation if they cannot rely on their supporters: witness the failure of the Labour Government of 1966–70 to enact the proposed Industrial Relations Bill because of its inability to secure the consent of the Parliamentary Party.

Modern Parliaments do not provide a forum for ventilating grievances of a general kind. In a House of Commons controlled by the executive, government need not offer to redress grievances in return for the voting of funds as in the classic model of parliamentary government. At most, Parliament remains a forum in which individual grievances can be ventilated if other means of securing government's attention have failed. Questions to ministers and the Parliamentary Commissioner for Administration's work in probing cases of maladministration only represent a part of the modern grievance procedure; for it is not

Parliament upon which the aggrieved citizen relies but his local MP, and the MP's intervention will normally entail direct contact with the department or agency which has occasioned the complaint.

Most of what an MP does in his constituency 'surgery' could be done by someone else appointed for the purpose, and it is only the personal and political rewards which MPs believe they obtain from such activities – as well as a sense of personal satisfaction – which prevent them from shedding this function. The alarm in the House of Commons when it was thought that the Parliamentary Commissioner might be petitioned directly like his Scandinavian counterparts shows how important this responsibility is in MPs' minds. It is almost the only duty, of course, which brings an MP into direct contact with his constituents, although the amount of time taken up by such work and the importance attached to it will vary enormously among MPs. What is perhaps surprising is that the function of advising and helping constituents at the local level has survived for so long without adequate secretarial facilities: many MPs write a good deal of their own correspondence and it would be unusual to find more than one secretary employed on constituency matters alone.

The Legislative Process

Legislation is divided into two broad kinds – public legislation and private legislation. Public legislation, which is far more important in terms of volume and character, is sponsored by government in the case of major measures but may also be sponsored by back-bench MPs through what are called private members' bills. Private legislation is a very different thing: it deals with matters affecting the interests of named individuals or bodies. In the nineteenth century, such private Acts of Parliament were very common as a method of dealing with matters for which general statutes did not provide, such as divorce. Today most of these things can be dealt with under the provisions of general statutes. However, private legislation is still employed when a local authority wishes to acquire some new function which is not covered by existing powers granted to local authorities, or when some local authority or other public body needs to acquire land by compulsory purchase.

The procedure which private bills must follow is more akin to that of judicial proceedings than to the adversarial method of passing public legislation. A private bill must clear a number of preliminary hurdles, which give ample opportunities for local objectors to a measure to be heard and which may involve public inquiries, a town poll, or a town meeting. Only after the completion of this expensive and time-consuming process can the first reading be taken. If the bill is unopposed progress will be rapid; but an opposed bill after second reading has to go to a Private Bill Committee of MPs, which operates rather more like a court than an ordinary standing committee in that the promoters and opponents of the bill are represented by counsel and call witnesses to give evidence on their behalf. The committee can deal both with the desirability of the bill itself and with its details. If it rejects the measure the rejection is taken as final; if approval is given subsequent procedure is like that for a public bill. Private bills must go through both Houses of Parliament according to the same procedures.

In questions of public legislation, the pre-eminence of government has long been accepted. All important bills are presented to Parliament by the appropriate minister after being drafted on the basis of departmental instructions to one or more parliamentary draftsmen. These draftsmen are the thirty-five or so barristers who make up the office of Parliamentary Counsel. The minister, aided by his civil servants and the draftsmen, will pilot the bill through the various stages of parliamentary scrutiny, aiming to secure the passage either of the original bill or at least of one which has been amended only in accordance with governmental wishes. Government will normally have a majority in the House of Commons and that majority will be reflected in the composition of standing committees; this means that the executive can control both the principles and the details of a bill.

In recent years there has been criticism of the way bills are drafted and amended because, it is argued, the statutes which emerge from the legislative process lack simplicity and clarity. A committee established to look at the legislative process in 1973 found that little could be done to improve the situation as long as MPs insisted on examining bills in considerable detail. Apart from suggesting an increase in the number of parliamentary draftsmen – many bills are thought to be ill-considered and the office of Parliamentary Counsel is generally overworked – the committee made few substantial recommendations.[7] Thus the problem of the quality of legislation remains a perplexing one. Incoherent or ambiguous legislation can be tidied up by the judiciary when they come to apply a statute, but of course the judges' interpretation of the law may reflect a quite different understanding of the purpose of an enactment from that originally intended. Equally, it has to be admitted that an opposition may well find it politically advantageous to allow faulty legislation to reach the statute book so that technical difficulties can later be exploited. This will be especially true where the legislation is of a novel kind, as with the Race Relations Acts or the Sex Discrimination Act.

Apart from financial legislation, government bills are the result either of government commitment to a party programme – most manifestos now have long 'shopping lists' of bills which the party intends to enact – or of departmental initiative. Departmental initiative may arise when practical experience in working a piece of legislation prompts the need for amendment; it may be the result of pressure-group consultations; or it may occur when some new problem appears which is thought to require legislative intervention. Some measures simply consolidate or tidy up existing statutes: latterly the Law Commissions have stimulated government departments into reviewing several areas of the law which it was thought deserved comprehensive overhaul.

Private members' bills may be the product of a variety of factors, but they frequently result from the urging of some pressure group or 'lobby'. Sometimes they will involve considerations of morality or religion where government will be wary of identifying itself too directly with the legislation for fear of losing votes; yet if the Government is sympathetic to such a measure it can do much to ensure that it reaches the statute book. The opportunity to introduce a bill is determined by a ballot of MPs for the time available – Fridays are traditionally set aside for private members' bills – but even those MPs who are initially allocated time know that their bills are unlikely to become law unless government makes some of its own legislative time available for the later stages of the bills. Normally a government will only do this when it is both sympathetic to the aim of the bill and when there has already been substantial collaboration between the private member sponsoring it and the appropriate government department, which will have to administer or enforce the law. Private members' bills introduced into the House of Lords have even less chance of becoming law than such bills introduced into the Commons. However, the point of introducing a private member's bill is often simply to gain publicity for a cause; the remoteness of the possibility that such a bill might reach the statute book is illustrated by the fact that bills are often formally introduced without even a prepared text.

When it adjourned in August 1978 the Parliament elected in October 1974 had passed 48 private members' bills into law. This number represented 11.5% of the 417 private members' bills introduced over those four years. Of government bills introduced in the same period, nearly 93% became law. In a Parliament with a clear government majority – for example that of 1966 – the executive did even better: in 1966–7 it was successful with all of its 103 bills; in 1967–8 it was successful with 63 out of 65 (96.9%); and in 1968–9 the figure was 51 out of 54 (94.4%).[8]

The difference made to bills by the legislative process is usually not very great. As has been pointed out, the main negotiations with any interests concerned will have taken place before a bill is introduced into the House of Commons and ministers can therefore always argue that any amendments to the text of a bill would upset accommodations already made. The formal stages of the legislative process are thus of less political significance than those which occur before the bill is introduced.

The parliamentary stages of the legislative process are known as readings. The first reading is a purely formal process in which the title of the bill is put down on the order paper. The second reading, however, provides an opportunity for the general principles of a proposed measure to be debated. Since the ultimate vote of the House of Commons is usually predetermined because members normally vote according to party instruction, this debate takes the form of an appeal by government and opposition to the electorate on the basis of their rival philosophies. It is at this stage that the adversarial style of British politics is most obvious and it is also this dramatic ritual which is highly prized by many traditional defenders of parliamentary procedure. The result of the second-reading debate will determine whether the bill is to proceed. If the vote is positive the bill will go on to its committee stage, which involves a clause-by-clause discussion; this will normally take place in a standing committee of the House of Commons. (Non-controversial bills may also have their second reading in committee, but this is relatively rare.) Only bills of unusual importance or of a constitutional nature – government decides which bills fall into these categories – and the main provisions of finance bills are dealt with at the committee stage by the whole House of Commons – 'in committee of the whole house' or 'on the floor' as this procedure is known.

It is significant that 'standing committees' are no longer what is usually meant by this designation in other contexts. They are not committees in existence with a defined membership so that business can be allotted to them as need arises: the membership of a standing committee depends upon the particular bill under discussion. While the whips on both sides of the House of Commons may well choose members of standing committees from MPs who have a special interest in the subject matter of a given bill, the essential requirement is that the balance of votes on the committee should reflect party strength in the house. Thus except when there is no overall majority in the house – as was the case between 1976 and 1979 – a government can almost always rely on being able to defeat any amendment to which it takes exception. The minister reponsible for a bill also has an important advantage over its critics: he has his civil servants available to brief him on the implications of a proposed amendment. Sometimes, however, the occasional amendment will be produced, perhaps from a government backbencher rather than the opposition, which will raise new issues; however, in theory committee amendments must be in harmony with the overall purpose of a bill.

After the committee stage comes the report stage when a bill as amended in committee is reported back to the House. This stage gives a government a further opportunity to put forward its own amendments to the bill, to reverse amendments made in committee or to endorse the treatment accorded to a bill by the standing committee or committee of the whole House. As at the committee stage, the introduction of government amendments here may reflect party or interest-group representations made between the formal introduction of the bill and the detailed consideration of it; alternatively they may reflect changed circumstances which make such an alteration desirable.

The final stage in the House of Commons' consideration of a bill is the third reading, which involves discussion of the principles of the bill again, though now in its amended version. The outcome, like that of the second reading, will usually be determined by a government's majority; however, of course it is possible that a revolt within the governing party may have grown by this stage and thus on some occasions there may be a setback. The total impact of the House of Commons on the details of legislation is very slight in proportion to the amount of time devoted by members to legislative matters. A detailed study of the fate of government bills over the three parliamentary sessions of 1967–8, 1968–9 and 1970–1 revealed that only thirty-nine amendments were successfully pressed home by opposition members or by government back-benchers, despite the fact that thousands of such amendments were moved. Of the thirty-nine in question not more than nine were substantial.[9]

Once a bill has passed through all its stages in one House it must then be considered by the other. The House of Lords may thus make further changes to a bill introduced into the House of Commons; however, as has been seen, the House of Commons can ordinarily overrule such changes so that those carried often simply reflect the fact that government itself has had second thoughts.

The foregone conclusion of standing-committee deliberations, and the technical level of such serious argument as takes place, mean that standing-committee proceedings receive little publicity and are hence relatively unattractive to MPs. It is because the influence of the House of Commons is thus essentially an indirect one, depending primarily on the relationship between governments and their back-bench supporters, that would-be reformers of parliamentary procedure have not on the whole devoted much attention to the legislative functions of Parliament. Parliament's weakness in matters of legislation is further demonstrated by the fact that the control of the parliamentary timetable rests with the government itself, unless its lack of a majority forces it to make concessions to the opposition. Lack of parliamentary time is a serious matter for governments with a heavy legislative commitment.

The total output of public legislation rose steeply after 1945, fell again during the 1950s and has shown a substantial rise since then. In 1957, 1,103 pages were added to the statute book; in 1973, 2,248 pages. In order to save time special procedures have been developed. To avoid filibustering, either a guillotine motion – one which closes debate – or a timetable motion – one which allocates the amount of time to be devoted to discussion of groups of clauses in a bill – is usually required. However, the opposition will usually contest these motions itself, which may mean a further loss of time; it will claim that it needs further time to discuss the details of a bill, but what it will really want to do is to proclaim again its opposition to the bill on principle. In the case of the Industrial Relations Bill of 1971, 111 of its 150 clauses were not discussed either in committee or at the report stage. The failure of the House of Commons to debate many of the clauses of the devolution bills in 1978 was one reason for the freedom with which the Lords sought to amend them.

Parliament also finds it difficult to deal with the growing output of delegated legislation, in other words legislation made by the executive by virtue of powers conferred by statute on the Crown, departments or individual ministers. The principal form used is that of the statutory instrument. Statutory instruments are published serially by the year and can be used for instance to vary the amount paid in social benefits, as in number 475 of 1978 – 'mobility allowance uprating order, 1978'. Other subordinate legislation includes the rules made by public corporations, local authorities and other public bodies.[10] The figures concerning delegated legislation are once again revealing of a general trend. After reaching a peak in the 1940s the number of statutory instruments declined in the 1950s but started to rise again in the mid-1960s; they now average between 1,000 and 1,300 a year. Their length has increased even more markedly. In 1955 they filled 3,240 pages; in 1965, 6,435 pages; and in 1974, 8,667 pages.[11]

Formal parliamentary control over delegated legislation is maintained by a variety of procedures. Acts may require that instruments made under their provisions should be laid before Parliament; the usual procedure then means that an instrument will become effective after a given time – usually forty days – unless a negative resolution has been passed by either House. In the case of some instruments which are regarded as of special constitutional significance or which impose taxation – an area dealt with by the House of Commons alone – an affirmative resolution is required. Affirmative resolutions are a significant check on executive activity, for the appropriate minister may have to defend the substance of an instrument. Negative resolutions are only a limited protection against executive action: the sheer volume of delegated legislation and the usual limitations upon time make it difficult for Parliament to supervise delegated legislation. Of course in both the affirmative and the negative procedures a government will use its majority to enforce the delegated legislation if necessary.

The role of committees is a significant indication of the actions of Parliament in this sphere. The House of Commons' Select Committee on Statutory Instruments which existed until 1972 was limited in its terms of reference to dealing with the technical aspects of the delegated legislation examined; it was chiefly important for making departments pay attention to clarity and consistency in their drafting and for preventing them from straying beyond the bounds of the parent Act. The corresponding House of Lords' Special Orders Committee had wider powers when it considered statutory instruments that required an affirmative resolution. The Lords' one rejection of a statutory instrument – the instrument renewing sanctions against the Smith regime in Rhodesia – was an important factor in the events leading to the abortive Parliament Bill of 1968–9 which attempted to reform the House of Lords. Since February 1973 the consideration of statutory instruments from the technical point of view has been the responsibility of a joint committee of both Houses of Parliament. This in itself is a rather rare device in the British system, though a joint committee also exists to consider bills that merely consolidate existing legislation. The House of Commons has in addition a standing committee which is entitled to look at the merits of certain statutory instruments, although this committee finds it hard to make its views effective. The whole problem of delegated legislation has been further complicated by Parliament's desire to have its say on legislation made by the European Economic Communities. In fact much of this legislation is not strictly speaking delegated or secondary legislation; however, as will be seen in Chapter 13, the responsibility for scrutinizing it now rests mainly with the Select Committee on European Legislation etc.

Financial Procedure

Equally important is Parliament's role in finance. Traditionally Parliament has operated on the theory that it will first consider what government needs to spend in the ensuing financial year and then make provision for such expenditure through taxation. Parliament's instruments of control, such as the Public Accounts Committee which is backed by the Comptroller and Auditor General and his staff, are designed to check in detail that money has been spent only on the purposes for which it has been voted by Parliament, as well as to guard against corruption. It is thus assumed that Parliament's interest lies in checking executive extravagance. However, although these elements of parliamentary control have their uses they have become relatively minor in relation to the role of government in an advanced industrial society.

From the point of view of civil servants the traditional annual estimates and revenue decisions are artificial divisions in programmes which either make permanent demands on the Exchequer, as in the case of the main government services, or, where capital expenditure is concerned, are based on a five- or ten-year 'forward look'. Basic decisions about expenditure are taken long before the estimates or the finance bill come up for parliamentary discussion, and usually only minor adjustments are possible by that stage. Decisions about raising money in particular ways, whether by taxation or by loan, will be affected not only by government requirements but also by calculations about the effect of such steps upon the general level of economic activity. Taxation and borrowing now perform the dual function of providing for services and controlling demand and the level of investment; however, the historic procedures of Parliament predate recognition of this general economic responsibility.

From the Whitehall perspective the important aspect of public expenditure – including local-government expenditure and expenditure by the public sector of the economy – is its effect in the long term. Whitehall now takes for granted the necessity of economic forecasting, and of allowing for changes in technology and the external economic environment. From another perspective however, that of individual departmental ministers, the vital decisions are those which cause the expansion or contraction of particular branches of government, again not so much in the immediate future but in the medium or long term. For Parliament, the supreme arbiter of the nation's fortunes, the essential question is whether or not it can participate in this process effectively; much of the unease about Parliament's role is influenced by a general suspicion that it cannot.

In recent years governments have become rather more willing to reveal in white papers and through other channels the basic presuppositions of their economic thinking and their consequent projections of the future demands likely to be made upon total resources by public expenditure. The Treasury remains reluctant about extending this experiment in open government further, although more progress could probably be made if there were sufficient public demand. Discussions of changes in taxation are difficult to initiate because the economy is extremely sensitive to speculations about such amendments; however, even here there is possibly room for more openness. In May 1971 one step was taken when a select committee was established to consider government proposals for the reform of the corporation tax; the detailed consideration of the proposed wealth tax announced in 1974 was also submitted to a select committee. The difficulty perhaps does not lie so much in the recalcitrance of the administration as in the indifference of parliamentarians; there seems to be no direct relationship between the importance of an issue and the interest which MPs are likely to show. Debates upon such general questions as the long-term pattern of public expenditure – which must to some extent affect all parties since decisions taken may become operative only in an ensuing Parliament or even the one after that – will neither attract Members of Parliament nor receive much public attention. They do not provide the occasion for one of those gladiatorial clashes which can occur when Parliament is at its liveliest. Mere discussion upon which no immediate decisions hang does not attract party politicians, and Parliament is not well equipped as a forum for the discussion of economic ideas.

However, some commentators have argued that Parliament could play an effective part in the control of public expenditure if the parliamentary timetable were changed. The way the annual estimates are put through the House of Commons is complicated by the fact that the financial year, which runs from 5 April, is not the same as the parliamentary session which runs in most years from October to October, of which period the last three months or so cover the summer recess. As a result the House of Commons may at various times be considering estimates covering the previous year, the current year and the forthcoming year. The supply days given for dealing with these estimates are by convention used to debate subjects of general interest chosen by the opposition; in fact recent changes have even made it unnecessary to relate the subjects to specific heads of expenditure. The authorization to spend the money which is approved is incorporated in three consolidated fund bills in February, in March and just before the summer recess. Members can raise matters of general or constituency interest in these debates; once again there is little serious consideration of the expenditure itself.

The opportunity to deny supply, although it exists, is normally unlikely to be taken seriously, for a government defeated on major portions of its estimates would be obliged to dissolve Parliament. It is perhaps significant that a defeat on the annual expenditure white paper, such as the Government sustained in 1977, is not considered an occasion for dissolution. A backbencher can in theory challenge items in the estimates on the days when they are placed on the order papers, but the whips

will not encourage him to do so. Moreover he has no opportunity to force votes on individual items at the consolidated
fund bill stage, while the annual debate on the report of the
Public Accounts Committee is also too general for this purpose.
The introduction of 'cash limits' in the 1977–8 session as a
method of limiting certain forms of public expenditure added a
further complication to the budgetary process, for the elements
of expenditure to which 'cash limits' apply are fewer than those
of the estimates; they also differ from the estimates both in
structure and in the way in which they are calculated to take
account of inflation. The 1979–80 defence estimates were,
according to the 1978 defence white paper, to be put on the
same price basis as the cash limits. Whether some new procedures bringing expenditure and income together can be
devised remains an open question after a decade of experiment.[12]

The difficulties of dealing with these problems would exist
even if the parties were as little divided in their economic
attitudes today as they were in the second half of the nineteenth century. However, the difficulties of promoting useful
economic debate are exacerbated by the deep ideological
divisions in Parliament. The would-be parliamentary reformers
often ignore the reality of party and of factions within parties
which, together with ambition for office, represent the motor
force of the parliamentary system. Such reformers believe
that Parliament can rationally allocate public expenditure in
the light of an accepted set of national priorities, for which
belief neither history nor observation gives them warrant.

Select Committees and the Limits of Reform

Many of the obstacles to reforming Parliament's financial procedures also prevent Parliament from establishing greater control over the general processes of administration. Specialist
Select Committees for Agriculture and for Education and
Science were set up as an experiment by Richard Crossman
when he was Leader of the House in 1966. Other similar devices
have subsequently been adopted, particularly since the replacement in 1971 of the old Estimates Committee by a new
Committee on Public Expenditure, which works through subcommittees with specialized fields of investigation. On the more

technical side of their inquiries the members of such committees have been able to stand back from the party struggle and frequently produce unanimous reports. Also, while in the nineteenth century the desire to keep public expenditure down was a unifying factor, now the desire for efficiency in administration has to some extent replaced it.

The growth of specialist-committee activity can be measured statistically. In the 1965–6 session, 8 select committees were appointed; in the 1977–8 session there were 17 select or joint committees and 22 subcommittees. While in 1961–2 there had been 294 meetings of select committees of all kinds involving 206 MPs, in 1976–7, a lighter year than the two preceding ones, there were 673 meetings involving 254 MPs. In 1975–6, the heaviest year to date, no fewer than 294 MPs took some part in committee work. Some select committees, for instance the Privileges and Selection Committees, deal with the internal organization and working of the House of Commons. The existence of a government majority on the Selection Committee can make a vital difference; this was especially true when in 1976 there was a dispute over the interpretation of the rules governing committee membership in circumstances where the Government did not command an overall majority in the House of Commons.

Of the committees which deal with matters of substance rather than procedure, the Committee on Nationalized Industries is of long standing; the Select Committee on Science and Technology represents the legacy of the Crossman approach to parliamentary reform; the Committee on Race Relations and Immigration scrutinizes the operation both of government departments and of the bodies especially devised to deal with the problems of discrimination; and the Committee on the Parliamentary Commissioner for Administration serves as a recipient of the Parliamentary Commissioner's reports and as an instrument for reviewing the PCA's operations. The Select Committee on the PCA has also been able to follow up many of the points made in his reports; it provides a mechanism for ensuring that his recommendations are followed by political and parliamentary pressure if they are initially ignored by government.

The key select committee since 1971 has been the

Expenditure Committee, which operates through its general or steering committee and five subcommittees covering most of the areas of government. It is difficult to say how far this apparatus represents an advance over the pre-1971 Estimates Committee. Like the old Committee it is primarily concerned with *post facto* inquiries on specific topics which may or may not prove fruitful; although there has been more experiment with outside advisers of late, the Committee is still hampered by the staffing restrictions which the Government places upon it. Certainly, there is none of the counter-bureaucracy which helps to make congressional committees so effective; nor can the House of Commons build up a fund of expertise, although individual members may contribute experience gained outside Parliament. What may in the long run prove important, however, is that MPs are in direct contact more than before with ministers and civil servants in the context of select-committee investigations.

Committee work of this kind is also becoming increasingly important because of the declining significance, in contrast, of parliamentary questions, which used to be seen as one of the unique advantages of the British parliamentary system. It is not that parliamentary questions are fewer in number – on the contrary – or that the need to answer them no longer takes priority in the allocation of work within a department; it is rather that the length of time which elapses between the turns of a particular minister to appear at Question Time means that questions cannot ordinarily be used to deal with matters of urgency. Oral questions are used not so much to call attention to administrative failings or individual grievances as to make party points, while the twice-weekly appearance of the Prime Minister at Question Time has become the occasion for mini-battles between the party leaders of a kind which borders on frivolity.

The additional burden of committee work has strengthened the case for a greater provision of research and secretarial assistance for MPs. To some extent the purse strings have already been loosened both for individual MPs and for the oposition parties in Parliament, although Britain is hardly lavish by comparison with other legislatures. Members must still make use of the clerks of the House of Commons and the staff of the House of Commons library, and both are limited in number. It remains noticeable that only a minority of members have shown much desire to participate actively in committee work. Initially pressure to extend the committee system came from younger members, particularly the Labour intake of 1966. However, it is the older MPs with little hope of office who bear the brunt of such duties: in the 1975–6 session 60% of all MPs were under 50 years of age; of MPs who served on more than one select committee only 35% were under that age. As long as ministerial office represents the principal goal of parliamentary activity, many MPs will either not seek select-committee work or try to prevent their committees from embarrassing their own governments if this is likely to damage their party standing. Admittedly there have been a few cases where MPs have seen the role of committee or subcommittee chairman as one which could enhance their political status, but in most cases this is because they have for various reasons become resigned to remaining back-benchers.

A study of a decade of innovation in the use of committees suggests that any serious attempt to expand parliamentary participation in government can only work if back-benchers are prepared to regard their parliamentary duties as full-time employment. However, perhaps only a minority so regard them. The failure of Crossman's experiment with morning sessions of the House of Commons, the difficulty of ensuring committee attendance in the morning and the insistence that much of Parliament's business should take place after normal working hours prove that the tradition lingers that membership of the House of Commons is an addition to ordinary employment. No doubt much of an MP's activity outside Westminster is related to political obligations, for example constituency business, which can be extremely time-consuming if the constituency is not within easy reach of London. However, much of it is work offered as a result of the prestige and expertise which an MP has acquired through his presence in the House of Commons, the most obvious examples of occupations being company directorships, consultancies and journalism. Members of Parliament must indicate if they have a personal interest in any matter on which they speak; the danger of corruption has been further acknowledged by the introduction of a register of interests, although this is voluntary and has been objected to by some as a violation of an MP's right to privacy. The income which these pursuits generate is obviously attractive to MPs, who are poorly paid by Western European standards, but there is no evidence that more generous salaries and allowances for MPs would necessarily bring about an alteration in the disposition of parliamentarians' time or make more room for committee work.

It is against this background that one must note the important suggestions for change in the organization of parliamentary business which were contained in the First Report from the Select Committee on Procedure for the 1977–8 session. In many respects this report, published in August 1978, was negative: it rejected changes in Parliament's hours of work; the general use of pre-legislative standing committees except in areas remote from party controversy; a return to specialized standing committees; and the device of outline or enabling bills, that is to say bills which dealt with their subject matter in very broad terms, leaving all the details to be filled in by the minister under powers granted to him by the bills. Instead it devoted a good deal of attention to suggestions for strengthening the House of Commons' control over delegated legislation. Moreover, it rejected the suggestion for a comprehensive method of timetabling for bills and upheld the present system of the guillotine.

Its positive suggestions related mainly to two matters – the procedure in standing committee and the range of select committees. First, in order to give Parliament more control over the content of bills the Report proposed that standing committees should be free to have a limited number of sittings in which they could, like select committees, take evidence from witnesses before proceeding to the normal committee stage. Such committees would be called public bill committees. More striking is the suggestion that the whole system of select committees should be recast. The Committee did not feel that the Expenditure Committee and its subcommittees permitted a comprehensive coverage of the work of the executive. According to its recommendations, while the Public Accounts Committee would survive and indeed be made more independent, the Expenditure Committee and its subcommittees would disappear as would the Committees on Nationalized Industries, Science and Technology, Overseas Development, the Parliamentary Commissioner, and Race Relations and Immigration. To replace them twelve new subject committees would be created and they each would be allotted the supervision of one or more government departments. In addition to their general functions these committees might acquire others including the supervision of some EEC activity. It would be normal for standing committees dealing with bills within their subject area to be drawn in large part from the relevant select committee. Pressure on government departments to reply promptly to the committees' reports would, it was thought, be one way of making them more effective. It was also envisaged that these committees would gradually find ways of dealing with delegated legislation in their subject area. They would each consist of about ten members so that the total numbers of MPs involved would not greatly exceed those active in committees in the present system. Arrangements would have to be made for cooperative action between committees since so many topics span the concerns of more than one government department. There would also be a committee of chairmen, which might come to play an important part in the House's general arrangements for scrutiny of the executive.

The Procedure Committee was well aware that only a minority of reports from select committees are debated in the House, and that attendance at such debates is sparse. Between 1970 and 1977 select committees issued 316 reports to the house, of which 115 were from its domestic committees. Forty-four reports were debated, half from the domestic-committee lists and half from committees dealing with public business. The Procedure Committee suggested ways of increasing the time available for debating reports and rejected the view that the only MPs who take part in such debates are the members of the select committees concerned. Yet it remains true that the transference from the committee to the House as a whole is the crucial stage for determining the impact which an individual committee report will have on the public. It is at the stage, too, when the bi-partisan atmosphere of the committee is replaced by the adversarial arena of the chamber, that the rationale of select committees is most strained.

The Labour Government was unenthusiastic about the Report, but the Queen's Speech to the new Parliament in 1979 indicated that the incoming administration might look on it with a kindlier eye, and that the proposed new subject committees would be set up.

Parliament and the Road to Office

In addition to Parliament's functions as a legislative body and as a body concerned with the scrutiny of executive activity, it has two other distinct roles. First, it is the source from which ministers are chosen. The possibility of obtaining office is one of the factors which compensates back-benchers for many of their mundane and routine activities such as marching through lobbies where the outcome of the vote is predictable. To impress the party leadership in Parliament an MP must show the House that he can shine in the peculiar arts demanded there: exchanges at Question Time, or perhaps in standing committee, matter more in this respect than technical expertise or intellectual ability. Members of Parliament must thus, if they wish to advance their careers, call attention to themselves; this requirement gives procedural changes which allow back-benchers to discuss topical issues at short notice a particular appeal.

This has become easier since the debates on the adjournment of the house at 10 p.m. after the completion of government business can now be used for raising topical matters with fewer restrictions than used to be the case. Also with increased committee activity MPs may in future be able to make reputations by committee work which will be reported via the whips to the party leadership; however, it is likely that such activity will aid MPs on the opposition side most since a government may be expected to disapprove of back-benchers who hold up its legislative business by frequent intervention in standing committees or assiduous questioning before select committees.

Parliament and the Public

The second remaining activity, the educative function of Parliament, is perhaps the role which it fulfils best although it is in many ways a by-product of its other and more obvious ones. The great set-piece debates over legislation, the endless reports which rarely get noticed by government or even fellow MPs, and the variety of procedures available for scrutinizing administrative activity – all these have their ultimate justification in the extent to which they make available to the public information about the workings and quality of the British governmental process.

The importance of this educative function perhaps in itself justifies the survival of many of the traditional and ceremonial aspects of Parliament. The great occasions such as the state opening of Parliament by the monarch emphasize the legislature's link with the whole of the country's history. The constitutional responsibility of the executive to the legislature is highlighted by the twice-weekly appearances of the Prime Minister at the despatch box, and the formal presentation of the budget to the House of Commons underlines the connection between taxation and representation. Above all there is the role of the opposition which provides the chairmen of key committees such as the Public Accounts Committee, the Committee on the Parliamentary Commissioner for Administration and the Statutory Instruments Committee. The opposition also has the right to choose the subjects for debate on certain days. For all the control which government now has over the House of Commons the operation of the system is shown to depend upon compromise and accommodation, upon members sharing at least a number of common values and upon the importance of stylized conventions of behaviour, regardless of party or ideology.

The most important example of the operation of these conventions and informal understandings, apart from the role of the official Opposition, is the position of the Speaker. The Speaker was originally the voice of the Commons, declaring the House's wishes to the monarch or to ministers. When ministers themselves began to figure prominently in the House of Commons, the Speaker might have become a party leader operating from the vantage point of the chair as in the American House of Representatives. Instead in the nineteenth century there developed the idea of a wholly neutral chairman who would hold the balance between factions and parties in the house and ensure that debates recorded all shades of opinion. The Speaker must thus see himself as a referee and as the natural protector of minorities. What is remarkable is the way in which this role can be successfully assumed by the Speaker and his deputies, despite the fact that they have often been previously immersed in party politics, frequently at a ministerial level. Also the impartiality of the Speaker and his deputies is almost always taken for granted by MPs. The definition of parliamentary privilege – the rules which protect MPs against outside interference with their freedom of action and bind them to certain codes of conduct – is determined by a committee and applied by it to particular cases. However, the Committee on Privileges acts upon references to it from the Speaker, and it is at his command that any action upon any report from that Committee is taken.

Given the parallel non-partisan role of the civil service it is not surprising that the servants of the House, the Clerk and his team, and the officials of the library should also regard their services as available to all MPs. Thus MPs do have assistance both in ensuring that they frame their questions in accordance with the rules of the House and in acquiring material for their speeches. In committee work also, the capacity of the clerks to regard themselves as servants of the entire House and not just of the majority party is extremely important.

On the other hand it would be absurd to ignore the fact that much of the business of the House assumes the existence of party. The main institutional form which this party element takes is the office of the whip. The whips of each party perform two roles which, although apparently contradictory, in fact complement each other. They are first the principal assistants of the party leader in organizing debates and ensuring the necessary turn-out of votes in the division lobbies. But they are also the principal channel through which back-benchers' views are conveyed to the leadership and the leadership's views conveyed to back-benchers. It is for this reason that the Chief Whip of the majority party normally attends cabinet meetings by invitation when he is not himself a member of the Cabinet. The whips are thus at the very heart of the power struggle between the parties, though by longstanding convention they are silent in debate. Yet without effective communications between the parties they could not do the job effectively. The timetable is usually arranged between the whips – though government could impose its will if it wished – and it is the whips who arrange the 'pairs' through which MPs can miss divisions, for political or personal reasons – that is to say, agreements between members on opposite sides by which they can both absent themselves since their votes, if cast, would cancel each other out. If what are called the 'usual channels' are blocked – that is if whip cannot talk to whip – Parliament cannot function properly. The payment out of public funds of salaries to the principal opposition whips is a recognition of the importance of this for the smooth working of the system.

The operation of Parliament is thus at once facilitated and constrained by party divisions and party organization. Yet despite the ambiguous role which Parliament performs in the political system and the diversity of views about how it might be reformed there is no shortage of men and women who wish to become MPs. Indeed, it could be argued that the effectiveness of Parliament depends less on its internal procedures than on the quality of MPs. Attention should therefore now be directed away from the House of Commons and towards those factors which determine its composition – the electoral system and the political parties themselves.

5 The Electoral System

The body of rules governing the British electoral process has often been seen as one of the keys to understanding the causes of the country's political stability. The gradual evolution towards universal adult suffrage, and the elimination of various forms of electoral corruption, occurred as ruling elites were forced to acknowledge the need for the political system to accommodate concrete social changes. Abstract discussions of electoral equality and democratic theory were much less important in reforming this aspect of the British constitution than the shrewd realism of practising politicians. The United Kingdom's electoral arrangements are thus suffused with the spirit of pragmatism and with an awareness that imperfections are bound to exist in machinery so intricately involved in the struggle for power between the parties.

The fact that the British have a long tradition of tolerating anomalies in their electoral system should not, however, be allowed to obscure the fact that recently the electoral system has been the subject of criticism. Particular controversy has surrounded the British method for translating votes into seats – the so-called 'first-past-the-post' or 'simple plurality' method – and the experience of the Parliaments of 1974–9, as well as the publicity given to the methods employed by other European countries, did much to heighten that controversy. Although most arguments about the merits of the British electoral system now focus on this aspect of the system, it is important to remember that what principally concerned nineteenth- and early twentieth-century politicians was the actual extent of the franchise. Indeed every successive change in the franchise was a matter of party controversy as well as a stimulus to debate about the foundations of the constitution itself (though Bagehot was moved to describe the coming of the Second Reform Act as 'the most silent of revolutions').[1]

The primary feature of the extension of the electorate in the nineteenth century was its slowness. Compromise and the tolerance of anomalies ensured that even when the principle of universal adult male suffrage was implemented in 1918, vestiges of older theories of representation lingered on. Corporate or group representation in the House of Commons survived in the form of university constituencies until the Representation of the People Act of 1948 abolished them along with the provisions for additional voting on the basis of occupation of business premises.[2] (The notion of corporate, as opposed to individual, representation is actually still apparent, of course, in the composition of the House of Lords.) Women achieved the vote only in 1918, and even then fear that they would be a numerical majority in the electorate induced Parliament to differentiate between the sexes in relation to the age at which the vote was acquired: men could vote at twenty-one, but initially women had to wait until the age of thirty for their chance to participate in the electoral process. The Representation of the People Act of 1928 abolished this anomaly, but it was a deeply divisive issue, and many Conservative politicians later thought that this so-called 'flapper vote' had lost them the general election of 1929.

The most recent alteration in the franchise occurred in 1969 when the Representation of the People Act of that year increased the size of the electorate by lowering the voting age to eighteen, following the Report of the Latey Committee on the Age of Majority.[3] (A Speaker's Conference which had examined the question had suggested that the age should be lowered to twenty, but its advice was ignored.)[4] It is tempting to speculate about the extent to which this extension of the franchise contributed to the electoral volatility of the 1970s; but certainly the change, coming as it did at the end of a decade in which images of student unrest and direct action had received much exposure in the media, was a symbolic one.

Youth, like women half a century earlier, had been incorporated into the political system, and the country's politicians had to reconcile themselves to constituencies made marginal by large university populations and to the task of canvassing schools.

Apart from age, the right to vote in Britain is dependent upon inclusion in the electoral register and the absence of any formal legal disqualification from voting. Since 1918 the compilation of the electoral register has been the responsibility of local authorities whose electoral registration officers supervise all aspects of the process of recording those who are entitled to vote; this process includes the annual house-to-house canvass on which the register is based. The fact that this responsibility now rests with the officials of local authorities reduces the likelihood of many of the defects which occur when registration is the personal responsibility of the citizen from occurring here. Voluntary registration discourages the poorest and least educated sections of society from voting; in the United States until very recently it has also had the effect of reducing the registration of ethnic minorities. (Even in Britain, with its system of semi-automatic registration, it is probable that a significant proportion of the immigrant community is unregistered: one study of Nottingham immigrants found as many as 27% unregistered and commented that it was the 'poorly educated, unskilled and recently arrived amongst them who were least likely to have been registered'.[5])

The fact that the registration function is undertaken by the local authority is an enormous advantage to the political parties, who would otherwise have to devote their own energies and finances to the task of encouraging registration through costly advertising campaigns. As the cost of compiling and maintaining the electoral register – outside Northern Ireland – was £6,025,000 in 1973–4, according to the Houghton Committee on Financial Aid to Political Parties, this is a particular advantage to small parties who have neither the financial nor the membership resources to undertake sustained organizational activity.[6] The disparities in wealth and membership which mark British political parties do matter at later stages of the electoral process, for example when it comes to organizing the postal vote; here Conservatives are generally thought to be superior to other parties – but it is important that they do not affect the basic function of registration.

A few categories of persons are disfranchised in Britain. The right to vote is not granted to aliens – those who are neither British subjects nor citizens of the Republic of Ireland. British nationality law and its accompanying franchise restrictions are a legacy of the country's experience as an imperial power. For a long time there was a concept of common citizenship prevalent throughout the Empire and Commonwealth; however, the need to restrict immigration to the United Kingdom, and the changes in the nature of the Commonwealth which have occurred since 1945, have eroded much of the freedom of movement and settlement which used to exist within that organization's member states. But one characteristic which remains is that citizens of member states of the Commonwealth resident in Britain can vote on the same terms as the indigenous population. More peculiar at first sight is the situation of citizens of the Irish Republic, which left the Commonwealth in 1949 but whose citizens can still vote in the UK. Again the explanation is largely historical – Eire was a component part of the United Kingdom until 1922 – but in addition it would be very difficult to restrict the rights of Irish citizens living in Britain while there is free movement of labour between the two countries and an open border with Northern Ireland. Also, the Irish vote is politically significant for the Labour Party in some constituencies. It is possible that, if there is any attempt to effect a comprehensive revision of British nationality and citizenship law, this anomaly will be corrected. Ultimately some rationalization may occur because of pressure to grant certain civic rights to citizens of other members states of the European Communities, all of whom have the right to work anywhere in the Communities.

Peers may not vote at elections to the House of Commons. The logic of this disfranchisement is that peers have the right to sit in the House of Lords in person and thus do not need, or qualify for, indirect representation in the House of Commons. Since 1963 it has been possible to renounce a peerage, and peers who do so – for example Anthony Wedgwood Benn and Sir Alec Douglas Home – thereby acquire the right to vote in parliamentary elections and to be elected to the House of

Commons.[7] Peers may nevertheless vote at local elections and at elections to the European Parliament, just as they may stand for these elections.

Disfranchisement also occurs when a person is in legal custody serving a prison sentence or when a person is in a mental hospital as defined by the Mental Health Act of 1959.[8] The latter provision has been the source of some controversy since it has become apparent that the law effectively disfranchises some fifty thousand voluntary patients in mental hospitals and psychiatric clinics who may be there only because they would otherwise be homeless. A Speaker's Conference in 1973 recommended a change in the law to allow patients in mental hospitals to be given the equivalent rights to patients in general hospitals in this respect and the Home Office and Department of Health and Social Security set up a working party in order to examine the implications of that recommendation. Although the working party had not reported by August 1978, it seems likely that some modification in the law will occur, especially since in 1976 there was a successful challenge to the existing legal framework when several inmates of a hospital in Warrington questioned in the county court the refusal of the local registration officer to treat the hospital as a residence for registration purposes.[9]

Persons who are convicted of 'corrupt or illegal electoral practices' in the United Kingdom are disfranchised for a period of five years, although in the case of illegal practices – which are in effect technical breaches of electoral law – the disfranchisement relates only to the constituency in which an offence occurred. Since 1883 there have been stringent limits placed on the amount of money which candidates may spend in the course of an election campaign and these legal restrictions, together with the strictly enforced procedures for reporting election expenses, have meant that Britain has been relatively free of this form of corruption. Indeed, it has been convincingly argued that the British electoral system had eliminated all forms of corrupt practice by the eve of the First World War.[10] However, as will be seen later, the strict regulation of expenditure really covers only money spent during the limited period of a campaign. Moreover there is also plenty of opportunity for governments, as opposed to individual candidates, to indulge in activities which could well be interpreted as electoral bribery. The most obvious example of governmental ability to affect the voters' choice on this scale is an administration's power to manipulate the economy to make an atmosphere of financial prosperity coincide with a general election. This problem is clearly a more intractable one than the simple question of how best to ensure that the electoral machinery itself does not permit corruption; it is perhaps salutary to bear in mind, as the third Marquess of Salisbury suggested in the 1860s, that the elimination of old problems of political morality does not preclude the emergence of novel ones.[11]

Voting at parliamentary elections in the United Kingdom is now done entirely through single-member constituencies. Many defenders of the existing electoral system see the unique link between a single well-defined constituency and its MP as one of the great merits of the British electoral machinery. Most forms of proportional representation would require larger constituencies returning at least three MPs. The form of proportional representation most discussed as a feasible experiment for the United Kingdom – the West German additional-member system – does not, however, destroy the bond between an individual representative and his constituency. (The West German system retains the single-member constituency for half of its MPs, and the distortions are corrected when the remaining half are allocated between the parties on a straight party list system.) The United Kingdom's attachment to the single-member constituency is, however, of relatively recent origin. Until 1885 double-member constituencies were the norm, and at the general election of 1945 a large number of boroughs including Dundee, Preston, Sunderland, Bolton, Blackburn and Southampton were still double-member constituencies; the last double-member constituency disappeared only in 1950.[12] In part the double-member constituency survived because of the reluctance of those areas to see their separate identities disappear even when population growth justified the creation of additional seats. But what this mystique of the constituency with a distinct identity underlines is the tenacious belief that representation in the United Kingdom should in some way be connected with a coherent territorial unit and not simply based on the mathematically calculated allocation of individual voters.

The British electoral system's remoteness from the idea of representing the population *per se* may be traced back to the form taken by the earliest Parliaments. These Parliaments were summonses from the monarch to representatives of the counties and the boroughs, as well as the peers of the realm, to attend at Westminster; thus the idea of representing a town or shire rather than people goes back to the Middle Ages. However, it is not this tradition alone that has shaped the British approach to such questions as constituency boundaries: it must be admitted that, in addition, factors of party self-interest have played a prominent role in precluding the consideration of reforms which might remove some of the anomalies associated with the existing system. British politicians are not merely untroubled on the whole by the lack of representation which the system affords to minorities; they also display little of that concern for minimizing discrepancies in constituency size which has so strongly characterized the United States' districting process since 1962. Individual electoral equality is not the holy grail in the United Kingdom that it has become across the Atlantic; as with the arguments surrounding the simple plurality system, the problem of boundary revisions has been discussed in a spirit which seeks a rough-and-ready fairness rather than an absolute equality imposed by a slide-rule.

Until quite recently no machinery existed for securing a regular review of constituency boundaries. In the nineteenth century it was common to revise constituency boundaries following an extension of the franchise, but the upheaval was often so great that the procedure was not institutionalized until the end of the Second World War, when steps were taken to provide for regular attempts to relate constituencies to population. (The criticisms of the pre-1832 system had largely centred on the fact that many of the ancient boroughs which enjoyed parliamentary representation had by that stage been depopulated, while new centres of population created by the industrial revolution were completely without political representation at Westminster.) The House of Commons (Redistribution of Seats) Act of 1944 established four Boundary Commissions for the four component parts of the United Kingdom, whose duty it was to review their respective areas to ensure that within them constituencies did not vary from an electoral quota by more than 25%. This electoral quota, obtained by dividing the number of seats available to the area into the electorate for that area, appeared somewhat meaningless as a norm if deviations as large as 25% were to be allowed. Yet even this formula came to appear too mechanical, so that when a new Act was passed in 1958 to accommodate objections to the procedure, the obligation to observe the 25% variation was abandoned altogether.

The Commissions themselves are nominally chaired by the Speaker of the House of Commons but are now effectively composed of a High Court judge – who sits as deputy chairman – together with two other members who must not be Members of Parliament. For the English Boundary Commission the Registrar General and the Director General of Ordnance Survey sit as assessors, while for the other Commissions their equivalents perform the same task. In addition to the power to make general recommendations and revisions every five to seven years, each Commission was given authority to make interim recommendations about specific problems. The Act of 1944 also introduced a procedure whereby local objections to proposed boundary changes could be heard. Once local objections have been taken into account the Commissioners make their reports, which must be laid before Parliament with a draft Order in Council to give effect to their recommendations; Parliament may then decide whether to approve them by affirmative resolution or to reject them.

It has already been seen how, despite the Boundary Commissions' theoretical task of producing equal constituencies, there has been an unwillingness to translate this requirement into an imperative with precise numerical implications. Since 1954 the Boundary Commissions have been urged to produce constituencies with electorates as close to their quota as is practicable, bearing in mind the need to respect such factors as local-government boundaries and any special geographical features of the constituency. Needless to say, this still permits the existence of substantial variations in size between constituencies. Thus at the first general election after the redistribution of 1970, constituencies in England ranged from Meriden, which had

96,380 electors, to Newcastle Central, an inner-city area, with only 25,007 electors. While the average constituency had 64,077 electors, there were 5 constituencies with over 90,000 electors, 49 with over 80,000, 79 with under 50,000 and 7 with under 40,000.[13] (In the general election of 1979 the disparity between English constituencies was even greater: Bromsgrove and Redditch had 104,375 voters while Newcastle Central had only 23,678.) Yet marked though the disparities were after redistribution, they were far worse at the general election prior to redistribution, as there had been no revision of boundaries to take account of population movements between 1954 and 1970, largely as a result of the Labour Government's refusal to implement boundary changes prior to the 1970 election.[14] Since 1958 the maximum interval between reviews has been increased to fifteen years – a delay which means the gross discrepancies in constituency size are likely to remain unless arrangements are made for interim adjustments on a more systematic basis than at present.[14]

The redistribution machinery has been identified as one of the instruments that perpetuates the over-representation of Scotland and Wales in the British Parliament. The 1958 House of Commons (Redistribution of Seats) Act clarified the question of whether the electoral quota should be calculated by each Boundary Commission on the basis of the electorate of its area or on the basis of the electorate of the United Kingdom as a whole; however, as one authority has emphasized, it did so 'at the expense of enshrining permanently the under-representation for England'.[15] The mal-apportionment of seats between the component parts of the United Kingdom stemmed from the instructions to the Boundary Commissioners contained in the 1944 Act that Scotland should have a minimum of 71 seats and Wales a minimum of 35 seats. The existence at that time of a separate Parliament for Northern Ireland was held to justify the continued under-representation of the Province at Westminster; but the suspension of Stormont in 1972 has led to a reassessment of this situation, and Northern Ireland will therefore have its allotted number of seats increased from 12 to 17 or 18 in time for the next election. The effect of this mal-apportionment of seats between the component parts of the United Kingdom is shown in Table 2: in October 1974

England had one MP for every 64,634 electors while, at the other extreme, Scotland had one MP to every 51,927 electors. The expansion of the English electorate made it necessary to create 5 extra English seats in the redistribution that followed the 1970 general election. The House of Commons, which has fluctuated greatly in size over the centuries, has thus stood at 635 since 1974, although after the next election it will be even larger to take account of additional Ulster members.

The over-representation of Scotland and Wales within the United Kingdom became a significant issue in the period 1974–9 when the Labour Government's devolution proposals seemed likely to be implemented. (This theme is further discussed in Chapter 10.) The continued over-representation of

Table 2
Ratio of Electors to an MP *in Great Britain at the General Election of October 1974*

Scotland	51,927:1
Wales	55,798:1
England	64,634:1
Northern Ireland	86,377:1

Source: Report of the Hansard Society Commission on Electoral Reform (1976).

Scotland and Wales in addition to separate Assemblies for those regions appeared illogical to many observers, especially bearing in mind the Ulster precedent. However, the matter was not simply one of logic: the anomaly benefited the Labour Party, and it declared itself unwilling to reduce the numbers of Scottish and Welsh seats at Westminster even to the point of equity with English representation. The abandonment of both the Scotland and the Wales Acts in the light of the referendum results of 1979 means that this issue has been defused for the time being, although it would undoubtedly surface again if new suggestions for devolving power were brought forward.

The establishment of permanent machinery to review constituency boundaries has therefore not been able to remove many of the anomalies associated with the process of electoral districting in the United Kingdom. The slowness of its operations and the slowness with which the changes are made mean that by the time suggested improvements have been made, further demographic change will already have occurred. Yet more frequent reviews would be unpopular with those who have to work the system, since even parties who are beneficiaries of boundary changes dislike the disruptive effect which reorganization has on their activities. The efficiency of local parties depends upon thorough local knowledge, and the cooperation of inhabitants and the voluntary organizations of an area are difficult to sustain if the constituencies themselves are perpetually changing.

It is, moreover, important to repeat that, while the neutral personnel of the Boundary Commissions might suggest otherwise, the procedure of redistribution can never be entirely divorced from calculations of party self-interest. Partisan considerations can enter at a number of points. The Conservative Party benefited from the survival of plural voting in Britain until 1948, and it may be that the more even spread of Conservative votes still gives the Tories a slight advantage in England at least. But as far as the politics of redistribution are concerned it seems clear that the slow revision of constituency boundaries aids Labour.

Other parts of the country's electoral machinery are perhaps less controversial than the redistribution machinery. Although there are occasional independent candidates and a range of candidates for small parties, the contest at a general election is essentially between the standard-bearers of the major political parties. They will have chosen their candidates far in advance of the election in most cases and will usually have a well-oiled machine ready to swing into action as soon as the date of the poll is announced. (The selection of candidates is further discussed in Chapters 6 and 7.) In contrast to the position in the United States and France, specifically local issues play only a limited part in British general-election campaigns. Campaigns do, it is true, assume a slightly different character in Scotland and Wales; and, of course, Northern Irish politics have become increasingly isolated from those of the mainland. On the whole, however, national issues predominate in the candidates' election addresses, and in England at least the geographic origins of a candidate are fairly unimportant. Candidates do not, for example, have to fulfil any formal residence requirements, although frequently they will have to comply with informal pressures and expectations generated by activists in their constituencies on such matters as where candidates should live. Equally, if the constituency is one which has special characteristics – if mining, fishing or farming play a significant role in it, for example, or if it is one of the twenty or so constituencies where the student vote exceeds 5% – then of course a candidate will be well advised to familiarize himself with these specialist features. But often the constituency for which a candidate ultimately stands will be determined by sheer chance rather than as the result of any objective assessment of suitability for the area or even because of local roots. Scotland is to some extent an exception to this rule, and after the loss of the February 1974 general election and the threat from the SNP there was a determined effort by Scottish Conservative associations to choose candidates with explicitly Scottish rather than English backgrounds.

Once the candidates have been chosen they must be formally nominated by ten electors, and a deposit of £150 must be paid. The deposit is forfeited if the candidate fails to receive more than one-eighth of the votes cast and is thus allegedly a deterrent to frivolous candidacies. Given the relatively low value of the deposit, which has been eroded by inflation since 1918, it is doubtful whether it really does have this effect, and each election produces its crop of frivolous eccentric candidacies.

Certain categories of persons cannot sit in the House of Commons – peers who have not renounced their peerages, clergymen of the Church of England, ministers of the established Church of Scotland, Roman Catholic priests, persons serving prison sentences or in custody under the Mental Health Act of 1959, and the holders of certain offices of profit under the Crown. The House of Commons (Disqualification) Act of 1975 lists those offices which are deemed incompatible with membership of the House of Commons. Judges, members of the armed forces, persons on the boards of nationalized industries, and civil servants, for example, are thus all precluded from sitting in the House of Commons, although members of these professions who resign are entitled to stand for Parliament. The aim of the restriction was initially to secure the independence from party politics of the professions concerned, and to ensure that the House of Commons was not a body dominated by persons in the pay of the Crown who would hence have a less than disinterested outlook when the survival of the government was at issue.

During the election campaign itself – which lasts for legal purposes from the announcement of a dissolution of Parliament until the close of the polls at 10 p.m. on election day – there are strict rules governing the amount of expenditure that may be incurred on behalf of an individual candidate in his constituency. These rules used to be of great concern to the political parties, but the increasing impact of national political propaganda and growing doubts that expenditure at constituency level affects votes to any great extent have perhaps rendered these elaborate restrictions somewhat artificial. Nevertheless these rules form an important part of the ritual of election campaigns since each candidate must appoint an agent – an institution unique to Britain – who is responsible for recording all expenditure on behalf of the candidate. The maximum level of expenditure is determined in accordance with a formula which has constantly to be amended because of the impact of inflation on the value of the sums concerned. At present the maximum expenditure per constituency is £1,750 plus 2 new pence per registered voter in a county constituency, or plus $1\frac{1}{2}$ new pence per registered voter in a borough.[16] In addition to these sums there are certain indirect grants in kind to candidates which, as well as registration, the Houghton Committee viewed as indirect state support to the political parties. Candidates are each allowed to send one piece of literature through the post to each constituent free of charge, and are entitled to use, free of charge, any publicly owned meeting hall or school in their constituency during the campaign.

This legal framework was perhaps more appropriate to an age when there were distinct campaigns in individual constituencies and when the formal election period, which is regulated by law, was not preceded by a period of intense pre-election speculation and campaigning. If a Parliament runs to almost its full term – as the 1959–64 one did – there will inevitably be a period in which the major parties are campaigning furiously at the national level. Yet this spate of expenditure, which almost certainly has more electoral impact than expenditure during the formal campaign, is completely unregulated. Mrs Thatcher's decision to launch a full-scale publicity campaign in the summer of 1978 when there was much speculation – erroneous as it happened – about an autumn election highlighted the contradictions of an approach to political campaigning in which strictly regulated expenditure is but a footnote to a much longer essay in the techniques of influence and conversion. On the one hand, as the Conservative Party leader's opponents argued, the campaign broke the spirit if not the letter of the election laws because the posters used were inevitably sited within constituencies, and would therefore have fallen within regulated expenses after an announcement of an election. Mrs Thatcher's campaign – which was managed by a professional public relations firm and was alleged to have cost over two million pounds – fell outside any regulations because the posters were distributed outside a formal election campaign although, as was thought at the time, immediately prior to one. On the other hand, it could be argued that governments themselves have superior opportunities for the publication of their arguments, and do not hesitate to use them even during an election campaign. One of the few legal cases in this complex area decided that a prime-ministerial broadcast could not be counted as an item of illegal election expenditure, even though the Prime Minister was then fighting a by-election at Kinross and West Perthshire in order to enter the House of Commons.[17] The concept of an election budget also indicates how much it is taken for granted that the Chancellor of the Exchequer will adjust the levels of taxation and public expenditure in order to create a favourable climate for his party in an election period.

One peculiarity of British election law in relation to illegal expenditure should be noted. The agent of a candidate is the only person who may legally spend money on his behalf. In law this means not only that a sympathizer of a candidate may not spend additional money on a candidate's behalf but also that any organization or group which seeks to persuade the electorate of the uniform unacceptability of all the candidates will be liable to prosecution. This rule affects organizations such as the National Front, which sometimes intervenes at elections without itself putting up a candidate. In August 1978, the Director of the Society for the Protection of the Unborn Child was charged with an offence under the Representation of the People Act of 1949, for issuing leaflets during a by-election in which the abortion issue had been raised.[18]

One aspect of national election campaigns which excites special controversy is the allocation of broadcasting time between the parties. Television first became an important force in general-election campaigns in the 1959 general election because between 1945 and 1955 the so-called 'fourteen-day rule' had prevented the media from commenting on election issues during the final fortnight of a campaign. The sensitive question of how to allocate broadcasting time is decided by an *ad hoc* semi-formal committee, the Party Political Broadcast Committee, on which are represented the major parties and the broadcasting authorities. The distribution of time has generally been made on the basis of the parties' respective share of the votes at the previous election, except that the Government and the official Opposition are usually accorded equal amounts of broadcasting time. The rise in the Liberals' and nationalist parties' electoral support in 1974 complicated the situation and underlined the often-ventilated grievances of minor parties with respect to this system. Since then a minor-party representative has been admitted to the Committee, the Liberal share of broadcasting time has been increased, and special arrangements have been made to take account of the fact that nationalist parties have a more significant position in their own regions than their share of the total United Kingdom vote reveals. Also, both the National Front and the Workers' Revolutionary Party were allowed short pre-election broadcasts in recognition of the number of candidates they were fielding. What distinguishes the British approach to election broadcasting, however, is that access to broadcasting time is seen as a special problem to be resolved on entirely non-commercial criteria: radio election broadcasts are free, and only minimal charges are made for television broadcasts. It may be that the influence attributed to television in this area is exaggerated, especially given the discovery during the October 1974 election that there had been an increase in the number of viewers who thought the amount of television coverage of the election had been excessive; it may be that the whole approach to party broadcasts is in need of re-examination. Yet as long as it is thought that television and radio have an impact on political attitudes and electoral choice, it is desirable that efforts continue to maintain some degree of all-party agreement in this area.[19]

ELECTIONS TO THE EUROPEAN ASSEMBLY

The need to hold elections to return the British representatives to the European Assembly in June 1979 presented the British electoral system with a novel set of difficulties. First, the number of 'Euro-MPs' or MEPS – Members of the European Parliament – meant that the constituencies in which these 81 MEPS were elected would have to be very large: a typical European constituency covered the territorial area of eight Westminster constituencies. (There are, however, discrepancies in the population size of European constituencies: two seats – Glasgow and Kent West – have electorates of over 550,000 while Highlands and Islands has only 279,521 electors.)[20] Secondly, the additional size and cost of a European election campaign raised the question of whether the regulations governing such matters as the candidate's deposit or the necessary number of nomination signatories should be changed from those in force for Westminster elections. In the end it was decided that candidates for the European Parliament should be required to deposit £600 with the returning officer and that thirty signatures in support of a nomination would be necessary for it to be valid. The limits on the amount of money that might be spent in the campaign were initially fixed at £5,000 plus 2 new pence for every elector in the constituency.[21] In these matters, as with such related question as the payment of Euro-MPs, the Government's final decision revealed a reluctance to move too far away from existing British practice, although it was eventually recognized that all British political parties could and would seek aid from the European Communities for their expenses incurred while publicizing the elections.

Conformity to established British electoral practice was of course most marked in relation to the electoral system itself. The countries of the Communities are committed to using the same electoral system for choosing their MEPS, but were free to select their own system for the first election in June 1979. There was no majority in the British Parliament for any form of proportional representation, and the United Kingdom, alone among the nine, used the first-past-the-post method for European as for Westminster elections. The only exception to the retention of the simple plurality system concerned the three seats allocated to Northern Ireland where, in order to ensure representation for the minority Roman Catholic community, proportional representation was used.[22]

The Impact of the System

Between 1918 and 1979 the British electoral system has on most occasions delivered a government with an overall majority in the House of Commons, although many governments have had to operate with very small majorities. Only in 1924, 1929 and February 1974 has there been no single party with an overall majority of seats at the start of a new Parliament. (After the election of October 1974 the Government had a majority of three, but its majority was eroded by defections and by-election defeats, so that by 1976 it was in a minority.) Yet beneath the apparent clarity of the results there are concealed a number of distortions in the system. The first such distortion is that the majoritarian government which the system ostensibly produces so smoothly is in reality a minority government in terms of the votes cast. Indeed, only the National Government of 1931 and its more Conservative-dominated successor of 1935 achieved more than 50% of the total vote at any general election since 1918. The overwhelming control of the House of Commons enjoyed by the Labour Governments elected in 1945 and 1966 and the Conservative Government elected in 1959 were acquired on the basis of the support of less than half of those voting.

The minority position of most British governments might perhaps be easier to reconcile with democratic theory if it were not for the rise of the doctrine of the mandate in British politics. By this doctrine a political party which secures the right to form a government by the quirks of the electoral system also claims the right when in power to put through any legislation it thinks fit, so long as it is based on some policy statement contained in the party's election manifesto. So deeply embedded in the major parties' consciousness is the assumption that the electorate has somehow endorsed not merely a government but all its programme, that it survives even if a government has only a tiny majority of seats, or even no majority at all. For example, the Labour Governments of 1974-9 took office with the support of 37.1% and 39.2% of the voters at each election, but the rhetoric of the mandate persisted when the Governments' legislative proposals were discussed in Parliament and the country.

The fact that the system is not truly majoritarian is evident also at the constituency level, where the increasing number of Liberal and other minor-party candidacies have made it more likely that those elected will not have an overall majority of the votes cast in their constituencies.

Apart from the inequity of conferring such a concentration of power on parties even when they have minority support, the electoral system generates other anomalies. For example, it is possible for the party which achieves the largest number of votes to end up with a smaller number of seats than its rival. This occurred in 1951 when Labour obtained 295 seats for its 13,948,605 votes while the Conservatives won 321 seats from only 13,717,538 votes and duly took office. This distortion arises largely because under the simple plurality system it takes an advantage of only one vote to capture a seat, and any additional votes are in one sense wasted. The tendency has been for Labour to pile up huge majorities in safe seats while the Conservative vote has been somewhat more evenly spread. In February 1974, the system worked to Labour's advantage: Labour won fewer votes than the Conservatives (11,639,243 to 11,868,906) but more seats (301 to 297). Possibly, if it had not been for the fragmentation of the party system at that election and such factors as the severance of the tie between the Ulster Unionists and the Conservatives, the Tory electoral advantage would have been paralleled by an advantage in seats in the House.

Perhaps the most conspicuous distortion of the system, however, remains its treatment of the minor parties. The two major parties, Labour and Conservative, may accept the anomalies of the system, feeling that whatever they lose in one period they will gain in another. Both assume they will have an opportunity to benefit from the system and to participate in government. But for minor parties the system is a barrier to effective parliamentary representation. The Liberal Party has suffered most patently as a result of the electoral system's effects since, although it has frequently been successful in attracting votes, its support has been distributed across the country rather than being regionally concentrated, as the SNP or Plaid Cymru vote is. Liberal representation in Parliament has not risen above 14 since 1935, despite the regular achievement by the Party of a share of the total vote which would justify many more seats under a proportional system.

The February 1974 general election results indicate the extent of the disadvantage which the Liberal Party has to overcome. The achievement of over half the votes cast for either of the two major parties brought the Liberals less than one-twentieth of the seats gained by either of the major parties: for 23.6% of the votes, 14 Liberal MPs were returned. And, although at that election regionally based parties such as the SNP were able to make a breakthrough, the Party still only won 7 seats in return for 21.9% of the Scottish vote. (The Welsh nationalist party, Plaid Cymru, won only 2 seats in February 1974 on the basis of 10.7% of the Welsh vote, and it is an interesting indication of the peculiarity of the system that Plaid Cymru retained 2 representatives in May 1979 despite a drop in the total share of the vote.)

The distortions of the system and its unfairness to minorities were given great publicity after the February 1974 election because even against the odds an unusually high number of MPs who did not adhere to the major parties were returned to Parliament. There were 37 such MPs in the Parliament of February to October 1974, and the number rose to 39 in the following Parliament. Attention was also drawn to the advantages of other electoral systems by the need to decide what method to employ for direct elections to the European Assembly and for the proposed devolved Assemblies in Scotland and Wales. Even the continuing tragedy of Northern Ireland highlighted the arguments against the simple plurality method, and the link between a country's electoral system and its style of politics since the abolition of proportional representation in Ulster in 1929 was clearly a factor in alienating the minority Roman Catholic community from the Province's devolved political institutions.

The relationship between the electoral system and the character of British government and politics was elaborated, as has been seen in Chapter 1, in a range of academic writings of the post-1974 period.[23] The defenders of the existing system could only reiterate what they saw as its virtues. Those virtues – comprehensibility, familiarity and clarity – enabled the voter to cast his vote for his preferred candidate and to see immediately the basis on which a seat had been awarded. By comparison with the intricacies of even the additional-member system or the alternative vote the method was intellectually undemanding, and the fact that it has survived has given it a legitimacy which can be balanced against its evident anomalies. It is, however, interesting that opinion polls taken during the 1974–9 Parliament revealed a majority of public opinion in each age group in favour of a proportional-representation system rather than the existing one.

Debates about the merits of rival systems will doubtless continue, and the requirements of uniformity in European elections will add fuel to the flames of the debate. However, abstract arguments are not likely to prove decisive in this particular case, for while it is easy to point to anomalies in the system, the procedure for changing it is exclusively in the grip of the two major parties. Certainly there have been occasions in the twentieth century when the electoral system seemed on the verge of substantial amendment (a Royal Commission recommended its replacement in 1910, a unanimous Speaker's Conference condemned it in 1917 and another Speaker's Conference urged electoral reform in 1929), but it has always proved possible to resist the logic of the case for change with more pragmatic arguments. The results of the last general election confirmed the Conservative Party's belief that the system still served both major parties well, and while that belief persists the structure will not be changed and wider arguments about the quality of British democracy will be ignored.

The customary method of altering electoral arrangements, it should be noted, is the device of the Speaker's Conference, which is constructed to reflect existing party strength in the House of Commons and existing attitudes towards parliamentary life and electoral reform. The bias of those attitudes is against change to such an extent that even when the Labour Government had promised under the terms of its pact with the Liberals to promote proportional representation by allowing a free vote on the electoral system to be used for Europe, a combination of Labour and Conservative MPs defeated the proposal by ninety-seven votes. It will clearly take a great deal to convince the majority of MPs to amend a system of which they are the principal beneficiaries.

6 The Political Parties I: Policy Divisions and the Party System

The British system of government is essentially one of party government. The major British parties determine many of the specific policies which emanate from government and they also exert a profound influence on the general style of British public life. It is the British party system's success or failure as a mirror of the social and ideological divisions in British life which will determine how far the institutions of government can command general public support and how far the changing demands of the various sections of society are translated into party policy. British political parties are thus vital to the democratic process as a whole and to the legitimacy and stability of the constitutional structure. Moreover, the British party system provides almost the only source of recruitment to political office; in contrast to the situation in France or the United States where members of the executive are frequently appointed despite a lack of political experience, the elevation to government office of businessmen, civil servants, academics or trade unionists in the United Kingdom has been rare and generally unsuccessful. Thus it is likely that the individuals primarily responsible for policy making at a number of different levels of the political system will have been immersed in an environment of party politics. Partisan considerations will therefore affect the treatment of issues and institutional relationships in the British system of government and inevitably any developments in the internal politics of the parties may have repercussions on the organization of government itself and on the constitutional values underpinning it.

In this chapter it will be necessary to examine the range of parties which compete for the voter's attention, the specific policies and philosophies which they espouse, and their role in the structure of party competition. In the next chapter the internal politics of the parties will be examined, and their structure, organization and finance. Finally, it will be necessary to outline some of the criticisms which have been made of the role of political parties in the contemporary British system of government and to examine some of the catalysts for change.

The Conservative Party

The Conservative Party – officially titled the Conservative and Unionist Party: the 'Tories' – is the oldest of the political parties of modern Britain. The intellectual origins of the Party can be traced to the debates occasioned by the French Revolution but most historians prefer to locate the formation of the Conservative Party in the period of Sir Robert Peel's ascendancy, between 1834 and 1846.[1] It was in that period that there emerged an identifiable body of Conservative supporters united behind a single leader and broadly attached to common policies. The policy of the Conservative Party in this early part of the nineteenth century was to support the agricultural interests, the Church, and the established constitutional order. Its electoral strength was rooted firmly in the counties and the smaller boroughs rather than the larger cities, and in the southern part of England. The significance of Peel's leadership was that he acknowledged the need for the Conservative Party to make a broad general appeal to the electorate, and the Tamworth Manifesto of 1834 perhaps marks the beginning of the modern system of party competition. Peel's dilemma, however, was how to reconcile the Party's need for a national electoral appeal with the vested sectional interests of the Party. His commitment to the reform of the Corn Laws in 1846, against the evident interests of his agricultural supporters in the country, split the parliamentary party so that the cohesion which he had introduced was short-lived. Under Disraeli's leadership, however, the Conservative Party was gradually rebuilt; and the extension of the franchise in 1867 reinforced party unity in the House of Commons and stimulated the formation of an extra-parliamentary machine in order to mobilize the new voters. By the time of the third great reform of the franchise in 1884 the skeleton of the modern Conservative Party was clearly visible. There was a distinct and increasingly cohesive Conservative group of MPs in the House of Commons, a National Union linking the local-constituency associations and a party bureaucracy at Conservative Central Office to deal with electoral arrangements, including candidatures, on a professional basis.

The major opponent of the Conservative Party in the period after 1867 until the end of the First World War was the Liberal Party. However, at the general election of 1918 the Labour Party obtained the status of principal opposition party and gradually thereafter party conflict in Britain has been dominated by the contest between the Conservative and Labour Parties. It is important, however, to remember that minor-party representation in the House of Commons has persisted throughout the twentieth century and indeed in the two general elections of 1974 rose quite considerably.

The fact that the 1918 Representation of the People Act introduced full male suffrage for the first time in Britain accelerated the displacement of the Liberals by Labour and forced the Conservatives to appeal to a wider spectrum of society than previously as well as to develop modern techniques of party electioneering. By and large the Party's electoral record has been extremely successful: for almost three-quarters of the period since 1918 the Conservative Party has been in government, either alone or in coalition with other parties, as during the 1918–22 and 1931–45 periods. Indeed, one of the features of the Conservative Party, at least until the post-1964 experience of Labour government, was that it was accustomed to think of itself as the natural party of government.

The Conservative Party's success in surviving the challenge of socialism and a mass electorate has been attributed to a number of factors. Most important, perhaps, is the point that it has never become the captive of any single section of British society, despite its early identification with some of the country's most established groups and causes. It has thus retained enough flexibility to be able to add to its supporters new groups and classes made powerful by social and political changes. In the nineteenth century, as has been seen, its major concerns included the protection of the agricultural interest, which Peel tried unsuccessfully to defy, the defence of the Anglican Church and the maintenance of the traditional constitutional structure. Yet the Party quickly realized the importance of gaining the backing of the country's financial and commercial interests as well as of newly enfranchised but perhaps weakly politicized groups such as women after 1918. Conservative leaders have thus tended to deny the sectional aspects of their policies and to emphasize instead their concern for the national interest. They have stressed the virtues of common sense and pragmatism over ideology and have generally applauded patriotism. In the nineteenth and early twentieth centuries, the Conservative Party placed great emphasis on its support of Britain's imperial role and it retains a strong strand of opinion which seeks to expand Britain's overseas influence.

Discussion of what the Conservative Party represents in contemporary British politics must take into account two factors which make its policy orientations rather more difficult to characterize than its main opponent's. First, the rise of the Labour Party to national-party status has meant that for much of the twentieth century the political agenda of the United Kingdom has been set by that Party while the Conservative position has in general been a defensive one. One reason for this aspect of the Conservative Party's political stance is that Labour has normally been the opposition party attacking the government's record. But Labour is also more likely to be the initiator of policy challenges because it brings to politics a critical and relatively comprehensive theory about the existing balance of power in British society and this automatically places on the Conservatives the onus of justifying existing social and economic relationships as well as that of advocating specific, if more modest, reforms. The general election of 1979 was rather unusual in that the Labour Prime Minister, James Callaghan, conducted a campaign in which he projected an image of almost conservative stability in contrast to the radical challenge offered by Mrs Thatcher. This development in part reflected the situation of fettered power which the Labour

Government had experienced as a result of its minority position in the House of Commons; however, it also reflected the more aggressive intellectual Conservatism espoused by the opposition leader.

The second point to notice about Conservative policy is that a Conservative manifesto will very much reflect the personal style of the party leader rather than, as in the Labour Party, being the product of a complex process of political accommodation and collective decision making. The Conservative leader enjoys a great deal of autonomy and authority throughout the Conservative Party so that although specific commitments such as support for British membership of the European Communities or for strengthening the forces of law and order may be found in a series of manifestos, the emphasis on them will vary from leader to leader. Policy making in the Party will be aided by the leader's closest colleagues, but ultimately the tone and the priorities of party policy are as much personal as reflective of party opinion generally.

Several recurrent themes can be discovered in recent Conservative manifestos, policy statements and actions when in power.[2] The Conservative Party in the twentieth century has become the party committed to the maintenance of free enterprise and private property, although initially the nineteenth-century Liberal Party was rather more identified with *laissez-faire* capitalism than were the Conservatives. Although its preference is for a free-market economy, the Conservative Party has generally adopted a pragmatic attitude towards the acts of nationalization undertaken by Labour. Thus it did not, for example, de-nationalize many of the industries which Labour had taken into public ownership during the 1945–51 period and, despite its theoretical hostility towards nationalization, the Conservative Government of 1970–4 itself, as has been seen, nationalized both Rolls-Royce and Upper Clyde Shipbuilders on the grounds that the former had an international reputation and the latter firm provided numerous jobs in an area already scarred by heavy unemployment. The disillusionment with Edward Heath's leadership, and the successful proselytizing activities of free-market economists and adherents of monetarism within the Conservative Party, have made the Tories' hostility towards governmental intervention in the economy more strident as well as more ideological in character since Margaret Thatcher assumed the leadership in 1975.

Defence of free enterprise goes hand in hand with a defence of private property which has a number of implications for Conservative policy and, as will be seen, for the sources of Conservative support. Thus Conservatives prefer to subsidize home ownership through mortgages rather than to subsidize the construction of houses for local authorities to lease at low rents. Indeed the Conservative Party has recently adopted a policy of selling existing local-authority houses to the sitting tenants at favourable prices by comparison with the open market. Defence of free enterprise is also linked with a desire for lower direct taxation: the Party sees high taxation rates as an impediment to enterprise and creativity. This desire to keep taxation as low as possible inevitably makes the Party suspicious of high levels of public expenditure. As far as the social services are concerned, the Conservatives have come to advocate a selective approach to the distribution of welfare benefits which, from their perspective, means restricting them to those in real need rather than distributing them to all citizens without regard to financial circumstance. In the last decade the Conservative Party has often seemed almost to be moving away from the Beveridge principles which inspired the modern welfare state. These principles formed an important part of the consensus on social and economic matters between 1951 and 1964 which was known as 'Butskellism' from the names of the moderate Tory R.A. Butler and of Hugh Gaitskell, the social democratic leader of the Labour Party between 1955 and 1963. In practice many of the differences between Conservative and Labour policy appear to be ones of emphasis. Conservatives do not wish to use welfare-state programmes to advance the substantive goal of equality and they give greater priority to freedom of choice in such fields as medical provision. Conservative policy accordingly advocates the retention of a flourishing private sector alongside the publicly provided programmes, in contrast to Labour's increasing advocacy of the abolition of the private sector. The experience of a period in which expansion of government expenditure on the social services can no longer be assumed has also caused Conservatives to re-examine their priorities in relation to welfare provision and to economize wherever possible in terms of organization and staffing.

One argument which Conservatives deploy against high levels of public expenditure is that such levels encourage inefficiency and create additional power for the bureaucracy. Thus the Party doubts that governments can contribute greatly to the solution of certain sorts of social problem, such as elimination of racial or sex prejudice, and it has even become sceptical about the extent to which poverty should be viewed as an objective phenomenon removable by government action. The state's resources, in the Conservative Party's opinion, should be concentrated on what have long been seen as the basic functions of government: defence against external attack and the maintenance of law and order. The theme of law and order has come to be emphasized heavily in Conservative manifestos, and Mrs Thatcher's earliest decisions on taking office in May 1979 were to bring forward rises in police pay and to improve the salaries of the armed services – symbolic decisions which reflected the priorities of her administration.[3]

The importance attached to defence expenditure in the Conservative Party is closely linked with the Conservative perception of the United Kingdom's role in the world. The opportunities for global influence offered by the Empire have largely been replaced by an emphasis on the potentialities of the European Communities as a forum for British diplomacy. Certainly the tone and character of Conservative statements on foreign policy are both more realistic and more pragmatic in relation to foreign policy than Labour's approach; Conservative defence strategy is not complicated by doubts about the morality of nuclear weapons or the cold war, and this again is a contrast to Labour attitudes where there remain strands of opinion hostile both to the United States and to Britain's possession of nuclear weapons.

The Conservative Party's attitude towards the non-English parts of the United Kingdom is complicated. Until the First World War the maintenance of the Union with Ireland was a central tenet in the Party's creed.[4] (The Party was known popularly by the name 'Unionists' until the Irish settlement removed the issue from the mainstream of British politics.) The Conservative Party's support for Ulster forged a link between the Protestant Ulster Unionists and the Conservatives for a large part of the period between 1921 and 1974, but the recurrence of violence in Northern Ireland led to Westminster's adoption of a bipartisan policy towards the Province, which divided the Ulster Unionists from their erstwhile Conservative allies. (This topic is further discussed in Chapter 10.)

The recent resurgence of nationalism within the British Isles also created difficulties for Tory strategy and policy. The Conservatives were by no means entirely hostile to Scottish aspirations for greater decentralization, but after an initial flirtation with the idea of a directly elected Assembly, the sentiments of English back-bench Conservatives and of Mrs Thatcher herself brought a large section of the Party down against the Labour Government's devolution proposals. However, the organizationally separate Scottish Conservative and Unionist Association (a name which replaced that of the Scottish Unionist Association only in 1965) was deeply divided by the problem of devolution, and the Conservative shadow spokesmen on Scotland, Alick Buchanan-Smith and Malcolm Rifkind, resigned their shadow portfolios rather than accept the leader's change of policy towards an Assembly. In the administration formed in 1979 both Buchanan-Smith and Rifkind were given posts, and these appointments, together with the poor performance of the SNP at the 1979 election, may enable the Party to sidestep divisions on the question for the time being. However, it is unlikely that the issue will completely disappear, and the potential for disunity over it remains.

Mounting Conservative suspicion of devolution reflects, partly, the Party's affection for the traditional unity of the Kingdom and the desire to preserve the essential character of Great Britain. These sentiments perhaps also account for the increasingly strong resistance to further immigration from the New Commonwealth. Although race relations and the immigration issue now play a role in the electoral strategies of both major parties, it is the Conservative Party which is perceived by the public as having the tougher policy in this area.[5] Paradoxically, one of the first problems which Mrs Thatcher's new Government had to face in 1979 was the future of refugees from Vietnam rescued by British ships and brought to Hong Kong; despite the possibility that they might prove the forerunners of larger numbers, the Government decided to allow them into the United Kingdom on humanitarian grounds. Conservative philosophy is thus difficult to characterize definitively. At some periods ideas such as individual freedom will be clearly articulated and may even produce concrete policy proposals designed to promote such values. At other periods the Party may seem to embody so wide a range of political ideas that few distinctive doctrinal features can be detected. The recent experience of opposition has led to a reappraisal of the Conservative Party's policies and some movement towards the neo-liberal economic doctrines of Milton Friedman and the libertarian political theories of Hayek. At the same time the Party's neo-liberalism has to be combined with a strong conviction that the authority of the state must be preserved and that firm, if not paternalist, government is a virtue. That such contradictions rarely reach the surface of debate within the Party may be attributed as much to the Party's general impatience with ideology as to its normal willingness to accept the compromises fashioned by its leaders.

The Labour Party

The birth of the modern Labour Party dates from the formation in 1900 of the Labour Representation Committee which was designed to bring together a number of disparate forces in British political life so that manual labour could be directly represented in Parliament. Twenty-nine Labour Party MPs were elected in 1906 when Keir Hardie became Chairman of the Parliamentary Labour Party, the PLP. The fact that the Labour Party had its roots in organizations external to Parliament has shaped its subsequent constitutional and political history: there is no parallel assumption to that found in the Conservative Party that the balance of power within the Party will be tilted towards the parliamentary representatives. It is extremely important also to bear in mind that from the begining the Labour Party has been a coalition or confederation of distinct groups and interests and this diversity, combined with the Party's traditions of internal democracy, has produced an alliance which contains a variety of political tensions.

One group in the amalgam of forces which came together in 1900 was the trade-union movement. Indeed it was as a direct result of a resolution passed at the Congress of the Trades Union Council in 1899 that the efforts to establish a Labour Representation Committee were made. This element in the Labour Party has been the dominant influence in the Party's structure, although it is not an influence that has been exerted consistently throughout the Party's history. The trade-union movement in Britain has always been heterogeneous. It only became closely identified with the cause of a single party with the threat to union organization which occurred in the latter years of the nineteenth and the early part of the twentieth centuries. Even after the establishment of the Labour Representation Committee the miners' union continued to maintain its distinct representation in Parliament.

The second element in the alliance forged in 1900 was the band of small socialist societies, each of which had evolved its own interpretation of the creed of socialism. Especially significant here was the Independent Labour Party, which had also played a significant role in bringing the new alliance into being. The ILP realized that these small socialist societies needed the financial and membership strength of the trade unions in order to be able to compete with the Conservative and Liberal Parties. Yet in this pragmatic compromise between groups inspired by varieties of socialist theory and the essentially defensive trade-union movement there was created a fertile source of controversy and conflict. In addition to the ILP, which came to be seen as 'a party within a party', two other socialist societies represented at the initial conference to form a Labour Representation Committee deserve special mention. The Fabian Society, although it claimed only 861 members in 1900, was to have an immense impact on the future of the Party, and Fabian intellectuals – especially Sidney and Beatrice Webb – were to leave their marks on the whole constitution and ethos of the Party. Secondly there was the Social Democratic Federation, which in 1900 claimed nine thousand members compared with the thirteen thousand claimed by the Independent Labour Party.[6]

The original advance of the Labour Party in terms of parliamentary seats had been the result of a secret electoral pact with Herbert Gladstone, the Liberal Chief Whip. But, once the entire working class was enfranchised in 1918, the Labour Party gradually displaced the Liberals as the Conservatives' main challenger. It was in 1918 also that the Webbs, together with Arthur Henderson, succeeded in persuading the Party to pass a new constitution for itself. It provides a convenient starting point for the analysis of Labour's contemporary political position, since it was then that Labour committed itself to socialism as an objective. Moreover, the end of the First World War saw the resolution of a number of political issues which had troubled pre-war Britain and thus marks something of a fresh political agenda for the parties.

The commitment to socialism was enshrined in Clause IV of the Labour Party's new constitution, which now declares as one of the Party's objects 'to secure for the workers by hand or by brain the full fruits of their industry, and the most equitable distribution thereof that may be possible, upon the basis of the common ownership of the means of production and the best obtainable system of popular administration and control of each industry and service'.[7] This commitment to socialism and to public ownership of the means of production have thus been linked in Labour politics, and Labour's 1945 manifesto, *Let Us Face the Future*, committed the Party to taking several basic industries – coal, gas, electricity and inland transport – into public ownership. To those industries already on the party list for nationalization were added the sugar-refining industry and the cement industry in 1950. By then, however, it was clear not merely that nationalization was an issue of controversy between the parties but also that it was extremely unpopular with the electorate at large. In 1974 a public-opinion survey still found that over 66% of the population was opposed to further nationalization of any kind, while only 10% favoured further nationalization.[8]

The unpopularity of nationalization was identified by Hugh Gaitskell as a major factor in Labour's run of election defeats in 1951, 1955 and 1959; he duly attempted to persuade the Party to modify clause IV. The failure of this attemp to steer Labour towards social democracy persuaded Gaitskell's successor in the leadership, Harold Wilson, that, while it was necessary to reduce the Party's emphasis on nationalization, this should be done pragmatically and not by attempts to persuade activists to expunge the doctrine from their creed. Very little further nationalization in fact occurred during the Labour administrations of 1964 to 1970. Instead the Labour Party tentatively initiated an experiment with new forms of intervention and public ownership, in which the state acquired controlling interests in the shares of leading firms in the private sector. It was hoped that such 'back-door nationalization' would allow the Labour Party to prove that the state could contribute to the profitability of industry as long as it was not confined to the already declining sectors of industry which had provided the traditional candidates for nationalization. It was also hoped that this new style of intervention would enable government to influence policies in the private sector, especially when they concerned pricing and investment.

The machinery by which this intervention was secured initially was a body called the Industrial Reorganization Corporation; this was abolished in 1970 and during Labour's 1970–4 period of opposition the idea of a state holding company was elaborated and defined under pressure from the left wing of the Party. Accordingly, when the Labour Party again returned to government in March 1974, it established the National Enterprise Board, which is designed to oversee the process of extending state interests in the private sector of industry. By the middle of 1978, the NEB had holdings in fourteen large companies including Ferranti Ltd, International Computer (Holdings) Ltd, and Rolls-Royce, the last of which had been nationalized by the Conservatives. Thus although there is pressure for the extension of traditional nationalization, the main thrust of future Labour involvement in this area is likely to come in the form of NEB activities, which do not of course entail the nationalization of a whole industry.

Commitment to public ownership is only one policy consequence of Labour's adherence to socialism. It is also committed to the redistribution of wealth through a progressive system of direct taxation. The February 1974 Labour manifesto defined Labour's aim as to 'bring about a fundamental and irreversible shift in the balance of power and wealth in favour of ordinary working people and their families'; the October 1974 manifesto reaffirmed Labour's belief that 'taxation must be used to achieve a major redistribution of wealth and income'. The same manifesto promised to introduce a wealth tax on wealth above £100,000 and to legislate for a Capital Transfer Tax.[9]

This belief in a high level of direct taxation has been complemented by a commitment to a high level of expenditure, especially in the fields of social welfare and education. Moreover, the experience of the inter-war period has made the Labour Party hostile to attempts to relate the provision of benefits to financial need and to most forms of means testing.

One peculiar feature of the British Labour Party is its ambivalent attitude towards international affairs. Many supporters of the Independent Labour Party were pacifists during the First World War, and the Labour tradition absorbed some of the old Liberal Party's attitudes towards international cooperation.[10] The Labour Party was thus marked at the beginning by anti-militarism as well as by a belief in decolonization. However, in the inter-war years there were many advocates of supplying arms to the Republicans in the Spanish Civil War and, with the coming of the Second World War, most doubts about the legitimacy of fighting were destroyed. Some Labour Party MPs were reluctant at the end of the Second World War to enter into an alliance against the Soviet Union and on the left of the Party there remains a considerable sentimental attachment to the Soviet Union. The question of foreign policy has thus been a deeply divisive one in Labour's ranks, and during the period 1945–63 foreign policy matters were frequently the issues which separated moderate from left-wing factions.[11] The controversies over British membership of the European Communities have highlighted the potential of non-domestic matters to disrupt unity in the Party, just as the Labour movement's somewhat insular outlook contrasted strongly with the internationalist perspectives of socialist parties in the rest of Western Europe.

The Labour Party has also displayed a strong concern for civil liberties in the recent past and has been responsible for a number of changes in the law concerning abortion, divorce, female equality, homosexual practices and censorship. However, the Party is by no means overwhelmingly secularist – the well-known remark that it owes more to Methodism than to

Marx underlines the Party's intellectual debt to religious Non-conformity – and concern about offending religious sensibilities has generally to be balanced against the claims of libertarian or secular causes.

The Party's electoral prospects have latterly been affected by its association with the trade-union movement, and there are some socialists who now query whether the connection is still in Labour's interests. The Party, as has been seen, came into being partly as a result of a TUC resolution and political protection of the trade unions remains a part of Labour's *raison d'être*. In 1969 the Labour Government attempted to legislate on the basis of a white paper, *In Place of Strife*, which suggested the introduction of greater legal control of industrial relations backed up by sanctions. The proposal violated the unwritten rule that no Labour Cabinet should interfere with trade-union immunities and the informal system of industrial relations which Britain possesses. The result was a humiliating defeat for senior cabinet ministers, with the exception of James Callaghan who had led the opposition to the proposals in Cabinet, and the creation of a new mood of hostility between the Labour Cabinet and the trade-union movement which lasted throughout the 1970 general election. The sides drew together again after the Conservatives passed their Industrial Relations Act and in 1972 there emerged from their joint opposition to that legislation a strengthened mechanism for consultation between the TUC and the Labour Party – the Liaison Committee – and a much closer involvement in Labour's policy-making processes.

The TUC–Labour Party Liaison Committee, which one authority has gone so far as to call 'the vital decision-making body in the Labour movement', was established as a result of a TUC initiative.[12] Given the circumstances in which the Committee began its life it was not perhaps surprising that its first priority was the co-ordination of industrial relations policy and the elaboration of alternatives to the approaches embodied in the wide-ranging Industrial Relations Act of 1971. The series of legislative measures passed after Labour returned to power in 1974 and the establishment of the ACAS machinery for dealing with industrial disputes reflected agreements worked out in large part in the monthly Liaison Committee meetings. The area of Liaison Committee discussions was not confined to industrial relations policy, however. As the scope of the TUC's interests broadened into the whole field of economic and social policy, so the Liaison Committee came to seem a suitable forum for pressing its views upon the Labour Shadow Cabinet. The 'social contract' was the result of these discussions and the Liaison Committee maintained its importance even following the Labour Government's movement back towards a rigid control of pay increases. The tension between the TUC's concern to foster a close relationship based on common opposition to Conservative policy, with its opportunities to influence policy, and the TUC's reluctance to get caught in a situation where it could no longer advocate to government the policies which its members really wanted, was but one paradox of the new relationship between Labour and the pressure group which had been largely responsible for the Party's creation. Another was the fact that the TUC as a body was being drawn into an ever more intimate relationship with the Labour Party at precisely the time when its clientele was changing. The TUC in 1976 had 113 trade unions affiliated to it, but only 59 of these unions were also affiliated to the Labour Party. Joint policy statements with a political party in these circumstances seemed anomalous, even if the newly unionized white-collar workers could hardly expect the TUC to shed its emotional links to the Labour movement overnight. Perhaps the final paradox was that the events of the 1970s had pushed the theme of the defence of unions back to the centre of the public's image of Labour just as the Labour Party itself was establishing its credibility as a national rather than a sectional party.

The results of the 1979 general election, which suggested that groups traditionally loyal to Labour had swung heavily to the Conservative Party in the south and Midlands, again emphasized the cross-pressures on the Labour Party. It could either look to the electorate first and risk unpopularity with activists, financial supporters and allies; or it could exploit its special relationship with the unions to promote an industrial and economic strategy which, if successful, could prove electorally popular but which could also, as in 1978–9, collapse, to the enormous electoral disadvantage of the Party. History, it appeared, had spun a web of relationships which it would prove very difficult to cut through.

The Liberal Party

The Liberal Party is now a minor party in terms of its parliamentary representation and its share of the popular vote. For much of the nineteenth century, however, it was a party of government, and until 1922 it was the major challenger to the Conservatives.

As in the case of the Conservative Party, the point at which the Liberal Party was formed is difficult to date with precision, but certainly by the time of the general election of 1868 there was a distinct Party with a coherent set of policies and a leader – Gladstone – who was in many ways the personification of nineteenth-century Liberalism.[13] Yet the Liberal Party, although it appeared unified in doctrine, was always composed of at least two conflicting elements – the traditional whig and the radical – and, while it could cover up its differences when some fundamental tenet of the Party such as free trade was attacked, the potential for disunity was always present.[14]

Free trade – the dogma that allegedly kept the people's food cheap – was the central issue at the general election of 1906. The result was the last spectacular Liberal victory at the polls, and after that landslide Liberal fortunes declines. Between 1906 and the outbreak of the First World War, however, the Liberal Party effected a significant shift in the balance of power in the British constitutional system. It laid the foundations of the welfare state, provided trade unions with legal immunities, disestablished the Church of Wales, limited the powers of the House of Lords and finally achieved the passage of legislation granting Ireland Home Rule. Unfortunately from the Liberal Party's point of view, the expansion of the electorate in 1918 meant that it would be Labour and not the Liberals who inherited the political benefits of these measures, and by the time of the 1935 general election few commentators would categorize the Liberals as anything but a third party in a system increasingly polarized between the Conservatives and the Labour Party.

The decline of the Liberal Party after 1918 has not been completely steady. The number of seats won in the post-1945 elections has fluctuated little: they reached a low of six in the general elections of 1951, 1955 and 1959 and a high peak of fourteen in the general election in February 1974. The Liberal share of the popular vote has, however, been rather more varied, as Table 3 shows.

Table 3
The Decline of the Liberals, 1906–79

General Election	% Popular Vote	Seats
1906	49.0	400
1910	43.2	275
1910	43.9	272
1918	25.6*	161*
1922	29.1**	116**
1923	29.6	159
1924	17.6	40
1929	23.4	59
1931	10.7***	72***
1935	6.4	21
1945	9.0	12
1950	9.1	9
1951	2.5	6
1955	2.7	6
1959	5.9	6
1964	11.2	9
1966	8.5	12
1970	7.5	6
1974 (Feb.)	19.3	14
1974 (Oct.)	18.3	13
1979	13.8	11

* Coalition Liberal and Asquithian Liberals added together.
** Lloyd George and Asquithian Liberals added together.
*** Simonite Liberals, Samuelite Liberals and Lloyd George Liberals added together.

By-elections have frequently offered the Liberals opportunities to make gains at the expense of the major parties and sometimes have created hopes of an incipient Liberal revival. The Liberal Party appears to have difficulty in retaining its converts, however, so that such upsurges in Liberal support as have occurred have generally proved short-lived. The two general elections of 1974 represented a marked advance from the 1970 position, but analysis of the Liberal vote suggested that it was relatively volatile and largely unrelated to Liberal Party policies,[15] and by 1979 Liberal support had again ebbed away – largely it seemed, to the advantage of the Conservatives.

Despite the fact that much Liberal support is only weakly linked to Liberal programmes, the ideas and strategies of the Liberal Party have been important both as a statement of what appears wrong with the two major parties and as a source of ideas for other groups in the political system. Three themes seem to have dominated Liberal politics at least in the post-1945 period. First, Liberals have attacked corporatism and the concentration of power in the British state. Liberals have advocated policies which extend the opportunities for individuals to control their own lives and this concern with individualism, which is nourished by a strong intellectual tradition within the Party, has led to such specific proposals as worker co-partnership in industry, a bill of rights and decentralization of government leading ultimately to the organization of the British system on a federal basis.

The second theme which runs through many contemporary Liberal arguments is a rejection of the existing system of adversary politics and partisan confrontation. The Liberal Party would like to see the existing electoral system replaced by proportional representation and the present style of politics replaced by a new partnership between the different groups in British society. Quite clearly the transformation of British political debate in the twentieth century into a dialogue between two class-based parties was not to the Liberals' advantage; they have therefore sought ways of diminishing the connection between social class and politics.

A third theme of Liberal politics is internationalism. Liberals in 1970 declared that while the Party's position was to stand up for the individual against the 'big battalions' at home, abroad the Party's goal was world cooperation. Thus its manifesto urged the strongest support for the United Nations, the entry of Britain into the European Communities and the democratization of European institutions, as well as the greatest freedom in international trade. The Liberal tradition has placed great emphasis on the need for a moral dimension to foreign policy – witness Gladstone's Midlothian campaigns and

163

the issue of Chinese labour in the South African mines – and its contemporary approach to world affairs maintains that tradition by manifesting concern with such issues of conscience as apartheid and human rights.

These policies may well contribute towards the Liberals' image as a classless Party, but its primary problems – how it can retain the support which it from time to time acquires and what strategy it should adopt in relation to other parties – remain questions of debate within Liberal ranks. In the normal parliamentary situation of the post-war period, one of the two major political parties has been able to dominate the House of Commons by virtue of its overall majority. In the period 1974–9 the parliamentary arithmetic was, however, such that the Liberal Party's parliamentary votes could influence legislative policy and the character of the Government itself.

In essence the Liberals have had to choose between three strategies when defining their relationship with other parties, and the post-1918 period has seen them experiment with all three at various times.[16] First there is the option of formal coalition. Senior Liberals might participate in government and legislative policy would then be worked out jointly between the Liberals and their coalition partners. The problem is that such experience of this option as there has been suggests that formal coalition tends to divide Liberals and to obscure the Party's identity. Thus the coalition effected with the Conservatives in 1915, and still more the Lloyd George coalition of 1916–22, split the Liberal Party internally when the threat from Labour was already severe. The 1931 coalition was short-lived as far as the wing of the Liberal Party led by Sir Herbert Samuel was concerned, although Liberals remained in the National Government under the leadership of Sir John Simon. The wartime coalition of 1940–5 was followed by a general election in which the Liberals' parliamentary seats were reduced in number from twenty-one to twelve. Thus when Edward Heath offered the Liberals a formal coalition in March 1974 the Liberal Party was hostile to the idea, although it seems that the Liberal leader, Jeremy Thorpe, might have favoured the scheme.

The second option for the Liberal Party in a confused parliamentary situation is a selective support of those measures with which it agrees. This strategy was employed during Harold Wilson's first administration from 1964 to 1966. The tactic provides the Liberal Party with the equivalent of a veto, but puts the onus on the governing party to arrange its legislative programme so as to maximize its chances of parliamentary survival. From the Liberal perspective, opportunities for influencing legislation can be combined with the retention of independence. The disadvantage is that such a strategy is often difficult to sell to the electorate and too negative to make much impact at the hustings.

The third tactic is the kind of formal pact to which David Steel committed the Liberals when Labour lost its parliamentary majority in 1976. The two parties agreed to establish a consultative committee so that the Liberal leadership and the relevant ministers could discuss measures prior to their introduction into the House of Commons. The consultative committee, which was chaired by Michael Foot as Leader of the House, was also intended to examine Liberal legislative proposals. In addition, it was agreed that there should be regular meetings between Steel and Callaghan on a personal basis, and between the Chancellor of the Exchequer and the Liberal economics spokesman, John Pardoe.

The arrangement thus appeared to place Liberals in a privileged position regarding the business of the House of Commons, and to offer Liberal MPs opportunities for access to government which might have enabled them to exert influence on a wide range of policy matters. The agreement also made a number of concessions to Liberal opinions, including a pledge that the Government would speedily bring forward bills to establish direct elections to the European Assembly and for the establishment of Assemblies in Scotland and Wales. Moreover the Liberals were able to secure a free vote on the electoral method to be used for the European Parliament, and to gain additional time for a private member's bill on homelessness which the Liberals wished to see enacted. Finally the Liberals were able to persuade the Government to modify a bill designed to extend local-authority powers to undertake construction work by employing direct labour.

Doubts about the wisdom of such a close alliance with the Labour Party – which was twice renewed but allowed to lapse in 1978 – were expressed within the Party, especially as the Liberal vote at by-elections seemed poor and the concessions to Liberal opinion ultimately amounted to very little. Certainly the unpopularity of the pact was one factor in explaining the loss of Emlyn Hooson's seat at Montgomery and John Pardoe's in Cornwall North in the May 1979 election.[17]

From the Liberal Party's point of view the pact was therefore something of a mixed blessing. David Steel, the Liberal leader, had to defend it by staking his leadership on it before the Liberal Assembly. On the other hand, the Liberals were in a weak financial and political state to fight an election in the period 1976–8 and so had a motive for propping up the Callaghan Government. The Liberal leaders received additional publicity and arguably came closer to the centre of decision making than they had been for many years. Above all the arrangements introduced into British political life, if only for a short period, the atmosphere of open political bargaining which is customarily associated with countries in which formal coalitions are the norm. The Liberal decision to vote against its erstwhile Labour ally in the March 1979 vote of confidence was, however, strong evidence that the pressures of the system tend to permit coalition-style behaviour for limited periods only, and that Liberal tactics are difficult to sustain or accommodate within an adversarial electoral system.

The Communist Party

The British Communist Party was formed in 1921 from the amalgamation of a number of small and fragmented Marxist groups.[18] Its membership has always been small and its parliamentary representation has similarly been minimal. At the Third Congress of Comintern in 1921, the Communist Party of Great Britain claimed ten thousand members and its total membership as reported to the annual Congress of the British Party in 1977 was 25,293.[19] No Communist MP has been elected to Parliament since 1945 when P. Piratin was elected for the Mile End division of Stepney. Thirty-eight candidates stood at the general election of May 1979 and all lost their deposits.[20]

The sorry state of the Communist Party's orthodox political activity in the nation's formal representative institutions is not, however, the only indicator of its strength. For the Communist Party enjoys some support in industry since many of the large trade unions have at one time or another been influenced by members of the Communist Party. At the 1977 Congress there were 337 delegates representing a number of major trade unions, and one commentator suggested that some 10% of all officials in the unions are Communists.[21] There were then, however, only two Communist Party members of the TUC's General Council, and at the higher reaches of the trade-union movement there are probably as many strongly anti-Communist officials as there are Party members.

The strength of the Communist Party is not necessarily concentrated in individual unions, although the Amalgamated Union of Engineering Workers has a particularly heavy concentration of Communists on its executive – over one quarter usually – and perhaps a thousand of its thirty-thousand shop stewards are Communists.[22] There is also a strong Communist presence in the National Union of Mineworkers where, in 1977, 6 of the 27 Executive Committee members were Communists. Although the industrial climate of the 1970s, and especially the Industrial Relations Act of 1971, may have moved all unions to the left of their original position, there is still reckoned to be a good deal of distrust of Communist Party tactics in industry which lingers from the 1950s experience of ballot rigging and fraud in the Electrical Trades Union, a distrust which restricts the scope of Communist influence.[23]

The British Communist Party used to be very subservient to Moscow and this caused it to lose some seven thousand members at the time of the Russian invasion of Hungary in 1956.[24] Its attitude towards the Russian invasion of Czechoslovakia in 1968 was more critical of the Soviet Union, but its long association with a blind pro-Moscow stance was damaging and membership figures at all levels continued to decline. In 1977, inspired perhaps by the example of Communist parties in other parts of Western Europe, the British Communist Party decided to revise and modernize its doctrine and Congress, after a long debate, endorsed a new version of *The British Road to Socialism*.[25] This suggested that the Party should abandon the doctrine of the dictatorship of the proletariat and guaranteed that a Communist government would maintain the freedom of all political parties, including those hostile to socialism, to contend for office. The Communist Party also expressed its willingness to work with other groups to create a socialist society in Great Britain. It is doubtful whether this evidence of a change of heart within Communist Party ranks will have much impact either on the electorate or on the Party's critics; but certainly it caused dismay to the hard-line Stalinists within the Party, who broke away to form a New Communist Party to maintain the old dogmas.

The National Front

The National Front was founded in 1967 as a result of the amalgamation of several small right-wing groups including the League of Empire Loyalists and the British National Labour Party. Its roots are thus very much in what one writer has called the British 'fascist tradition', and it is often overtly anti-semitic.[26] In 1967 it seemed unlikely that membership of the National Front could be more than two thousand overall. However, the emergence of race as an issue in British politics, and the vacuum created by the apparent unwillingness of either major party to take strong action to prevent further immigration, caused the National Front's membership to increase.[27] Yet there is an imbalance between the claims made for the National Front's influence – and its coverage in the press – and the electoral success which it has achieved.

Certainly the performance of the National Front in three by-elections between March 1977 and April 1978, when it beat the Liberals into fourth place, and its achievement of an average vote of 4.4% in the 18 by-elections which it fought between 1975 and 1978, appeared ominous. But by-elections are not general elections and at the October general election of 1974 the National Front only secured an average of 3.1% of the vote in the seats it contested. That level of electoral support has remained relatively stable over the decade since the Front's formation so that it may well be that, despite the publicity, the potential appeal of the National Front is limited, especially where another party, for example the Liberals, is also available to capitalize on the protest vote.[28] Certainly the Front's poor showing at the general election of 1979 (when it gained o.6% of the total vote) suggests that earlier fears of a 'fascist' advance were unfounded.

What the Front's activities did over the period 1967–9 was to call into question traditional practices with regard to political demonstrations and meetings. Street marches formed an important part of the National Front's propaganda campaign, but the staging of such marches in areas of heavy immigrant concentration – especially the east and south-east of London – provoked counter-demonstrations and violence, such as that at Lewisham in August 1977, and at Southall in the 1979 election campaign, which the police found difficult to control (see Chapter 11). Moreover, the widespread doubt which has been expressed about the ethics of the Front's policies in a plural society committed to the ideal of racial harmony has led some to wonder whether the National Front should be allowed access to television and radio at election times.

The Extreme Left

Two smaller parties of the extreme left may be mentioned. The Socialist Workers' Party or SWP has a Trotskyist affiliation. The Party put up several candidates in by-elections, although none of them achieved more than a negligible percentage of the vote. On the other hand, the Party, both in its own right and through the Anti-Nazi League which the SWP largely sponsored, engaged in demonstrations and counter-demonstrations to those of the National Front, and had some importance in industrial conflicts and student politics. The Workers' Revolutionary Party put up sufficient candidates in the 1979 election to warrant an election broadcast but their total vote was negligible.

The Scottish National Party

The Scottish National Party was founded in 1934 as a result of the merger of John MacCormick's National Party of

Scotland and the rather more conservative Scottish Party which had been formed in 1932. The Scottish National Party could draw on a tradition of nationalism and agitation for Home Rule which went back at least to the beginning of the nineteenth century. (This topic is further discussed in Chapter 10.) The SNP has, however, been deeply divided over tactics in the course of the twentieth century, with some of its leaders favouring alliances with other parties deemed sympathetic to Scottish aspirations and some in favour of independent political action for an independent Scotland. The Second World War brought many of these divisions to a head, and the Scottish National Party in 1942 split into two groups – a moderate Scottish Convention designed to build all-party support for devolution, and the Scottish National Party which became a separatist party.

The SNP's electoral record during the 1950s was one of slow growth, but during the 1960s the Party made rapid advances, to become at the election of October 1974 the second-largest party in Scotland in terms of its share of the popular vote (see also chapter 10). The overriding goal of the SNP remains independence, but the circumstances of the 1974–9 Parliament induced the SNP to support the Government's devolution proposals as a step towards independence. The SNP has experienced internal divisions once it has had to construct policies across the range of social and economic questions, since it is unclear whether it should be oriented towards a left-of-centre programme or a right-of-centre one. The initial successes of the SNP were in Conservative-held seats, but to proceed further the SNP must appeal to Labour voters, especially in the heavily populated Strathclyde region around Glasgow. Yet it appears that the leadership is not entirely committed to socialist-style policies; and indeed the SNP has not always voted together in the House of Commons, although it was united in voting against the Labour Government in March 1979 in protest at the Government's refusal to implement the Scotland Act. The SNP was perhaps the major casualty of the May 1979 election when its representation in Parliament was cut to two seats, and its share of the total Scottish vote slumped to 17.3%, putting it way behind both Labour and the Conservatives again.

Plaid Cymru

Plaid Cymru was founded in 1925, but it did not develop a political platform of Welsh independence until 1932. Its programme has always been heavily cultural and oriented towards the preservation and promotion of the distinctive Welsh traditions and the Welsh language. Its goals have therefore tended to be divisive since, unlike Scottish nationalism, Welsh nationalism has until recently been perceived as the preserve of the minority of the Welsh population which can actually speak Welsh. Since 1966, however, Plaid Cymru has tried to broaden its appeal from rural and middle-class Welsh-speaking parts of the electorate to the non-Welsh-speaking and younger groups in the industrialized south of Wales. Its parliamentary representation at Westminster has been small – three seats in the Parliament elected in October 1974 – and the party has conveyed the impression of greater sympathy for the Labour Party than has the SNP. At the general election of 1979 it lost its leader's seat to Labour, although the party's decline in terms of the percentage of the total Welsh vote – from 10.9% to 8.1% – was less dramatic than the SNP reversal. (The topic of Welsh nationalism is further discussed in Chapter 10.)

The Political Parties of Northern Ireland

Northern Irish party politics differ from politics elsewhere in the United Kingdom. Here the sectarian divisions are the most important factors shaping electoral choice: the issues of political debate centre not on social or economic policy alone but also on the very existence of the border and the constitutional unity of Northern Ireland and Great Britain. Because the community is so polarized by religious affiliation, the scope for genuine party competition is small; parties are typically confined to their own religious constituency for electoral support and any attempt to broaden the appeal beyond a 'natural' religious base risks alienating a core of party sympathizers. Northern Irish politics thus tend to be isolated from those of the rest of the country, and this isolation has become more marked since 1974 when the fragile bonds which linked the majority Protestant

171

Ulster Unionist Party to the Conservatives snapped completely in the wake of the suspension of Stormont and the experiment with power sharing. (The complexities of the Ulster situation are further discussed in Chapter 10.)

Until the Northern Ireland Civil Rights Association campaign in the late 1960s and the changes occasioned by the return of violence to the Province, Ulster's party politics were frozen into a mould of competition between a solid Ulster Unionist Party, the symbol and vehicle of the Protestant majority, and a group of fragmented and somewhat stagnant opposition parties. These parties drew their support mainly from the alienated Catholic minority in the Province, but there were also occasional attempts to erode the solidity of the Protestant support for the Unionist Party. In general, however, such attempts were unsuccessful. The distinction between opposition to the Unionists and opposition to the constitutional settlement was at best imperfect, and this automatically restricted the room for manœuvre of such parties as the Northern Irish Labour Party. Protestants feared to join it lest by weakening the Unionist Party they should thereby weaken the instruments of Protestant ascendancy; the Roman Catholics would not join it because it was committed to the existing constitutional framework.[29] Also, the Party's concern with social and economic issues made its relevance dubious in a situation where religious questions dominated the political agenda.

The political party which most Roman Catholics supported until the end of the 1960s was the Nationalist Party. This party was the survivor of the pre-1918 Irish Parliamentary Party, but with partition in 1920 its position in Ulster became increasingly difficult. Clearly the goals of the Nationalist Party were anathema to the majority in the new political unit of Northern Ireland, while to participate in the politics of the Province in a constitutional manner would entail the Nationalist Party's acknowledging the legitimacy of the Ulster institutions and partition. Moreover the border between the Republic and Northern Ireland severed the organization of the Nationalist movement as surely as it created two polities and, although bonds of sympathy remained, it was difficult to support a coherent party in the very different circumstances of the North and the South. This disorientation of the Nationalist Party in

Ulster meant that the party to which, *faute de mieux* perhaps, most Catholics gave their natural support until 1970 was not an effective vehicle of political action. Indeed its primary characteristics, as one authority has noted, were its tendency to abstain from the formal politics of the Province, a lack of efficient organization and, above all, a tendency to concentrate on the single issue of the border even when, as in the late 1960s, new issues of importance for the Catholic population had appeared on the agenda of Ulster politics.[30]

Competing with the Nationalist Party for Catholic votes were two much smaller anti-partition parties – the National Democratic Party, which originated in 1965 and had its roots in a group called National Unity, and the Republican Labour Party. The Republican Labour Party had been formed when the Northern Ireland Labour Party split in 1949 over the issue of the link with the United Kingdom. The Northern Irish Labour Party remained 'unionist' and thereafter its appeal was in effect limited to Protestants; the Republican Labour Party was formed and was able to blend opposition to partition with socialism.

The changed situation of Northern Irish politics in the 1960s stimulated a realignment of political forces in the Province and the formation of new political parties. Although the situation is still extremely fluid, there are now at least three groups of importance competing for the Protestant vote and two competing for the Catholic vote as well as one non-sectarian party.

THE UNITED ULSTER UNIONIST COUNCIL

This was founded in 1975 in an attempt to regain the unity which the old Ulster Unionist Party had enjoyed until the political developments of the late 1960s began to divide it. It consisted of three political groupings, the Official Unionists, the Democratic Unionist Party and the Vanguard Unionist Party.

The Official Unionists have existed since the possibility of Home Rule forced Protestants to organize in defence of the union. The party traces its history back to 1892 and, although the divisions over power sharing have weakened it both electorally and organizationally, it can still claim to be the nucleus of Protestant political organization in Northern

Ireland. Its leader from 1974 to 1979 was Harry West and among its five MPs at Westminster in the 1974–9 Parliament was Enoch Powell, who was offered a seat there after resigning his Wolverhampton constituency. The Democratic Unionist Party is distinguished by its loyalism and extreme evangelical Protestantism. It is a party organized to give political expression to the sentiments voiced by the Reverend Ian Paisley, who is the leader of a body called the Free Presbyterian Church. Paisley has gained notoriety by his demonstrations against the ecumenical movement and by his organization of Protestants against the civil rights movement. The Party was formed in 1971 and enjoys considerable popularity among working-class Protestants because of its economic and social concerns. It has three seats at Westminster.

The defunct Vanguard Unionist Party was led by William Craig, who formed the organization as a result of disagreement with Brian Faulkner's decision in 1973 to accept the idea of power sharing in Northern Ireland between Protestants and Catholics. Craig lost his seat as an Official Unionist in 1979. The Vanguard Unionist Party is determined to maintain Ulster's distinctive traditions, and if this cannot be achieved by the maintenance of the union with Britain then it is prepared to see an independent Ulster, although such a state would obviously be extremely vulnerable to internal terrorism and international pressures.

In addition to the groups united under the umbrella of the United Ulster Unionist Council there is the Unionist Party of Northern Ireland, a moderate group formed by Brian Faulkner in 1974 in an attempt to break the sectarian impasse of Ulster politics. The distinguishing feature of the Unionist Party of Northern Ireland is its desire to promote moderate policies and reconciliation between the religious communities. Its assumption is that the union is necessary to Northern Ireland and its constitution commits it to the principle of coalition government. It has no seats at Westminster, and secured only 1.1% of the votes cast in the Province in 1979.

The opposition to the parties whose strength is rooted in the Protestant community now comes primarily from the Social Democratic and Labour Party which was founded in 1970 as a coalition of Catholic political groupings. (At the 1979 general election it gained 19.9% of the votes cast in Northern Ireland and one seat.) Its ultimate ideal is the reunion of the whole of Ireland, but it is prepared to accept that this must be dependent upon the wishes of the population of Northern Ireland. In the meantime it wants greater Catholic participation in the state and equal civic rights. It was therefore anxious to support the idea of power sharing and the constitutional settlement worked out in 1973.

In the same year that the Social Democratic and Labour Party was founded, in 1970, there was also a movement to found a non-sectarian party which came into being as Alliance. Its primary feature is its attempt to rally moderate opinion on a bi-confessional basis, a goal which rather sadly means that its electoral support has been small – 11.9% in 1979, which was insufficient to give it any seats.[31]

Minor Parties and Independents

In addition to the political parties which base their appeal on issues specific to the peripheral areas of the United Kingdom, a history of British parties would reveal a range of tiny parties and organizations which have fielded candidates at parliamentary elections. Usually these candidates have no chance of success unless they have already acquired the support of the local organization of one of the major parties or there is a pact between the major parties not to contest an election – a rarity except in wartime by-elections. The return of minor-party and independent candidates is, of course, more likely at a by-election than at a general election because the government of the country is not at stake and maverick candidates acquire more publicity if the contest is an isolated one. However, the general election of February 1974 saw the return to Parliament of two independents – E. Milne and Dick Taverne – who were denied the support of their party organizations, so that, although rare, such an achievement is not totally impossible. Equally, the candidacy of independents and minor-party representatives may be significant in a constituency not so much because there is the chance of such a candidate's actually gaining the seat but because the challenge may split one of the major parties or so divide its vote as to allow the other major party to win the seat.

The Basis of Voting and the Character of the Party System

The British party system has been seen as a classic example of a system of two-party competition, whether that competition has been between the Conservative and Liberal Parties or, as after 1918, between the Conservative and Labour Parties. Yet although it would be absurd to deny that on one level the United Kingdom does conform to the criteria for determining when a two-party system exists – for example, that two parties are in a position to compete for an absolute majority of seats; that one party is expected to achieve such a majority and be willing to govern alone; and that the parties are sufficiently balanced in electoral strength to make alternation in power a possibility – recent events and the Parliaments of 1974–9 require a few reservations to that generalization to be made.[32]

First, the United Kingdom's party system is a two-party system at the parliamentary level only. At the electoral level support is very much more divided, whether one looks at unusual elections, like those of 1974, or at more normal ones, like those of 1959, 1966 or 1979. The domination of the two-party system is in many ways a product of an electoral system which is insensitive to dispersed minority preferences.

Secondly the label of a two-party system is accurate only if one takes an overall view of the United Kingdom and ignores the peculiarities of Ulster. The presence of nationalist parties in Scotland and Wales is one aspect of the diversity of party competition within the United Kingdom: at the general election of 1979 it was noticeable that Scotland behaved very differently from the rest of the country by registering a swing to Labour while Wales and England swung heavily towards the Conservatives. Regardless of the presence of minor parties, the balance of strength between the parties in each component area of the country is different, and politics in each area reflect distinct social patterns and assumptions. In Scotland the Labour Party dominates the industrial west and the Conservative Party is generally weaker than in England; in addition the Scottish

National Party has been electorally significant, and the Liberals also retain some islands of strength. Wales, despite an unusually heavy swing towards the Conservatives in the 1979 general election, is dominated by the Labour Party. In addition, Northern Ireland's pattern of party competition and its sectarian voting behaviour make it as distinctive a sub-system of the United Kingdom as the South once was in the United States.

Finally it should be noticed that even if the two major British parties continued to dominate British politics, that continuity should not be allowed to conceal subtle changes in the basis of their support. The 1960s and the 1970s were years in which the simple model of class as the basis of British voting behaviour was called into question. The striking decline in the two-party share of the vote over the period 1964–74 led some commentators to speak of the phenomenon of 'partisan de-alignment', while a high degree of electoral volatility suggested a weakening of the links between some sections of the population and their natural class parties. It is perhaps too early to say whether the results of the 1979 general election can provide any clues to the social changes underpinning these developments, but at the very least they should serve as a reminder that the relationship between class and party affiliation is a complex one. A manual worker in Leeds may behave very differently at the polls from a manual worker in Southampton or Oxford and younger manual workers in both areas may have quite different assumptions from those of their fathers about the relationship between their occupation and politics. The importance of the period 1974–9 from the point of view of the two major parties may be, in retrospect, that it alerted them to the possibilities of such changes in the electorate's perceptions of the party system, even if it provided them with no easy solutions.

7 The Political Parties II: Internal Structure

The internal relationships of each of the major British parties can best be understood in terms of tensions between the leader of the parliamentary party, the members of the parliamentary party as a whole and the party organization in the country. The relationships are of course fluid and will change as different personalities occupy key offices and as different political issues grip the attention. The analysis of the relationship between the different elements in the Labour Party is in addition markedly more difficult than in the case of the Conservative Party, because Labour is a 'federal' party comprising several distinct elements so that tensions between, for example, the trade unions and the constituency parties can cut across simple antagonisms or differences between the PLP and the NEC.

The style of politics within Britain's political parties varies enormously because each individual party has been shaped by its peculiar traditions and history, although the fact that both Labour and Conservative Parties have to operate within the framework of the British constitution to a certain extent produces a degree of similarity between those parties' internal relations. The standard interpretation of modern British parties in the 1960s, Robert McKenzie's *British Political Parties*, emphasized the similarity of the distribution of 'power' in the Labour and Conservative Parties despite the fact that they appear to have very different constitutions and very different assumptions about the degree of internal democracy to be encouraged within their ranks.[1] That analysis has since been subjected to extensive criticism, although it should be remembered that it was very convincing when it was first written precisely because it reflected aspects of the party system at that time. Its current weaknesses stem primarily from the fact that the character of the parties has changed in the ensuing period.[2]

The contemporary need to revise the account of British parties which was popularly accepted in the 1960s should not be allowed either to conceal the merits of McKenzie's thesis or to produce accounts which veer too far in the opposite direction. Political parties in Britain do still share a number of common features and assumptions, which affect such questions as the autonomy of the parliamentary party from external control, and limit the extreme interpretations of internal democracy in the Labour Party. At the same time, however, the British constitution – as was seen in Chapter 1 – may be adapting itself to the pressures generated within the Labour Party, and it could well be argued that the referendum device and the more flexible interpretation of collective responsibility are both instances of this trend. Also one of the striking features of party politics in Britain in the 1970s has been the extent to which a number of problems such as limited finance and the loss of membership have been common to all political parties. The internal norms of the parties are nevertheless subtle and complex; they do not readily fit into a simple intellectual or conceptual framework.

The Conservative Party

The most conspicuous aspect of the pattern of relationships within the Conservative Party is the prominent part played by the parliamentary leader. The Conservative Party's leader has a dominant role in the policy-making process, and has virtually unlimited powers to appoint both cabinet colleagues when the Party is in power and shadow cabinet colleagues when the Party is in opposition. This is not to imply that Conservative leaders enjoy security of tenure in their office, for their considerable autonomy entails a corresponding responsibility for whatever electoral successes and failures the Party experiences. Twentieth-century Conservative leaders have several times been obliged to resign, but the process is rather different from that in the Labour Party because until very recently the mechanism for ousting a leader who had lost the Party's confidence was an informal one rather than the formal machinery of annual re-election which has long existed in the Labour Party.

The relationship between the Conservative Party leader and his parliamentary colleagues was radically altered in 1965 when formal election machinery was created so that thereafter leaders would be chosen by vote of the whole of the Conservative Party in the House of Commons. The Conservative Party's attitude towards elective party leadership had until then been hostile; because it had been in government for so much of the twentieth century it had usually proved possible to avoid the issue of leadership selection by accepting as leader of the Conservative Party the person invited by the monarch to form the administration. That person in turn would have been recommended to the monarch on the advice of a small group of senior Conservatives who would have taken soundings to ascertain which eligible individual would be most likely to command the most support or create a consensus behind him. However, this situation would only arise when a Conservative Prime Minister died or resigned in the middle of a Parliament so that a new Prime Minister had to be found. If the Party had a leader and the new administration had to be formed as a result of a general-election victory, then the monarch's choice was limited: since 1911 it has been generally assumed that the monarch must send for the leader of the Conservative Party in the House of Commons.

A vacancy in the leadership had not occurred in opposition since 1911, when Bonar Law was elected leader at a time when the Party was deeply divided over tariff reform. During the Party's shorter spells of opposition prior to 1964 the Conservatives usually had a former Prime Minister, who could automatically become the leader of the opposition.

The decision to change to an elective procedure stemmed from the events and controversy surrounding the selection of Sir Alec Douglas Home as Prime Minister in 1963. Sir Alec Douglas Home's selection as successor to Harold Macmillan was unusual, since at the time of his selection he was a peer and there was a much more attractive candidate from the point of view of many Conservative M Ps in the person of R. A. Butler. After the Party lost the general election of 1964 a new and more open procedure was devised and the successor to Sir Alec Douglas Home was chosen by this method in 1965. The procedure now involves a ballot of all Conservative MPs; to be elected on the first ballot, a candidate must win an overall majority plus an additional 15% of those eligible to vote. If no candidate achieves this on the first ballot, there is a second ballot in which new candidates may stand and in which only an overall majority is necessary for victory. If there is still no winner on this ballot, a final ballot is held; only the candidates with the three highest votes at the second ballot may stand. Electors rank candidates in order of preference, and the winner is determined by adding the number of first preferences to the redistributed second preferences on the papers of the third candidate.[3]

Initially the system was intended for use only when the leadership was actually vacant – in other words when a leader had already indicated his intention of resigning. However, after the Conservative Party had lost two elections in 1974 there was increased back-bench dissatisfaction with Edward Heath's leadership and a demand for a revision of the rules to allow for annual elections in which the incumbent could be challenged. This change was made in 1975, and in that year Edward Heath was beaten by Margaret Thatcher in the election.

The change in the basis of the Conservative leader's authority – the fact that his or her position is now no longer determined by the arcane process of nomination but by an open election – has perhaps yet to be fully appreciated by the Conservative Party. Edward Heath's style of leadership and the unexpected election victory of 1970 made his period of office as Conservative leader very similar in pattern to that of earlier leaders. There was little concern with cultivating the back-benchers by whose votes he had been elected; indeed one of the reasons for his defeat in 1975 was that he was thought to have been authoritarian and aloof in his handling of back-benchers.[4] Margaret Thatcher's leadership on the other hand does reveal an awareness of the mechanism by which she attained her position, and since 1975 she has taken great care to involve the back benches more in policy discussions. Her style of leadership is thus very much one in which communication with the rank and file of the Party in Parliament plays a central part. It is not so much that the Conservative Party has suddenly discovered the power to depose leaders but rather that the machinery of annual elections makes the possibility of displacement more evident to leaders and followers alike. It is inevitably more likely that the kind of leader selected by this machinery will be a clearer reflection of back-bench sentiments than in the past, and perhaps even of the outlook of constituency activists; previously the advice given to the monarch could take into account not merely a candidate's acceptability within the Party but also his potential vote-winning capacity among the electorate at large.

When the Conservative Party is in opposition the leader will appoint a number of front-bench spokesmen to assist him in his parliamentary duties; the most senior of those appointments will form a Shadow Cabinet. These spokesmen are the personal choices of the leader; if they appear successful in their tasks they are likely to form the core of any future Conservative administration. The leader also appoints the key officers in the Party's central bureaucracy. The Conservative Central Office was founded by Disraeli in 1870 in order to help organize the Conservative Party's electoral efforts in the circumstances of an expanded electorate. The Office is normally regarded as the personal preserve of the leader, who will appoint both the Chairman of the Party – a position which will go to someone on whose personal loyalty the leader can count – and the Director. The Chairman of the Party is a full-time politician, and if the Conservatives are in power he often has a seat in the Cabinet. The Director of Central Office is responsible for the routine administration of the Party's activities and exercises general supervision of the Central Office's various subdivisions such as finance, organization and publicity. The leader is also responsible for appointing the Director of the Conservative Research Department, which was founded in 1930 and acts as a support service for Conservative spokesmen by contributing material for speeches and policy making. This function is much more important when the Conservative Party is in opposition and senior spokesmen have no access to the Civil Service for briefing. The Research Department also provides a secretariat for some of the Conservative Party's policy committees, including the Shadow Cabinet itself. In 1979 the decision was taken amidst much controversy to bring the Research Department under the control of Central Office.

The second element of importance within the Conservative Party is the whole body of Conservative MPs. The character and composition of the Parliamentary representation of any political party is significant for at least two reasons. First, the image and appeal of a party is the product not merely of the specific policies and issues with which it is identified but also of the kind of men and women who are seen to represent that party. The electorate's perceptions of the parliamentary party are perhaps the most important element in determining the party's image; and, as far as the major British parties are concerned, the social and economic characteristics of each party's MPs will be of special relevance in shaping the image presented to the electorate. The second reason for attaching significance to the composition of the parliamentary representatives of a party is that divisions of opinion and ideology may well be compounded by social heterogeneity and thus make the task of leadership more difficult. It is therefore important to ask of a party not merely what range of ideas are reflected within its ranks and how ideologically cohesive a group it is, but also how diverse are the people selected.

An examination of the background of Conservative MPs reveals that they are a relatively homogeneous group. Indeed there can be little doubt that the image which the modern Conservative Party indirectly projects is still that of an upper middle-class or 'patrician' party.[5] One index of the upper middle-class character of the Conservative parliamentary representatives is the percentage of its members who attend a public, (in other words a fee-paying), school. The proportion of Conservative MPs with this educational background has not fallen below 60% since 1945, and in 1945 it was as high as 83.2%. The most famous English public school, Eton, alone provided between 16% and 27% of the Conservative Party's MPs over the period 1945–79. The number who attended the two ancient universities – Oxford and Cambridge – has never fallen below 50% in the post-war period, although it must be remembered that access to Oxford and Cambridge has long been possible via education at a state school and that both Edward Heath and Margaret Thatcher are products of the former state grammar schools rather than of the private sector of education. The occupational background of Conservative MPs has also not changed greatly during the past thirty-four years. The vast majority of Conservative MPs are drawn from the ranks of business, commerce and farming, as well as from such professions as the law and accountancy. However, some slight shifts in the occupational groups most prominent in the Tory Party may be discerned. There has, for example, been a decline over the post-war period in the number of Conservative MPs with a landowning or farming background and an increase in the number of businessmen, who have come to represent the largest group. (There are, however, reasons for suggesting that the Conservative Party's identification with the interests of the business community is by no means perfect, and that in many ways the policies advocated by the Party are out of step with those advocated by the financial and business interests outside Parliament.) The proportion of barristers in the parliamentary Conservative Party has also declined slightly; however, the Bar still constitutes one of the most numerous professions within the Tory ranks. Taken together, the three occupations of farming, business and the Bar accounted for 55% of Conservative MPs elected in October 1974, which, although a decline from the 1945 figure of 61.4%, remains a substantial portion of Westminster's Tories.[6]

It thus appears that the stereotype of a Conservative MP is an individual with a public school and/or Oxbridge education whose working experience has been in business, in farming or at the Bar. It should also be noted that the typical Conservative MP is also likely to be male. Women, along with candidates of working-class origin, are heavily under-represented in the parliamentary Conservative Party. Indeed, in the election of October 1974 only seven female Conservative MPs were returned – a fact which suggests that not only are selection committees less likely to choose women candidates but also that the few women who are selected as candidates tend to be selected either for hopeless seats or for seats which are vulnerable if there is a swing towards Labour.

The Conservative leadership has at times tried to encourage

local constituency associations to adopt candidates who might contribute greater social diversity to the parliamentary Party. Constituency associations are, however, notoriously jealous of their right to select a candidate of their choice, and despite the efforts of Central Office it appears that selection committees still find the attributes associated with a public school and Oxbridge education and a career in business or the Bar impressive; certainly individuals with these characteristics are likely to find their chances of a Conservative seat greater than those of applicants from less orthodox backgrounds. The Conservative Party's parliamentary representatives are thus very different both from its electoral supporters and from its Party activists.

The fact that certain educational and professional backgrounds are common to a large number of Conservative MPs has been seen by some commentators as an explanation of the cohesion of the parliamentary Party. Social homogeneity has, it was thought, reduced the likelihood of party division and faction. Certainly the internal divisions of the Conservative Party are different in kind from those in the Labour Party. For whereas the Labour Party has within its ranks a number of well-organized groups who regularly meet and vote together usually on the basis of some shared ideological approach to policy issues, divisions of opinion within the Conservative Party have been altogether more fluid, less durable and inspired by broad similarities of outlook rather than sharp disagreements of principle. This distinction regarding the form which differences of opinion and attitude take in the two major parties has been described in terms of a distinction between faction and tendencies – Labour's back-bench groups being sufficiently tangible to warrant the use of the term 'faction' while the Conservative Party's overlapping and inchoate divisions have had to be analysed in terms of 'tendencies'.[7] Yet although it is true that such divisions as exist within the Conservative Party are less clear-cut than those which mark Labour politics, the cohesion of the Conservative Party should not be exaggerated. Some clear divisions of opinion do exist within the Party, and there has been evidence since 1970 that Conservatives are becoming much more willing than hitherto to express their dissent from the official party line by defying the advice of the whips and voting against the leadership in the lobbies.[8]

Political attitudes within the Conservative Party are difficult to place on a simple right–left spectrum. It is necessary instead to consider opinion within the Conservative Party in terms of at least two divisions. The first division, which reflects a long-standing polarization in the Party, is that between the traditionalists and the progressives. On such issues as social and penal reform, as earlier on colonial matters, the Party is thus divided into those who see Conservatism as a means of defending the existing social order and those who regard it as a method of promoting gradual and non-dogmatic change. The second distinction cuts across this one; for it reflects the increasing significance of economic policy in recent British political debate. At one end of the spectrum of economic policy stand the monetarists, who have, they believe, a coherent explanation of how inflation has occurred and a comprehensive theory of what the state's role in the economy ought to be. At the other end of the spectrum are what might be called the 'pragmatists', who do not feel convinced of the truth of any single economic doctrine and who assert the need for various forms of state intervention in industry and the economy as circumstances demand.

In the 1950s and early 1960s such issues as de-colonization and penal policy were the touchstones for assessing the strength of the divisions within the Conservative Party; in the 1970s it is the second division over economic policy which has become more significant, and the general balance within the Conservative Party has probably moved in the monetarist direction, although it is doubtful how many MPs really understand the intricacies of Milton Friedman's doctrines.

The Conservative Party, although traditionally suspicious of organized groups within its ranks, does contain some pressure groups which can claim adherents at the parliamentary level. The Bow Group, for example, which was founded in 1951, used to be seen as an organization on the far left of the Party because of its attitude towards de-colonization in Africa and its problem-solving approach to social policy. Now, it has developed a strong monetarist element, and its diffuse research activities mean that it rarely seeks to exert any pressure as a group or to speak with a single voice. The fact that it has some sixty-five Conservative MPs among its membership – including twenty-eight ministers – does not therefore mean a great deal in terms of the Bow Group's influence.[9] The Monday Club was founded in 1961 to combat the influence of liberals and progressives in the Conservative Party, especially on foreign policy and colonial questions. However, it is now almost as divided as the Bow Group on economic policy: it combines a dislike of high taxation and government intervention in the economy with an authoritarian and paternalistic conception of the role of the state. The replacement of issues connected with de-colonization by such questions as coloured immigration on the agenda of the right wing of the Party in the constituencies, where the Monday Club has been strongest, made membership of the Club something of an embarrassment for Conservative MPs, and by the late 1970s its parliamentary adherents were few in number. Two other organizations deserve mention as examples of the style of Conservative pressure groups. One is the Selsdon Group founded in order to promote free-market doctrines enshrined in the Conservatives' 1970 election manifesto and rapidly jettisoned in the light of the experience of office; the second is the Tory Reform Group which aims to promote the progressive strand of Conservatism that used to be associated with the Bow Group. It is doubtful whether either of these groups has a great deal of influence although their research activities are sometimes significant. In the case of the Tory Reform Group it is possible that its existence provided a focus for those whose intellectual sympathies were not with Mrs Thatcher and who saw the hostility between the former leader, Edward Heath, and Mrs Thatcher in policy as well as personal terms.[10]

These divisions of opinion have not normally produced regular defiance of the party whips. Although there have been spectacular examples of intra-party dissent in the past – for example over the Government of India Act 1935 which extended self-government for India against the wishes of a large section of the Conservative Party including Winston Churchill – the norm in the Conservative Party is internal cohesion. Indeed, it was the Conservative Party which in many ways was responsible for the extension of party discipline in the House of Commons at the end of the nineteenth century. The degree of cohesion in both major parties can be gauged from the figures of cross-voting.[11] Between 1945 and 1970 cross-voting – defined as an occasion when a member of one party defies the whips' instructions and votes in the opposite lobby – occurred in no more than 12% of all divisions. However, between 1970 and 1974 – a single Parliament – there was some cross-voting in at least 20% of the divisions. This increase was especially marked in the Conservative Party, and the increase challenged many of the orthodox assumptions about the Party's ideological cohesion.[12] For there was evidence not merely of a greater degree of dissent within the Party, measured by the willingness of Conservative MPs to take their disagreement with the leadership to the level of voting against the party line; there was also evidence of a much greater degree of congruence between dissidents on different issues. In other words, dissent within the Conservative Party seemed to have been hardening and, although Tory dissenters took no steps to build a formal organization on the basis of their emerging common intellectual and emotional outlook, the development was a significant one. It revealed at the very least the existence of a group of MPs whose shared opinions could provide the basis within the Conservative Party for a factional grouping akin to those with which the Labour leadership has to contend.

Back-bench opinion in the Conservative Party is formally organized through a body known as the 1922 Committee.[13] This is the channel of communication between back-benchers and the leadership and, although it does not use formal votes and resolutions as the Labour Party's committees do, the character of its discussions conveys to the leader the impact which his policies are having in the parliamentary Party. The 1922 Committee meets weekly, and when the Conservatives are in opposition the leader and the front-bench spokesmen attend the meetings. If the Conservative Party is in power, however, the members of the administration do not attend and the Committee becomes the forum solely of back-bench opinion. The 1922 Committee's influence is veiled and discreet but nevertheless extensive. It can be assessed from the experience of the leadership crisis of 1974–5 when it was this Committee which initiated the change in the rules for election to the leadership to enable an incumbent leader's position to be challenged.[14] And of course the Committee's name commemorates what was probably the most important exercise of back-bench power in twentieth-century peacetime history – the decision by Conservative MPS not to support the continuation of a coalition under Lloyd George.

In addition to the 1922 Committee there are a range of subject committees for the various policy areas of the Party. Their operations also provide a mechanism for the expression of back-bench opinion; although there is no formal role for them in the policy-making process, there is usually a good deal of interaction between the specialized study groups which a leader may establish in opposition and these committees, which obviously serve also to inform MPS on the details of a subject area. Mrs Thatcher's general desire to keep her back-benchers in touch with the progress of her policy ideas has led to some institutionalization of these contacts between back-bench committees and the special study groups. It was interesting, however, that in 1979 the left of the Party – the wing thought to be out of sympathy with some of Mrs Thatcher's policies – made a clean sweep of the elections to back-bench committee chairmanships.

The third element in the Conservative Party organization is the National Union of Conservative and Unionist Associations. Each parliamentary constituency will have a constituency Conservative association, and these associations, when grouped together, comprise the National Union of Conservative and Unionist Associations of England and Wales. (The Scottish Party is a distinct organization and the Ulster Unionists, although linked to the Conservatives until 1974, are separate yet again.) The National Union was founded in 1867 as part of the drive to mobilize Conservative sympathizers in the country at large – especially in the boroughs – behind the Party leadership in the wake of electoral reform. The primary feature of the constituency associations is their freedom from central control and their self-sufficiency. They largely raise their own funds through a variety of social activities based on the subordinate units of each association, the branches. (The branches are organized on the smallest electoral division – the ward – and it is through these smaller units that much of the routine political work of the constituency association is effected.) The constituency associations also employ their own agents and select their own candidates for local, parliamentary and – in conjunction with other constituency associations combined for the purpose – European Assembly elections.

This relative degree of independence and autonomy is accompanied by subservience to the parliamentary leadership in respect of policy making. The National Union does hold an annual conference to which all constituencies are entitled to send representatives, but its debates on policy are frequently anodyne and its resolutions are advisory, not binding on the leadership. The Conservative Party's tradition with respect to the relationship between the Party's parliamentary leadership and the voluntary wing of the Party has thus been to emphasize the autonomy of the former and the supportive but subordinate role of the latter. Recently some commentators have noticed a certain change in style in the relationship, and certainly the annual conferences have become more obviously political occasions as opposed to semi-ritualistic and social ones. The change has been indicated by the increased frequency of votes, especially on issues such as immigration control which arouse the sentiments of some constituency representatives, the greater willingness of speakers to disagree with the platform, and additional fringe-group activity. Yet if the atmosphere at Conservative conferences has become more controversial, of late the role of conference in the Party is quite distinct from that of the Labour Party: in Labour's constitutional theory, conference is the sovereign policy-making body of the Party, but for Conservatives the major functions conferences fulfil relate to propaganda, publicity and the general integration of the various groups within the Party into a corporate whole.

The leadership has from time to time attempted, via Conservative Central Office, to exert control over the constituency associations. The question of candidate selection has been a particularly delicate issue, since the parliamentary leadership would like to be able both to influence the kind of person selected to represent the Party at an election and, on occasions, to place certain individuals in safe seats. The power to influence the quality of candidates is to some extent possible because every candidate must, before he can be officially adopted, be endorsed centrally. Theoretically, this means that constituency parties must select their candidates from a list maintained by the Standing Advisory Committee on Candidates and the Vice-Chairman of Party Organization, although it is always possible for a constituency to consider the name of an individual prior to his inclusion in the central list.[15] The point of the central list is to exercise some influence over the individuals who will carry the party banner at a parliamentary election, since 'whether he wins or loses, the candidate's bearing and behaviour will affect the reputation of the Conservative Party in the constituency' and could affect the result in a marginal seat.[16] However, in practice such sanctions as are available centrally are not very great: the list is large, and local associations have proved so determined to maintain their freedom of action concerning candidate selection that such attempts as Edward Heath's efforts to ensure a greater social mix by tightening the vetting procedure have been unsuccessful. (Indeed the Heath initiative caused such criticism within the Party that Margaret Thatcher suspended the review of the central list as soon as she became leader, and any names which had been dropped were replaced.)[17]

The central organization has on occasions attempted to erode the autonomy of constituency parties with respect to the employment of agents. From the central-party perspective it is inefficient to have so little control over the deployment of agents, for these individuals are in many ways the key to sound electoral organization, and it would be beneficial for the Party as a whole if the best agents could be sent where they were most needed at a general election – that is, to the marginal seats on which the overall result will depend. From the constituency point of view, however, local employment of an agent is important, both because the funding is raised locally and because the agent could become – in circumstances of dispute between a constituency and its MP or between a local MP and the leadership – an instrument through which central pressure could be applied. Indeed, agents were used to communicate the leader's displeasure with MPs who rebelled over the Common Market issue during the 1970–4 Parliament, and some dissident MPs greatly resented these intrusions via the agent into their relations with their constituency parties. The agent is inevitably in a delicate position in any dispute between local MP and local constituency or between the local MP and the leadership; constituency parties have not unnaturally preferred to make it quite clear what they view as an agent's primary loyalty by employing him themselves. Thus, although attempts were made to start a central agency scheme whereby a certain number of agents would be employed by the Party at the national level, the idea was both unpopular in the constituencies and costly. It was therefore abandoned.

The Labour Party

The internal relationships of the Labour Party are very different in character from those of the Conservative Party. The fact that the Labour Party originated outside Parliament and that at times in its history its parliamentary representation has been very small has meant that the Parliamentary Labour Party, PLP, has never enjoyed that autonomy in policy making which Tory MPs have been accorded. The greater attention which the Labour Party has given to the values of participation and internal democracy has also contributed to the style of Labour politics. Together with the fact that ideology and doctrine have frequently divided the Party, these features of the British Labour Party make the tasks of party management more complicated than in the Conservative Party, and present different problems for the Party leadership.

The leader of the Parliamentary Labour Party has been elected since the Party first formed a distinct group at Westminster following the 1906 general election. There was initially some ambiguity over whether the leader or chairman of the PLP was also the leader of the Labour Party as a whole, but gradually the superior position of the PLP leader was recognized. Thus, although this has recently been the subject of some controversy, election to the Party leadership is by the vote of Labour MPs alone.

The members of the PLP also elect the committee of twelve (the parliamentary committee) who aid the leader in carrying out the Party's parliamentary duties when the Party is in opposition.[18] These twelve members thus form the core of a Labour Shadow Cabinet and, although the Labour leader may deploy them as he thinks fit and may add to their number, the fact that careers within the parliamentary Party can be built up on the basis of popularity and esteem in the PLP as a whole is a significant difference from the situation in the Conservative Party. Initially at least, it is sufficient in the Conservative Party for an aspiring front-bencher to gain the support of the leader, and any front-bencher who loses that support will be in danger of losing his position; in the Labour Party a Labour leader may have to keep as a front-bench spokesman someone in whom he has lost confidence.

The fact that Labour elected its front-bench spokesmen could have suggested the use of a similar arrangement when Labour first took office in 1924. However, Ramsay MacDonald had no hesitation in following the normal constitutional convention and appointing his own Cabinet without further reference to the PLP. Indeed one of the peculiarities of Labour Party history has been the alternation between periods of opposition, in which the norms of intra-party democracy have bound the leadership to a greater or lesser extent, and periods of office, in which the leadership has appealed to the conventions of the constitution against the practices and expectations of the Labour Party.

The composition of the Parliamentary Labour Party is of special interest because one of the explicit purposes for founding the new Party was to secure the representation of the working classes in Parliament. In the opinion of the Labour founding fathers the defence of labour interests would be best carried out by sending into Parliament individuals with experience of manual occupations. However, the Labour Party in Parliament has become an overwhelmingly middle-class party, and the working-class element in its ranks has been steadily depleted as the century has worn on. The trend to replace MPs from working-class occupations who have very little formal education with university lecturers, school teachers, broadcasters and journalists can easily be followed.[19] It should be noted that the mix of occupations in the Labour Party is of course different from that in the Conservative Party in that the traditional professions and business are much less evident in the PLP than in the Conservative Party. However, it can hardly be said that the Labour Party at the parliamentary level remains in any sense reflective of the Party's electoral base.

Labour's complicated constitution reflects the federal nature of the Labour alliance. In order to understand the Party's internal politics it is necessary to appreciate that the varied interests in the Labour coalition are subject to very different pressures.

In theory the ultimate and sovereign policy-making organ in the Labour Party is the Labour Party Conference. Conference has the dual function of debating and framing Labour policy as well as electing the Party officers who, as members of the National Executive Committee, are to be responsible to Conference for the routine administration of the Party's affairs between Conferences. (It is normal for Conference to meet annually, although it may not meet if there is an election in the offing; additional Conferences may be called if – as occurred in relation to the issue of British entry into the EEC – the Party wants to devote time to a particular issue.) The different elements in the Party – the trade unions, Constituency Labour Parties (CLPs) and socialist societies – may send resolutions to Conference, and if passed by a two-thirds majority they become official Party policy.

Because the resolutions sent to Conference are too numerous for the time available for debate, resolutions on similar subjects are grouped together in an obscure process known as compositing.[20] This process is performed on the eve of the Conference, although all the original resolutions are printed in full for delegates to read. The mere fact that a resolution has been passed by Conference with the requisite majority does not mean that it will be implemented by the parliamentary leadership. Conference endorsement can make a proposal official Party policy. The Labour Party's election manifesto is, however, drafted by the National Executive Committee in conjunction with the Labour Cabinet or Shadow Cabinet and the parliamentary leader recognized was as having a veto over until 1979 items he disliked. Equally, of course, an item which does succeed both in being adopted as official Labour policy at Conference and in being included in the Party manifesto will not automatically be enacted as soon as Labour is returned to power. The legislative timetable is solely dependent on the discretion of a Labour Cabinet, and the Party as a whole can exercise no control over it. The fact that official Party policy is not the preserve of the parliamentary wing does create conflicts within the Party, because the leadership will generally be concerned with the electoral popularity or practical wisdom of a programme, while Conference delegates – in whose hands responsibility for Conference decisions resides – may be motivated by different considerations. They may for example be more impressed by the ideological justification for a proposal, or they may be responding to pressures at the grass roots of their own union or CLP. The adoption of extreme or impractical programmes by Conference clearly offers Labour's electoral opponents ammunition with which to attempt to frighten the electorate and so, even if Labour leaders know they need never implement the proposals, there is always an incentive to try to influence Conference policy decisions.

The Conference is composed of the representatives of the different sections of the Party: trade unions, CLPs and the small socialist societies. In addition to the attendance of delegates to Conference some provision is made for *ex officio* attendance, which does not carry voting rights. Labour MPs and adopted candidates who are not present as delegates attend in this capacity, as do members of the Party's National Executive Committee.

The trade-union movement is the dominant force at Labour Party Conferences in terms of electoral strength. The number of votes cast by delegates reflects the affiliation fees which they pay to the central Party organization. What this means in the trade-union movement is that each individual trade union can cast at Conference a number of votes equivalent to the number of members the union affiliates to the Labour Party. In trade unions which affiliate to the Labour Party each trade unionist pays a political levy which is a sum added to trade-union dues for the union to spend as it likes on explicitly political purposes. (Historically, the levy has been controversial because Conservative governments have in the past sought to make it effectively optional by legislating to require trade members to opt *into* the scheme; Labour governments, on the other hand, have put the onus on the individual to opt *out* of the levy if he prefers not to pay it. Needless to say inertia means that the trade unions have a much larger sum of money available to them when members have to opt out than would be the case if opting in were the rule.) The trade unions do not need to affiliate on the basis of their total membership, and trade-union membership is in most cases larger than the number of affiliated members reported to the Labour Party. However, the important point is that by counting as a member of the Labour Party every trade unionist who pays the levy, the paper membership of the Party is made very much higher than that of any other British political party, although of course this means very little in terms of active participation in the affairs of the Labour Party. And it is the distribution of membership between the trade unions and the individual CLPs which gives the trade unions their enormous influence over Conference and its decisions.

In 1977 the trade unions had a membership of 5,913,159 as compared with a total individual membership of 659,737 in the constituency parties.[21] Together with the 43,375 members of the socialist and cooperative societies this gave the Labour Party in 1977 a total membership of 6,616,271. Because votes are allocated on the basis of one vote per thousand members or part thereof, and because the votes have to be cast as a block – in other words there is no question of a union with a large number of votes dividing them in proportion to the opinions of its delegates or its members – the decisions of one or two big unions can be vital in any policy dispute at Conference. There have been some changes in the voting weight of the largest unions at Conference over the past fifteen years, but the two unions with the largest votes are still the Transport and General Workers with over a million members and the Engineering Workers with over 915,000 members.[22] In 1970 the six largest unions represented at Conference cast 3,518,000 votes out of a total membership of 6,222,580, so that it is not simply that the unions as a group can dominate Conference; a very few large unions can determine the outcome of policy debates in most cases.[23]

The trade unions do not only dominate the policy-making aspects of the Conference; they also have a significant impact on the composition of the National Executive Committee. The extent of the trade unions' influence in elections is a product both of their superior numbers and of the peculiar constitution of the Labour Party. The NEC is constructed to reflect the different sections of the Labour Party, and for some sections election to the NEC is confined to the particular element in the Party which has to be represented. For some posts, however, the election is by the Conference as a whole and this inevitably has the effect of placing the election in the hands of the trade-union membership.

The National Executive Committee currently has twenty-nine members. As might be expected given the unions' importance within the Party, the trade unions are the largest single group represented on the NEC, with twelve out of the twenty-nine seats. Positions on the NEC are usually used to satisfy trade-union officials in the second rank of the union hierarchy, as most professional trade-union organizers will see a seat on the TUC General Council as the summit of their ambitions. Labour Party Standing Orders prevent the holding of office on the NEC and the TUC at the same time, so that one frequently finds a union putting its General Secretary on the TUC and some less important officer on the NEC.

The Constituency Labour Parties elect seven members in their section, and these are chosen by delegates representing the CLPs alone. (Until 1937 the representatives in this category were chosen by Conference as a whole, but the anomaly of having trade unions dominating the CLPs even in this respect was too marked, and the constitution was amended to provide for separate voting.) The smaller affiliated societies can elect one member to the NEC in their section, and this seat is virtually within the gift of the largest of them, the Royal Arsenal Co-operative Society. A final division is that of women members, who have five seats on the NEC, although these are elected by vote of the Conference as a whole and thus by a process in which union strength is decisive. In addition to these twenty-three seats, the Labour Party Young Socialists are entitled to one seat on the NEC, and the Leader and Deputy Leader of the PLP sit *ex officio*. There is also the Party Treasurer who is elected by the whole Conference, and whose position is regarded as a 'virtual trade-union appointment'. Thus the trade unions – though they do not necessarily act in concert – could decide the result of the elections to eighteen of the twenty-nine seats on the NEC.

Initially the influence of the trade unions was seen, for good or ill, as a moderating force within the movement, since until the 1960s trade unions appeared to have limited political objectives and to be content to follow the policies of the parliamentary leadership. In addition they displayed a marked suspicion of the more ideological style of politics which often marked the CLPs. The explicit opposition by the union leaders of the

1945–55 period to left-wing sentiment, and the strategic use of their block votes to support the platform and the leadership whenever it was challenged at Conference, did indeed earn the unions a lot of criticism. The left-wing CLPs greatly resented the fact that a group of union leaders – such as Deakin of the Transport and General Workers' Union and Carron of the Engineering Union – could prevent the operation of internal democracy within the Party. However, the pattern of politics in the 1950s – in which moderate union leaders could be counted on for numerical muscle in any crisis within the Party – has been succeeded by one in which a different and more complex pattern of Labour politics has emerged. It would be simple and accurate to typify the change as a shift by the unions from a right-wing to a left-wing policy stance within the Party; but such a description would conceal the heterogeneity of the trade unions and the complexity of their internal developments over the past fifteen years.

Several factors have contributed towards the change in the role of the unions within the Labour Party. The most visible change has been the replacement of a number of key union leaders whose politics were of the centre by a number of left-wing figures. Certainly it is no longer safe for any party leader to assume that personal loyalty will prompt any of the men who control the largest unions to deliver their votes in support of the leadership. The trend towards the left among union leaders may perhaps be dated from 1956 when Frank Cousins became General Secretary of the Transport and General Workers' Union following the retirement of the right-wing Arthur Deakin and the premature death of the latter's successor, Jock Tiffin. Because it was the largest union this change in the character of the TGWU's political leadership was bound to be significant, and the tradition of left-of-centre leadership was maintained by Jack Jones, who became General Secretary in 1969, and by Moss Evans, who took over in 1978. During the late 1960s other unions acquired a left-of-centre leadership: Hugh Scanlon was elected President of the traditionally left-wing Amalgamated Union of Engineering Workers in 1967, with Communist support, and Alan Fisher became General Secretary of the militant National Union of Public Employees. The latter union was to a large extent responsible for the industrial unrest in the United

Kingdom in the winter of 1978–9, unrest which damaged the electoral prospects of the Labour Government and was a direct challenge to its policy of wage restraint.

Changes in the character of union leadership in recent years should not be seen as the only factor affecting the role of the trade unions inside the Labour Party. Of more direct importance has been the change in the agenda of British politics, and the fact that for much of the period since 1964 it has been a Labour Government with which the trade unions have had to deal. The ambiguity of the trade unions' position within the Labour Party is to some extent concealed while the Party is in opposition; but when Labour is in power there are inevitable conflicts of loyalty when the priorities of the Labour Government appear to be different from those of the trade-union movement. The fact that incomes policies played such a large part in the Labour Government's economic strategies after 1964 was the primary cause of tension within the Labour Party. The unions were forced to work out their own defensive positions and policies, and sometimes the passions engendered by the resultant arguments have prevented general cooperation with the leadership on other issues, or at least made it unsafe for the leadership to count on union support in a crisis. The decline of voluntarism in industrial relations policy, too, and the 1966–70 Labour Government's flirtation with the idea of legal regulation – as well as the 1970–4 Conservative Government's actual implementation of industrial relations legislation – meant that another issue touching the fundamental interests of trade unionists was at the heart of British political debate. In the 1950s the Labour Party's most bitter divisions were over foreign-policy issues rather than over domestic policy and this fact meant that on the whole the leadership could assume the unions would not have an independent line of their own to pursue in any confrontation between left and right. By the late 1960s, however, the touchstone of the Party's ideological divisions was the whole range of economic policies, and here the unions were bound to be active participants in any debate. Indeed one of the first responses of the TUC to Mrs Thatcher's election victory in 1979 and her subsequent budget was to outline an alternative economic strategy which it was felt would be able to command trade-union support.

The final aspect of the changing relationship between the Labour Party and the trade unions is related to this change in the Party's agenda. The trade unions were of course induced to cooperate with the Labour Governments of the 1964–79 period on the issue of incomes control; but in return they claimed a greater voice in determining a wide range of social policies. The experience of opposition to the Conservative Industrial Relations Act of 1971 generated new machinery for consultation between the unions and the Labour Party. This was the so-called TUC–Labour Party Liaison Committee, and after 1971 much of the trade-union influence in the Labour Party's policy-making processes was exerted through this Committee. The initial development of a united front against the Industrial Relations Act of 1971 was broadened into a more comprehensive agreement on economic and social policy in the general election of February 1974. This commitment – the so-called 'social contract' – was unusual in that its implications for Labour policy were worked out in the Liaison Committee rather than in the formal policy-making apparatus of the Party – the NEC and its subcommittees. The Committee continued to meet regularly and the NEC's 1978 Report to Conference recorded joint discussions between the TUC and the Labour Party on such matters as priorities in the use of North Sea oil revenue, the wealth tax proposal, child benefits, the common agricultural policy of the EEC, overseas investment, trade and investment with South Africa, and manpower and employment policies. A new agreed joint statement of policies – *Into the Eighties* – was presented to the 1978 Conference in addition to this detailed investigation of specialized policy areas.[24]

It should be noted that the Liaison Committee brings together representatives of the TUC, the NEC and the PLP. In other words the Committee offers a forum for influence on Party policy for the trade-union movement as a whole and not just for the influence of those unions which are affiliated to the Labour Party. (The number of unions affiliated to the Labour Party is only a small proportion of the total number of trade unions, but the affiliated unions are the largest in terms of membership; however, the rapidly expanding white-collar unions include some which are politically neutral.) The existence of the Liaison Committee means that in addition to the influence which the trade unions can exercise within Conference as a component part of the Labour organization, the trade-union movement as a whole has another point of access into Labour policy, and one where the whole range of the trade-union movement's interests can be promoted. Together with the fact that the subject matter of political debate more directly concerns the major unions than in the 1950s, it seems likely that this further institutionalization of trade-union influence will increase the weight of trade unions in the Party, at least on those issues where a common trade-union perspective exists. On a number of topics, however, the unions are themselves divided; and the likelihood of this potential influence on Party policy's being consistently mobilized is not perhaps very great.

The fact that the Labour Party has a greater concern with ideological questions than the Conservative Party, and the fact that it is not socially homogeneous, have both contributed to the proliferation of factions within it. While the issues which have occasioned such factional groupings within the Party have varied with the passage of time, there has usually existed at least one group which has organized itself to push Labour policy to the left. Sometimes its activity has provoked a reaction by right-of-centre Labour members as controversy stimulated the formation of the Manifesto Group in the 1974–9 Parliament; but increasingly in recent years one has had the feeling that it is the left wing of the Party which is setting the issues for debate within the Party. The left-wing groups thus take on the role of the Party's intellectual driving force and conscience; the counter-organizations frequently find themselves having to fight a rearguard action to keep the Party on moderate lines in order to maximize its appeal for the electorate.

The post-1945 period has seen a number of identifiable left-wing factions emerge in the Labour Party. The Keep Left Group of 1946 elaborated distinct positions on a number of foreign-policy and domestic issues and those positions were for much of the 1950s associated with the personal supporters of Aneurin Bevan. The revisionist debates within the Labour Party in the period 1955–63 – in which Gaitskell tried to persuade the Party to amend many of its fundamental tenets and modernize its version of socialism – in order to enhance

Labour's electoral appeal, stimulated the leader's supporters to found their own organization to promote Gaitskell's policies. That faction – the Campaign for Democratic Socialism – was able to mobilize a number of the Party's leading intellectuals such as Anthony Crosland, and Party members outside and inside the parliamentary Party who were sympathetic to the cause of moderate socialism. In that sense the CDS is an unusual example of an aggressive faction on the right of the Party which was able to seize the initiative from the left-of-centre critics of Gaitskell.

In the period since Harold Wilson became leader of the Labour Party groups on the left of the Labour Party have been significant. The first was the Tribune Group which was founded in 1964, and which was able to claim a membership of sixty-seven in 1967 among Labour MPs, although it may be that membership of the Tribune Group was by 1979 no longer the sign of militant left-wing socialism that it once was and that the Group had become an orthodox and anodyne organization within the Party. The second faction which should be mentioned is the Campaign for Labour Party Democracy, which was founded in 1973 with the explicit objective of transferring power from the Parliamentary Labour Party to the Party as a whole – a movement which would inevitably mean greater influence for Conference in the policy-making processes of the Party and greater control by constituency activists over their MPs. Together these changes would produce a leftward shift in Labour politics, although it is not entirely clear that all trade unions would be in favour of such radical structural changes in the Party.

Because the goal of the Campaign for Labour Party Democracy involved a reduction in the autonomy of Labour MPs, it is perhaps not surprising that the group has found more enthusiastic support in the extra-parliamentary organs of the Party than in the PLP. At the end of 1978, the CLPD had as its President the left-wing MP Joan Maynard, and its Vice-Presidents included Alan Sapper of the Union of Cinematograph, Television and Allied Technicians who was also a member of the General Council of the TUC.

The Campaign for Labour Party Democracy tried to implement its philosophy by the promotion of two practical movements within the Labour Party. The first cause to absorb its energies was the attempt to change the procedure governing the selection of parliamentary candidates. The CPLD wanted constituencies to be able, if they found themselves with MPs whose views did not coincide with those of constituency members, to displace sitting MPs and replace them with people whose views were more in accord with those of the activists. The second crusade which the CLPD conducted was an attempt to change the rules governing election to the party leadership. Instead of election of the leader by all Labour MPs, it was suggested by the CLPD and others that election should be either by Conference as a whole or, preferably, by a specially constructed electoral college which would not be dominated, as Conference is, by the trade unions with their block votes. Such a move would obviously increase the chances of a left-of-centre candidate's winning the ballot, since the PLP is still inclined towards the centre-right of the political spectrum, as well as being mindful of electoral consequences of any decision it takes, while constituency delegates might be expected to prefer a candidate whose views were nearer theirs than the electorate's.

The Campaign for Labour Party Democracy launched its operations at a particularly embarrassing time for the PLP. Although many Labour supporters would admit the argument for extending the participation of the Labour rank and file in key political decisions, many others were also aware of the ease with which the extra-parliamentary Party can be infiltrated by far-left factions whose aim is to colonize the Party for their own purposes – purposes which it is suspected are basically undemocratic. The process of infiltration by the far left (Communists, Trotskyists and others) has long troubled the Labour Party, and from 1930 it kept a list of proscribed organizations, membership of which was incompatible with belonging to the Labour Party. The practice was abolished in 1973, but in the period 1975–6 the Labour Party again became concerned that the frequently moribund Constituency Labour Parties were being taken over by well-organized groups who did not fully subscribe to the traditions of the Labour Party. An investigation of such allegations was eventually ordered by the National Executive Committee in January 1977 and, although the authors of its report on 'entrism' – the process of infiltration of the Party – were anxious to play down the extent of the phenomenon, they did call for renewed membership and political-education campaigns to alert the solid Labour Party supporters to the dangers of the so-called Militant Tendency in the Party.[25] The implications of according the constituency parties greater control over their MPs had been discussed in the early 1970s when a number of celebrated disputes between MPs and their local parties occurred. In a number of cases, the readoption of a sitting MP was refused for non-ideological or policy reasons; and in some cases the dislodged MP's only defence was to accuse his attackers of an ideologically inspired conspiracy. In other cases, however, the motive was simply that the constituency party felt itself unable to continue supporting MPs such as Dick Taverne and Reg Prentice when the MPs' views on divisive issues, for example British entry into Europe, differed so markedly from their own. Taverne's dispute with his constituency party was unusual in that he took the step of resigning the seat once denied re-nomination and fighting the ensuing by-election as an Independent Labour candidate. Although he won the seat both at the by-election and at the general election of February 1974, an official Labour candidate was returned in October 1974. A number of sympathizers with Taverne inside and outside the Labour ranks had taken his by-election victory as a signal to form a new social democratic party, but the idea was crushed when the fledgeling party's few other candidates were heavily defeated at the general election of February 1974.

The cases of Reg Prentice in Newham, and to a lesser extent, of Frank Tomney in Hammersmith and of Neville Sandelson in Hayes and Harlington, confirmed the determination of many constituency parties to regard their MPs as delegates rather than trustees. The Newham case was unusual not merely because Prentice was at the time a member of a Labour Cabinet but also because the constituency became the subject of litigation as warring factions tried to test in the courts the credentials of delegates to the constituency party's annual general meeting. In the aftermath of these cases, the NEC decided to review the rules of local constituency parties to ensure that members who belonged to a constituency party by virtue of membership of an affiliated organization – usually a trade union – were also resident in the constituency, and to iron out ambiguities surrounding the appeals procedure.

The broader question of the automatic re-selection of MPs came before the Labour Conference in 1978, and a compromise NEC motion was narrowly passed as an alternative to the rank-and-file demand, spearheaded by the CLPD, that a fresh selection procedure should automatically be held during each Parliament. Instead, a sitting MP must now go through a re-selection procedure only if he first loses in a vote of no confidence moved against him in the constituency. The fact that this compromise proposal was widely regarded as a retreat from an NEC pledge on the question, in part explained Ian Mikardo's failure to be re-elected to the NEC; and the suggestion that Hugh Scanlon cast his union's votes behind the NEC proposal in error meant that the issue was not regarded as closed; in 1979 the CLPD proposal was passed.

The question of broadening the electoral college for the party leader arouses as much passion as the ability of selection committees to oust a sitting MP. It has already been seen that by comparison with his Conservative opposite number, a Labour leader is more constrained by the need to balance various elements of the Party in his Cabinet and by the fact that in opposition his senior colleagues are elected by the PLP as a whole. A Labour leader's success thus rests on the agility with which he can unite very different opinions and personalities in a collective body which is electorally credible. The basis of the leader's position would, however, be transformed if it were to rest not on the support of the PLP but on an electoral college reflecting the values of constituency activists and the trade unions. For then a leader elected on a left-wing platform by votes of the extra-parliamentary elements of the Party could easily prove unable to command the support of his parliamentary colleagues, and the Labour Party might find itself, *mutatis mutandis*, in the same difficulty as back-bench Tories in 1963, when their new leader, the Earl of Home (who disclaimed his peerage and became Sir Alec Douglas Home), was chosen by an inner circle of Conservative leaders without reference to the Tory back-benchers.

A working party of the NEC which had been examining the suggestion of broadening the electorate in leadership contests reported to Conference in 1978. The suggestion that Conference itself should elect the leader of the Party attracted hardly any support, largely because the unions themselves do not appear to want such a responsibility. The alternative proposal – for a specially constructed electoral college – was defeated, and again in 1979 by 4,010,000 to 3,076,000. Although the Campaign for Labour Party Democracy's two causes thus appeared not to have advanced very far by 1978, it would have been a mistake to see the set-back as necessarily permanent, and certainly the issues which the CLPD has raised seem likely to remain live ones on the agenda of Labour Party politics.

It can thus be seen that divisions within the Labour Party can occasion a variety of alliances involving the PLP, the trade-union movement and the constituency parties in different combinations at different times. The tension between Labour's theoretical commitment to internal democracy and the practical problems of party management is a tension which Labour leaders have to accommodate but which perhaps has implications not just for the Labour Party but for the political system as a whole.

The loss of the 1979 general election occasioned new divisions in the Party. Both the left-wing (Tribune Group) faction and the right-of-centre Manifesto Group put up slates of candidates for election to the Shadow Cabinet, and although the right swept the board the situation was peculiar for two reasons. First, two leading left-wingers, Tony Benn and Eric Heffer, declined to serve in the Shadow Cabinet in order to be able to pursue an independent strategy. This was taken to mean not merely a redefinition of socialist policies but also the advocacy of fundamental constitutional reform in the Party, including a proposition even more radical than those advanced in 1978, namely that members of a Labour Cabinet should be elected by the PLP as a whole, and not simply selected by the Prime Minister. Secondly, the fact that it was the first time that formal slates had been constructed by party factions and the fact that both sides were looking to a future leadership contest gave the exercise of portfolio distribution as well as PLP voting a significance which in normal years it would not perhaps have had. Yet whereas the post-1970 Parliament saw Labour's policy-making processes falling into the hands of the left, the 1979 Parliament seemed very different. The right had experienced and accommodated the tactics of the left and held a secure majority in the PLP, if not in the Party as a whole; and the PLP left for its part seemed somewhat divided as to tactics, especially given the emphasis of the former Prime Minister Mr Callaghan on the importance of acknowledging the electoral victory of the Tories. Thus while the balance of power in the Labour Party as a whole in 1979 was very favourable to the left, it was not clear what the policy or personality consequences of this would be, nor how able the left would be to mobilize the advantage it clearly held by the 1979 Conference.

The Liberal Party

The relationship between the parliamentary element in the Liberal Party and the extra-parliamentary Party is conditioned by the fact that the Party's parliamentary representation has been so small in recent decades. Profound disagreements about electoral strategy have marked Liberal Party politics as a result of the different approach to policy questions adopted by the Young Liberals and those sections of the Party which espoused 'community politics'. (Community politics theorists urged the Party to concentrate on the local level of politics and to give low priority to Westminster where an 'unfair' electoral system made it unlikely that a third party such as the Liberals could have much impact.) The strength of the extra-parliamentary wing of the Liberal Party by comparison with its tiny band of MPs was reflected in the introduction of new rules for election to the leadership of the Party. These new rules were introduced immediately prior to Jeremy Thorpe's resignation from the leadership in 1976 and they are unique among the British parties in that they make formal provision for rank-and-file participation in the process of electing the leader of the Liberal Party and, indeed, give the extra-parliamentary Party the major voice in that appointment.

Candidates for the Liberal leadership must obviously be MPs. Each constituency association affiliated to the Liberal Party is entitled to exercise ten votes plus a further ten if it was affiliated for the previous year plus one further vote for every five hundred votes, or part thereof, cast for a Liberal candidate in that constituency at the previous general election. (A constituency may opt to count a more recent by-election vote or an aggregate local election vote if that is higher.) By this complicated procedure – which produced David Steel as leader in 1976 – the choice of leader of the parliamentary Party is given to the constituencies and weighted towards the areas of Liberal strength.

The Liberal Party is, strictly speaking, a federation of four distinct and semi-autonomous parties for each of the units of the United Kingdom. Its major institutions are the National Executive Committee, the National Council and the Finance and Administration Board. There is an annual Assembly of the Party which has the function of electing Liberal officers and members of the Council. It also hears progress reports from the various administrative committees of the Party and considers resolutions on public policy. The general style of Liberal politics has become increasingly 'open', and the emphasis on participation by all sections of the Party in policy making has made it difficult to tell how much control the officers of the Party could exercise over the parliamentary leadership. David Steel had to defend his strategy of a coalition with Labour before the Liberal Council and the Liberal Assembly in 1977, and it seems clear that unless a major Liberal revival takes place the balance of power within the Party will continue to move towards the grass roots and away from Westminster.

Party Finance: A Catalyst of Change?

During the 1970s one problem became especially acute for all the party organizations – how to find the money to pay for their various activities. The cash problem was especially serious in the Labour and Liberal Parties, and it led to the establishment of a committee, the Houghton Committee, to examine the basis of party funding in the United Kingdom.[26] That Committee, as will be seen, recommended a major change in the methods of financing party activities and, although its proposals have not been implemented, there would probably have been a move in this direction had Labour secured an overall majority at the 1979 general election. Any alteration in the methods of paying for party politics would of course change the power structure within the parties substantially. Before examining the reasons for the financial difficulties of the parties in the 1970s it is necessary to outline the current sources of party income.

At the national level the Conservative Party's money comes from a number of sources and there will be fluctuations in the amounts raised from year to year. It can, however, be roughly estimated that a third of its income will come from constituency payments, including the 'quotas' levied on the constituency parties on the basis of Conservative voting strength; about two-thirds will come from donations from individuals and business; and a minute proportion will come from investment income. In 1976 the Conservative Party's central income was £1,739,0000, of which £1,137,000 came from donations (65.4%); £574,000 came from the constituencies (33%), and £28,000 came from investment income (1.6%).[27]

A major source of Conservative Party income is thus the money which it derives from individual or corporate donations. The donations which public companies give directly for political purposes have to be declared in the company accounts, so that it is possible to monitor the amounts given by individual companies to the Conservative cause. In 1977 the largest donation was £25,000, but many companies do not give merely to the Conservative Party; they also channel money into other promotional organizations which conduct campaigns thought to be beneficial to the company interest. Thus in 1977 one of the most regular donors – Rank Hovis MacDougall – gave £41,000 in donations to all anti-Labour campaigns but only £20,000 of that went directly into the Conservative Party's coffers.

The Conservative Party estimated that in 1975–6 its net expenditure at the central level was £1,724,000, of which the largest element was spent on headquarters and regional administration. About 71% of expenditure went on salaries and wages and only 12% went on research. The amount spent on publicity clearly varied from year to year, with expenditure on advertising and propaganda reaching a peak in an election year.

By contrast the Labour Party in 1976 estimated that its

annual income was £1,211,000, of which £1,150,000 came from subscriptions – primarily from the affiliation fees paid by trade unions; £51,000 of central income came from donations and appeals and a mere £10,000 from investment income.[28] It can thus be seen that the trade unions provide the major source of the Labour Party's annual income. This, it has been suggested, constitutes another important weapon in the unions' hands if they wish to exert their influence over Labour Party policy. Indeed the financial dependence of the Labour Party upon the trade-union movement is greater even than the annual income figures suggest; for in addition to the affiliation fees – which in 1978 were 24p per affiliated member – the unions, like major companies, are likely to give out of their own political funds additional money in an election year or for special purposes such as the construction of a new Party headquarters. The unions also sponsor candidates for Parliament, in which case they may contribute up to 80% of the maximum legal election expenses of that candidate, may contribute to the constituency party's funds and may contribute between 60% and 65% of the salary of an agent in that constituency. (There were 148 sponsored MPs elected at the election of May 1979.)

Labour expenditure at the central level was similar to the Conservatives' in magnitude – £1,280,000 – but over 90% of it was spent on regional, area and headquarters services. It estimated that some £64,000 would be spent on publicity in 1976 and some £82,000 on research and policy formation.

The income and expenditure of the smaller parties, including the Liberals, is much less than that of the two major parties and is mainly derived from individual subscriptions and small donations. The Liberal Party, according to the Houghton Committee Report, had an income of £96,000 in 1975, while the Communist Party appeared to have an average annual income of £88,000. The Scottish National Party in 1976 had an estimated central income of £61,000 while Plaid Cymru expected to have an income for that year of £85,000.[29]

At the constituency level the situation of all the parties is extremely complex, but the Houghton Committee's survey found that Conservative constituency associations had approximately twice as large a financial turnover as Constituency Labour

Parties, and they in turn had double the financial turnover of constituency Liberal associations. Money at the constituency level was raised by a variety of methods and from a variety of sources – social events, bazaars and lotteries as well as individual membership subscriptions.

The level of party membership in Britain and the general state of party activity are not only extremely low but have been declining steadily over the past decade. A major survey of electoral attitudes in the period 1963–70 confirmed the impression that the only form of political activity engaged in by the majority of British citizens was the simple act of voting at parliamentary elections. The degree of participation in other forms of political work such as canvassing was minimal, as was the level of party membership. The survey also found that, low though the level of political activity was in 1964, it had probably declined still further by 1970. For whereas the portion of the sample who were conscious of belonging to a party had stood at 14% in 1964, it had fallen to 10% by 1970.[30]

The Houghton Committee discovered a similar pattern of decline: only 11% of the 100 constituencies sampled in a specially designed questionnaire thought that their membership figures were satisfactory, while 89% thought that the level of membership was either unsatisfactory or very unsatisfactory.

The Houghton Committee's survey found an average constituency membership in 1974 of 2,400 for each Conservative constituency party, 500 for each Constituency Labour Party and 300 for each constituency Liberal association. If uniform across England, Wales and Scotland, these findings would suggest an individual membership for the three largest national parties as follows:

Conservative Party	1,495,200
Labour Party	311,000
Liberal Party	186,900

The problem of ascertaining the accuracy of party membership figures such as these is exacerbated by the fact that as far as the Conservative Party is concerned no national membership totals are collected. And, although Labour does keep membership figures, it is generally agreed that the official numbers are inflated by the rule which requires a local constituency party to affiliate to the central Party on the basis of a minimum of a thousand members – a figure which most Constituency Labour Parties in practice do not attain. Thus although the annual report of the Labour Party gives numbers for individual and trade-union affiliated members, these figures must be read against the background of a tradition of flexible interpretation of membership. But even if one takes the inflated figures given by the Labour Party itself there is still clear evidence of a decline (see Table 4). Indeed, the Labour Party launched a membership campaign in June 1977 to try to arrest this decline and

Table 4
Individual Membership of the Labour Party, 1928–77

Year	No. of Members
1928	214,970
1935	419,311
1945	487,047
1950	908,161
1955	843,356
1960	790,192
1965	816,765
1970	690,191
1975	674,905
1976	659,058
1977	659,737

Source: *Labour Party Annual Conference Report*, 1978.

commented that 537 out of the total of 623 constituency parties had affiliated at the minimum level of one thousand members, so that only 86 constituency parties could be presumed to have a membership of one thousand and above.[31]

The Liberal Party in its evidence to the Houghton Committee acknowledged that its membership had declined from the 1964–5 peak of 250,000 but pointed out that the number of Liberal organizations in the constituencies had increased since that date even if their membership remained small.

The problems which the three largest of Britain's political parties have faced in maintaining a stable level of party membership over the past few years has made it difficult for them to keep in existence efficient machinery for fighting elections. Thus the most basic task of any political party is becoming difficult to perform as membership levels fluctuate and constituency parties become moribund. Equally, party officials have become concerned that the routine tasks of party organization at the grass roots have to be performed by a dwindling band of people. Political parties perform a number of functions, not the least of which is the selection of a parliamentary candidate who may ultimately become a member of the House of Commons. In addition the political parties have a role to play as channels of communication between the institutions of government and the governed. The efficiency and legitimacy of that role will, however, be determined to a very large extent by the degree to which the party organizations themselves are representative of the wider community. Declining membership suggests that not merely are these organizations becoming smaller and more exclusive but that the major British parties are also in danger of becoming isolated from the mainstream of opinion in the country as a whole.

The loss of vitality in British political parties implied by declining membership was aggravated by the problem of finance. The maintenance of even a rudimentary organization at the constituency level requires both members and money. A loss of membership impedes a party's ability to raise money by undertaking fund-raising activities as well as reducing the amount which can be raised directly from subscriptions. The Houghton Committee thought that party organization at the local level was generally on a 'pitifully inadequate' scale – in terms of accommodation, equipment, trained staff and resources. The Committee also found that a large number of constituency associations could not afford to employ a paid full-time agent, although the Conservative associations were generally better off than the Labour and Liberal Parties in this respect: whereas only one-quarter of Conservative associations were without either a full-time or part-time agent, three-quarters of the Constituency Labour Parties and 90% of the Liberal associations were without the services of an agent on either a full- or part-time basis. The fact that so many constituency associations could not afford the salaries of paid professional agents was obviously serious for the parties, and both the Labour and the Conservative Parties experimented with schemes whereby the salary of the agent could be met in part out of central funds. However, in both parties the scheme has been something of a failure because in the 1970s they both found themselves in financial difficulties at the central level as well as locally. Moreover, as has been mentioned, there was in the Conservative Party a great deal of resistance to the central employment of agents since this was thought to undermine the jealously guarded autonomy of the constituency associations. Thus by 1976 only one-third of all Labour agents – twenty-six out of eighty-six – were being paid from central funds while the Conservative Party was phasing out its central employment scheme.

The reasons why the political parties were in financial difficulties at the national level during the 1970s are not hard to identify. The high level of inflation had eroded the values of their reserves while it had also pushed up the salaries of the staff employed by the parties. The general economic climate meant that individual and corporate donors had less money to spare for political purposes and many public companies became increasingly sensitive about their shareholders' attitudes towards direct gifts to the Conservative Party. The Labour Government's Companies Act of 1967 which forced disclosure in company accounts of donations for political purposes undoubtedly made many boards prefer to make donations to pressure groups such as Aims (formerly Aims of Industry) rather than the Conservative Party. And the trade-union movement, the traditional source of much Labour Party income, was increasingly keeping its money in its own coffers. The financial strains which these developments imposed upon the political parties were exacerbated by the fact that the parties had in 1974 to fight two general elections within a short space of time.

The first steps in the direction of a subsidy from the state to arrest the spiral of decline in British parties was taken when in 1975 the House of Commons authorized a grant to opposition parties to enable them to fulfil their parliamentary functions more effectively; but the idea of a more general subsidy to all political parties to finance the whole range of organizational and propaganda activities constitutes a radical change in thinking about the role which parties play in the political system of Britain.

The Houghton Committee's Report of 1976 thus confirmed a general impression of weakness in British party organization and underlined the extent to which economies had generally been made at the expense of the parties' research and educational activities as well as of their organizational functions. The majority report recommended an injection of public funds as a means of reviving the parties' sagging morale and enabling them to fulfil the tasks required of parties in an advanced democracy. Unfortunately from the point of view of the Labour and Liberal parties who had most to gain from the proposals, there was no unanimous welcome for the Houghton proposals which suggested grants should be made to parties at both the national level (for general purposes) and the local level (for election expenses). The Conservative Party was confident of its ability to survive financially, and took the strong ideological line that the taxpayer should not be burdened with the cost of such a subsidy, although the professional staff of the Conservative Party – the agents – whose salaries seemed most at risk in the harsh economic climate seemed somewhat less sure of the enormity of the suggestion. The nationalist parties were spirited in their criticism of the idea of propping up declining parties no longer able to inspire enthusiasm among the general public. And the Communist Party, while willing to accept a small extension of state aid in kind, such as free postage, rejected the idea of cash grants to the parties. As we have seen, the objections to the proposals prevented their implementation during the life of the 1974–9 Parliament. But the way may have been opened for a fundamental change in the relationship between the state and the political parties, since if public money were to be handed out to the parties there would have to be some degree of public accountability in return.

Greater public control and accountability was indeed one of the features of state aid which some of its advocates found most attractive. Subsidies would provide the lever whereby, it was argued, the insulated party structures could be prised open to allow a greater amount of internal democracy and electoral participation. That this argument should be used was itself revealing of the extent to which the internal processes of the parties – especially the selection and repudiation of candidates and Members of Parliament – had created an image of party activists as extremists remote from the values of the general public. Whether the acceptance of state grants would really do very much to make the political parties more responsive to the electorate at large is questionable, and for some critics the more radical remedy of electoral reform remains the only way of reasserting public control over the party system. But some people felt that state financial aid would serve to remind the parties that they are institutions of vital significance to the functioning of government and that the values they espouse are a proper subject for public scrutiny, and claimed that the cost to the taxpayer would be worthwhile.

8 Public Servants or Ruling Elites? Influence and Bureaucracy in Modern Britain

In any society those who exercise political influence will be less numerous than those who do not. In an advanced industrial society such as the United Kingdom the arenas in which such influence can be wielded will be diverse: the worlds of finance, industry, government, education and religion may all generate their distinctive elites or ruling groups.[1] From the point of view of the student of government, what is important is to determine precisely what opportunities each group has for access to the decision-making process and hence for influencing its outcome. Secondly, it is important to know whether a group has any distinctive social characteristics and how far these features are shared with other groups enjoying influence in the political system. Finally, it is important to ask to what extent a group is cohesive, how much it is characterized by shared social features and homogeneity of attitudes. The latter question is important because its answer will affect the ability of leaders to control their followers; however, it is somewhat difficult to answer with any precision since, as yet, little information is available on which such an answer could be based. Impressions and inferences from objective information about an elite's social composition will normally have to suffice, although it would be a mistake to draw too many hard-and-fast conclusions from simple facts about education, family background and so on.

It is not only because a country's political elites exercise influence on the substantive decisions which public authorities take that they are significant, although clearly that is one reason for studying pressure groups such as the trade unions, the

Confederation of British Industry and the plethora of promotional organizations which the United Kingdom possesses. In addition the characteristics of a country's elites will to a large extent determine the legitimacy of the whole governmental structure. If recruitment to elite positions is based on criteria which are no longer acceptable to society at large or if the persons recruited to them hold values which are out of phase with those of the wider society, then the basis of the whole political order may be undermined. Although many of these questions go far beyond the scope of this chapter, it is important to keep such broader issues in mind as the more concrete aspects of bureaucracy and interest-group activity in modern Britain are discussed.

In assessing the degree of influence which particular groups can exercise in a society, two questions immediately arise. First, is the general political environment conducive to group activity and influence? Secondly, to what extent does the structure of pressure-group activity reflect the distribution of power within the governmental system as a whole? As far as the general political environment is concerned, it appears that in relation to two groups – big business and the trade unions – the public is distinctly hostile to their perceived influence. A survey of public attitudes between 1963 and 1970 found between 59% and 48% of respondents agreeing that big business had too much power and between 53% and 66% feeling that the trade unions had too much power. In 1970 a full 72% thought that trade unions should stay out of politics.[2] At the very least one may infer from these figures, which receive frequent confirmation in the opinion polls, that in relation to these two groups, which appear to wield more influence than any others in British politics and which have in the context of 'tripartism' – close association in policy making between government, the unions and the CBI – almost been seen as candidates for incorporation into the machinery of government itself, public attitudes are less than friendly.

The distribution of power in the governmental system will affect pressure-group activity because the groups themselves will seek influence and access at the points where decisions are actually taken. In the United Kingdom this means that the major interest groups will seek access at Cabinet level and to the departments and will view their contacts in the legislature as fall-backs, spokesmen who may be of use in a publicity campaign when attempts to persuade a department to change its mind on an issue have failed. Because many of the issues on which pressure groups seek to influence government are technical and detailed, their relationships with the bureaucracy will be more important than those with cabinet ministers, for the chances of a group obtaining regular contact with a minister are usually small. The bureaucracy is of course important in its own right, for the influence which it can exert in the governmental structure makes its members both a significant constraint on sectional influence and an independent source of governmental policy. The ability of civil servants in the modern British state to contribute both positively and negatively to the decision-making process has, not surprisingly, focused attention on them. This is especially true since disillusionment with government has grown and party theoreticians have sought to explain why their remedies for every area of politics, from the economy to homelessness, have proved indequate.

All aspects of the ruling elites have been subject to critical examination but perhaps none more so than the means of recruitment. Two methods have until very recently enjoyed a particular, and indeed almost exclusive, legitimacy. The first is popular election. In an earlier chapter it was shown that certain kinds of social background find especial favour when the major political parties are recruiting their candidates for parliamentary contests. Thus the mere fact that an office is dependent upon popular election is no guarantee that its incumbents will reflect the social and economic attributes of the population at large, though there remains a lingering aspiration to make democracy representative of both these attributes. Political office at the national and the local levels is now largely dependent upon elections, as is office in the larger pressure groups. Inevitably the further one moves away from the centre of political attention the more likely it is that many of the elections will be nominal. Even at local-government elections public participation is appreciably lower than at general elections; elections for office in a trade union or other pressure group reveal even smaller degrees of public participation.

The second method which has acquired a certain legitimacy

for recruiting individuals to places of influence within the governmental system is selection on the basis of merit. This method is most significant politically in relation to the bureaucracy or civil service, although it dates only from the middle of the nineteenth century. By contrast with some of her continental neighbours also the United Kingdom is unusual in that this particular route to positions of influence does not apply to the judiciary which, as will be seen later, is selected from among practising lawyers, mainly barristers, who in the United Kingdom have traditionally maintained a separate ethos from that of the civil service.

A generation ago it might have been possible to argue that these two methods alone were relevant in a study of the country's governmental system. The hereditary element in British politics was weakening in importance and had few defenders in principle whatever pragmatic reasons might be advanced for maintaining a hereditary element in Parliament's upper House. But patronage – the filling of posts by ministerial nomination – has experienced a remarkable resurgence and today the holders of such posts could not be ignored in any survey of Britain's political elites.

The Civil Service: Fulton and After

Some aspects of the background and social characteristics of parliamentarians have to a large extent been outlined already. However, it is now necessary to examine how far the Civil Service in its classical form exhibits common characteristics and to assess the changes which took place within it between the Fulton Report of 1968 and the Eleventh Report of the House of Commons Committee on Public Expenditure in 1978.[3] It will be necessary to look at the effect of the revival of patronage on the Civil Service and at developments foreshadowed in more recent discussions of the Service.

One reason why the Civil Service has attracted so much political attention in the past decade is the expansion in its size, occasioned partly by the state's assumption of new functions and partly by the extension of existing governmental activities. It is not easy to present this process statistically since not everyone whose ultimate employer is the state is covered by the label 'civil servant' in the strict sense. Employees of the Post Office and other public corporations are not civil servants, for example. Nevertheless, according to official figures the Civil Service grew from 470,573 persons on 1 April 1968 to 571,130 persons on 1 April 1977. Given the inflation which marked the period it is not surprising to find that the cost of employing them rose sharply from £578 million in 1968–9 to over £2,000 million in 1976–7. If only the top echelon of the Civil Service is considered – Permanent Secretaries, Second Permanent Secretaries and Deputy Secretaries – their number went up from 147 on 1 April 1968 to 200 on 1 April 1976.[4]

Although the permanent Civil Service has a long history – some of its contemporary features were visible by the seventeenth century, as the diary of Samuel Pepys abundantly illustrates – the modern history of the Civil Service starts with the Northcote–Trevelyan Report of November 1853. It was significant that the Fulton Committee reprinted that Report in full: the Service under examination in the 1960s owed its principal features of recruitment, structure and training to the recommendations laid down over a century before.

The principles governing the higher reaches of the Civil Service as it existed in the 1960s can be summarized without much difficulty.[5] First, government service was a commitment normally entered into for the whole of a working career, and it was remunerated with this fact in mind. Entrance demanded proof of suitability through the satisfaction of objective tests, which at the highest levels were open and competitive examinations. Patronage, the necessity for nomination for entry to such a competition, was gradually eliminated; however, it survived longer in the Diplomatic Service, and until the integration of the Diplomatic Service with the Foreign Office in 1919 it was essential for would-be diplomats to have a private income. There was thus something of a social divide between the Diplomatic and the Home Civil Service.

The work of the Civil Service in its upper strata was broadly administrative: it was concerned with organizing and carrying out the business of the various departments and with advising ministers on matters of policy, including the preparation of primary and secondary legislation. The qualities sought – order, method and the ability to work with others – did not include the entrepreneurial talents. It was thought that such work called for little specialized knowledge or expertise and it was assumed that particular training could be acquired on the job. The examinations for entry into what was known in the pre-Fulton era as the 'Administrative class' were thus tailored to those who had recently graduated from a university without regard to the subjects which they had studied there. The written examinations had largely given way since the Second World War to the so-called 'Method II' mode of entry which involved a shortened written examination and extended interviews. Recruitment was central, not departmental, and the Civil Service Commission was thought of as an independent body not directly subject to ministerial or departmental control. While it was necessary to recruit specialists of various kinds – lawyers, scientists, technologists, statisticians and economists – it was not initially thought necessary to fit them into the general framework or to make the most senior posts available to them. They remained part of distinct hierarchies of specialists separate from the general administrators who ultimately controlled their work.

A civil servant's qualifications at entry would determine the level at which he would work throughout his career. The Administrative class was, as has been seen, drawn from university graduates; entry into the Executive class demanded completion of the secondary-school curriculum, and earlier school-leavers could join the Clerical class. However, by the time the Fulton Committee conducted its inquiries there had been a change in the British educational system so that a higher proportion of those who completed secondary school were going on to universities. Because the entry into the administrative class was still very limited, many of these graduates were now competing for places in the Executive class. Although promotion between classes was not unusual, the general expectation was still that a recruit's future career would be within his class.

By comparison with the pattern of recruitment of future civil servants in continental European countries, the most striking difference was the absence of any demand for legal training or economic expertise. Also, because entry into the Civil Service usually followed directly after the three- or four-year undergraduate course, the age of entry was lower in Britain than in the European administrative *corps*. Because of the general importance of finance and the particular significance attached to economy in public expenditure when the system was created in the generation following the Northcote–Trevelyan Report, the Treasury was recognized as the senior department, entitled to be consulted on all matters relating to expenditure and staffing. It was thus understandable that the Permanent Secretary to the Treasury should have been styled in addition 'Head of the Civil Service' by the Treasury circular of 15 September 1919.[6] Senior Civil Service appointments were thereafter made by the Prime Minister on the advice of the Head of the (Home) Civil Service; this made it possible for the whole Service to acquire a common ethos, although the Foreign Office successfully maintained its independence.

The Fulton Committee's inquiry followed a period of questioning of some accepted practices. Influenced by the mood of the time it had two broad goals in view. First, it wanted to expand access to the higher Civil Service and reduce the advantage which graduates of Oxford and Cambridge had in the entrance competition. On the other hand, it was conscious of the criticism that the lack of a proper role for scientists and technologists, and the absence of adequate facilities for post-entry training, made the Service incapable of meeting the demands made upon it in the context of a society which it was hoped was about to need guiding through a 'white-hot technological revolution'. It was also believed that the central departments could be relieved of some of their responsibilities for routine management functions by a process known as 'hiving off'. However, even before the Report appeared it was clear that the Committee's terms of reference would hardly permit it to deal with one of the central weaknesses of British government – what one of the present writers called at the time 'the appalling speed of the ministerial merry-go-round'.[7] Ministers, like 'transient and embarrassed phantoms', stayed in office for too short a time to learn the business of vast departments and could only function properly if their senior official advisers were at least chosen from within the department – not, as was by then normal, from a different one. No change was made in this respect by the Report, and the same criticism of the British method of administration was voiced by Lord Crowther-Hunt, himself a member of the Fulton Committee, in a memorandum to the Expenditure Committee in June 1977.[8] The Fulton Committee did recommend by a majority that preference in the recruitment of civil servants should be given to those with degrees in relevant subjects, especially the social sciences; however, this recommendation was rejected by the Government, which preferred the traditional view that ability could best be tested by measuring achievement in any university discipline and that special governmental needs should be covered by in-service training. In other respects, however, the Committee's recommendations found more favour. It recommended the establishment of a Civil Service Department which would take over that part of the Treasury's work related to personnel and staffing and performed by the Pay and Management Group and which would be under the Prime Minister. The Committee also recommended that the system of classes – Administrative, Executive and Clerical – should be abolished and replaced by a unified grading system which could cover the whole of the non-industrial part of the Service. Among the new administrators, the counterparts of the old Administrative and Executive classes, there should be specialization – economic and financial administrators on the one hand and social administrators on the other. The scientists, engineers and other professionals should be given opportunities to rise to managerial positions; the importance of training should be recognized by the establishment of a Civil Service College which would also have research functions; and while it was assumed that the Civil Service should remain predominantly a career Civil Service, there should be greater mobility between the Civil Service sector and other forms of employment. Such interchange, it was thought, could be achieved by greater provision for late entry to the Civil Service and the selective use of devices such as temporary appointments.

Other recommendations of the Fulton Committee related to the machinery-of-government aspect of its inquiries rather than to the intrinsic nature of the Civil Service itself. For example, it recommended – echoing the Haldane Report – that all departments should have planning units and that at the head of each of these units there should be a senior policy adviser to assist the minister. Inquiries into a number of other subjects such as 'hiving off' were also suggested. In addition the Report attacked the general aura of secrecy which unnecessarily surrounded a great deal of government.

The post-Fulton decade has seen the implementation of some of these recommendations, but such progress as has been made has not silenced critics. It was obvious that it would take some time to bring many of the proposals into effect, and that in making changes affecting the careers of individual civil servants regard would need to be paid to the opinions of the Civil Service unions, which would be voiced through the elaborate negotiating machinery of the Civil Service Whitley Council. The most important step was the setting up of the Civil Service Department as the instrument for bringing about the other changes. It officially came into being on 1 November 1968. At the time the headship of the Civil Service was vested in one of the Treasury's two Permanent Under-Secretaries; he then moved over to become Permanent Secretary of the Civil Service Department. Although the nucleus of the Department was formed from the Treasury group which had been transferred to it, it came to be manned largely by short-term appointments from other departments, rather in the manner of the Cabinet Office. The intention was to prevent it from losing contact with the rest of Whitehall. However, it may have been less effective in making its views respected than would have been a department with a powerful specialized staff. The Prime Minister was made the formal head of the Department but most day-to-day responsibilities were devolved upon another cabinet minister, a member of the House of Lords. Splitting up the Treasury in this way was not altogether acceptable to some civil servants, and in 1976 a former civil servant who had been a member of the Fulton Committee argued publicly that since the main period of reorganization was over, the headship of the Civil Service should revert to the Treasury.[9]

The Civil Service Commission was brought within the Civil Service Department. At the same time it was argued that since the Commission derived its authority from the latest relevant Order in Council – that of 1956 – and since individual members of the Commission were appointed not simply by ministers directly, but also by Orders in Council, the independence of the Commission was fully preserved under the new system. While this is no doubt true where individual cases of selection are concerned, there is some reason to doubt whether the Commission is as free in deciding upon recruitment policy as it would have the public believe.

The Civil Service College, which took over part of the work of the existing Centre for Administrative Studies, was opened formally in June 1970.[10] Its role, however, has not been as important as that envisaged for it by the Fulton Committee. It has been preoccupied largely with the provision of specialist skills required in the more routine tasks of civil servants, and it has not made major innovations in the training of the upper echelons of the Service – partly because the more senior a civil servant is, the more difficult it is to release him for study or training. Nor has the College been involved to any considerable extent in research.

Most important of all were the steps taken to implement the Fulton idea of a unified Civil Service with a uniform grading system and maximum opportunities for promotion irrespective of a recruit's starting point. The reorganization began with what the Fulton Report had styled the Senior Policy and Management Group, the seven hundred or so top posts at Under-Secretary level or above. This Group was henceforth to be treated as a single unit and the posts within it were to be open to those with general or specialist skills, including scientists. When a scientist engineer from the Farnborough Research Station and the old Ministry of Supply became, after a spell in the Cabinet Office, the new Permanent Secretary of the Department of Education and Science, this was hailed as 'the first real fruit of the Fulton reforms in this area'.[11] However, the same example was also used by Lord Crowther-Hunt to make the point that the Fulton reforms were intended to give specialists the opportunity of reaching top positions in their own specialist subject areas rather than in other fields where they had no relevant expertise. Despite its name, the Department of Education and Science has very little to do with science.

The decision to abolish the historic tripartite division between the Administrative, Executive and Clerical classes was gradually implemented. The most obvious immediate effect was to abolish direct entry for some seventy to eighty graduates a year into what had been the Administrative class. Under the new system, the old rank of Assistant Principal, which had been the first rung on the ladder of the Administrative class, was replaced by a larger category of entrants known as administrative trainees. Although under this revised system the number of successful graduate entrants doubled, only a proportion of them – mainly the starred entrants – could expect rapid promotion to the senior levels of the Service while the remainder were left to strengthen the middle levels of the structure. The British Civil Service thus introduced, perhaps without intending to, something similar to the French distinction among graduates of the Ecole Nationale d'Administration between those chosen for the *grands corps* and the rest.[12]

The Civil Service and the Foreign Service nevertheless remain the most obvious examples of the dominance of certain educational criteria among Britain's governing elites. Despite the observations by the Fulton Committee about the undue prominence of Oxbridge graduates and its suggestions about how this imbalance might be corrected, there was no great change in the situation in subsequent years. The statistical bias towards graduates from the ancient universities in part reflected the unwillingness of graduates from other universities to consider the Civil Service a desirable and profitable career. Yet the predominance of Oxbridge graduates at the highest levels of the bureaucracy created an impression of social as well as educational bias because the two ancient universities have traditionally recruited a larger proportion of their students from the independent schools than have other universities, though this feature of the Oxbridge intake is diminishing. Also the high proportion of Oxbridge graduates in the Civil Service caused concern because it was believed that the emphasis on general culture in those two universities, as opposed to specialist training and knowledge, was inimical to the demands which a modern Civil Service would have to meet. It is not surprising that when in 1978 the Expenditure Committee came to look at developments in the Civil Service since the Fulton Committee's Report it found that some of the evidence presented to it re-echoed the Fulton themes.[13]

By 1978, however, two other elements in the situation had to be taken into account. One was the return of patronage in the process of appointing to governmental and quasi-governmental bodies. Since experience outside government was often a necessity for such positions, the ordinary Civil Service preference for recruiting people at the outset of their careers was obviously difficult to apply to these cases. A directory of such appointments by ministers which was published in April 1976 contained 4,900 appointments. Of their holders, 3,300 were paid by fees and 1,600 by salaries of which a quarter were sums of less than £1,000 per year.[14] There were also 5,300 unpaid appointments. Parliamentary answers in June 1978 revealed 8,411 paid appointments and 25,000 unpaid ones where only expenses were paid.[15]

The criteria used for such appointments became a vexed issue in 1977–8 when it was claimed by the opposition that Labour ministers were using their power to displace experienced members of, for example, area health boards in order to make way for Labour Party members. It was also ascertained that no impediment existed to prevent individuals holding a plurality of such appointments and that indeed a number of senior trade-union officials and academics, active or retired, appeared on the list again and again. Ministers can also add to the numbers of such appointments without reference to Parliament. The Central Arbitration Committee, which has compulsory powers deriving from the Employment Protection Act, increased its numbers between May and September 1977 from a chairman, 8 deputy chairmen and 25 part-time members to a chairman, 18 deputy chairmen and 63 part-time members.[16] Questions have also been raised about the competence of some of the appointees from the political world who are placed on the boards of nationalized industries, and about the conflict of interests which may arise in the case of individuals who hold appointments on more than one of them. Finally civil servants, when retired, can hold such posts, which undermines their independence of government.[17]

Despite the fact that retired civil servants have been among the beneficiaries of the system, suggestions for making it more open have come from within the Civil Service itself. Harold Wilson was worried about the limited range of people from which appointments were made and founded the Public Appointments Unit in the Civil Service Department. The directory already mentioned was the first result. Early in 1978 a scheme was prepared by the Unit which would have enabled people to nominate themselves or others and which would have encouraged people to come forward by advertisement; this would have been especially useful in the regions. A standard form would have been provided to obtain comprehensive data about the qualifications of all candidates. However, opposition from within the Cabinet prevented any action from being taken.[18]

Even so, ministers can now – as in the past – turn if they choose to their civil servants to suggest names for public appointments if they do not wish to use such appointments for rewarding party services. The Civil Service is known to keep a list, officially known as the central list, of 'the good and the great', which it is believed contains about six thousand names. While the Conservative Opposition was in 1978 attacking the Government's political use of such appointments, it was reported to be drawing up a list of its own of individuals available for appointment and likely to be sympathethic to an incoming Conservative government.[19]

The other change since 1968, which is likely in the long run to have even greater significance, is the return to political patronage of appointments within the departmental machinery itself. The Fulton Committee approved the idea of ministers introducing of experts who could help them in their own departments. To a minor extent this was taken advantage of both in the first Wilson administration and the Heath administration. Heath's appointments were few and largely from business. However, the practice was extended, especially after Wilson's return to power in 1974 when one began to see the appointment of individuals not as experts, selected for some ability to contribute special experience or academic insights to the work of particular departments, but as political advisers. Drawn as some are from the interest groups, they may handle interest-group representations better than regular civil servants. It was assumed that such individuals, who were often quite young, would help to keep ministers in touch with the Party or sections of it. Cabinet ministers were confined to a maximum of two special appointments each; the policy unit established by Wilson in the Prime Minister's Office has varied in size from five to seven.[20] The status of such appointees is that of temporary civil servants: they sign the Official Secrets Act and must resign if they wish to enter active politics. The degree of permissible involvement in politics short of actually campaigning for election remains somewhat obscure. In February 1978, for instance, the list of so-called 'special advisers' was for the first time included in *The Labour Party Directory*.

The original assumption was that such appointments would in any event terminate at the close of the administration under which they were appointed. In 1972 there was an agreement between the Government and the Civil Service that such appointees could not remain as civil servants for more than five years without facing open competition. When Harold Wilson resigned in March 1976 there were twenty-eight holders of such posts and all resigned. Many were, however, reappointed under the Callaghan administration. In August 1978, when there were twenty-five such temporary ministerial advisers, it was announced that the five-years rule would no longer apply. Such advisers were excluded from the operation of the 1969 Order in Council whereby all persons proposed for permanent appointment to the Civil Service had to receive a certificate of suitability from the Civil Service Commission. The reason given was that the advisers could not be treated as permanent since their tenure of office would come to an end with that of the Government itself.[21] It is understandable that the Civil Service unions should try to limit what might otherwise appear a form of back-door access to the Service and a departure from the rules of open competition. At the same time there have been attempts to widen the right of permanent civil servants to engage in political activity, but as far as civil servants with political responsibilities are concerned this development has been resisted.[22]

Not only had there been changes in the public service in these and other respects by the time the Expenditure Committee conducted its inquiries in the 1977–8 session of Parliament; it was also the case that the atmosphere was quite different. In the 1960s, when it was thought that there would be great economic expansion, the accent was heavily upon finding the most efficient personnel and forms of organization. In the 1970s, when the growth of public expenditure as a factor in inflation was a general preoccupation, the priorities became different. There was a much greater volume of criticism of the whole governmental machine and the political system in general as Britain's economic failings became increasingly apparent. At least one school of thought – foreshadowed in the Crossman diaries which cover the period 1964–6 – placed emphasis on the resistance by the Civil Service to the reforms of ministers. The centralization of the Civil Service made it impossible for ministers of their own volition to move out of the departments civil servants whose abilities or opinions they mistrusted. The Head of the Civil Service, and behind him the Prime Minister, stood in the way of such action. There is reason to believe that similar feelings were entertained by some ministers in the Heath Government. The Civil Service as a whole felt itself on the defensive, and it was revealed in August 1978 that a committee of civil servants had been set up in October 1977 to discuss ways of improving the public image of the Service.[23]

The Expenditure Committee thus found itself confronted with both arguments that the Fulton reforms had not been fully implemented and a number of additional suggestions for change. Like the Fulton Committee, it concerned itself with questions of machinery and also with staff and training.[24] The work of inquiry was done by the general subcommittee but when the report was presented to the Committee as a whole deep divisions were revealed. An alternative version of its first chapter was proposed and supported by eleven members of the full Committee led by Mr Brian Sedgemore, who had actually served on the subcommittee. Those eleven Labour members were defeated by the vote of the Conservative members combined with the rest of the Labour members, a total of fifteen votes. The minority had wished to report that the real problem of the Civil Service as they saw it was the unresponsiveness of civil servants to the democratically chosen ministers whose wishes it was their duty to implement. Civil servants were seen as men of 'superior intellect' who, however, lacked the training or experience relevant to the tasks they had to perform, and who had therefore invented for themselves the role of 'governing the country'. According to this view civil servants acted together across departmental boundaries and took advantage of ministers' difficulties to pursue policies of their own. The amendment continued by saying that it would 'be as wrong to accuse top civil servants of overt party political bias as it would be foolish not to recognise that Labour governments seeking to alter society in a socialist direction have more difficulty with civil servants (who are seeking in conjunction with other establishment figures from the City, the Bank of England, industry, the established Church and the monarchy to maintain the status quo) than do Conservative governments who wish to leave things roughly as they are'. But the radical policies of even the Heath Government had in this minority's view encountered obstruction from the Civil Service. In the case of the existing Labour Government, the amendment alleged that civil servants at the Department of Industry had frustrated its interventionist policies and its proposals for industrial democracy as embodied in the Bullock Report.[25] It also drew attention to the Home Office which was allegedly 'stuffed with reactionaries' and to the way in which some Foreign Office officials interpret being a good European as being 'synonomous with selling out British interests'.

The recommendations to remedy these alleged deficiencies in the system related in part to the future composition of the higher Civil Service:

Whether through the appointment of powerful ministerial back-up teams or 'cabinets' chosen by ministers and including Members of Parliament if ministers so desired and to whom civil servants at Deputy Secretary and Under Secretary level would be accountable, or through the developing role of political advisers, or through political appointments of top civil servants at Under Secretary level and above, or through other devices Ministers must inject more party political clout into the upper echelons of the administration.

This minority group also advocated the strengthening of the House of Commons committee system with the aim of placing 'far more power than at present in the hands of back-bench Members of Parliament in general and in the hands of back-bench members of the majority party in particular'.[26]

The majority report itself was far less radical. The Committee was obviously worried by the continued predominance of Oxbridge over other universities in the competition for places at the administrative trainee level and by the success of candidates from independent schools who, it was held in some quarters, were especially favoured in a system based on interviews. However, all the Committee asked for was better statistical information so that the possibilities of bias could be monitored. The Civil Service Commission of four civil servants was held to be too inbred and the Committee recommended that they should be balanced by outside part-time commissioners who would form the majority. The membership of the Final Selection Committee should also be widened. The Committee also recommended an examination of the work of the Civil Service College to see whether this could not be done by individual departments or by institutions outside the Civil Service. It was thought that the administrative trainee scheme should be abolished. Holders of good degrees should be allotted directly to jobs and should compete on equal terms with other graduates and non-graduates for entry to a new higher management training course. Completion of this course – to which candidates from the National Health Service, local government and the Diplomatic Service would also be admitted – would be a prerequisite for promotion beyond the rank of Assistant Secretary or its equivalent. The unified grading structure should be extended downwards through the Service and there should be further restraints on the employment of ex-civil servants by companies in a contractual relationship with government.

Some attention was also devoted to the remuneration of civil servants, a topic of much controversy since civil servants complained of the suspension of the Pay Research Unit which had been designed to establish comparability with jobs in the private sector. A new independent Pay Research Unit was proposed and it was left that government would take upon itself any refusal to pay the salaries recommended if restraint was necessary in the interests of incomes policy. The 'inflation proofing' of public-service pensions under the Pensions Increase Act of 1971 and the Superannuation Act of 1972 was criticized; however, given the existence of inflation-linked pension schemes elsewhere, it was not suggested that inflation proofing should now be abandoned – although review of the whole policy was, in the Committee's view, desirable.

The Committee accepted the view that ministers should

normally be responsible for changes in the management of their departments, that special advisers had become an accepted feature of the system and that a Cabinet minister should no longer be limited to two such advisers. A minister should be able to associate with himself a group of advisers – or even of back-bench MPs, though without executive authority – if he thought this conducive to efficiency.

As far as the machinery of government was concerned, suggestions were made for improving efficiency and for monitoring the effect of changes by a new system of financial accounting to Parliament. It was also proposed that the office of Comptroller and Auditor General should be strengthened and his department made more directly responsible to the House of Commons. A reconsideration of the relationship between the Civil Service and local-government service was also recommended. The Prime Minister and the Leader of the Opposition, the Committee suggested, should jointly consider a modification in the rules about non-disclosure of the papers of one administration to its successor.

On one main point the Committee's report represented a retreat from Fulton's proposals. It was now felt that the separation of the functioning of manning the Civil Service from the function of monitoring its efficiency undertaken by the public-expenditure divisions of the Treasury had not proved useful; the Committee therefore recommended that personnel functions should be returned to the Treasury. The Civil Service Department would thus be left only with limited personnnel functions, including recruitment, training, pay and pensions responsibilities. The Government took some time to respond to these recommendations and when it did so its reply was a tentative one. In its white paper of 15 March 1978 it stated that it had accepted wholly or in part thirty-one of the Committee's fifty-four recommendations but it remained undecided as to whether the division of responsibilities between the Treasury and the Civil Service Department should be changed. For the moment therefore the Fulton formula held good. The white paper emphasized the traditional doctrine of ministerial responsibility for the policies of departments and therefore insisted that the advice of civil servants to ministers should be 'confidential and objective' and that it was for ministers, not civil servants, to defend government policy before select committees. While accepting that special advisers should become an accepted feature of the constitution, the Government reiterated its adherence to the long-established tradition that the British Civil Service should remain a non-political permanent career service.

Many of the criticisms of the Home Civil Service, especially the alleged bias in the selection process and the alleged inadequacy of existing training for the tasks of bureaucracy in the modern world, were also voiced in the 1960s and 1970s about the Diplomatic Service. In the strict sense this was a new organization, which had been formed in 1965 as a result of the Diplomatic Service Order of 1964 amalgamating the Foreign Service, the Commonwealth Service Commission and the Trade Commission Service. Recruitment is in the hands of the Civil Service Commission, but the Civil Service Department has less control over the Foreign Service's grading arrangements than it does over those of the Home Civil Service, although the Department does have a say in the Foreign Service's overall manpower ceilings. The Diplomatic Service is of course a much smaller corps: those occupying what would be regarded as administrative posts in the Home Civil Service are proportionately more numerous than those at the executive level – one to three compared with one to thirty. When the Central Policy Review Staff looked at the matter in 1976–7, they thought the Diplomatic Service took in more highly qualified persons than were needed to discharge some of its functions and that far too little attention was given to any form of expertise other than linguistic ability.[27]

In fact there has been some broadening of the Diplomatic Service's intake if schooling is taken as the criterion for assessing social background. In the early part of the Second World War, all ministers responsibile for foreign affairs, economic warfare and intelligence were Etonians, as were the principal officials in the Foreign Office and the heads of two secret services, MI5 and MI6; also many leading diplomats were Etonians. By the time the Duncan Committee looked at the situation in 1969, the effects of earlier reorganizations had begun to be felt and variety had been brought in by the recruitment of men with experience in the Commonwealth or the colonies.[28] Of the 77 ambassadors serving in 1969, only 8 were Etonians. On the other hand 50 were public-school products, and the domination of Oxbridge was even clearer: Oxford supplied 32 and Cambridge 26 of the ambassadorial contingent, leaving only 19 who had been at other universities or who were – usually because of war service – not graduates at all.

The view that at the very top in British government there was a similarity of experience, particularly at the university level of education, was a commonplace of discussion in the 1970s. It was obviously not without truth and was not very greatly altered by changes in the political complexion of governments. In the Cabinet with which Harold Wilson went into the general election of 1970, 16 of its 21 members were university graduates, of whom no fewer than 10 had been at Oxford. 6 had been to public schools, independent schools outside the state system. Of the 5 non-graduates, 3 had been to grammar schools, of whom 2 had then acquired professional qualifications while 1 went into the wartime Royal Air Force. Only 2 out of the 21 thus shared the educational experience of the majority of the Party's supporters. In April 1972, Heath's Conservative Cabinet numbered 18. 14 of these were graduates, 10 from Oxford and 4 from Cambridge. Of the 4 non-graduates 1 had gone from school to the Royal Military College, Sandhurst, 2 direct into the fighting forces in the war and 1 straight from grammar school into business and politics. The only real difference was at the school level: 13 of the Heath Cabinet had been to well-known public schools and 4 of these to Eton.

On the Civil Service side, if one takes the 21 heads of principal departments whom Heath inherited from Wilson in June 1970, the educational careers of 20 are known. 18 were university graduates, including 10 from Oxford, 7 from Cambridge and 1 from the London School of Economics. On the other hand, the public-school element is closer to the Labour than to the Conservative proportion – 7 out of the 20, including one Etonian.

Thus, taking the leading figures of the two main parties and the top civil servants as the core of Britain's governing elite at the beginning of the 1970s, one has a tally of 58 men and 2 women – 60 in all. Of these, exactly half – 30 – were Oxford graduates and 11 were Cambridge graduates. Oxbridge thus accounted for just over two-thirds of the total. Post-Fulton developments did not seem likely to alter this situation much in relation to the Civil Service: 21% of the applicants for admission as administrative trainees in 1973–5 were from Oxbridge, yet Oxbridge graduates represented only 12% of the graduates from all universities in the United Kingdom. Among successful applicants the proportion of Oxbridge graduates was a startling 57%. Nor was there any very obvious change at the apex of the political world. When Callaghan was elected leader of the Labour Party, and so became Prime Minister in succession to Harold Wilson, all his 5 rivals were Oxford graduates.

The difficulty facing those who argued that Britain suffered from the narrowness of the range of educational experience in the higher ranks of the Civil Service was that the French system, with which the British was so often compared to its disadvantage, was – making allowances for the obvious difference between the educational systems in the two countries – if anything even more restricted in its intake.

A Plural Society?

The sense of close-knit intimacy which foreign observers have noted as characteristic of Britain's ruling elites is fortified by the fact that the same educational background – particularly the predominance of Oxbridge – extends to the leaders of the legal profession, to important sectors of the commercial and financial worlds and to the editorial staffs of the quality press and the media. Industry, too, while clearly giving more opportunities for internal promotion from the shop floor, has in its leading positions a high proportion of men with similar educational advantages. Taking directors of large companies in industry, finance and commerce together, some two-thirds have been found to be from public schools, and of the graduates among them, about two-thirds from Oxbridge. Company chairmen are even more likely to be in these categories. In banking this is more marked than in industry and the range of experience becomes even more limited if one looks at those who have been at one of the more prestigious public schools.

The establishment of links of educational experience or social origin between members of different elite groups does not necessarily get one very far in determining how they are influenced by each other. However, it may suggest to the outsider, and to those groups with a different background, an ease of communication which those without such shared experiences are denied. The business world is represented in a multitude of consultative committees within the framework of the National Economic Development Council and, along with representatives of the trade unions, has been relied upon by government to administer such organizations as the Manpower Services Commission, the Central Arbitration Committee and the Health and Safety Commission. However, business itself has not seen its position in the 1960s and 1970s as being particularly favoured with respect to government. The larger firms, which operate a recruiting mechanism not so different from that of the Civil Service, have continually complained that the universities have not encouraged their best graduates to enter industry, and that there is a strong cultural bias against the productive sector and the profit motive in the educational system. At the same time smaller businesses tend to feel that the relationship between the larger industries and government is now altogether too intimate and detracts from true entrepreneurship. Whether the increasing recruitment of young graduates with a business background to the ranks of Conservative parliamentary candidates will gradually produce greater sympathy between business and government remains to be seen.

The tendency to identify the cbi as a business pressure group whose influence is equal to that of the tuc is misleading. The cbi does enable the opinions of business to be collected but since its members include the nationalized industries it has some difficulty in developing a coherent strategy which can suit all of them. Moreover the cbi is clearly representative more of manufacturing than of retail interests and its membership tends to be biased towards the larger firms rather than small businesses. These divisions mean that it cannot often speak with the unity of conviction which marks the tuc when the latter is backed by the bloc votes of the major industrial unions. Furthermore the organic link of trade unions with the Labour Party has no counterpart in a similar link between the cbi and the Conservative Party, although private industry does provide financial support for the Party. Indeed, divisions over policy between the CBI and the Conservative Government of 1974 were frequently apparent and a speech by the CBI's Director General two days before polling in the February 1974 election was regarded by some observers as a contributory cause in the Conservatives' defeat. A major study of the CBI, while pointing out that it enjoyed access to government at the cabinet level and that senior CBI officials and company chairmen shared a common social and educational background with politicians and administrators, concluded that the CBI had 'little consistent direct influence over the policies pursued by government'.[29] It could affect the details of legislation and policy but not their substance.

Other pressure groups in British politics, with the exception of organized labour, are in an even less secure position. Although they are able to develop contacts with their sponsoring ministry and to give their views on proposals affecting their area of concern, they have little direct access to the legislative process itself or to the Cabinet. If their channels of access to the department are poor or they do not successfully transmit the necessary influence on a particular issue, then recourse must be had to influencing public opinion and trying to persuade one or other of the main parties to take up their cause. The more successful a pressure group, the less necessary it will be to engage in publicity campaigns, and the goal of interest-group activity will remain regular contact with a government department. For less successful pressure groups the recent development whereby some Labour advisers were selected from former officials of social welfare pressure groups such as Shelter or the Child Poverty Action Group was important as an opportunity for access to government at the highest levels which had previously in general been denied.

On the British scene in the 1970s the trade-union movement provided the only exception to the general rule that Britain's governing elites share a common social background and educational experience. Although in one sense trade-union leaders are integrated in the country's political elite through their Labour Party connections, in another sense they are separated from it by background, education and life-style. The most important feature of the British trade-union movement may be its historic link with the Labour Party which was originally formed to enable working-class voices to be heard in Parliament. However, as the unions grew stronger there was an unwillingness to allow leading trade unionists to seek political careers for themselves. Except in wartime they were not encouraged to seek parliamentary seats or to become ministers. The quota of Labour MPs with a trade-union and working-class background has been diminishing, as has been seen, despite the fact that the general election of May 1979 returned 148 trade union-sponsored MPs. The trade unions, while treating the Labour Party as their own and giving it great financial and personal support, also need to pursue their objectives through negotiation with governments, whatever their political colour. What to a large extent distinguishes the trade-union movement from other pressure groups is the preference which union leaders have for promoting their policies through contacts between union leaders and ministers rather than through contacts between union leaders and officials.[30]

All this may change with the growth of trade unionism in Britain in the last decade, which has doubled the number of trade unionists to over twelve million in unions affiliated to the TUC. The growth has largely been in the white-collar occupations and in service trades, whose leaders have a different outlook from those in the more established unions for mining, manufacturing and transport. So far, although the unions do employ some graduates for research, they remain dominated and controlled by their elected officials, who are closer in many ways to the unions' rank-and-file membership. Although electoral participation is low in most unions, the authority of trade-union leaders does not appear greatly dimished by this. Also, while the TUC has little power over individual unions it can often muster a great deal of support on those issues which it thinks important.

One aspect in which the trade-union elite clearly differs from its political, Civil Service and business counterparts is its relative insularity – although here too there are signs of change as the need to deal with multinational companies on an international basis comes to be felt. For the moment, however, the movement's self-image is largely confined to the context of

British industrial relations. It has been a major source of resistance to greater participation in European affairs through the European Communities and relatively indifferent even to trade-union questions in the Soviet Union and the Third World.

In domestic matters it could be argued that the trade-union movement's horizons are broadening. Its policy pronouncements now cover not merely the traditional issues affecting trade unions but almost the whole range of economic and social policy. The experience of the 'social contract' in which trade unions and the Labour leadership reached a concordat on what policies would be implemented in return for wage restraint may seem a turning-point, but in reality the process of achieving trade-union influence has been a cumulative one. It could be argued that if a turning-point existed it came not under the Labour Government of 1974 but under Edward Heath's Government of 1970–4, when there was a comprehensive attempt by the Conservative Government to bargain with the trade-union movement over incomes policy; also, significantly, the idea of pressure groups' nomination of representatives to a body such as the Manpower Services Commission, which can then frame and execute policy, was explicitly acknowledged by Conservative ministers as a way of giving such groups both opportunity for influence and the responsibility for decisions taken.

In raising the question of greater trade-union involvement in government – and indeed greater involvement by certain sections of industry – one must inevitably ask how far such a development can go and also how far such a close association with government is representative of the wishes of the groups' memberships. For the sorts of arrangements which might be concluded on a range of issues, from incomes policy and wage restraint to employment protection and industrial strategy, may be little more than accommodations reached between leaders who are themselves incapable either of convincing their members of their utility or of ensuring that such bargains, once made, are kept.

It is important, however, not to exaggerate the influence of trade unions. For all the examples pointing in the direction of trade-union incorporation into the decision-making process there are examples of governments not following trade-union preferences, for example TUC economic policy. (Callaghan's policies between 1976 and 1978 in the economic field were worked out in conjunction with the IMF and were almost diametrically opposed to the expansionist and protectionist policies favoured by the TUC.) In addition there is evidence that the trade unions are anxious not to lose their right to bargain freely with employers over wages, whatever the returns in terms of a social wage.

The United Kingdom may now be a society in which groups do not merely expect to be consulted when legislation affecting their material interests is contemplated, but in which some groups may have an effective veto on certain sorts of political action. However, few of them are necessarily prepared to sacrifice their freedom of action to pursue their sectional concerns (which after all motivated their organization in the first place) in order to exercise power over their members, other pressure groups and the general social and administrative processes which are properly the functions of government. To this extent labels such as 'corporatism' are as misleading as they are useful.

9 Government on the Ground I: Local Government

A large number of the services which citizens of the United Kingdom have come to expect are provided, as has been seen, not by central government directly but by local authorities. Such major responsibilities as education, which is local government's most expensive service, roads, housing, planning, libraries, museums and galleries, social services and refuse disposal fall to a network of elected authorities which are distinct from the central government. These maintain a substantial degree of autonomy despite the inroads made upon local independence, for example by the Treasury's efforts to exert more stringent control over local-government expenditure in the interests of overall economic management. The importance of local government in the political and economic system of the United Kingdom is illustrated by the fact that in the period 1975–6 local authorities were responsible for spending some £15,000 million, had a capital debt of £23,000 million and employed $2\frac{1}{2}$ million people.[1] Local-government expenditure was reckoned in 1977 to represent some 30% of all public expenditure and 13% of Gross National Product.[2]

It is not merely the level of local-authority spending that makes local authorities important, nor even the fact that their policies can significantly affect the standard and style of provision in certain key areas of welfare and regulatory activity. They are also important because they offer additional opportunities for individual and group activity of a political kind, and together form a distinct arena of politics and decision making.

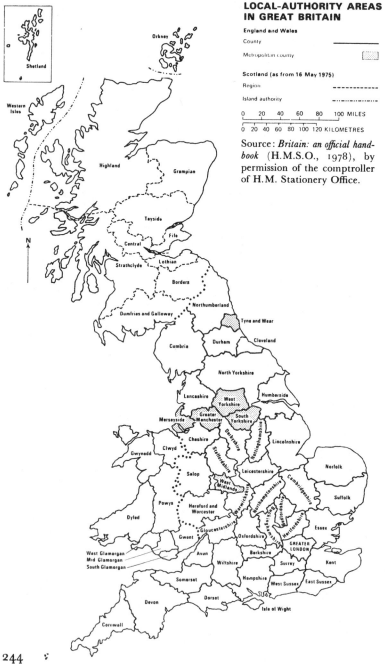

LOCAL-AUTHORITY AREAS IN GREAT BRITAIN

England and Wales
County ————
Metropolitan county [▦]

Scotland (as from 16 May 1975)
Region ------------
Island authority —··—··—··—

0   20   40   60   80   100 MILES
0 20 40 60 80 100 120 KILOMETRES

Source: *Britain: an official handbook* (H.M.S.O., 1978), by permission of the comptroller of H.M. Stationery Office.

Orkney

Shetland

Western Isles

N

Highland

Grampian

Tayside

Fife

Central

Lothian

Strathclyde

Borders

Dumfries and Galloway

Northumberland

Tyne and Wear

Cumbria

Durham

Cleveland

North Yorkshire

Lancashire

West Yorkshire

Humberside

Merseyside

Greater Manchester

South Yorkshire

Cheshire

Derbyshire

Nottinghamshire

Lincolnshire

Gwynedd

Clwyd

Staffordshire

Salop

Leicestershire

Norfolk

West Midlands

Cambridgeshire

Powys

Hereford and Worcester

Warwickshire

Northamptonshire

Bedfordshire

Suffolk

Dyfed

Gloucestershire

Oxfordshire

Buckinghamshire

Hertfordshire

Essex

Gwent

GREATER LONDON

West Glamorgan
Mid Glamorgan
South Glamorgan

Avon

Berkshire

Surrey

Kent

Wiltshire

Somerset

Hampshire

West Sussex

East Sussex

Devon

Dorset

Isle of Wight

Cornwall

The last decade has seen a radical reorganization of the units of local administration and yet another reappraisal of the basis on which local-authority expenditure is financed. Together these developments have generated a debate about the role which local government should play in the wider political system – although by comparison with the more explicitly constitutional questions of devolution and regionalism that debate may appear a minor theme in a much larger movement.

The modern structure of local government in England and Wales dates from the Local Government Act of 1972, except for London which has a slightly different structure of local administration since it was reformed in the early 1960s. The basis of local government since 1972 is that the country is divided into forty-five county authorities outside London, and these counties are in turn subdivided into smaller units known as districts. The county authorities exercise all major functions except housing; the district councils deal with housing, refuse disposal, traffic control and lesser matters. There is a variation to the pattern in six county authorities known as metropolitan authorities because these areas – Merseyside, Greater Manchester, the West Midlands, West Yorkshire, South Yorkshire and the north-eastern conurbation of Tyne and Wear – are heavily populated and present different problems from those experienced by the majority of counties. In these areas, the principle that major functions such as education ought to be exercised by the county does not apply, and the lower-level authorities – metropolitan district councils – are sufficiently populous to administer education and some other functions reserved to the counties elsewhere. In 1974, when the system became operative, the metropolitan authorities were subdivided into 36 district councils while the remaining 39 counties were divided into 296 districts.

In London the old London County Council had already been replaced by a Greater London Council covering the area of the old LCC and the surrounding suburbs. The GLC has a wide range of functions relating to planning, highways, traffic and so on. The staple functions of local government – housing, education, social services, etc. – are however exercised by thirty-two London boroughs, except that in the old London County Council area a joint education authority, ILEA, administers education.

In Scotland, which was reformed by the Local Government (Scotland) Act of 1973, the system is different yet again: the Wheatley Commission recommended a structure based on large regional councils and, at the lower level, district councils. The anomaly in the Scottish local-government system, which has made discussion of devolution somewhat more difficult than it would otherwise have been, is that one region – Strathclyde – contains over half of Scotland's total population.

The difficulties associated with local-government reform in recent years, and the controversy produced by attempts to alter the financial relationships between local and central government, originate in part from the ambiguity of the British tradition of local democracy. That ambiguity permeates the whole field of central-local conflicts and makes it difficult to assess the role which the system of local government is supposed to play in the constitutional structure. It has been said for example that one of the most important features of British local government is the *ultra vires* rule, which means that local authorities have no independent legal competence as they do in France but derive all their powers from Parliament; if the local authorities should step outside the realm of authorized activities the courts could intervene and control them.[3] This doctrine has been criticized as being unduly restrictive on local-authority enterprise and innovation. Yet it is by no means clear that all local authorities have been hamstrung by it. The eighteenth and nineteenth centuries were periods when local authorities were extremely active as promoters of private Acts of Parliament which would enable them to engage in new activities; and in the twentieth century – especially under the stimulus of Fabian views about the role of local authorities and the activities of councillors – local authorities produced a number of experiments in municipal activity. The prominence of the *ultra vires* doctrine has been combined with a fierce concern for local values and a belief that local self-government was an ideal at least as important as either economic administration or equality of provision.[4]

The contradictions inherent in the British political system's treatment of local affairs partly reflect the absence of a comprehensive written constitution prescribing the relationships between the different levels of political authority. They are also a product of the haphazard growth of local-government functions and arrangements for administering services. The norms which came to govern the provision of educational facilities were thus not necessarily the same as those which guided the administration of the police or the social services.[5] Moreover the fact that until very recently Britain was assumed to be a political system in which geographical and regional divisions were relatively unimportant has meant that claims for local autonomy have found few echoes of a consistent or unambiguous kind within the major political parties. While a party in opposition may take up a local cause from time to time, the considerations which are likely to prevail when that party is in government are those of administrative convenience, equality of treatment and the national interest.

It is hardly surprising that with this situation of ambiguity the pattern of local government's structure, functions and powers displays no more logic today than it did twenty or even fifty years ago. In the absence of a clear consensus about the role of local authorities, the local dimension of British government is inevitably subject to two pressures. First, as the Layfield Committee pointed out, it is subject to creeping centralization, for to maintain the status quo in local government's position *vis-à-vis* the central departments is to endorse a partnership in which central government has an increasingly strong hand.[6] Secondly, the position of local authorities is bound to appear unstable, since the temptation to adjust the structure is always present. It might have been thought that the plethora of committees and Royal Commissions established to reform, and allegedly to strengthen, local government in the 1960s – to say nothing of the costly and disruptive effects of the reorganization itself between 1972 and 1974 – would have assuaged the enthusiasm for institutional change in this sphere. However, the dynamic of political interest is such that a transfer downward of functions between levels of authority is envisaged by the Labour Party in respect of education and the social services, while the Conservatives are concerned with over-government as well as with the reduction of expenditure. This makes it likely that both major parties will continue to tinker with the machinery of local government even if the process is obscured by such descriptions as 'organic change'.[7] Such sporadic intervention is not new; there could be no better monument to the changing tides of administrative fashion than the catalogue of functions which local government has acquired and lost in the twentieth century alone.[8]

Although the basic structure of the United Kingdom's system of local government was completely revised by the reforms of 1972-4, it is necessary to set these measures against the background of the earlier system, for some of the traditions of local government can be explained only by reference to the pre-1972 pattern of authorities.

The Modern History of Local Government

The Municipal Corporations Act of 1835 applied only to the larger boroughs; the rural parts of England were still at that time administered as they had been since Tudor days by the Justices of the Peace assembled in the county Quarter Sessions. It was not until Salisbury's unenthusiastic acceptance of the need to introduce the elective principle into the system of county government in 1888 that the whole country was covered by the authorities elected by the ratepayers.

The reorganization of local government which took place between 1888 and 1894 laid the foundations of the system of local government which was to endure until the 1972 Local Government Act. Yet the structure was deeply flawed even after the reforms of 1888; for although the 1888 Act made the county the major unit of local administration, it excluded from the county's jurisdiction the larger towns, which were accorded a degree of autonomy similar to that enjoyed by the county. These towns were given what was known as 'county-borough status'; although the 1888 Act had originally limited the number of county boroughs, the legislation was amended to provide that additional towns could become county boroughs immediately and that other towns could apply for this status in the future. Moreover, towns which already possessed county-borough status were allowed under this legislation to seek an extension of their area. Thus the division between town and country, which was to play such a prominent part in the Redcliffe-Maud Commission's analysis of the defects of local government in the 1960s, was established as a relationship marked by jurisdictional competition: the counties' and boroughs' existence thereafter was characterized by suspicion that any increase in the independence of the boroughs would mean a loss of jurisdiction and income for the counties. The system established in 1888–94 may have appeared stable, but the search by the larger towns for county-borough status was a cause of great instability.[9] The tension between counties and county boroughs was also heightened by the different styles of politics which prevailed in the two kinds of authorities: in the boroughs, organization of the council and its committees was increasingly on party lines; in the counties, apolitical organization and uncontested elections were much more frequent, except in such counties as Glamorgan and Durham.

The level beneath the county council was organized by the legislation of 1894 into a structure of district councils so that the minor functions of local government could be administered at a level that was closer to the urban or rural community.

Because reform of the local-government system was delayed for so long in the nineteenth century there were, in addition to authorities which were organized as part of the structure of local government explicitly, a series of *ad hoc* authorities for special purposes which had been created as the need arose. Localism was not greatly admired by the utilitarian reformers of the mid-nineteenth century, who were inspired by Benthamism and saw in the existing structure of local administration only an irrational set of authorities inimical to the efficient provision of services. The special needs of the poor were taken into account in 1834 when the Poor Law Amendment Act grouped parishes together on principles which took little notice of historic boundaries. The poor-law union later became the administrative unit for a number of other purposes including the registration of births, marriages and deaths. When public health authorities were instituted following deep public concern over the incidence of cholera, the pattern imposed upon them was that of the earlier poor-law unit. The advantages of the functional authorities over the traditional units of local government were that they facilitated uniform administration and could be constructed to accommodate the special features of the particular problems which had to be tackled. An obvious example here is that of the sanitary area, which needed to be constructed to cover the whole drainage area of a town regardless of local-authority divisions. Above all, the functional authority promoted a greater use of expertise and allowed a greater element of central supervision than did local government proper. The weaknesses of traditional local authorities in this respect have been pointed out by S.E. Finer, the biographer of Edwin Chadwick, the public-health reformer who was a great admirer of the highly centralized administrative system which Napoleon had established in France:

> To a middle-class Radical, this new administration contrasted favourably in every respect with the historic patchwork of local franchises and parishes that served in England for the exercise of local government, and with the chaotic efforts of unprofessional officials and self-elected local bodies who, from fear or self-interest and complete independence of the centre, mal-administered the vital social services of justice, Poor Law, public health, police and highways throughout the countryside.[10]

With the simplification of local-government structure in 1888 and the introduction of elections into county government, it might have been expected that many of the tasks performed by specially constituted authorities could now be transferred to local authorities. There was some move in this direction when education was transferred to the county and county-borough councils in 1902, and the poor-law guardians were abolished and their functions transferred to the local authorities in 1929. However, the trend towards giving the new local-government system more responsibilities was by no means a uniform one, and it was also the case that from the beginning of the twentieth century more intervention in local authority matters was exercised by central government. Sometimes this was intervention on the grounds of efficiency and economy, sometimes it was intervention to maintain minimum standards, but the overall effect was clear. By the inter-war period, the defenders of locally based administration had become concerned that central-government control was debilitating the whole structure of British local government.

The literature which analyses local government's weaknesses and urges reform has its twentieth-century origins in the inter-war period immediately after local government had acquired massive new responsibilities in the form of poor-law duties.

Such writers as W. A. Robson identified, among other weaknesses in the existing structure of local government, the continuing removal of functions from local control, either to central government directly or to updated versions of the specially constituted authorities of Chadwick's day.[11] Such a transfer of power and loss of functions was like a slow process of bloodletting which weakened and debilitated the patient and proclaimed his unsuitability for arduous tasks. Between the publication of Robson's early work on local government in 1931 and the transfer of power to newly created authorities in 1974, local government had lost the responsibility for trunk roads, hospitals, public assistance and for many public utilities including water, which was made the responsibility of a network of new water authorities after the Local Government Act of 1972. The argument for these transfers was that local authorities were unable to perform these specific tasks proficiently because of their limited resources in terms of finance and in terms of area. (It was ironic that water and ancillary health services were transferred closely on the heels of legislation designed to remedy these defects in the system.)

The transfer of local-government functions to specially created *ad hoc* authorities in the twentieth century differed from the nineteenth-century establishment of authorities for special purposes because in many twentieth-century cases the element of popular control was lost. The twentieth-century authorities – unlike the Boards of Guardians, the Highway Boards, the Sanitary Boards, the Burial Boards and the School Boards – were not elected and were not accountable to any democratically elected bodies for their day-to-day transactions. Indeed, even in policy matters their accountability left much to be desired. The inevitable result of this process of transfer was that not only were important services being removed from popular control altogether, but that those services which were left under local administration were affected by a consequent lack of confidence and deterioration in morale. The less local authorities retained in the way of major social and regulatory functions, the more difficult it became to recruit able professional administrators and talented councillors. Equally, the less the direct impact of local matters on the lives of the electorate, the less likely it was that enough interest in local affairs would be generated even to ensure the casting of votes at local elections. In the late 1950s it therefore seemed that many of the elements which had given British local government its distinct style and vigour were rapidly disappearing and that British democracy at the grass-roots level was very frail. Thus the idea of reform was generated in part as a way of arresting this spiral of decline and preventing the local arena of politics in the United Kingdom from being transformed into a simple outpost of regional administration.

The election of a Labour Government in 1964 meant that reform of the structure of local government was likely to be initiated. Socialist policies were bound to draw attention to the weaknesses of the existing structure since any measures aimed at improving the quality of welfare services would largely depend for their success on the administrative efficiency of local bodies. The Labour Party had come to power with a programme which highlighted the need for institutional reforms of a comprehensive kind in a number of areas of British life, and there was within the Labour Party a distinct impatience with the improvised remedies which had marked the Conservative Government's approach to local-government matters between 1951 and 1963. There was also an awareness that – as the reform of local government in London in 1963 had shown – there was a distinct party advantage to be gained from being the initiator and controller of such changes.[12] If local government were to be reformed at some point in the future, better from the Labour Party's viewpoint that it be done under Labour guidance than to wait until another general election allowed the Conservatives to decide the principles on which reform was to be executed.

The desire to tackle the anomalies in the structure of local government in a systematic and comprehensive fashion was translated into political action largely as a result of the personality of Richard Crossman, the Minister of Housing and Local Government in Wilson's 1964–6 administration. Local-government reform was something to which he claimed to have a strong personal commitment, despite knowing little about it, and it seems that Crossman managed to commit the Labour Government to major reform before the matter had been discussed in Cabinet.[13] Yet the likelihood that any reforms which might emerge from this initiative would contribute substantially to revitalizing local government, or indeed do anything to redress the balance between central and local power, was greatly reduced by the decision to exclude the problem of finance from the terms of reference to the two Royal Commissions established in 1966 to investigate the problems of local government in England and in Scotland.[14] Thus the financial relationship which was in many ways the major determinant of the extent to which local autonomy could survive in the context of the second half of the twentieth century, and which reflected the weaknesses of the British local-government structure, was separated from the reform of that structure in a way which, as the Layfield Committee later remarked, made it unlikely that reforms in either sphere would prove satisfactory.

The exclusion of finance from the ambit of the Royal Commissions' inquiry underlined one of the major difficulties which confronts any government seeking to reform local government – the enormous interest which existing authorities and personnel have in maintaining the status quo. Indeed, the very membership of the Royal Commission on Local Government in England under the chairmanship of Lord Redcliffe-Maud highlighted this difficulty; for it was necessary for the Secretary of State to include on the Commission representatives of the existing authorities and to ensure that the perspective of the county boroughs was balanced by representatives of county opinion. The Commission, when it reported in 1969, recommended the complete abolition of the old structure of local government and the establishment of a quite different pattern of authorities. Its majority report had followed on from its analysis of the weaknesses of local government, but when legislation was ultimately introduced to amend the system it was done in a way which seemed to ignore the force behind the Commission's reasoning.

The Commission was convinced that the most important fault in the system of local government at that time was the structural one, and that the jungle of areas and jurisdictions was too complicated and also failed to reflect the habits of life of contemporary British society. It attacked the fragmentation of England into forty-five counties and seventy-nine borough authorities which, it said, had made 'the proper planning of development and transportation' impossible. Moreover the Commission attacked the division of responsibility within the county areas between the county council itself, which performed some major functions such as education, and district councils, which performed minor functions such as refuse disposal and some major ones such as housing. In effect this division meant that services which should have been administered in the framework of a consistent policy were in the hands of several authorities. A strong supportive relationship ought, it held, to exist between such services as housing, education and the personal social services, but this was impossible while responsibility was thus divided; the structural divisions, which precluded a co-ordinated approach to social welfare matters centred on the family, were also an impediment to a rational and integrated approach to policy in the fields of housing, traffic and planning. The analysis by the Commission of the problems of English local government was therefore characterized by the belief that the functions of local authorities were interdependent and ought to be exercised in as close a conjunction as possible. The logical extension of this approach was that, as far as possible, the local authorities, outside the large city areas where different principles might be applied, ought to be unitary and multi-purpose, and not, as they were outside the county boroughs, divided into tiers.

The principle that the ideal authority would exercise all local-government functions had the obvious implication that local authorities would have to be large enough to exercise the number of functions involved and to provide the range of services previously provided by the counties. Indeed, the Commission saw the determination of the correct size for a local authority in terms of population and area as one of the most significant of its tasks. Yet here the conflict of values within the system as a whole became most apparent. For insofar as the survey data commissioned for the Redcliffe-Maud inquiry yielded any information about the unit of administration with which people most readily identified – a criterion which could be used to establish the optimum size of an authority for facilitating civic interest and participation – the results suggested that the majority of the electorate identified with their community in terms of smaller rather than larger units of administration. The implications of this information ran counter to much of the argument made elsewhere in the Commission's report, which suggested that increased mobility in twentieth-century Britain justified a corresponding expansion of scale in local authorities without any danger of impairing the sense of local community. The search for an ideal size of authority also placed in sharp relief the incompatibility of a reorganization based on the assumption that high priority ought to be given to the managerial aspects of local administration with one designed to heighten the sense of local control and self-government of a given neighbourhood or area.

The search for the answer to the problem of what size of authority can best combine the requirements of managerial efficiency and economies of scale with a sense of local control was not an easy one. The need to provide a large number of services in the Commission's view pointed to a minimum population of 250,000, although representation from officials concerned primarily with education suggested that as far as education was concerned 500,000 was the minimum figure for the provision of a full range of services. At the other end of the scale, the Commission felt that it would become difficult to organize services efficiently, and to maintain proper liaison between a councillor and his constituents, if an authority exceeded one million in size. The Commission concluded by urging that the existing two-tier system of authorities should be replaced by fifty-eight unitary authorities which would cover most of the country. In three metropolitan areas, however, responsibilities would be divided between the metropolitan area, which could plan the city's overall development, and large district authorities, which would exercise responsibilities in the fields of education, the personal social services, health and housing. The Royal Commission's report was published in 1969 and the Labour Government, although it made one or two amendments to the scheme, fundamentally accepted the analysis and proposals of the majority. But those proposals did not command universal support and there was much criticism of the assumption that small authorities could not be efficient. When the time to introduce legislation came, it was a Conservative Government that was in power, and the legislation was based not on the coherent analysis of the Commission but on the basis of a compromise which rationalized the system of county authorities but retained a division of responsibilities between two tiers of government. The Conservative Government's decision to maintain a division of responsibility between county and lower-level authorities was based on the argument that the size of authority envisaged by the Redcliffe-Maud Commission would be too large to foster a sense of association with the decision-making process. Fear of remote authorities thus significantly influenced the rejection of the Commission's principles. It should, however, be noted that the Royal Commission on Local Government in Scotland – the Wheatley Commission – had favoured a two-tier rather than a unitary system and that Derek Senior's minority report to the Royal Commission on Local Government in England had also favoured a two-tier system, although one based on the concept of the city region. But in opposition to the natural political instincts of the Conservative Government to strengthen existing county and local-government loyalties, it was argued that the cost of reorganization – both in crude financial terms and in terms of the disruption caused to local-authority staff and voluntary associations whose activities were focused on local government – could really be justified only if the opportunity were taken to remedy major flaws in the system in a radical and comprehensive manner. (The impact of piecemeal reform and reorganization inevitably was such as to affect the quality of the service provided, and at the very least to limit the ability of an agency to plan or co-ordinate efficiently. One indicator of this effect of the administrative fashion for reorganization was that an investigation into the operations of statutory social services and their response to New Commonwealth immigration found that no less than seven of the eight types of agency approached were to some extent distracted from their primary duties by the prospect of an impending reorganization.)[15]

A structure was now created in which functions were divided between two levels of decision making and in which the second level, the district, exhibited the weaknesses identified in the old system by the Commission which thought areas of that size were incapable of sustaining important services such as housing. The integration of the personal social services with education and housing functions, which the Seebohm Committee had recommended and which the Redcliffe-Maud Commission had endorsed in principle, thus became impossible.[16] Also, the functions of planning and housing, which had acquired additional significance since 1945, remained divided – although the Conservative Government acknowledged the need to draw the exercise of these functions together, and accordingly introduced a special device – the structure committee – to co-ordinate district and county authorities in the process of planning the area as a whole. Thus 'reform' when it came was very much a patched-up affair and the new system, while it has settled some problems, has been an object of continuing criticism.

The New System

The great majority of the county areas created under the 1972 Act were based on the old shires in order to retain the links with the past which the Conservative Party and many of the county authorities themselves thought important. (Indeed it was largely due to the county authorities' successful lobbying that the 1972 Act created metropolitan areas far less extensive in scope than those envisaged by Redcliffe-Maud, though this saving of areas for the county effectively undermined the principle which had run through the Royal Commission's thinking – that the dichotomy between town and country ought to be obliterated.) In three areas, however, new county authorities were established – Avon, Cleveland and Humberside – which represented the subordination of historic loyalties to administrative convenience, as did the abolition of the smaller counties – Herefordshire, Rutland and Westmorland – in order to produce county areas which conformed to the new population norm. (Another small county, Middlesex, had been abolished in the wake of the reorganization of London government in 1963.)

In addition to these basic changes there were many minor boundary alterations in order to ensure that as far as possible local-government boundaries did not partition natural social and economic areas and did reflect the pattern of life of their inhabitants. This goal is of course always a difficult one to achieve, for the pattern of life can alter substantially over quite a short period of time in response to such factors as the growth or decline of local industry, the siting of new roads or an airport or even changes in preferences for inner-city living or suburban dwelling.

The Royal Commission on Local Government in England had recommended that in addition to the proposed multi-purpose authorities which constituted the core of its ideal system there should be two additional levels of authority. In order to meet the criticism that its new pattern of unitary authorities would be too large for real democratic participation and responsiveness, the Royal Commission had proposed a system of elected parish councils which could function as the organs of local communities below the unitary authority. These parish councils would have advisory powers and could develop into vehicles for the expression of community feeling on such issues as recreational amenities and planning applications. The Royal Commission had also envisaged a tier of councils above the unitary authorities; it thought that these regionally based councils could exercise responsibility for the range of planning functions which demanded larger areas than the unitary authorities covered.

It has been suggested that the separation of the reform of the structure of local government from the reform of regional administration – like the separation of the reform of local government structure from that of local government finance – reduced the chances of success in either sphere, and meant that a comprehensive and integrated approach to the problems of decentralization was impossible. In the context of Welsh and Scottish administration, the reforms were rapidly overtaken by the demands for more radical devolution. The question of parish councils, on the other hand, has to some extent remained a live issue in the politics of local government because although the 1972 Local Government Act did not adopt the Royal Commission's proposed unitary authorities it did make provision for the creation of parish councils, as well of course as for the secondary tier of councils, the metropolitan and non-metropolitan districts.

The need for parishes was a two-fold one in the view of the Government: they had the role of transmitting community feeling to higher authorities and they played a significant part in the practical function of small-scale administration. Rural areas were automatically divided into parishes but the provision of small-scale units of representation was not confined to rural or semi-rural areas: the district councils of urban areas were allowed to seek 'successor parish status' and some have done so. The problem in relation to an urban area, however, was to identify the community upon which the parish could be based; whereas it was envisaged that parishes would normally have a population of between ten thousand and twenty thousand the Department of the Environment recognized that in some cases it might be appropriate to grant parish status to a community with slightly more inhabitants than these guidelines suggest. In urban areas, neighbourhood councils, which unlike parishes are non-statutory bodies, are an alternative form of community organization. These neighbourhood councils are extremely diverse in scope and constitution and by no means all of them are elected. However, they have allegedly proved particularly useful in conveying local sentiment to housing authorities and in facilitating the participation of residents in planning matters. Both parish councils, of which there are well over ten thousand, and neighbourhood councils provide an arena in which the various local residents' and amenity groups, as well as more general pressure groups such as those concerned with the problem of homelessness, can promote their activities on a very small scale.[17]

The review of parish boundaries and the consideration of applications for successor parish status are functions of the Local Boundary Commissions. The establishment of permanent Local Boundary Commissions as a result of the reforms of 1972 eased the task of reconciling the discrepancy between local-government boundaries and population patterns. The English Commission was responsible for the initial delineation of district boundaries; county boundaries, which were much more contentious, had originally to be settled by the Department of the Environment but henceforward revision of county boundaries will be the responsibility of these Boundary Commissions, as will all other local-government boundaries. In 1978 the English Local Government Boundary Commission announced that its programme over the period 1978–83 would involve a consideration of the reports from district councils on their parish reviews and over 1984–9 the general review of all county, metropolitan and London borough districts, as required by the Local Government Act of 1972.[18] (This Act provides that the Boundary Commissions should undertake a comprehensive review of boundaries every ten to fifteen years, although the Commissions could also undertake priority reviews in exceptional circumstances.)

Internal Structure

It was not only the structure of local-government areas and functions which had been subjected to rigorous scrutiny in the 1960s and 1970s. The internal organization of local authorities had also given rise to criticisms, which had in turn led to experiments with the apparatus of local decision making.

The traditional manner of organizing local-authority work was through committees. There were some committees which were mandatory: education and police matters are examples of subject areas where local-government Acts have reflected the necessity of ensuring that the relevant local authority establishes some forum for dealing with specific business. In a committee organized on party lines, the chairmanship used invariably to be taken by a member of the majority group on the council; indeed, Labour's model rules explicitly forbid members of a council Labour group from entering into any pact or arrangement which breaks this understanding. A committee was staffed by the local authority's full-time officials, who were organized in a departmental rather than a comprehensive local-government service.

At the apex of the professional local-government service under the old system stood the Town Clerk. His training was almost invariably a legal one – he was usually a solicitor – and his pre-eminence in the local bureaucracy symbolized the extent to which the *mores* of local-government service differed from those of the civil service at the national level. For whereas recruitment to the civil service has been dominated by the Oxbridge graduate in a general discipline, the recruitment to local government was on professional lines; in addition the development of a sense of a general administrative local-government service was very late in coming, and is by no means universal even now. In part the difference reflects the constitutional distinction between the two strata of government. The civil service at the highest levels has always been oriented towards advising ministers, and a great deal of its decision making has involved the exercise of discretion. In local government, on the other hand, the *ultra vires* rule and the concept of illegal expenditure made it important to ascertain that any decisions taken were in conformity with statutory authority.

The fact that traditionally local authorities were organized on committee lines means not merely that power was diffused but that it was often difficult to foster a sense of local-authority identity and responsibility for the whole range of functions within an authority's jurisdiction. The Maud and the Mallaby Committees of the 1960s recommended a number of reforms in the internal structure of councils, and both suggested that in future the Town Clerk should be regarded as a figure with a general administrative role and that his training should emphasize the managerial rather than the legal aspects of local-authority affairs. When local government's structural reforms had been decided, a further committee – the Bains Committee – was set up, in 1971, to determine what opportunities the imminent reorganization offered for general reform in the internal structure of the new authorities.[19]

The Report of the Bains Committee placed a great deal of emphasis on the need for corporate management as opposed to the compartmentalization of administration by committee subject. The Report also advocated a change in the general administrative hierarchy. Instead of a Town Clerk, the local authority should have as its senior official a Chief Executive, and each authority, it was suggested, should have a general policy committee, as some authorities already did. This committee could set priorities, assess resources and monitor the effectiveness of policy in a way which would give some unity to the diverse activities of the local authority. The concept of a Chief Executive had been pioneered by T. Dan Smith in Newcastle in the 1960s; the theory was that he would have no formal department, or indeed departmental responsibilities, of his own, but would be responsible for co-ordinating the work of other departments. In this he would be advised and supported by a team of management officers. This recommendation reflected the Bains Committee's concern to change the style of local administration by giving greater attention to personnel and policy matters as opposed to legal and financial ones, although it may be doubtful whether such concern has survived the financial stringencies of the late 1970s.

The idea of a general strategy committee has become quite common among the new local authorities. The Local Government Act of 1972 reflected the view, inherent in the Bains Report, that local authorities should be made freer of central controls on their internal organization. Thus there are now fewer committees which are mandatory, although a local authority must still appoint an education committee, a police committee and a social services committee if it is the authority administering that service. (In most cases this will be the county authority.) As well as these statutory committees there is likely to be a range of subject-oriented committees, and in addition some joint committees with other authorities for such purposes as planning. (There are also arrangements for councillors to be nominated to water and area health authorities so that the latter authorities are interlinked with local government.)

One of the functions of local government in the wider political system is to offer an opportunity for participation in the country's public life below the level of national affairs. This role writers such as Mill considered to be extremely important, for it was at once educative and an insurance against benevolent despotism. One of the most marked features of local politics in recent years has been the growth of pressure-group activity centred on the local level of administration and concerned specifically with the quality of services provided locally. Thus the activities of such groups as Shelter, the Child Poverty Action Group and Age Concern have given a new dimension to local participation which complements the role of more orthodox party activity in providing a channel for civil and political activity.

The Local Government Act of 1972 made four years the period of office for both county and district councillors, although there is no uniformity in respect of electoral districts.

Thus while county councillors are re-elected *en bloc* every four years in single-member constituencies, district authorities can choose whether to elect their councillors in staggered elections or as a whole. They can also choose whether to elect them through multi-member or single-member constituencies. The provisions for the metropolitan districts were different again: these now elect one-third of their councillors in single-member constituencies in each of the three years in which there is no election for the metropolitan county council.

Since reorganization in England and Wales, the vast majority of elections have been organized on party political lines, although in some areas there remains a reluctance to extend the concerns of national politics to the local electoral level. Indeed, even where politics at the local level are apparently organized on party lines, the party label may conceal the fact that the political orientations and beliefs of councillors are much more local than national; the interpretation of a party's values may be modified considerably by the specific problems of a particular area.

The reasons why reorganization led to an extension of party politics are not hard to find. The amalgamation of the style of county politics with that of the boroughs meant that the distinct ethos of the rural areas, where independent councillors are most commonly found, was submerged in the new units. The survival of independent politics can be partly explained in terms of isolation from the issues and personnel of national parties, but that isolation could no longer persist when town and country were integrated for administrative purposes. Equally important, the process of reorganization created new prizes for the parties, and the temptation to control the new structure promoted an extension of party activity and party contests. Also, because the county exercises such important functions as education and social services under the new system there is a very real reason to contest county elections from the point of view of a Labour group which might hitherto have had control of education in a county borough and therefore not been so concerned with county policies. The decline of independent local politics is greatest where urbanization is highest; thus over half the district councils which were still controlled by independents in 1976 in England and Wales were in the seven western counties of Cornwall, Devon, Shropshire, Hereford and Worcester, Powys, Gwynedd and Dyfed.[20]

Local government can therefore be increasingly regarded not merely as a means of extending civic participation but as a new field of partisan activity. Indeed, service on the local council provides a training and recruiting ground for national politics. In the United Kingdom it is rare for local politics to be used as a power base from which an individual may enter national politics, and only the highly unusual careers of Joseph Chamberlain and Herbert Morrison spring to mind as ones in which long service on a local authority has been followed by cabinet office. One term of office as a local councillor as a means of developing credit with the local party is a much more common background for an aspiring MP than a decade or two spent administering local-government functions. Moreover, there is here a substantial difference between the parties: the tradition of municipal politics as a background for Westminster is much more common in the Labour Party than in the Conservative Party. As one authority has shown, of all Conservatives elected during the period 1945–October 1975 the percentage with experience of local-government office was 25.8% whereas the Labour figure for the same period was 45.3%. The number of Conservatives who see local government as a suitable preparation for parliamentary politics has increased recently, it is true; but the influence of such work on the choices made by Conservative selection committees is not entirely clear.[21]

Yet whatever the value of local government in the general process of civic education and political training, it has long been recognized that the system of local government is heavily dependent on its personnel. The structural reforms of the 1972–4 period were intended partly to make local-authority service a more attractive career for officials and to ensure that the staff recruited in the future had the appropriate level of managerial and technical skills. If reorganization inevitably entailed a substantial increase in the level of salaries paid, at the time it thought to be merely a belated recognition of the scale of local-government activities and the need to change the assumptions about employment in the service as a whole. Concern about the quality of recruits to local government was not, however, solely directed towards the permanent employees of the service. By the 1960s it was also thought that it was becoming increasingly difficult to persuade talented and competent people to stand for election as councillors; and councillors, it appeared, were unrepresentative of the community in that there was generally among their numbers a much higher percentage of retired and middle-class people than the socio-economic characteristics of the society as a whole would warrant.

Detailed surveys of the characteristics of councillors, the hours devoted to council activities and the financial implications of their membership of a local authority have been undertaken since the 1960s. The most recent study by the Department of the Environment attempted to compare its findings with those of the surveys done for the Maud Committee on the Management of Local Government and in 1965 for the Royal Commission on Local Government in Scotland.[22] It was interesting to compare developments across the decade partly because in the period between the two surveys the need to encourage people to stand for election to their local authorities had prompted the introduction of attendance allowances. Such payments, it was thought, would improve the representativeness of local councillors by ensuring that council service did not carry a financial disincentive in addition to the difficulties of combining council duties with normal employment.

The general impression given by the 1976 Department of the Environment survey is that, although the broad picture of the typical councillor has remained accurate over the period 1964–76, there have been some slight changes. Women councillors have increased as a proportion of all councillors from 12% in 1964 to 17% in 1976, although this is, as the report points out, still grossly out of line with the proportion of women in the population as a whole. Councillors remain older than the general population. However, by 1976 it seemed that the proportion of councillors in the younger age-groups had increased; London boroughs had the highest proportion of young councillors; the English and Welsh counties tended to have slightly older councillors. The proportion of economically active councillors had also increased since 1964, and this trend was reflected in a corresponding decline in the proportion of retired councillors and the change in the age distribution. How-ever, as far as distribution between occupations is concerned, the Department's survey found that manual workers were still seriously underrepresented in the ranks of local councillors: seven out of ten councillors either were or had been involved in non-manual occupations, and councillors included more than twice the proportion of administrators, managers and technical workers than existed in the population as a whole.

One marked change in the characteristics of councillors as a group over the period 1964–76 concerned educational qualifications. Whereas only 23% of all councillors in 1964 were graduates, by 1976 that figure had risen to 50%. Perhaps this change reflects in part the increase in higher educational opportunities, but it may also reflect a change in the kind of individual whom local selection committees are anxious to recruit for council membership.

The Department of the Environment's 1976 survey made a distinction between council members and 'leaders' – defined as councillors who held major jobs such as Chairman or Mayor, Vice-Chairman or Deputy-Mayor, majority party leader and committee chairman or convenor. The survey found women far less well represented among council 'leaders' than among councillors as a whole and it found that 'leaders' tended to be somewhat older than other members. It also found that the self-employed represented over a third (35%) of economically active councillors.

One interest of the survey was to ascertain how council members distributed their time and whether more hours were being devoted to council work than in the past. It emerged from the survey that more time was being spent by councillors on council activity in 1976 than in 1964 and that the increase had been in the order of 50%, from a level of 52 hours per month to 79 hours per month. The vast majority of that extra time was spent on council and committee work and on electors' problems rather than on such activities as serving on nominated authorities such as water boards, serving as school governors or attending semi-social functions related to the council.[23]

This increase in the amount of work associated with local-government service is probably not explicable by reference to any single factor. Undoubtedly the size and complexity of local-authority functions make it necessary to devote more time to their routine administration, while the expansion of competitive party politics has provided an impetus for additional contact between councillors and electors. On the other hand the trend of the last decade – particularly the introduction of attendance allowances – has been to emphasize the need for councillors to approach their tasks in a professional manner so that the councillors elected in that period may expect to spend more time on council affairs. (It was noted that the average councillor claimed an attendance allowance for 42% of the time spent on council work.) Certainly the rise in the proportion of councillors with higher educational qualifications suggests that local-authority service is attracting its fair share of the best-educated sections of society – although a fall in the number of manual workers elected might make some voters feel that local authorities might be remote from them and so unresponsive to their needs.

The need to secure a greater proportion of economically active councillors was perhaps not the only reason for introducing attendance allowances for local councillors as part of local-government reform in 1972. Another problem which had worried many observers of local authorities in the 1960s was that of corruption. The standards of probity at the national level of politics in the United Kingdom are relatively high, by comparison for example with the United States. In part this could be because British central government has limited direct commercial responsibilities – a feature of it which may diminish as government departments intervene in more areas of the economy. At national level, the alternation of parties in government is a disincentive to stray too far from an agreed code of ethics, although again in relation to appointments and honours the situation may be changing. Corruption has long been a feature of some local authorities, however, partly because the functions which local authorities perform, particularly the granting of building and planning permissions, create opportunities for financial gain which do not exist at the national level. The Royal Commission on the Standards of Conduct in Public Life, reporting in the aftermath of the Poulson affair, which produced evidence of corruption in the awarding of public contracts, was preceded by a special committee headed by Lord Redcliffe-Maud to examine local-government law and practice in relation to situations where a conflict of interest existed between members' and officers' positions in local government and their private interests. The Redcliffe-Maud Committee recommended that a register of the interests of a council should be kept and that this should include information about such matters as paid directorships, consultancies, shareholding and the tenancies both of a member himself and of his spouse. The Royal Commission, which was a much more far-reaching investigation of the field, thought that the national code of local-government conduct recommended by the Redcliffe-Maud Committee should be amended to emphasize the dangers inherent in the attendance at social functions organized by outside bodies liable to undertake business with a local council; it suggested that a councillor's attendance at such functions should always require authorization.[24]

The machinery for objections to a council decision was improved by the Local Government Act of 1974; this introduced a network of local ombudsmen under the direction of a collegiate Commission for Local Administration in England and a Commission for Local Administration in Wales. (A Commission for Local Administration in Scotland was established a year later with a slightly different constitution.) The Commissions' jurisdiction covers local authorities, water authorities and police authorities as well as any joint board of which local authorities are constituent parts; the Commissions may examine any complaint made by or on behalf of a citizen who claims to have experienced 'injustice' in consequence of 'maladministration'. Thus the local ombudsmen, like their parliamentary counterpart, are restricted to an examination of procedural irregularities rather than the merits of decisions.[25] It is perhaps too early to tell how successful the institution has been in the process of improving the quality of local administration, but one significant development occurred in 1978 when Parliament passed legislation amending the 1974 Local Government Act to empower authorities to incur expenditure for the purpose of making a payment to an individual found to have suffered an injustice at the hands of that authority.[26] Thus there is now not merely more elaborate machinery for detecting maladministration at the local level, but also the opportunity of providing compensation when such maladministration is discovered.

Relationships with Central Government

The relationship between central and local government is a difficult one to characterize, for it varies considerably with the different priorities of national governments and from subject area to subject area.[27] The formal constitutional position – that local authorities are entirely subordinate to Parliament – reflected in the traditional *ultra vires* doctrine, and the political subordination of local government to central government, is apparent from the range of controls which can be exercised by central departments over local authorities. Moreover, the importance of the Treasury's contribution to the revenue of local authorities means that, in financial matters, the relationship is one in which the central government is the dominant partner – a fact which has become increasingly apparent since the 1975–6 grant settlement. Yet alongside the overwhelming constitutional, political and financial domination of local by central government, there has to be set the fact that the normal mode of conducting central–local discussions is that of negotiation rather than coercion, and that the tone of most local authorities' discussions with central departments is one of cooperation and harmony rather than antagonism. The variety between the level of services offered by individual authorities has itself been taken as an indication of how little effort or success has marked central government's attempts to impose its own priorities upon local government so that, although the mechanisms for influencing local policy undoubtedly exist, they have not been systematically used to create uniformity of provision. Of course there will be topics – and the reorganization of secondary education on non-selective lines is one example – where central government's wish to force a controversial policy on recalcitrant local authorities may lead to bitter conflicts between individual local authorities and a central department. Indeed, in the case of secondary-school reorganization the dispute led not merely to political arguments but also to court action, as at least one local authority was determined to deny the Minister's

interpretation of his statutory powers.[28] The tensions generated
by such a conflict often of course reflect ideological divisions
between the parties, although it would be superficial to see the
major parties as unambiguously identified with either a pro- or
anti-local autonomy position.

Conservative governments have as often eroded the autonomy
of local authorities in the name of economy as Labour governments have eroded their autonomy in the name of social justice
or egalitarianism. What is important to note, however, is that
because local elections are frequently used to register popular
dissatisfaction with the party in government rather than as a
verdict on local issues, control of the majority of local authorities
frequently lies with the opposition rather than the government party. In order to see how central government could
exert influence over local-government policy it is necessary
to examine the range of controls and devices which central
government has at its disposal and to sketch the outlines
of the financial interaction between the two levels of government.

The formal constitutional position of local authorities, as has
been mentioned, is encapsulated in the *ultra vires* doctrine. This
doctrine means that local authorities may only lawfully engage
in activities for which they have express statutory authority or
in activities which are reasonably incidental to ones for which
they have statutory authority. Activity for which no statutory
authority exists can be challenged in the courts and pronounced null and void if in fact local-authority action is found
to conflict with the *ultra vires* rule. The most famous example
of this restriction on local initiative was a 1921 case in which
it was decided that statutory powers given to Fulham Corporation under the Baths and Washhouses Acts of 1846–7
did not give that body the power to operate a municipal
laundry.[29]

Expenditure incurred in the pursuit of an activity which is
ultra vires is illegal expenditure and the District Auditor, who
is responsible for the examination of local-authority accounts,
may seek a declaration from the courts if he thinks any item of
local-authority expenditure falls into that category. The legal
control of unauthorized expenditure has in itself given rise to
political controversy in the past. Thus in 1925 the Poplar

Borough Council, which had used its discretion to pay employees a minimum wage of £4 a week regardless of the work involved, was found to have incurred an illegal expenditure when the practice was challenged in the High Court. The financial loss to the authority thereby occasioned had to be repaid by the councillors, a procedure known as 'surcharge'.[30]

Surcharge has been criticized as an unnecessarily savage penalty, for the scope of the concept of 'legal expenditure' remains uncertain; doubts in this area can affect the whole style of local administration by acting as a brake on initiative and making councillors extremely cautious in their conduct of public affairs. It is doubtful whether this still holds true, for councillors are likely to reflect on the legality of expenditure before entering into it.

Perhaps the most controversial case of surcharge in recent years occurred in 1973 when the councillors of Clay Cross in Derbyshire refused to raise council housing rents in accordance with the provisions of the Housing Finance Act of 1972. The Secretary of State for the Environment ordered a special audit of the urban district council's revenue account and the District Auditor found the council to be in default to the sum of £6,985, a sum which he ordered to be recovered by surcharge. The councillors appealed to the High Court under the Act which at that time governed this aspect of local-authority finance, the Local Government Act of 1933, but the Queen's Bench Division held that the surcharge had been correctly imposed because the resolution of the council to refuse to implement the rent-rebate scheme contained in the Housing Finance Act constituted negligence or misconduct within the meaning of s. 228(1) of the 1933 Act.[31] As the Court put the position, 'no matter how sincerely they believed in the course they followed, no matter how strong were their feelings of moral obligation and no matter whether this was a matter of policy or politics, the inescapable fact is that they quite clearly broke the law'. Such was the political anger engendered by the case, however, that when the Labour Government returned to power in February 1974 it relieved the councillors of the obligation to make good the deficit by the Housing Finance (Special Provisions) Act of 1975.[32]

The scope for local initiative over expenditure was widened

to some extent by the Local Government Act of 1972 which gives any local authority, including a parish council, the power to incur expenditure which is, in the authority's opinion, in the interests of its area or any part of it or in the interests of some or all of its inhabitants; this can include purposes for which an authority is neither authorized nor required to make a payment by virtue of some other statutory provision. This discretionary power to spend money on the general interests of the area is controlled by the restriction of expenditure to the product of a rate of 2 new pence in the £, although the inflation rate persuaded the Government to include in the Act a clause enabling the Secretary of State for the Environment to vary the rate upwards or downwards by statutory instrument.

Other extensions of the scope of local initiative, although they do not fundamentally affect the *ultra vires* principle, give local authorities the power to acquire land if in their opinion it is for the 'benefit, development, or improvement of their area', and the power to dispose of land held by them in any way that they wish. (This additional flexibility in relation to land does not extend to compulsory purchase, which is still subject to strict procedures; nor does it necessarily prevent the intervention of central government in the sale of council houses – an issue of some controversy between the major political parties.) In addition, certain statutory requirements concerning the committees which a local authority must appoint were also amended by the 1972 Act.

There are a variety of formal powers which central government can use if it wishes to determine the policy of local authorities in specific areas. The two most important are the power to approve appointments and the power to hold inspections. The power to approve appointments is perhaps most important in relation to the police: the Home Secretary has to approve the appointment or dismissal of a Chief Constable in the various police authorities.

Central intervention in local government is, indeed, extensive in relation to the whole range of police functions, for the Home Secretary has a general responsibility for the level of pay and the training in the police force. Since the passage of the Police Act in 1964 the involvement of the Home Office in the management of the country's police has increased, and such matters as police pay, the increase of crime and the eruption of terrorism have reinforced the national dimension of police administration. The Home Secretary also has substantial powers to issue detailed regulations on such topics as pay and service conditions, hears appeals from disciplinary proceedings inside local police authorities, and can ask for reports on the activities of the police within particular police authorities. These powers are rooted in the fact that the Home Office pays half the cost of the police services from money raised nationally from taxation; in the case of police efficiency the threat to withhold the percentage grant is a real one which has been used on a number of occasions. To a much lesser extent the Home Office also uses its powers to regulate pay and employment conditions to ensure that local authorities provide an efficient fire service.

The power to regulate senior appointments has recently been considerably extended. It became important in relation to a whole new range of posts when the Local Government Act of 1972, s. 112(4)g, made the appointment of Directors of Social Services in the new authorities subject to the approval of the Secretary of State for Health and Social Security. This supervisory power was partly the result of the recommendations of the Seebohm Committee's Report on Local Authority and Allied Personal Social Services; this was followed by legislation in 1970 – the Local Authority Social Services Act – which represented a major attempt by central government to influence the long-term development of local provision in the field of social services and to introduce a more integrated approach to what had hitherto been a disparate group of services.

The power to inspect the manner in which local-authority services are being conducted and to intervene in cases of inadequacy is as important as the power to approve appointments. The use of this power of inspection is especially relevant in relation to probation, after-care services and education: the DES maintains a corps of some four hundred inspectors who visit the schools and institutions of further education within local authorities and report to the Department on their findings. Yet the educational service is a sector where devices such as circulars, consultations and discussions are used much more frequently to communicate departmental policy to local authorities than the formal mechanisms. Departmental circulars are a good example of communications which can vary enormously in import and tone: some are merely for information, while others, and this is especially true in the DES where such circulars as those of October 1966 (10/66) and October 1970 (10/70) have acquired notoriety, have almost the status of departmental fiats which local authorities will defy at their peril. The growth of concern about declining educational standards has prompted the Department of Education and Science to institute an Assessment of Performance Unit, which is also possibly symptomatic of a changing climate in which traditional ideas of local-authority and school autonomy over curriculum content will be replaced by a greater degree of central control.[33]

However, it is in relation to the various aspects of finance that central-government control is felt most directly. Here, the very recent past has seen an increasingly hostile relationship between local authorities and government in London. National concern with the overall level of public expenditure has meant that local autonomy in such areas as educational expenditure has had to be severely curtailed, and many local-education authorities have had to make sudden adjustments in their teaching ratios in order to comply with cuts which have been imposed with some suddenness on local budgets. Naturally what looks like a rational policy when viewed from a central-government perspective occasions deep resentment when seen from the perspective of an individual school or even an individual local authority. Similarly an authority which has had to impose sudden, quite sharp rent increases on its tenants as a result of a change in central-government policy will dispute the logic of the new policy, even though if viewed from the perspective of Whitehall it might conceivably be acceptable. However, the main problem is not that, in a period of financial stringency, cuts in public expenditure and the imposition of cash limits automatically mean a sudden reduction in the quality of local-authority services, or even that at such a time medium-range planning becomes difficult; nor is it even that local authorities resent being used as instruments of financial planning and investment control. It is rather that, regardless of the level of expenditure involved, central government is the major source of local-authority revenue, and local authorities can control the distribution of this money only to a very limited extent; this enforces and sustains the feeling of dependence upon central government, and acts as a brake on the development of a truly autonomous structure of local democracy.

Local-authority expenditure can be divided into two parts – capital expenditure, which is expenditure on some asset of long-term benefit to an authority such as a school, and revenue expenditure.[34] As far as capital expenditure is concerned, the major restriction on a local authority's freedom is that any loan required to raise money has to be sanctioned by the appropriate government department. Revenue expenditure is derived from three distinct souces, although the balance between them is extremely uneven. First, there is the income derived from the rates, which are a local tax on real estate. Secondly, there is the money which is paid out to local authorities each year in the form of grants. Some of these grants may be specific contributions which represent a percentage cost of providing a service, for example 50% of the expenditure on the police services. Most of them, however, are paid out to local authorities each year in the form of general money given to meet the shortfall between rates and total local-authority expenditure. Since 1966 such contributions have been known as the 'rate support grant'; once the money has been distributed between authorities on the basis of a complex formula, an individual authority is free to determine its spending priorities as it sees fit. This freedom is to some extent constrained by the need to meet minimum standards in some policy areas and by electoral expectations, but otherwise, once the money has been allocated to an authority, there is little government intervention. The third source of income is the money which the local authority itself obtains in return for some of the services which it provides. This source includes payments for council houses (rents and sales), school meals, transport and trading activities of various kinds. The balance between these different sources of revenue income has shifted throughout the post-war period as governments have laid more obligations on local authorities and have felt bound to finance themselves a higher proportion of the cost of local-authority services. The balance is now roughly that 61p for every £ of local-government expenditure comes from the Exchequer, 13p from receipts, and 26p from the rates.[35]

The calculation of the total amount of money available to all local authorities is done in consultation with them through a committee established in 1974 – the Consultative Council on Local-Government Finance. At this committee the major central departments concerned with local-government services – the Department of the Environment, the Department of Health and Social Security, the Department of Education and Science, the Home Office and the Treasury – meet with representatives of the local authorities to discuss the aggregate amount of assistance which the Exchequer can make available. This amount covers both specific grants, which are used primarily where the national government insists upon a minimum level of provision and where costs are uniform and high, and which amount to 10% of the total grant, and the rate support grant.

Once the total level of the rate support grant has been determined it is then distributed between the various local authorities according to a formula which can take into account the different social and economic characteristics of authorities. This formula has three elements known as 'domestic', 'needs' and 'resources'. The domestic element represents an attempt to compensate for the fact that rates are a regressive form of taxation and bear no relationship to the ability of a household to pay the sums demanded. National government therefore subsidizes the rates directly through the rate support grant; in 1974–5 this subsidy represented the equivalent of a reduction of 10p in the £ for householders. The needs content is based on general demographic factors and the socio-economic profile of the particular neighbourhood. This enables the basic allowance of each local authority to be weighted in proportion to such factors as population density, percentages of children of school age and percentages of old persons; it can compensate authorities where there are particularly heavy calls on their services.

The resources element in the grant attempts to ensure that local authorities which are relatively poor in terms of the money which they can raise from the rates – often precisely those authorities which have the greatest demands made upon them in terms of educational and social-service provision – are brought up to the national average in terms of *per capita* resources. Thus the overall formula for calculating the grant which each local authority will ultimately get has a strongly redistributive aspect; this contrasts strongly with the nature of the rating system itself, and represents an attempt by national government to iron out arbitrary inequalities between areas. Unfortunately the increasingly prominent role played by central government in the funding of local services has blurred the distinction between local and central accountability. Not only has increased central-government support been used to justify additional central-government intervention but often local authorities have felt unable to control their own policy areas and have sought to shift responsibility for the conduct of local services onto central government.

The pressures on local authorities and the major explosion in the rates in the years immediately following reorganization prompted the Government to establish an inquiry into the funding of local-government services. This Committee, the Layfield Committee, started from the assumption that the overall level of local expenditure would need to be carefully controlled, and suggested two broad ways of doing it. One method was further central intervention, although it should be noted that the Layfield Committee thought that the status quo was itself centralization by stealth. The alternative method which Layfield seemed to advocate as a way of strengthening and clarifying local-government accountability and responsibility was to reform the origins of locally based revenue by creating a local income-tax as a source of local finance in addition to the rate system. Such a proposal would have gone a long way towards arresting the erosion of local government, but the Labour Government evidently thought that such an innovation was too radical and in a green paper published in 1977 it rejected the proposals of the Layfield Committee, and indeed denied the analysis on which Layfield had based its recommendations. Instead the green paper chose what it called a 'middle way' between Layfield's centralist and localist solutions – a middle way which seems to be in effect a slightly centralized version of the existing arrangements.[36] The green paper did, however, make some recommendations for change.

It recommended a change in the mechanism of central control over capital expenditure, so that in future capital expenditure financed out of revenue and out of the proceeds of the sale of assets – as well as from loans – would need central-government approval, though this would not be on a project-by-project basis. It also proposed an extension of the District Auditor's role and an increase in the proportion of grants paid as specific grants or supplementary grants. Its major proposal – the substitution of a unitary grant for the rate support grant – seemed designed not so much to aid local accountability as to enable central government to exercise more direct control over local-authority spending.

The idea of a unitary grant, in which only the needs and resources elements in the formula would be taken into the calculation, stemmed from the desire of central government to have a less crude instrument of control than the rate support grant. At present, if government wishes to reduce the amount spent by local authorities it has to do so by reducing the overall level of the grant; this affects all authorities regardless of need or affluence, extravagance or financial caution. The unitary grant would enable government to make public its estimate of the necessary expenditure of an authority and, although an authority would be free to vary the amount of expenditure, if it overspent the shortfall would have to be met out of the rates. Such a system would probably increase central control and reduce the variation in expenditure levels which currently exists, for many councillors would find it hard to justify expenditure in addition to that recommended by government. Indeed it is the public nature of the proposed assessment which the local-authority associations have objected to so strongly.

The reform of local-government finance, like the reform of local-government structure undertaken earlier, seems calculated not so much to increase the independence and discretion of local authorities as to improve the machinery of administration according to the criteria currently fashionable in Whitehall. Perhaps the greatest chance for the survival of local-government independence lies in central government's inability to maintain a consistent and sustained view of what those criteria are to be, and its even greater inability to apply them with any rigour.

10 Government on the Ground II: The Diversity of the United Kingdom

The reassessment of the relationship between the component parts of the United Kingdom has been one of the most startling features of British politics since the 1960s. Until then most commentators had assumed that the country's highly centralized and unitary state reflected an underlying cultural homogeneity and political integration which was perhaps only to be expected in the world's first industrial nation. The first challenge to the unity of the United Kingdom, the demand for Irish Home Rule, might have been recognized as an indication that nationalism could be a disruptive and disintegrative force even in these islands; but somehow it has always proved possible to ignore the lessons of Ireland, and anyway it was for a long time confidently assumed that the remedy of partition had settled the Irish question. Developments since 1966 have, however, cast considerable doubt on the validity of the assumptions of homogeneity and have reawakened awareness of the diversity and variety within the United Kingdom and the possibility of political movements arising from this. The cultural, ethnic, and geographical divisions of the United Kingdom are not as multifarious as those that obtain in, for example, the United States; but nor are the sentiments of England – still less its political behaviour – identical to those of the rest of the United Kingdom.

The rediscovery of cultural diversity and the emergence of a series of claims for political treatment on the basis of these cultural and national divisions have generated a long debate about the constitutional arrangements of the United Kingdom.

In 1978, far-reaching proposals for change in the distribution of power between the centre of the United Kingdom and the periphery reached the statute book in the form of the Scotland Act and the Wales Act. If those acts had ever become operative, not only would the government of the United Kingdom have been even more complex than at present, but there would also have been considerable constitutional implications for the United Kingdom as a whole. For it is difficult to believe that the relationship between central, regional and local governments embodied in the Devolution Acts would not in due course have promoted at the very least a questioning of the existing relationship between central and local authorities in England, and it would probably have entailed more fundamental constitutional changes, for example in relation to the role of the judiciary. As it happened, the degree of support for the measures was not sufficient to warrant the implementation of the schemes and the Acts were repealed. However, at least in the case of Scotland opinion was very divided about the desirability of devolution, and the issue is likely to continue as a factor in Scottish politics, although it is of course unlikely that there will be any attempt in the immediate future to revive the 1978 scheme.

The emergence as serious influences on their countries' politics of nationalist movements in Scotland and Wales coincided with the resurgence of violence in Ulster. In a relatively short period of time, therefore, the political arrangements prevailing in the three non-English parts of the United Kingdom claimed general attention. (Indeed, the violence in Ulster was perhaps the main cause of writers' doubts that exclusively peaceful methods for the resolution of conflicts were still employed in the United Kingdom.)[1] Government policy did not, however, assume that these developments in the three non-English parts of the country had similar histories; it accordingly worked out separate strategies to deal with each of them, although the schemes for Scotland and for Wales seemed much more alike than the series of policies attempted in Northern Ireland after 1972.

The impression given by successive governments' handling of the devolution issue is thus somewhat untidy; it might have been preferable to have employed a comprehensive strategy for all the component parts of the United Kingdom rather than devising distinct arrangements for each of them. The absence of such a comprehensive approach is also rather surprising, for many of the arguments which the Labour Government previously deployed against a federal solution of the problem – that it might enhance judicial power or would be too rigid – were used against the final scheme accepted by the Government.

Yet in one way the arguments for not seeking to impose the same form of devolution on Scotland, Wales and Northern Ireland were sound: the separate regions or nations of the United Kingdom have different histories, and the political consciousness of each has been forged by specific experiences. To enable a proper assessment of the strength of nationalist demands within the United Kingdom, it is necessary initially to outline what those specific features are and how they have affected the political culture of each area.

Northern Ireland

Many of the same issues which have been raised quite recently in relation to devolution for Scotland and Wales, and their subsequent relationship with England, were raised long ago over the Irish question. Indeed, it was at the beginning of the twentieth century that the difficulties of governing Ireland and the solution of Home Rule prompted a general discussion of the merits of devolution for Scotland and Wales – 'Home Rule all round', as the slogan had it. In addition, the cause of devolution or Home Rule was taken up by a small all-party group of federalists who wanted to see a federal United Kingdom within the wider framework of the British Empire. The Irish question had bedevilled Westminster politics for much of the nineteenth and early twentieth centuries. Its return to the centre of the United Kingdom's political concerns has not perhaps been entirely admitted by politicians on the mainland, but it would hardly be denied that terrorism in Ulster itself and in England constitutes a radical challenge to the basis on which the Province is governed and a disruptive factor in the whole of the political system.

Between the Act of Union of 1800 and the Irish Treaty of 1921 the whole of Ireland was an integral part of the United Kingdom, although the colonization of Ireland had begun long before 1800. By the Act of Union of 1800, Irish MPs sat in the House of Commons at Westminster and representatives of the Irish peerage sat in the House of Lords. The Act had been modelled in many ways on the earlier and much more successful Act of Union with Scotland. Yet the attitudes which marked relationships between England and Ireland, and the form of government employed across the Irish Channel, suggested that Ireland was hardly on the same footing as Scotland in the eyes of the English. Indeed, in retrospect the treatment accorded to Ireland was strikingly similar to that which a colony would have received, and so were attitudes which supported that treatment. As formal head of the Irish administration there was a Lord Lieutenant, who was responsible to the Home Secretary, the formal channel of communication with the Crown. The Lord Lieutenant had relatively little responsibility for the routine administration of the country; this role fell to the Chief Secretary for Ireland, who sat in the House of Commons and was answerable to Parliament for the details of Irish administration and policy.

The difficulties of governing Ireland arose from the cultural conflicts which existed within the country; also, the hostility between the different communities there was translated into political antagonisms which other divisions within the society could not transcend. Basically, the complexities of Irish politics can be traced to three different communities, which differed in their customs, assumptions and values and which each regarded the values of the other communities as a threat to their own survival. First, there was the native population, which was marked by its adherence to the Roman Catholic religion and its Gaelic cultural heritage; its attitude towards the other groups was that of a dispossessed peasantry, for it considered the settlers to be alien colonists, the machinery of rule from Westminster to be illegitimate, and the true goal of Irishmen to be independence. Needless to say, it was this group which was to provide the backbone of the Irish nationalist movement, although not by any means all its leaders. The second group of significance was the Anglo-Irish component which had settled in Ireland and taken over its estates. Although quite different in cultural heritage and manners from the native Irish – the group was for one thing Protestant – it was sufficiently distinct from the English on the mainland to make identification with London imperfect. Indeed, the literature of the Irish renaissance and a great deal of the nineteenth-century agitation on Ireland's behalf owed as much to members of this section of the Irish population as to the native Irish. The final cultural entity in the country's triangle of conflict was the group which settled primarily in Ulster and which, although Protestant by religion, had Scottish origins and adhered to the Presbyterian faith rather than to the Anglican Church in Ireland. It was this group which settled and developed what became the industrialized parts of the country and which came to regard the development of Irish nationalism as such a threat to its economic status, political sentiments and cultural identity that violence was almost inevitable.

Between these groups there was little comprehension and still less social interaction. Religion was the badge of their distinct communities, but it also represented cultural divisions which went deeper than confessional differences alone. Also, just as the three communities were isolated from each other inside Ireland so there was a comparable distance, both intellectual and social, between the inhabitants of Ireland and the rest of the United Kingdom.

The spread of Irish nationalism in the late nineteenth century and the attempts from the 1880s to grant Ireland Home Rule stimulated the Protestants of Ulster to resist any settlement in which they might be left a small minority – no more than 27% – in a political system which would be dominated by the Roman Catholic Church. Indeed, on the eve of the First World War it was apparent that Ulster's Protestant population would resist Home Rule, if need be by force of arms.

As it became clear that only some form of partition offered any hope of a peaceful solution, Parliament in 1920 passed the Government of Ireland Act providing for separate Home Rule Parliaments, for six northern counties at Belfast and for the remaining twenty-six counties in Dublin. The subsequent strife in the South brought about the Irish Treaty of 1921 by which the South became a dominion, albeit a restless one, until in 1949 it became an independent republic outside the Commonwealth.[2] Meanwhile Ulster continued to operate the devolved institutions conferred upon it by the 1920 Act. Unfortunately for the ultimate viability of this solution the division between north and south did not eradicate the communal tensions: within Northern Ireland there was a substantial minority of Roman Catholics – about a third of the whole population – for whom the border was only a temporary solution, and in whose eyes the institutions of the Province enjoyed little or no legitimacy.

From 1921 until its Parliament's suspension in 1972 Ulster enjoyed a large measure of autonomy within the United Kingdom. The Ulster Parliament, which had both a House of Commons and a Senate, sat at Stormont Castle and there was a separate executive which dealt with a wide range of matters and was responsible to it. Westminster remained responsible for the defence and foreign policy of Northern Ireland and for its overall economic policy; naturally it remained the superior legislature.

The relationship between Northern Ireland and the rest of the United Kingdom was an extremely unusual one, both constitutionally and politically. For although there was theoretical subordination to Westminster and although there were twelve Northern Irish representatives at Westminster, the two political systems hardly interacted at all. This was partly the result of London's unwillingness to be drawn back into Irish politics, and partly because the constitutional settlement of 1920 had been quasi-federal in character. It had recognized a division of powers on the basis of subject matter and had established – as did the 1978 Scotland Act also – a special procedure for determining disputes about the proper allocation of powers between the two authorities. The special procedure was designed to decide constitutional arguments with the minimum of political friction; disputes were referred to the Judicial Committee of the Privy Council, a court which was the final court of appeal for Commonwealth countries with written constitutions.

The constitutional structure thus erected might have been expected to have reassured the Protestants of Ulster that the connection between the United Kingdom and their own way of life was safe. However, the degree of autonomy accorded them was balanced by the retention of formal legislative powers which could be used to amend the settlement at any time – though it was not until 1972 that Westminster used those powers to supersede the political wishes of the majority of the Province's population. Because of the doctrine of parliamentary sovereignty, Stormont could not be entrenched. At the same time, the differential birth rate between the Catholic and the Protestant populations provided another source of anxiety because it suggested that Protestants might not always be in the majority in the Province. Although the Ireland Act of 1949, which recognized the independence of the Irish Republic, affirmed that the status of Northern Ireland would not be altered without the consent of its Parliament, no piece of legislation could securely bind Westminster's hands in the future, so that Ulster's political system was based on less than firm constitutional ground. This insecure position largely explains the value attributed by Protestant militants, through such organizations as the Orange Order, to the symbolism of parades and marches, even when these are obviously inflammatory to the Catholic population. It also helps to explain why the apparently innocuous suggestion for a Council of Ireland which accompanied the abortive power-sharing constitution of 1973 aroused Protestant suspicions that the Westminster Parliament was abnegating its commitment to the continuation of Ulster's link with the United Kingdom.

It was not simply because of Ulster's constitutional status that its society and politics seemed anomalous to observers from the rest of the United Kingdom. Although Northern Ireland had been formed because the majority in the Province abhorred the idea of incorporation into a Roman Catholic Ireland, the majority of Protestants in the north made little attempt to conciliate those Catholics who remained within the Province's boundaries and whose dissatisfaction might threaten Ulster's stability. The 1920 Act had recognized the dilemma of a political system in which a third of the population was likely to look across the border for a government which possessed legitimacy; there was thus an attempt to incorporate into the constitution guarantees of equal treatment before the law for both communities in the north. The Act of 1920 specifically prohibited Stormont from giving 'a preference, privilege or advantage' or imposing any 'disability or disadvantage on account of religious belief, or religious or ecclesiastical status'.

Such a prohibition was, however, quite without force in the climate of mutual suspicion which prevailed between Ulster's religious communities. What has been very aptly called an 'institutionalized caste system' developed, and in that system the Protestant majority dominated the political institutions of Northern Ireland, maintaining its power through a variety of mechanisms, such as the gerrymandering of local-government boundaries – means which would have caused outrage had they been employed on the mainland of Britain. In addition to the political supremacy which they sustained through the Ulster Unionist Party, Protestants enjoyed a virtual monopoly of municipal jobs and housing facilities, while segregation on religious lines was evident on municipal and private housing estates, in private employment and in education. As in all modern societies where religious issues retain political importance, the character and control of education has always been a salient political issue in Ireland. The divisions caused by segregated education are mainly the product of Roman Catholics' desire to send their children to schools which are both willing to provide instruction in the Roman Catholic faith and sectarian in terms of teaching staff; however, these divisions have also suited the more militant Protestants.

The virtual insulation of the internal political system of Northern Ireland from Westminster's scrutiny over the past fifty years is perhaps the most eloquent testimony to London's weariness with Irish affairs. The Ulster MPs who came to Westminster were overwhelmingly Ulster Unionist in political complexion – and until 1974 were allied with the Conservatives – but few questions were ever asked about the nature of domestic government there between 1920 and 1966. Indeed, it was a convention that Northern Irish affairs were not proper subjects for Westminster's attention; from 1923 the Speaker refused to allow parliamentary questions dealing with matters devolved to Stormont. The other aspect of this convention was that Ulster's representatives in the Westminster Parliament tended to be docile, especially since most Ulster politicians with substantial ambitions would pursue them at Stormont rather than at Westminster.

Violence, which has marked so much Irish history and which forcibly reminded the majority of the population about the political complexities of the most remote part of the Kingdom, terminated the ignorance in which Westminster had chosen to live for so long. The year 1966 was, according to Conor Cruise O'Brien – later a minister in the Irish Republic and a notable analyst of international affairs – a watershed in the relationship between the two communities of Northern Ireland, and indeed between the two halves of Ireland. Dr O'Brien saw 1966 as a symbolic year, for it was the fiftieth anniversary of the Easter Rising of 1916, and that anniversary 'had to include the reminder that the object for which the men of 1916 sacrificed their lives – a free and united Ireland – had still not been achieved'.[3] Inevitably perhaps, the 1966 celebrations led to a revival of nationalist sentiment and a backlash on the part of Ulster Protestants who, according to Dr O'Brien, remembered 1916 not as the year of an heroic nationalist uprising but as the year in which Ulster divisions were cut to pieces in France in the fight against the German domination of Europe.

The revival of the cult of Irish nationalism inside and outside Ulster was complemented in the 1960s by a growing determination among the Province's Catholic minority to combat the political, economic and social discrimination to which it was subject. One dramatic form taken for this new articulation of minority grievances was that of mass protest and direct action, co-ordinated through a civil-rights campaign organization founded in 1967. The espousal of demonstrations and direct action by the Northern Ireland Civil Rights Association, and experimentation with the techniques and strategies used in the United States to combat discrimination against blacks, proved to be a catalyst for change in the political structure of Northern Ireland, as well as transforming the methods by which Roman Catholics in Ulster expressed their political demands. The concessions to the Catholic community and to the civil rights campaign made by the Northern Irish Prime Minister, Captain Terence O'Neill, since 1965, alienated his party. At the same time the experience of a new form of political activity provided an alternative to the old-fashioned policies and attitudes of the Nationalist Party which had previously claimed the allegiance of Roman Catholics in Ulster.

The decline of support for the Nationalist Party, which had abdicated its role as a champion of Catholic grievances in the social and economic sphere because of its overriding concern with the issue of reunification, cleared the way for the formation of a new party based on the changing demands of the Catholic community inside Ulster; for in the 1960s this community was less interested in the border than in economic opportunities and political rights. The Northern Irish general election of 1969 indicated how divided the Ulster Unionists were becoming and stimulated the opposition parties at Stormont to attempt some kind of alignment. The formation of the Social Democratic and Labour Party in 1970 was the fruit of that attempt; since then it has become the party which the majority of Catholics support, and an essential element in any solution of the Ulster problem.

However, by the time that new political solutions seemed to be emerging as viable options for Ulster's Catholic population, the key question in Ulster politics had become how far Stormont could handle the growth of violence in the Province. The turning point here was the civil-rights demonstration in Londonderry in October 1968, which led to a spiral of violence and ultimately to the prohibition of demonstrations such as those undertaken by the civil rights movement. By 1969 it was clear that the police force alone could not contain the violence, and the British army was sent in to restore order, especially in Belfast and Londonderry where inter-communal conflict had prompted the erection of barricades and the arming of the two communities.

The first fatalities in Ulster were in 1969 when thirteen people were killed; in 1970 the number killed rose to twenty-five. The killings at this stage were mainly the result of inter-communal fights – gang warfare with weapons ranging from stones to home-made petrol bombs. However, by 1971 guns became increasingly evident in the violence and the Provisional IRA, or Irish Republican Army, a splinter group which had broken away from the official, broadly pro-Marxist IRA because it thought more militant policies should be pursued, initiated a campaign of urban guerrilla warfare. As the number of bombings increased, the Ulster Prime Minister, then Brian Faulkner, persuaded the British Government to introduce internment without trial, which in turn exacerbated the situation. The viciousness of the IRA's reaction and the solidarity of its support among the Catholic population stunned the Stormont Government and Westminster. Altogether 59 people had been killed in Ulster between 1969 and August 1971; 231 were killed between the introduction of internment and the assumption of direct rule by Westminster in March 1972.[4] By September 1978 the death toll for the years since 1970 stood at 1,369.

The reasons for the assumption of direct rule related to the control of the security forces. British troops had originally been sent into Northern Ireland to keep the paramilitary forces on both sides apart, but as the violence escalated and the troops became the objects of attack from both sides it steadily became anomalous for British soldiers to be implementing a security policy framed by Stormont. The British Government's demand for sole responsibility for security matters was something which the Northern Irish Government could not accept and Brian Faulkner resigned. The Stormont Parliament was suspended and direct rule from London introduced instead. The suspension of Stormont was seen by many not as a temporary solution to Ulster's problems but as an admission that a form of government which had so patently failed to build up the support of a consensus had to be replaced.

The prorogation of Stormont was infinitely easier than the search for some method of government to replace it. It was perhaps ironic that it was the Conservatives – traditionally the Ulster Unionists' allies and initially the party that encouraged the Protestants to resist incorporation in the south – who were faced with the arduous task of constructing a new system which would effectively restore responsibility for Northern Ireland's government to Ulster politicians without being a blatant abnegation of responsibility for the area. The solution suggested at first was a new Northern Irish Assembly elected by proportional representation, with an executive which would exercise many domestic, but no security, responsibilities. This executive was to differ from the old one, however, in that its composition would be based on power-sharing – in other words it had to include representatives of the minority Catholic community, so that government could be seen to represent all groups in Northern Ireland. The use of the single transferable vote would, it was hoped, produce a majority for moderate parties. Perhaps the most controversial element in the proposals was the suggestion that a Council of Ireland should be created which would take account of the 'Irish dimension' of Ulster's affairs and facilitate discussions between Dublin, Belfast and London.

These proposals, enacted in the Constitution Act of 1973, split the majority Unionist Party in Northern Ireland. Elections to the new Assembly showed that Brian Faulkner's moderate and pro-power-sharing Unionists had won a slightly smaller share of the Unionist vote – 26.5% – than the hard-line coalition of so-called 'Loyalists' – 35.4% – who wanted a return to the old majoritarian Stormont. However, with the support of the SDLP, the non-sectarian Alliance Party and one Northern Irish Labour Party MP, a coalition Government could be formed with a majority in the Assembly. Pressure on Faulkner from his own Unionist Party was nevertheless strong enough to cause him to resign the leadership of the official Unionists only four days after the executive based on this coalition had been formed. The withdrawal of Unionist support from the power-sharing executive effectively doomed the constitutional edifice established by the Conservative Government; although the executive lasted for another four months, it was by then clear that the settlement had not taken root in Ulster and the triumph of the Loyalists at the February 1974 general election was taken as further evidence of this fact. The experiment with a power-sharing executive was eventually terminated when the Ulster Workers' Council, a hard-line Protestant organization, staged a general strike which forced Westminster to resume direct responsibility for Northern Irish affairs.

As a result of the strike it had to be recognized that no solution which could not elicit the consent of the major political forces in Northern Ireland would work. Thus the next initiative from London put the matter before the Northern Ireland Constitutional Convention of 1975–6; after long deliberations this merely revealed the political impasse into which the Province had stumbled.[5] No solution was likely to be acceptable to Westminster which did not provide adequate guarantees of equality for the Catholic community including some form of participation in government; no settlement would enjoy Protestant support unless it allowed the majority community to control the government of the Province. In the absence of a formula which can satisfy both sides it seems inevitable that Westminster's least favoured solution, direct rule, will continue and that the politics of the Province will remain in the forefront of the problems of British government.

The events of the 1970s thus destroyed the political formula which had been used to contain the Irish problem since the 1970s. Those events also caused a transformation of the political structures and alliances within Ulster itself and generated new political parties and movements. However, if the decade was clearly one in which the base of the Province's government had been shattered by violence and a political vacuum had been created, there were compensating administrative gains. The housing system had been reformed, the police and security systems had been reorganized, local government had been rationalized and procedures had been introduced to facilitate the protection of the citizen against arbitrary or unfair governmental action. The paradox of Northern Irish government may in retrospect turn out to be that in the years when her politics were becoming more sharply differentiated from those of the rest of Great Britain, the standards of administration in Ulster were becoming more like those that marked the rest of the country.

Wales

It may be considered ironic that just as events were tending towards the suspension of the United Kingdom's first experiment with a devolved system of internal self-government, two other areas of the United Kingdom were exhibiting a resurgence of nationalism and advancing claims for separate treatment from the rest of the United Kingdom. The different arrangements which the British Government at the time envisaged for the government of Scotland and that of Wales meant that had such schemes in fact been implemented, in accordance with the Scotland and Wales Acts of 1978, there would have been four distinct forms of government in the United Kingdom.

For one of the curious features of the whole devolution debate as it applied to Scotland and Wales was the purely pragmatic treatment given by the policy makers in London to the claims of the different parts of the United Kingdom. The notion that perhaps a logical and comprehensive treatment of all the parts of the political system might be preferable to a series of unequal arrangements which would themselves give rise to further complaint and instability seems to have been rejected out of hand. The politics of 'muddling through', here as elsewhere in the system, must appear endemic to observers.[6]

The according to Scotland and Wales of different treatment in their constitutional arrangements did have some justification in their very different histories and cultural complexities. Wales was first annexed to England in 1282 when Edward I conquered the territory, although the formal consolidation of that conquest was the work of the early Tudors, Henry VII and Henry VIII. The integration of Wales into the Tudor state was achieved by two major Acts of 1536 and 1542 – measures which also marked the beginnings of the long conflict between the Welsh and English cultures. The assertion of English superiority was enshrined in the provision in these Acts which forbade the use of the Welsh language in the administration.

Between the Tudor period and the onset of the Industrial Revolution, the relationship between Wales and England was a relatively harmonious one. The subordination of the principality to the United Kingdom was accepted and it was only with the changes engendered by industrial development that there emerged a new sense of a distinct Welsh identity. Yet the Industrial Revolution not only marked the beginning of a new period of Welsh consciousness but also caused new divisions within Welsh society. These internal divisions have contributed at least as much to the tensions occasioned by the devolution proposals as any differences of sentiment, culture and politics between Wales and England.

The Industrial Revolution produced two distinct patterns of politics, two cultures, in Wales. On the one hand it created the radical Nonconformist Wales which was for so long a bastion of the Liberal Party. This culture became increasingly conscious of the need to preserve the distinct Welsh identity, as expressed above all in the survival of the Welsh language, which was still the primary tongue of a substantial portion of the inhabitants of the country. On the other hand the Industrial

Revolution brought about a dilution of the Welsh identity by precipitating massive emigration from England into South Wales, where the coalmines and the steel industry needed workers. For such workers the links of class were to prove stronger than the links of culture or religion; those bonds of common class-interest were ultimately to find their expression not through Liberalism or nationalism but through the Labour Party. It is of course all too easy to oversimplify very complex patterns of attitudes and interests; however, the division between industrial and rural Wales, which broadly corresponds to a geographical division between the south of Wales, where most industry is concentrated, and the mid- and north Welsh farming communities, does seem to correspond to a real division in political outlook.

The industrialization of the southern part of Wales reinforced the fears of some Welshmen that their culture, especially their language, would be completely eradicated by the spread of English, which represented the language of modernization. The Act of 1870 which introduced compulsory education exacerbated these fears, for through it, ironically the product of a Liberal administration which might have been expected to be more sensitive to Celtic interests, English was established as the medium for all teaching in state schools. Indeed, it was only in 1889 that Welsh was allowed to be taught at all in grant-aided schools, even as a foreign language, so detrimental was the use of the native language considered to be to modern educational achievement.

However, the challenges to the survival of the Welsh tongue stimulated its supporters to organize in its defence, and opinion began to change on this issue so that by the early years of the twentieth century, partly as a result of pressures from the Welsh Language Society founded in 1885, there was a much stronger awareness of the need for facilities at all levels of the educational system for the study of Welsh language and literature. After the return of the Liberal Government in 1906 a reorganization of the Board of Education recognized the cultural autonomy of Wales by the formation of a specialized Welsh Department within it whose Secretary had direct access to the Minister. Also in 1907, charters were granted to the National Library of Wales and the National Museum of Wales, which together with the

University of Wales were thereafter to play an important part in the preservation of Welsh traditions and cultural identity. Today the Welsh language seems to have staged something of a come-back: in 1978 a survey of Welsh primary schools revealed that overall, 12.8% of all pupils in primary schools were fluent in Welsh, although there was great variation between the northern and western counties Gwynedd and Dyfed – where 63% and 33% of primary-school pupils were fluent – and the southern counties of Mid-Glamorgan, South Glamorgan and Gwent, where the proportions were 5%, 3% and 0.3% respectively.[7] In addition, since the Welsh Language Act of 1967, Welsh enjoys equality of status with English – for example in legal proceedings and official documents.

Resentment of the threats to Welsh cultural identity has fuelled political nationalism since the late nineteenth century, although its support has been uneven. The years between 1870 and 1920 saw substantial concessions to Welsh political sentiments: the Liberal Party, which was for so long the vehicle of the United Kingdom's special sectional interests, succeeded in disestablishing the Church of Wales – a minority Church in a country where the majority of the population subscribed to varieties of Nonconformity – and introduced special legislation to ban the sale of alcoholic drink on the sabbath. (Sunday opening of public houses in Wales is still immensely varied, for areas decide individually by periodic referendums whether they wish to be 'wet' or 'dry'. The number opting for prohibition has receded recently; the areas which favour closure on Sundays are the predominately rural areas of the north and west.) However, the decline of the Liberal Party after the First World War meant that Wales no longer had a champion at Westminster to advance its special concerns. The onset of the depression – which hit the areas of Wales dependent on basic industries especially heavily – then ensured that for a long period the politics of Wales were the politics of the Labour Party and that they were directed towards securing special economic treatment for the distressed areas.

Plaid Cymru, which had been founded in 1925 primarily as an instrument of cultural promotion, became an explicitly political organization in 1932 when it adopted the policy of self-government for Wales. Yet self-government was still seen as a means to an end – the protection of the language and culture which formed the basis of the nation. Because the numbers who could speak Welsh were and still are a tiny minority of the Welsh population as a whole, and because the cause was presented in a manner which reflected the perspective of the movement's initial activists – teachers, educationalists and lecturers – the mass appeal of the party remained small and excited suspicion among those who could not speak Welsh. In 1951 it put up only four candidates at the general election and it obtained only 10,920 votes. Although its votes between 1951 and 1966 showed a steady increase, this growth was more the result of Plaid's having contested additional seats than of any substantial increase in its popularity.

The by-election victory of Gwynfor Evans at Carmarthen in July 1966 seemed to suggest that a breakthrough might be imminent. Personal factors played a part in the victory in what had been Lady Megan Lloyd George's seat but the result was interpreted as more than a personal triumph for Gwynfor Evans, the President of Plaid Cymru. Also, in subsequent Welsh by-elections in very different areas of the country – Rhondda West and Caerphilly – Plaid Cymru's vote quadrupled. As one commentator put it, 'The moral for the Labour Party in Wales was clear. Labour hegemony in the Welsh Valleys had ceased to be automatic. Commitments to socialism had become blurred in the face of pit closures, economic insecurity and high rates of unemployment under a Labour government.'[8] At the general election of 1970, however, Plaid Cymru won no parliamentary seats at all. At the two general elections of 1974 the desertion of the major parties by the electorate resulted in two seats being won in February and three in October, and the anomalous electoral system allowed Plaid Cymru to retain two seats in 1979, although Gwynfor Evans' seat was lost. However, the cultural element in Welsh nationalism severely limits its appeal, and those who cannot speak Welsh feel that they would be second-class citizens if Wales were given a great deal more governmental autonomy. This fear explains the massive rejection by the Welsh of the devolution proposals in 1979.

Although in comparison with Scotland the administrative arrangements for Wales exhibit less difference from those of England, two features should be noted. First, a Welsh Office was created in 1964 when Labour was returned to power. Richard Crossman at the time declared it an 'idiotic creation' but its staff, although small initially by comparison with the ten thousand at the Scottish Office, numbered one thousand in 1974 and is now substantial. Secondly, a forum for the discussion in Parliament of specialized Welsh measures and problems was established in 1960 as the Welsh Grand Committee. It considers bills relating exclusively to Wales and any other matters referred to it by the House of Commons, and it consists of all MPs with Welsh constituencies together with no more than five other MPs nominated, for each topic to be considered, by the Committee of Selection.[9]

Scotland

Unlike Wales, which was subdued by conquest in the twelfth century, Scotland was never permanently incorporated into the United Kingdom by force of arms. In 1603 the succession of James I to the throne of England united the Crowns of England and Scotland. However, the union was thus a personal one at that time, and Scotland retained its own political system, its own Church and its own legal system. The establishment of a common Parliament occurred as a result of the Treaty of Union of 1706, whereby the Scots gained political representation at Westminster but were guaranteed that certain features of their administrative system could remain inviolate: the Church of Scotland, which is Presbyterian, would survive as the established Church, along with the Scottish legal system; in addition Scotland has maintained a distinct educational system and a different system of local government from that obtaining in England and Wales.

The Scottish legal system is perhaps the single most important factor explaining why Scotland has been accorded separate governmental treatment since the Act of Union. Unlike the English legal system, the Scottish system has depended rather more on the principles of continental jurisprudence and Roman law than on indigenous common law. Consequently, whenever a piece of legislation has been intended to apply to Scotland as well as to England and Wales this has had to be achieved either by a separate appendix to the measure or by a distinct Act for Scotland. There is therefore a certain amount of variation in the law between Scotland on the one hand and England and Wales on the other.

The growth of Welsh national sentiment and the recent success of Plaid Cymru have been fuelled by cultural factors, especially a fear of Anglicization, but this is much less true of Scotland. In part, this is because certain Scottish institutions are already protected and recognized by London as deserving of special consideration, and in part it is because although a very small minority of the Scottish people do have a distinct language, the vast majority speak English.

The particular political and administrative arrangements in existence in the 1960s and 1970s are really of nineteenth-century origin, although inevitably the twentieth-century expansion of government has had its impact upon them as it has upon so much else in the British administrative structure. Immediately after the Acts of Union, Scotland had had a Secretary of State to supervise and represent its interests in the British Parliament. But the abortive rebellion of 1745 put an end to that arrangement, and Scotland's special needs thereafter were largely the responsibility of the Lord Advocate, a law officer. The growth of governmental activity made the separation of administrative from legal functions necessary, and in 1885 it was decided that the Lord Advocate should concentrate primarily on his responsibilities for legal matters while administrative responsibilities in Scotland should be undertaken by a Secretary for Scotland and a separate Scottish Office.

The revival of the office of Scottish Secretary could perhaps be seen as one of the first steps along Britain's road towards administrative devolution. Already at the local level, however, as new governmental functions had emerged in the course of the nineteenth century, many specialized boards and *ad hoc* authorities for special purposes had been created to meet Scotland's needs. Since 1892 the Scottish Secretary has been a regular member of peacetime Cabinets, and the status of the office was enhanced in 1926 when the Secretary for Scotland was made a full Secretary of State.

The Scottish Office was moved to St Andrew's House in

Edinburgh in 1939; its internal organization today remains very much the same – a loosely co-ordinated structure of functional departments, such as those of agriculture, education and health together with a residual home department, presided over politically by the Secretary of State. The task of the Secretary of State for Scotland has indeed become increasingly ambiguous and politically difficult. The control of the Scottish Office, which has responsibilities equivalent to those of nine English departments, demands a greater range of expertise, even, than that required of ministers of the new 'super-departments'. (To some extent this is also now true of the Welsh and Northern Irish Secretaries of State.) However, in addition to his statutory responsibility for a range of subjects, the Secretary of State for Scotland gradually acquired the role of general spokesman for Scottish interests, irrespective of whether policy-making authority for the subjects concerned had been devolved or not. Yet the Secretary of State's role presented obvious difficulties. If his brief was for Scotland as a whole and he pressed Scottish interests in Cabinet successfully, in the field of economic policy in particular the claims of equally deprived English areas might be unjustly treated. Also, where ultimately did the responsibility of the Secretary of State lie? – with Scottish interests or with the wider interests of the United Kingdom if they proved incompatible with specific Scottish claims?

In addition to the existence of separate administrative machinery for Scottish affairs, Parliament at Westminster had even before the 1960s developed institutional arrangements to take account of the peculiarities of Scottish legislation. The Scottish Grand Committee, which is the oldest of the specialized committees dealing with Scottish affairs, was made permanent in 1907 and consists of all MPs for Scottish constituencies together with enough English representatives to bring the balance of party strength on the Committee into line with that in the House of Commons as a whole. In addition there have been experiments with smaller standing committees for the discussion of less important bills than seemed appropriate for the Scottish Grand Committee, and in the post-1966 period there was established a Select Committee on Scottish Affairs which produced reports on subjects such as economic planning and land use in Scotland.

The political challenge of the emergence of the Scottish National Party increased the amount of time which Scottish MPs felt obliged to devote to purely Scottish business within Parliament. Thus the period since 1964 has seen both the development of specialized parliamentary mechanisms for coping with Scottish matters and a growing tendency for Scottish MPs to concentrate in debate and Question Time on advertising their concern for Scottish matters. Perhaps this *de facto* specialization of Scottish MPs has isolated them to some extent from the major business of the House of Commons as a whole; certainly, constituency affairs weigh more heavily on Scottish MPs because of the distances between London and their constituencies.

Local government in Scotland was reformed in 1973 and the new arrangements became fully operational in 1975 in accordance with the recommendations of the Wheatley Commission. Scotland is now divided into regional, district and island authorities. There are only nine regional authorities in Scotland; these are divided into fifty-three districts including the cities of Aberdeen, Dundee, Edinburgh and Glasgow. The remote areas of the Orkneys and Shetlands and the Western Isles have single-tier authorities for most purposes but, as between the regions and the districts, functions are divided. The regions are responsible for major planning and related services including transport and water, as well as education and other local-authority functions. The districts are responsible for housing, local planning, building control and libraries except in the Highland, Dumfries, Galloway and Borders regions where these functions are exercised by the regional authorities.[11]

One of the arguments which was used against devolution proposals was that if an Assembly were to be added to the structure of local authorities Scotland would be over-governed, especially in those areas where the population is very sparse. (Population varies within Scotland from 99,000 in the Borders region to 2.6 million in Strathclyde, that is over half of the total.)[12] Yet although the Government in 1978 intended to transfer local-authority functions to the Assembly's overall control it did not envisage any immediate alteration of the local-government structure, but simply proposed to leave that for future consideration by a Scottish Assembly.

THE ROYAL COMMISSION ON THE CONSTITUTION AND THE DEVOLUTION DEBATE

The establishment of a Royal Commission on the Constitution was announced in the Queen's Speech of November 1968. According to Harold Wilson, the idea of the Commission had come from James Callaghan, a Cardiff MP and at the time Home Secretary. It was instructed to examine

the present functions of the central legislature and government in relation to the several countries, nations and regions of the United Kingdom; to consider, having regard to the developments in local government organization and in the administrative and other relationships between the various parts of the United Kingdom and to the interests of prosperity and good government under the Crown, whether any changes are desirable in those functions or otherwise in present constitutional and economic relationships; to consider also whether any changes are desirable in the constitutional and economic relationships between the United Kingdom and the Channel Islands and the Isle of Man....

The Commission could not look at the problems of the constitution in isolation from other institutional developments. In particular it would have to take account of the possibility that Royal Commissions might recommend major rearrangements of the local-government structure, and it would have to remember that violence had brought Northern Ireland back into Westminster's political calculations. However, from 1968 onwards it became increasingly difficult to treat Northern Ireland as anything except a unique political problem – to the extent that parallels between the Scottish question and the Irish problem were ignored.

The Royal Commission sat for four years; when it reported it produced both a minority memorandum and a majority report, for the members of the Commission disagreed about the nature of the problem which they had to investigate. The minority memorandum of dissent rejected the belief that there could be real divisions over policies and priorities between the centre of government and the United Kingdom's peripheral areas. In place of devising solutions to the limited problems of Scottish and Welsh nationalism, the minority memorandum advocated reform of the regional or intermediate tier of government – a course which, it was thought, would be quite compatible with increased planning of the economy and equality of provision of services throughout the United Kingdom. As the authors of the memorandum of dissent pointed out, it was not a question of creating that intermediate tier of government, for it already existed in the plethora of authorities which had been created as local-authority functions were transferred upwards and as central-government functions were devolved. If there could be a rationalization of what the memorandum called 'the jungle of boundaries', and the creation of a regional structure made democratically accountable, then, it was argued, the whole process of government would be democratized and brought closer to the people who were subject to it. The essence of the minority's scheme was therefore the creation of seven democratically elected regional assemblies and regional governments; five of these would be for England, with one each for Scotland and Wales. If they were elected on the basis of proportional representation – the single transferable vote was recommended – it was envisaged that such assemblies could exercise a wide range of the powers and responsibilities then exercised by *ad hoc* authorities and central government. Each regional government, it was suggested, should have its own civil service and its own ombudsman to hear complaints.[13] These changes in governmental structure were to be complemented by other reforms aimed at rejuvenating the British democratic system, including primaries in the process of candidate selection. The memorandum of dissent thus saw its proposals as part of a broader process of adjusting the British constitution to new demands, a process which would have to be implemented in stages.

It was perhaps not surprising that instead of grappling with a host of interconnected constitutional issues, the majority report chose to concentrate its attention on the government of Scotland and Wales, where the Commission recognized the 'added dimension of national feeling' had complemented the general dissatisfaction with government in the United Kingdom which had emerged during the 1960s. Yet however dramatic that upsurge of nationalist sentiment might seem, the Commission nevertheless based its recommendations on the assumption that there was not a majority for independence in either Scotland or Wales, and that the two countries' populations would want autonomy in government to remain balanced by the tangible economic benefits which government from London brought in the form of subsidies. According to the Royal Commission, there were three possible approaches which the Government could adopt. First there was separation, which the Commission roundly rejected, for it did not believe this was a policy for which the political will existed. The second solution, federalism, which has more recently come to seem the logical solution to some of the problems, was declared unsuitable. The only remaining option, devolution, came to seem the only policy which could accommodate both the essential unity of the country and the claims for more autonomy. Devolution was defined as 'the delegation of central government powers which would leave over-riding control in the hands of Parliament' and which, in 'its more advanced forms' would involve 'the exercise of powers by persons or bodies who, although acting on authority delegated by Parliament, would not be directly answerable to it or to central government for their actions'.[14]

Unfortunately from the point of view of the authors of the majority report, although they were united on the merits of devolution as a half-way house between centralism and federalism, they could not agree on a form of devolution or on whether, as a matter of principle, the same kind of devolution should be applied to Wales, to Scotland and to the English regions.

The Kilbrandon Commission's proposals were virtually ignored by the Government, but the general election of February 1974 gave new urgency to the Commission's subject of inquiry, if not to its precise proposals. For at the general election of February no single party had an overall majority, so that the seven SNP members and the two Plaid Cymru MPs in the House of Commons could play a significant part in deciding whether legislation would pass through the house. Yet the development of the minority Government's own legislative proposals was slow – partly because it wanted to see whether the number of SNP members and the 21.9% of the Scottish vote which the SNP had obtained indicated a permanent electoral shift away from the major parties in Scotland or whether it was simply a freak protest vote. The different schemes of the Kilbrandon Commission were accordingly published in order to generate discussion, although as it turned out the response of individual members of the public was 'disappointing', and the organizations which responded to the Government's invitation to write in about devolution were themselves deeply divided.[15]

The October general election did not produce the expected overall majority for the Labour Party which would perhaps have enabled the Government to control the content of devolution proposals to a considerable extent. Indeed, the number of SNP MPs rose to eleven and the Plaid Cymru contingent rose to three, which suggested a permanent and enduring challenge to the existing constitutional arrangements. The Government accordingly published in November 1975 its white paper *Our Changing Democracy*, with an outline of the powers and responsibilities which the Assemblies it recommended would have.[16] Even here, however, the Government had to give way to a much greater degree of autonomy than it had earlier envisaged by reducing the reserve powers of the Secretary of State on policy grounds; by transferring decisions about the legal power of any bill proposed by the Scottish Assembly to a neutral body, the Judicial Committee of the Privy Council; and by conceding that Acts of a Scottish legislature would of necessity be open to challenge in the courts after they had received the Royal Assent.[17]

A Scotland and Wales Bill introduced into Parliament in 1976 met heavy opposition, and eventually had to be withdrawn in early 1977 when a cross-party alliance defeated a guillotine motion. The Bill was thereafter divided into two.

THE SCOTLAND AND WALES ACTS OF 1978

After a difficult parliamentary passage, the Scotland and Wales Acts reached the statute book in July 1978. The principal concession made to opponents of the Acts within the governing party was an obligation laid upon the Government not merely to submit them to referendums but to lay orders for their annulment before the House of Commons if the 'yes' vote reached less than 40% of the total electorate.

In the Scotland Act provision was made for a directly elected, fixed-term Assembly which would have a wide legislative competence over devolved matters. The main areas of policy which the Act did not devolve were those of the conduct of international affairs, economic affairs and taxation. Legislative competence was to be transferred for such matters as the National Health Service: education, excluding universities; local government; transport, except for British Rail; social services, except for social security; and law and order.

Initially the Assembly was to be elected by Westminster parliamentary constituencies, with the heavily populated constituences returning three members and the more sparsely populated constituencies two members each. Peers and ordained ministers of the Church of Scotland were to be eligible for election to the Assembly – while they are not of course for election to Westminster – and peers could vote at such elections. The subsequent distribution of constituencies would be a matter for the Boundary Commission for Scotland; it was envisaged that ultimately there would be single-member constituencies on the Westminster model. The suggestion that the simple plurality system should not be used for elections to the Scottish Assembly found favour with some Conservatives for it was their Party which was likely to be a minority in Scotland, and there was a general fear that small movements of electoral opinion could easily result in an overall majority for the Scottish National Party. However, amendments to ensure that election was by proportional representation were rejected, so that the system applied to Westminster elections was to prevail in relation to the Scottish – and Welsh – Assemblies.

The Scottish Assembly would have power to regulate its own internal proceedings and to decide, for example, which committees to establish. However, the legislative process was not to be solely within the competence of the Assembly: the Secretary of State was to consider every bill passed by the Assembly to establish whether its provisions fell within the competence of the Assembly before submitting it to the Queen-in-Council for approval. If he was in doubt about the legislative competence of the Assembly with respect to a bill, he could refer it to the Privy Council for an opinion, and he was obliged to refer a bill if he considered that it was not within the Assembly's jurisdiction. The decision of the Judicial Committee of the Privy Council was binding: if it decided that a bill was not one which fell within the Assembly's competence, it could not be submitted for the Royal Assent; if it decided that a bill was within the Assembly's competence, the decision would become binding in all legal proceedings. The Secretary of State did not, however, have to refer a bill to the Privy Council if he thought a bill incompatible with the United Kingdom's obligations to the European Communities; in that case he was merely to certify that he was of that opinion to the Assembly, and would not forward the bill for assent. Similarly, if it appeared to the Secretary of State that a bill was one which might directly or indirectly affect a reserved matter – i.e. a matter for which Westminster had retained responsibility – and was against the public interest, he did not need to refer the issue to the Privy Council but might instead lay the bill before Parliament together with a reasoned statement of why in his opinion it ought not to be forwarded for the Royal Assent. If within twenty-eight days both Houses of Parliament resolved that it should not be submitted for the Royal Assent, then it would not become law.

These elaborate procedures for retaining an element of control over the legislative competence of the Scottish Assembly represented substantial reductions from the supervisory jurisdiction of the Secretary of State for Scotland as it was originally envisaged. Initially it had been suggested that he should both decide competence in strict legal terms prior to a bill's passage through the Assembly and retain the right of veto for reasons of broad policy. Later, however, his discretion was limited to a few areas which were strictly defined, and his power to veto bills of the Assembly could only be exercised with the concurrence of either the Privy Council or the Westminster Parliament, except where international obligations were involved.

The model on which the Scottish Assembly was to operate was that of the Westminster Parliament. Thus provision was made for the appointment of an executive, one of whose members was to be known as the First Secretary but who inevitably was also spoken of as the Scottish Prime Minister. The First Secretary's task was to advise the Secretary of State for Scotland on the appointment of the other Scottish Secretaries, who in effect would form the Scottish Cabinet; no one, except members of the Scottish executive performing the functions of law officers, could hold office without being elected to the Assembly. The Scottish executive would exercise all executive powers concerning devolved matters and would have the power to make subordinate legislation. The Assembly would not have the power to levy its own taxation, however, since the funds for the devolved services were to come from a Scottish consolidated fund. The level of payment from the Treasury to the Scottish consolidated fund would be determined by negotiation between the Scottish executive and Whitehall on the basis of a percentage of total UK expenditure. Originally the Government had envisaged annual negotiations but under Liberal pressure this was replaced by a percentage-based block grant which could be reviewed every four years. The absence of a taxing power underlined the general determination of the Government in London to retain overall responsibility for the management of the economy. The possibility of allowing the Scottish executive to levy additional taxation, for example by imposing a sales tax, was considered but rejected. The Government was adamant that no concessions would be made to the Scottish National Party's claim that proceeds from North Sea oil should be diverted to the Assembly. The existence of representation without taxation was odd enough, but also there was still the likelihood of tension between the Scottish executive and government in London in negotiations over the grant for devolved services even if these wrangles occurred at four-year intervals. Failures of policy or administration in Scotland could always be excused on the grounds that the cause was an inadequate grant, while Whitehall would be under constant pressure to raise the level of the block grant to 'buy off' criticism or difficulties in Scotland – and channels for the exertion of such pressure by Scottish representatives would be many, including the Secretary of State for Scotland, the Scottish executive and Scottish MPs at Westminster.

The Wales Act of 1978 was a much less far-reaching measure than the Scotland Act. The principal distinction between the proposed Welsh and the Scottish Assemblies was that whereas the Scottish Assembly had full legislative competence the Welsh Assembly was not to have such power; it was to be a body which could simply undertake some functions hitherto exercised by ministers in the fields of local government, housing, education, health and social services, planning and land use.

The powers of the Assembly as envisaged in the Act would be exercised not by a single executive as in Scotland but by mandatory committees to deal with the subjects devolved to it, although the Assembly might create other committees as well if it so desired. Each committee was to have a chairman and a leader – who would presumably always have been a member of the majority party in the Assembly – and the leader of the committee could be known as the executive member. The Assembly had also to appoint an executive committee, consisting of all the leaders of the various subject committees. The Secretary of State for Wales retained a great deal of control of the matters to be devolved to Wales because of the absence of independent legislative powers. He might direct whether an action was to be taken or avoided according to whether he considered that a reserved matter was directly or indirectly involved. He also had general powers to revoke an instrument made by the Welsh Assembly if he felt it would be in the public interest to do so or if the instrument affected a reserved matter.

The manner in which these two Acts would have operated would have depended first of all on the character of the Assemblies which were elected and secondly on the complexion of the government at Westminster. A Conservative government at Westminster would have been likely to have had a particularly difficult time since it would almost always have faced a Labour majority in Cardiff and, unless the Scottish National Party won a majority, would also have been likely to face a Labour majority in Scotland. However, tensions could have arisen even if a Labour government in London faced a Labour Scottish executive in Edinburgh, since the Scottish Labour Party, and indeed the Scottish TUC, have always been more left-inclined than their English counterparts; there would thus perhaps have been an even greater incentive for the Scottish Labour Party to show that it is not simply a subordinate of the Party in London.

The status of the two Acts raised interesting questions about entrenchment. The use of referendums gave the Acts a peculiar position, analogous to the legislation on the European Communities, and the fact that referendums had been held might have been interpreted by many to preclude easy amendment of them. It is perhaps significant, therefore, that clauses in the Scotland and Wales Bills pronouncing that their provisions did not affect the unity of the United Kingdom or the supreme authority of Parliament to make laws for it were deleted during the Bills' passage through Parliament.

Finally it should be noted that the creation of separate jurisdictions for Wales, Scotland and the surviving anomaly of Northern Ireland would mean that British government would become in many ways vastly more complicated as far as central government was concerned. Also, the variety of relationships at a territorial level would perhaps correspond more nearly to those found in a federal system than to those of a unitary state. And, as was mentioned in the first chapter, the increased role designed for the judiciary emphasized the extent to which the arrangements as far as Scotland was concerned were a departure from the normal internal arrangements of British government. The degree to which these changes would have satisfied the political aspirations of the Scots or indeed the Welsh is a matter for debate. However, one thing is certain: if provisions similar to those of the Scotland and Wales Acts were ever to become effective the pattern of political authority in the United Kingdom would have so diverged from the pattern of the 1950s as to justify the assertion that in essence one would be dealing with a new constitutional structure, whose full implications could not easily be estimated.

THE RESULTS OF THE REFERENDUMS

The referendums provided for in the Scotland and Wales Acts were held on 1 March 1979. The figures for the total electorate were adjusted to allow for deaths, double registrations and other eventualities. The results with the percentage figures for the adjusted electorates are shown opposite.

Two things stood out from the results. In Wales, turnout was very low and even the most Welsh-speaking counties did not return a 'yes' majority. In Scotland, turnout was higher but the 'yes' majority was due entirely to the voters of the central industrial area; rural and small-town Scotland was largely hostile.

Table 5
The Devolution Referendum Results

Wales	Scotland	
Clwyd	**Borders**	**Strathclyde**
Yes 31,384 (11.1%)	Yes 20,746 (27%)	Yes 596,519 (34%)
No 114,119	No 30,780	No 508,599
Maj., No. 82,735	Maj., No. 10,034	Maj., Yes 87,920
Dyfed	**Central**	**Tayside**
Yes 44,849 (18.3%)	Yes 71,296 (36.4%)	Yes 91,482 (31.5%)
No 114,947	No 59,105	No 93,325
Maj., No 70,098	Maj., Yes 12,191	Maj., No 1,843
Gwent	**Dumfries & Galloway**	**Western Isles**
Yes 21,369 (6.7%)	Yes 27,162 (26.1%)	Yes 6,218 (28.1%)
No 155,389	No 40,239	No 4,933
Maj., No 134,020	Maj., No 13,077	Maj., Yes. 1,285
Gwynedd	**Fife**	
Yes 37,363 (22.1%)	Yes 86,252 (35.4%)	
No 71,157	No 74,436	
Maj., No 33,794	Maj., Yes 11,816	
Mid-Glamorgan	**Grampian**	
Yes 46,747 (12%)	Yes 94,944 (27.9%)	
No 184,196	No 101,485	
Maj., No 137,449	Maj., No 6,541	
Powys	**Highlands**	
Yes 9,843 (12.3%)	Yes 44,973 (33.3%)	
No 43,502	No 43,274	
Maj., No 33,659	Maj., Yes 1,699	
South Glamorgan	**Lothian**	
Yes 21,830 (7.8%)	Yes 187,221 (33.3%)	
No 144,186	No 186,421	
Maj., No 122,356	Maj., Yes 800	
West Glamorgan	**Orkney**	
Yes 29,663 (10.8%)	Yes 2,104 (15.2%)	
No 128,834	No 5,439	
Maj., No 99,171	Maj., No 3,335	
TOTAL FOR WALES	**Shetland**	TOTAL FOR SCOTLAND
Yes 243,048 (11.9%	Yes 2,020 (13.7%)	Yes 1,230,937 (32.85%)
No 956,330 (46.9%)	No 5,446	No 1,153,502 (30.78%)
Maj., No 713,282	Maj., No 3,446	Maj., Yes 77,435

11 The Citizen and the Administration I: The Legal Order and Civil Liberties

The Courts and the Administration of Justice

The British legal system is a complicated structure. Even today it owes as much to the slow evolution of the political system between the Norman Conquest and the Great Reform Act of 1832 as it does to the attempts of nineteenth- and twentieth-century legislators to make the country's legal arrangements respond to the needs of an expanding and industrializing society. Thus, although an increasingly large part of the network of courts and jurisdictions is governed by reference to such recent statutes as the Courts Act of 1971, the historical perspective is still extremely important for a proper understanding of the role of law and its personnel in the British political system today. For although the British legal system has its defenders and the common law has been seen as one of England's finest intellectual exports, the role of law and the role of the judiciary remain controversial. It may be that recent constitutional developments and in particular entry into the European Communities will extend the part played by legal institutions in the British system of government; however, the exercise of additional powers will have to be delicately handled, for the attitude of politicians towards legal intervention in government is frequently one of suspicion and hostility.

The analysis in this chapter will cover mainly the pattern of legal institutions found in England and Wales. The English legal system has three features which distinguish its structure and style from most continental systems. First, there is the rigid division between barristers and solicitors. Solicitors are the lawyers who perform the routine non-litigious tasks and prepare the background material when litigation is necessary. They are the more numerous branch of the profession, and may form partnerships which can vary in size from a large London specialist firm to a small family solicitor's firm. It is the solicitor with whom the general public most comes into contact. The range of functions which a solicitor can perform is, however, limited. He may not argue cases in any of the higher courts; the senior and much smaller branch of the legal profession, the Bar, has the exclusive right of audience there. It is, moreover, from the ranks of barristers that the higher judiciary is recruited. Solicitors may become stipendiary magistrates and Recorders, and they are now also eligible to become Circuit judges though very few have in fact done so.

Whether this division of the profession is in the public interest is a fiercely debated question. Those who favour the retention of the division argue that this specialization – barristers are in effect specialists in the more difficult aspects of litigation and in advocacy – is beneficial to the client. Opponents say that this is but one of many of the restrictive features of the legal profession, and that the cost of legal services would be greatly reduced if a solicitor could see a case through all its stages instead of having to hand it over to a barrister when it involved litigation in the superior courts. A Royal Commission was established in 1977 to consider whether the provision of legal services in the United Kingdom was in need of reform, and one of the issues thoroughly investigated was the organization of the legal profession.[1] However, it rejected the idea of fusion and suggested only a number of minor amendments to the existing system and the acceleration of such trends as the development of a common professional organization for barristers and solicitors.

The second feature of the English legal system which distinguishes it from continental systems – though not from the American one – is that it is adversarial. Legal proceedings are conducted by the presentation of arguments on behalf of both the prosecution and the accused in criminal cases and on behalf of both the plaintiff and the defendant in civil suits. The function of the judge is to decide the case on the merits of the arguments put to him on behalf of each side. He does not, as in an inquisitorial system, intervene to ascertain the facts of the case himself, although small-claims procedures may constitute an exception to this rule.

The third significant feature of the English legal system is the absence of a separate jurisdiction for public law cases – cases which involve the state in some capacity as opposed to cases where only private citizens are involved. Until the late 1960s it was generally assumed that the British system of public law was underdeveloped, and certainly there is nothing which corresponds to the system of *droit administratif* in France; public-law issues are heard in the same courts as private-law cases, and few special procedures apply when government is involved in a suit (see Crown Proceedings Act, 1947).

The structure of civil and criminal courts is set out in Table 6 and Table 7. At the bottom of the civil-law hierarchy is the county court, which may hear only the kinds of cases assigned to it by statute – mainly disputes where small sums of money are at issue. The function of such courts is to effect a quick and inexpensive determination of legal cases. The existing network of county courts can trace its origins back to the County Courts Act of 1846, although there have been several rearrangements of the districts covered by the courts as the population has shifted and the distribution of cases has changed. The definition of a small dispute has had to be adjusted to take account of inflation, and this adjustment can now be done by Order in Council.[2] Prior to the Courts Act of 1971, which rationalized the whole system of courts in England and Wales, the county courts had been staffed by persons appointed as full-time county-court judges. However, the pressure of the number of cases and the difficulty of finding members of the Bar to act as county-court judges prompted a change in the system of recruitment to the judiciary at this level, so that after the Courts Act a new category of judges known as Circuit judges replaced the existing county-court judges. However, the Courts Act also opened the office of Recorder – as has been seen, an office previously confined to barristers – to solicitors, and allowed additional Circuit judges to be recruited from their ranks. Thus it is now possible for solicitors to reach the lower rungs of the judiciary.[3]

Table 6
The System of Courts Exercising Civil Jurisdiction

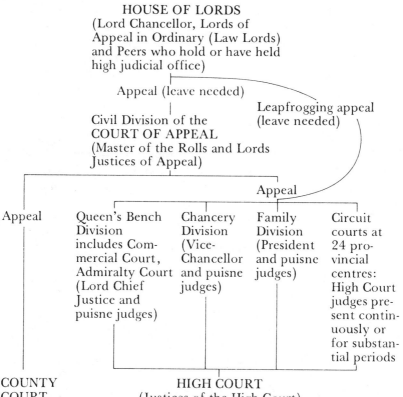

HOUSE OF LORDS
(Lord Chancellor, Lords of
Appeal in Ordinary (Law Lords)
and Peers who hold or have held
high judicial office)

Appeal (leave needed)

Leapfrogging appeal
(leave needed)

Civil Division of the
COURT OF APPEAL
(Master of the Rolls and Lords
Justices of Appeal)

Appeal

Appeal	Queen's Bench Division includes Commercial Court, Admiralty Court (Lord Chief Justice and puisne judges)	Chancery Division (Vice-Chancellor and puisne judges)	Family Division (President and puisne judges)	Circuit courts at 24 provincial centres: High Court judges present continuously or for substantial periods

COUNTY
COURT
(Circuit
judges)

HIGH COURT
(Justices of the High Court)

Source: R.M. Jackson, *The Machinery of Justice in England*, 7th ed.
(C.U.P., 1977).

313

Above the level of the county court there is the High Court, which has three specialized divisions – the Queen's Bench Division, which includes the Commercial Court and the Admiralty Court; the Chancery Division; and the Family Division. The Queen's Bench Division is headed by the Lord Chief Justice; cases are heard by him and the forty-four 'puisne judges', as High Court judges who are not heads of divisions are known. The Queen's Bench Division has original jurisdiction in civil matters, which means that a plaintiff may choose to begin his action there rather than at the county-court level. Obviously whether a plaintiff does this or not will depend on the seriousness of the suit, but a judgement from the High Court is more authoritative than a county-court one, and this consideration may outweigh the additional cost involved in pursuing the action there. Another civil function of the Queen's Bench Division is that it exercises a supervisory jurisdiction over the lower courts and the plethora of tribunals which deal with such subjects as rent assessments, employment disputes and social-security payments. The High Court exercises this control over subordinate jurisdictions through its ability to issue *inter alia* prerogative writs and orders.

The third function of the High Court is to act as an appellate court, hearing appeals from magistrates' courts and tribunals on points of law. In criminal matters it may also hear appeals from the appellate jurisdictions of the Crown Courts. The appellate functions of the Queen's Bench Division are usually exercised by the Divisional Court, which consists of five or three judges, but where a statute provides for an appeal to the Queen's Bench Division from a tribunal on a point of law, this appeal may come before a single judge.

The Chancery Division of the High Court had its origins in the development of a distinct set of legal processes and remedies known as equity, which was designed to supplement the inflexible common-law procedures. The two aspects of English law, common law and equity, have now been almost entirely merged, so that the plaintiff no longer has to choose whether to bring his action in common-law or equitable courts. The Chancery Division is still distinguished by the material it deals with: trusts, land, taxation and bankruptcy matters are the special concern of this Division, as well as contentious probate and succession matters. The Lord Chancellor is the nominal head of the Division but it is in practice presided over by a Vice-Chancellor and staffed by eleven puisne judges. The Family Division of the High Court was created in 1971 when the old Probate, Divorce and Admiralty Division was abolished and its functions redistributed. The Family Division, headed by a President and staffed by sixteen puisne judges, exercises jurisdiction in connection with the breakdown of marriage, the disposition of family property and the custody of children.

Above the level of the High Court is the Court of Appeal, which has two divisions – one for criminal and one for civil matters. The Court of Appeal was established to hear civil appeals in the late nineteenth century under the Judicature Acts of 1873–5: it provides a tribunal which can hear appeals from both the county courts and the civil divisions of the High Court. It is presided over by the Master of the Rolls and staffed by sixteen Lords Justices of Appeals who sit together usually in courts of three. (The Lord Chancellor, ex-Lord Chancellors, Lords of Appeal in Ordinary and the Presidents of the various Divisions of the High Court are also *ex officio* members of this Court and competent to hear appeals there.) Under Lord Denning, the Court of Appeal has acquired a reputation for being an innovatory force in English law; although its unorthodox approach to precedent has occasioned criticism from the House of Lords and from politicians, on balance it has made a unique contribution to law reform in recent years.[4]

Above the Court of Appeal is the highest domestic court in the country, the House of Lords. Under the Administration of Justice (Appeals) Act of 1934 the right of appeal to this body is limited: leave from the House of Lords itself or from the Court of Appeal must be given, and this will generally only be done when there is a substantial point of law in dispute. The House of Lords' judicial functions originated when medieval monarchs delegated routine aspects of adjudication to members of the Great Council and, although it took time for the legislative and adjudicative processes to become distinct, it is clear that by the end of the sixteenth century the House of Lords was a pre-eminent court in Britain. Lay peers participated in judicial proceedings until the middle of the nineteenth century; however, this habit was effectively ended with O'Connell's case in 1844.[5] Since that time the House of Lords has effectively reserved its judicial functions for specialists, although the appointment of professional judges to undertake them had to wait until the Appellate Jurisdiction Act of 1876. That Act provided for the appointment of paid Lords of Appeal in Ordinary, and their number has been raised to cope with additional judicial work so that it now stands at ten. As well as these specially created Law Lords – who are given life peerages – any peer who has held high judicial office may sit on appeals to the House of Lords. The Lord Chancellor himself does not normally participate in the routine judicial business of the House of Lords, although this very much depends upon the personal preferences of individual Chancellors: Lord Hailsham, who was Lord Chancellor in the Conservative administration of 1970–4, and again in the administration formed in 1979, enjoyed this aspect of his duties and participated in appeals on a regular basis.

Two further points should be noted about the appeal structure in civil matters. First, it used to be the case that the House of Lords was bound by its own previous decisions, so that where the house had considered a legal point already – even if a long time previously – in theory it had to follow the earlier precedent.[6] Of course there were ways of getting round this rule, but in 1966 the House of Lords decided actually to modify the doctrine and give itself the freedom to depart from earlier decisions when it felt that such a change would be justified. In fact it has made relatively limited use of the freedom thereby acquired.[7]

Secondly, the special role of the House of Lords in determining difficult points of law, especially in relation to statutory interpretation, has been recognized by a new procedure which enables the appellant to bypass the normal route for appeals, the Court of Appeal, and to go directly to the House of Lords from the High Court. To invoke this special procedure, which is known as 'leap-frogging', it is necessary for the trial judge to certify that a point of law of general public importance is involved, and for the House of Lords to grant leave to appeal in this way.

A word should perhaps be said here of the Privy Council and its Judicial Committee. Until 1833 there was no specialized Judicial Committee and the Privy Council's jurisdiction was exercised by its lay members. Now the Judicial Committee is composed of all those peers entitled to hear cases in the House of Lords together with some members of Commonwealth countries who have held high judicial office and the Lord President of the Council. Its special jurisdictions include appeals from outside the United Kingdom, mainly from Commonwealth countries which have chosen to retain this court and from the remaining colonies and protectorates; it hears domestic appeals from specialized tribunals, especially the General Medical Council; and from ecclesiastical courts. It may also hear special references on matters which are not strictly appellate, such as the validity of legislation in Jersey or eligibility to take a seat in the House of Commons.

The criminal law is administered through a rather different system of courts, and the whole structure of criminal jurisdiction has recently been subject to radical overhaul. Perhaps the most peculiar feature of the criminal law in Britain is the role played by lay magistrates or JPs.[8] The lay magistracy has a long history. Certainly by the end of the sixteenth century one finds a system in which minor offences could be tried by the gentry of an area, while more serious offences had to wait for visitations from the itinerant judges on assize. Administrative functions were also assigned to the magistracy, especially those concerning the poor law. Appointed on a county basis, JPs would assemble four times a year in Quarter Sessions to perform their judicial duties. However, as the burden of work increased magistrates developed the practice of dealing with trivial offences themselves at so-called 'petty sessions' without a jury. Magistrates' courts thus form the bottom rung in the hierarchy of criminal courts, and can perform a variety of minor judicial and administrative tasks.

First, JPs can decide cases which are triable summarily. This they do by majority verdict, sitting in benches of at least three Justices; there is no jury, but each court has a trained clerk to keep it informed on points of law. Secondly, with the consent of the accused they can try offences which are indictable but which may be determined summarily. Finally, they can decide in the case of an indictable crime whether the prosecution has determined that there is a case to answer, as well as whether bail should be granted if the accused is remitted for trial in the

Table 7
The System of Courts Exercising Criminal Jurisdiction

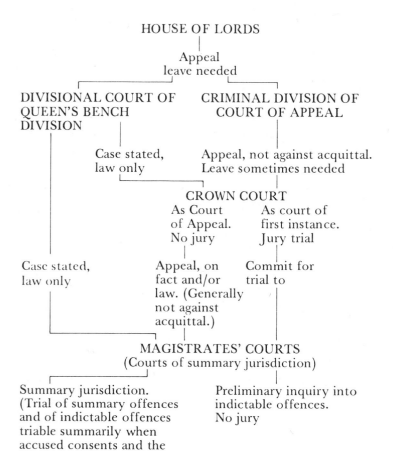

HOUSE OF LORDS

Appeal
leave needed

DIVISIONAL COURT OF
QUEEN'S BENCH
DIVISION

CRIMINAL DIVISION OF
COURT OF APPEAL

Case stated,
law only

Appeal, not against acquittal.
Leave sometimes needed

CROWN COURT
As Court   As court of
of Appeal.   first instance.
No jury   Jury trial

Case stated,   Appeal, on   Commit for
law only   fact and/or   trial to
                 law. (Generally
                 not against
                 acquittal.)

MAGISTRATES' COURTS
(Courts of summary jurisdiction)

Summary jurisdiction.
(Trial of summary offences
and of indictable offences
triable summarily when
accused consents and the
court thinks it expedient.)
No jury

Preliminary inquiry into
indictable offences.
No jury

Source: R.M. Jackson, *The Machinery of Justice in England,*
7th ed. (C.U.P., 1977).

Crown Court. In addition to these judicial functions magistrates still perform such administrative duties as granting licences to sell alcohol, and they have retained significant civil-law functions such as making affiliation orders. Juvenile courts are staffed by magistrates, who hold separate sessions to deal with young offenders and to make orders whereby children in need of care and protection may be taken into local-authority custody.

The argument in favour of substantial lay participation in the administration of justice is a complex one. Some would argue that such participation reinforces the idea that the whole community, not just the specialized agencies of law enforcement, are responsible for the prevention and punishment of crime. Lay participation may also be justified on the grounds that it enables the legal sanctions imposed to reflect the community's general values. By involving the public in the sentencing process, the law can thus become rooted in the opinions of a wider section of society than would be the case if paid full-time lawyers were exclusively responsible for it. In addition there is the more practical but weighty argument that a lay magistracy is cheaper than a professional system would be. The cost of training magistrates is much smaller than would be the salaries of professional magistrates – even if, which seems doubtful, the personnel were available for such a reform. The routine expenses of the legal institutions of the country are not popular items in governmental budgets – although the issue of law and order is frequently raised at elections – and it may therefore be hazarded that this factor alone will guarantee the survival of amateurs in the British court structure.

Against the arguments for a continuing lay element in the administration of the criminal law, it could be maintained that the system is biased. Although it is undoubtedly true that magistrates as a whole are more representative of British society than barristers and solicitors, the groups who become JPS are not exactly a microcosm of modern Britain. Some sections of society, notably the manual working classes, the young, and ethnic minorities, are under-represented on the bench – an under-representation which is especially unfortunate when the crimes involved are typically ones associated with these groups. Equally, the manner of appointment to the bench has often been suspect; although efforts have been made to eliminate the cruder aspects of political patronage, it is still doubtful whether this aspect of the system commands confidence. Above all, the question of competence arises. There is now much greater emphasis on training, and some aspects of the magistrates' work – specialized juvenile courts for example – provide sophisticated facilities for JPs to learn about such topics as sentencing, psychology and social welfare. However, the effect of these opportunities is by no means apparent and it could be argued that the justice which the bench imposes is still somewhat arbitrary. To some extent, the remedy for the deficiencies of the lay magistracy lies in the comprehensive appeals mechanism which exists, and in the variety of professional and welfare assistance which is available to the bench.

The trial of more serious crimes takes place at a level above the magistrates' courts, in what are known now as Crown Courts. Crown Courts were established by the Courts Act of 1971. In order to understand their role it is necessary to remember that prior to that date there were two places in which indictable offences could be tried. The first was at Quarter Sessions which until local-government reorganization were organized differently depending upon whether they were county or borough courts. In the boroughs, the court consisted of a Recorder sitting alone; in the counties, the Quarter Sessions were the lay magistrates – between two and nine in number – sitting with a legally qualified chairman. These courts had a wide jurisdiction, but usually they did not try offences carrying a maximum penalty of life imprisonment on first convictions; they could also hear appeals from magistrates' courts. More serious crimes had therefore to be tried at the assize courts.

Assize courts had been important since at least the reign of Henry II when officials travelling into the country to dispense royal justice were also able to extend the administrative jurisdiction of the Crown. Despite the delays inherent in the system, the practice whereby High Court judges travelled to major towns at fixed times each year survived until 1971. Then, following a Royal Commission on Assizes and Quarter Sessions, the system of Quarter Sessions and Assizes was abolished, and a single court above the level of the magistrates' court, the Crown Court, took their place in a number of court centres.[9]

The Crown Courts are staffed by High Court judges, Circuit judges and Recorders. Criminal offences are divided into those which must come before a High Court judge, in other words very serious ones such as murder and treason; those which would normally be tried by a High Court judge but which may be released for trial by a Circuit judge; those which can be tried either by a High Court judge or by a Circuit judge according to convenience; and those which would normally be tried by a Circuit judge. This reform thus combined the merits of the old system, which meant that no area was in danger of continual subjection to the peculiarities of a single judge, with a new flexibility which had become increasingly necessary because the old assize system took little account of the distribution of work between the different areas of the country.

Appeal from the Crown Courts in criminal matters is made to the Court of Appeal (Criminal Division) and, in very rare cases, to the House of Lords. A general right of appeal in criminal matters is actually a relatively recent innovation in the English legal structure, and the Court of Criminal Appeal was established only in 1907. It was merged with the Court of Appeal in 1966.[10] Appeal from the Court of Appeal to the House of Lords requires the former to certify that a point of law of general public importance is involved; the House of Lords or the Court of Appeal must give leave to appeal on the grounds that there is a point which the House of Lords ought to consider. There is no appeal against acquittal in the Crown Court, but since 1972 the Attorney General may refer a point of law to the Court of Appeal.

Since British entry into the European Communities it should be noted that cases which have an element of Community law in them may be subject to a further examination: there is provision in the European Communities Act of 1972 for a reference on a point of law beyond the country's domestic courts to the Court of Justice of the European Communities. The European Communities Act and Article 177 of the EEC Treaty makes a reference to the Court of the Communities compulsory when a case with such a European element has exhausted all domestic remedies and has reached the House of Lords; however, a case may be referred to the European Court by any court in the judicial hierarchy if a matter of European Community law is at issue and the British court would like a ruling on it.[11] Strictly speaking the court and not the parties to a suit refer the matter to the European Court, whose jurisdiction is designed to produce harmony and uniformity of approach throughout the member states of the Communities rather than to provide another opportunity for appeal. Possibly also an action will lie beyond the domestic legal system if there is any question of government or a public authority having breached the European Convention on Human Rights. This is administered by a Commission on Human Rights, and cases where an allegation is *prima facie* substantial are heard by the European Court of Human Rights as distinct from the Court of Justice of the European Communities. An important example of the Court of Human Rights' reaching a different verdict from that of the British courts occurred when *The Sunday Times*'s right to publish information about the drug thalidomide was upheld.

The network of institutions through which the law is administered obviously depends for its efficiency and fairness on the personnel who have to operate the system, and in particular the respect of the community at large for the machinery of law enforcement will depend upon two groups, the judiciary and the police. Although judges are in theory politically neutral, they all owe their appointment to politicians. The Prime Minister appoints the Lord Chancellor, who is a senior member of the Cabinet, presides over the House of Lords and is in theory the head of the Chancery Division of the High Court, although in practice he will perform his judicial duties in the Judicial Committee of the House of Lords. The Lord Chancellor is responsible for the vast majority of judicial appointments – High Court judges, Circuit judges and Recorders – and even magistrates are appointed on his advice. The Prime Minister, on the other hand, has a major voice in the appointment of judges to the Court of Appeal and the House of Lords, as well as to the office of Lord Chief Justice. It is an important feature of British constitutional theory that High Court judges have security of tenure, and cannot be removed from office except by an address to both Houses of Parliament. The retirement age for High Court judges is seventy-five.

Much criticism has been levelled at the social characteristics of the British judiciary.[12] Certainly, the vast majority of judges come from middle-class backgrounds, and a high proportion have been educated at public schools and the traditional universities of Oxford and Cambridge. Yet the argument that as a result judges will either be biased towards the interests of their class, or against certain sections of society, or display consistent political prejudices seems overstated. There is a wide range of opinion and outlook within the ranks of the judiciary on political matters, and it is doubtful whether this overall situation would be much changed by the addition of persons with a different social background. However, it is possibly true that the world of the Bar, from whom the senior judges are exclusively recruited, and that of the bench are atypical of British society as a whole, and that the kinds of problems which increasingly confront judges may be remote from their experience. Whether it is fair or not, many people in Britain do actually believe that the judiciary is biased against the working classes and in favour of established interests – a belief which largely explains the hostility of the trade-union movement to any attempt at introducing legal procedures into the conduct of industrial relations. A Gallup Survey conducted in May 1976 found that when people were asked whether the courts dispensed justice impartially or favoured the rich and influential, opinion was almost evenly divided, with 45% saying that justice was dispensed impartially and 38% saying that the courts favoured the rich.[13]

Obviously one factor in shaping the public's perceptions of how fair the courts are is cost; here the British provisions have deteriorated recently. Under the Legal Aid and Advice Act 1949 and its successors, a national scheme to meet the costs of poor litigants was established; in addition to this statutory scheme there is a voluntary scheme run by the Law Society itself. However, though well intentioned the statutory provisions have been greatly weakened by the rate of inflation, which means that now only a very small section of the population earns sufficiently little to qualify for assistance. The recent development of law centres may help but the position is still far from satisfactory.

The second important component of the personnel of law enforcement and administration is the police force. The British experience of an organized police force dates from 1829 when

Sir Robert Peel established the Metropolitan Police Force; in the succeeding decade both the boroughs and the counties were enabled to establish police forces of their own. The original organization of police forces on the basis of local-authority areas meant that for much of the nineteenth century there were over two hundred separate police forces in the United Kingdom. During the twentieth century this arrangement became increasingly anachronistic and inefficient, and in 1960 the Royal Commission on the Police urged the amalgamation of a number of forces, although it rejected in rather cavalier fashion the argument for a national police force. (A national police force in Britain has been seen as in some way a step towards authoritarian government, although it is quite clear that the increasing reliance on specialized services has shifted the balance away from localism and towards centralization in the 1960s and 1970s.) The implementation of the Royal Commission's proposals in the Police Act of 1964 set in motion a process of amalgamation, so that by 1978 there were fifty-one forces only.

The responsibility for the day-to-day operations of the police force is that of the Chief Constable of each individual force, and he is answerable for the performance of his duties to a local police authority composed of county councillors and magistrates. In London, however, a different situation applies: the Chief Commissioner of the Metropolitan Police is directly answerable to the Home Secretary for the conduct of his force's activities. The precise nature of the relationship between the Chief Constable and his local police authority is difficult to define; it seems that although during the nineteenth century local authorities frequently gave their police forces instructions on prosecution policy, this practice declined in the twentieth century, and the general view developed that police policies were not a proper subject for detailed supervision by local government. The Police Act of 1964 gave local authorities the power to request reports about the policing of their local areas but in practice these have been very little used. As far as the Home Secretary's powers are concerned he is subject to parliamentary questioning on the general level of policing in the country, although not on matters of detailed administration except in relation to the Metropolitan Police Force. As the financing of the police is effected through a percentage grant, and as the Home Secretary has a variety of powers to lay down conditions of service, there is a substantial amount of central-government influence in the administration of police forces.

The 1960s and 1970s witnessed a number of incidents of police corruption. In the Metropolitan Area this development led to the establishment of a special unit, A10, to root out such practices as bribery and protection rings. It also led to the establishment of a procedure for complaints against the police. Until 1976 the investigation of a serious allegation by a member of the general public would have been undertaken by the police themselves, albeit from another force. In 1976, however, a Police Complaints Board was established to provide an independent review of action taken as a result of complaints by the public against the police. The inclusion of an independent element in the Complaints Board had been bitterly disputed and some officers, such as the ex-Chief Commissioner of the Metropolitan Police, Sir Robert Mark, argued that it would undermine the morale of the police forces. Whether it will prove a success remains to be seen, but certainly by 1979 there was disturbing evidence that the public confidence in the police had declined – and this was especially true among ethnic minorities – while the police felt not only that they were being asked to perform a difficult job on poor pay but that machinery such as the Complaints Board would subject them to further criticism. In practice the operation of the Board seems to have given the police little cause for concern. Only fifteen cases had arisen by 1978 in which the Board recommended disciplinary charges when the police were opposed to them, and it seems more likely that the Board will fail to satisfy critics than that it will seriously disrupt the organization of the force.

Public Order and Civil Liberties

The fact that it was only in 1976 that the British Government felt it necessary to introduce machinery for securing independent review of complaints against the police perhaps underlines the general complacency which had previously existed in the United Kingdom about the country's arrangements for protecting the citizen from administrative error or excess. Indeed, although national and international developments have focused attention on individual rights to a remarkable extent in the 1970s, it is surprising how slowly this new sensitivity towards issues of civil liberties and accountability has been translated into legislative or administrative action. For the British tradition of thought in the area of individual liberties is still very much shaped by a longstanding hostility to abstract formulations of rights, and a reliance on common sense and common values to keep those in authority under control. Moreover, the preference for political rather than judicial protections for the citizen has meant that, even in those areas where legal safeguards are most important, such as police powers, the judiciary has sometimes been too deferential to executive claims of administrative necessity.

Satisfaction with the manner in which the British system of government provided for the protection of individual liberties and the more complex question of governmental accountability had a partly historical explanation: Britain developed a tradition of parliamentary democracy at a time when most European countries were still suffering the abuses of absolute monarchy. The early appreciation of the need to provide adequate and effective remedies against the executive can be indicated by a study of the range and depth of the constitutional debates of the seventeenth century – debates which left their imprint on American as well as English theories of constitutional government. Yet the sheer length of the British parliamentary tradition may have acted as a brake on the development of remedies to protect the individual in contemporary Britain. The peculiar concerns of the seventeenth century could not provide a set of constitutional principles appropriate to a period in which the balance between state and individual has been altered radically by the massive extension of governmental activity; moreover the rhetoric of parliamentary supremacy, which is the historic achievement of the seventeenth-century struggles between the Crown and the House of Commons, has served to disguise the extent to which the legislature itself can threaten individual liberty – especially since, in normal circumstances, the legislature is controlled by the executive through the discipline of the party system. Protection of the interests of individuals in British political debate has thus invariably been associated with the protection of majority interests expressed through political parties inside Parliament. The problem of how to balance minority interests against those of the majority has been either ignored entirely or resolved by appealing to the expectation that at least two political parties will alternate in government.

The alternation of parties in government and the diffused, if diminishing, spirit of compromise in British political affairs have generally ensured that the absence of a clear statement of individual rights and a coherent body of principles to govern executive action has not led to tyranny. A British citizen may find it difficult to predict the limits which a court will impose on his freedom of speech or to ascertain the circumstances in which he may challenge a government decision successfully; however, for the most part he may assume that governmental agencies in the United Kingdom will recognize fairness to individuals as an important value to be given weight in their decisions, even if they are not always consistent about applying it.

Discussions about formalizing the rights accorded to individuals have formed part of the wider debate about the general adequacy of British constitutional arrangements, in which lawyers have taken a prominent part. Both Lord Scarman in his 1974 Hamlyn Lectures and Lord Hailsham have advocated the introduction into the British system of government of an entrenched bill of rights as part of a comprehensive revision of the constitutional system.[14] Despite ambiguities in both major parties' approach to the problem of individual rights, the 1970s saw internal working groups on the subject set up by both the Labour and the Conservative Parties, as well as the publication of a Home Office discussion paper on the topic. And in 1977 following the introduction of a bill on the subject the House of Lords established a Select Committee to examine the question of whether Britain should enact a bill of rights. The House of Lords considered two specific questions in relation to the desirability of such a step. First, was such a measure desirable in principle? Secondly, if it was desirable what form should such an enactment take? The second question, which had been raised in the Government's discussion paper, really turned on whether Britain should acquire a bill of rights by incorporating the European Convention on Human Rights into United Kingdom law or whether it would be better to enunciate a bill of rights which could take account of Britain's own political system and the difficulties associated with the doctrine of parliamentary sovereignty.[15]

The status of the European Convention for the Protection of Human Rights and Fundamental Freedoms is rather anomalous as far as the United Kingdom is concerned. While the United Kingdom was one of the first countries to ratify the Convention, which she did in November 1950, it has not been incorporated into British law. The fact that the Convention does not form part of British law was made clear in a case before the Court of Appeal in 1976, although the case also found that it was legitimate where possible to construe Acts of Parliament so that they do not conflict with the Convention.[16] Moreover, although Britain gave early moral support to the idea of guaranteeing individual freedoms against state governments, it was not until 1966 that she was prepared to admit the right of individual citizens to petition the Commission on Human Rights directly and take what the Select Committee called 'the long road to Strasbourg'. Even now there is no guarantee that a complaint which reaches the European Court of Human Rights, and is upheld by it, will be remedied. The enforcement of the Convention depends upon the assumption that countries which have ratified the document will want to harmonize their approach to civil liberties, and that moral and political criticism from other European countries will be more effective than sanctions against a state found in breach of the Convention.

Certain references to the Commission on Human Rights have indeed proved highly embarrassing for the United Kingdom, which is in fact the only signatory of the Convention not to have incorporated its principles into its domestic law or to have a bill of rights of its own. One sensitive area which keeps producing conflicts is the question of the treatment of prisoners in Northern Ireland. After the introduction of internment in 1971 the Irish Government brought a number of charges against the United Kingdom and, although the Commission exonerated the United Kingdom on some of them and recognized the peculiar nature of the situation there, it also found against it on some charges. In particular some of the British security forces' 'deep interrogation techniques' were found to have violated article III of the Convention which states that 'no person shall be subjected to torture or to inhuman or degrading treatment or punishment'. The same provision of the Convention has also been invoked successfully to condemn the practice of birching as a judicially enforceable punishment in the Isle of Man.

The Select Committee reported in favour of introducing a bill of rights into British law, but it was a narrow majority decision of six votes to five. The Committee was, however, unanimous in its opinion that if the step to acquire such a formal statement of individual liberties was taken, the bill of rights should be based on the European Convention. One argument which was strongly used in favour of the introduction of a bill of rights was that by joining the European Economic Community Britain had already taken a step which would have a growing impact on her domestic law and give an extended role to the British judiciary – an argument which many libertarian critics of the judiciary do not favour. However, against the proposal were marshalled many arguments, including the proposition that, despite the absence of a bill of rights, there were no more than a few 'marginal situations' where such a change would bestow a remedy not already available under existing law. In the view of those opposed to a bill of rights for Britain, therefore, the traditional British approach to civil liberties was entirely justifiable, and unlikely to be improved by the device of a formal declaration.

The traditional British approach to civil liberties has been called a 'negative' approach in that it allows the citizen complete freedom to do anything which has not been specifically prohibited. Also, in a number of identifiable spheres such as freedom of the person it gives the citizen specific remedies to be used in case of an invasion of liberty. In order to see how this system operates it is necessary to look a little more closely at the spectrum of issues involving civil liberties in Britain, and the contemporary position in relation to them.

The liberty which has traditionally been seen as the most important item in Britain's catalogue of civil liberties is freedom of the person. American and British lawyers have traced its origins back to Magna Carta; Dicey gave it a special pre-eminence when he cast scorn upon the idea that formal declarations of rights were necessary and pointed out that had Voltaire been imprisoned in a country with Britain's legal remedies he would have been able to secure his release from the Bastille. The legal remedy most closely linked with the idea of freedom of the person is the prerogative writ of *habeas corpus ad subjiciendum*, which provides a procedure for effecting the immediate release of an individual from unlawful detention by either a public or a private authority. Initially the point of the writ was to prevent imprisonment without trial; it acquired an important status as a symbol of procedural fairness in the period of conflict between Crown and Commons in the seventeenth century. Today it is of relatively limited use, for its scope is restricted to circumstances where no legal process has been concluded and no alternative remedies are available. Thus it cannot be used to challenge imprisonment after a conviction. Moreover in Northern Ireland, where the writ might have been useful as a way of challenging internment, the Government has in times of crisis suspended the Habeas Corpus Act. (The whole question of civil rights in Northern Ireland is now supervised by a standing committee on civil rights.) Although the remedy of *habeas corpus* has occasionally been used to challenge detention in a mental hospital or by immigration authorities, it is thus of very limited use to the average citizen.

In part the infrequency of applications for habeas corpus writs underlines the general conformity of British administrative practice to the principle that there should be no detention without trial. Yet in relation to other aspects of the administration of law and order, Britain cannot claim so unquestionably successful a record. In particular such routine matters as the police powers of arrest and the questioning of suspects, as well as the related matter of the invasion of privacy and the seizure of potential evidence, vividly illustrate the weaknesses of the pragmatic British approach to civil liberties. The problem is not that a citizen who finds himself in the situation of confrontation with the police is likely to be treated less fairly than his American counterpart, even after the so-called 'due process revolution'. It is rather that the British reliance on the fair play of policemen, internal codes of discipline and the discretion of the courts places a tremendous premium on the consistent integrity of institutions which by their very nature are often subject to pressures and prejudices that may prove difficult to resist. Overworked policemen who suspect that someone is guilty are perhaps not the best protectors of suspects' rights, especially where those rights are somewhat obscure; the fact that British courts do not operate rigid rules to exclude improperly acquired evidence offers further temptations to cut corners.

The precise powers of the police in relation to arrest, interrogation, search and seizure are beyond the scope of this book, and only the outlines of the position will be attempted here. It is important to note that in England and Wales the citizen and the policeman enjoy statutory powers of arrest, although if the arrest turns out to be unjustified they may be sued for unlawful assault or false imprisonment. Most arrests, however, are made by the police with warrants from a magistrate. It was established in the seventeenth century that a warrant must be a specific one, naming the individual and the offence. The police and the private citizen also have powers under the Criminal Law Act of 1967 to arrest without warrant in connection with a range of serious offences known as arrestable offences. If the arrest is to be lawful the accused must be brought before a magistrate as soon as is practicable. The magistrate can then either remand the accused in custody or grant bail until full legal proceedings can occur. The conditions on which bail will be granted have traditionally concerned libertarians; the conditions under which it may be refused have been restrictively defined in the Bail Act of 1976. This Act no longer makes bail dependent on the ability of the accused to provide recognizances and gives a general right to bail except where it is thought that the accused might escape, commit further offences or try to interfere with witnesses.

The rules about police behaviour while a suspect is being questioned derive from the Judges' Rules and a number of administrative directions to the police. These rules do not have the status of rules of law but serve merely as guidelines for the police. The Judges' Rules and directives were re-issued in 1978 following general criticism that they were not well enough known even by lawyers and policemen, let alone the general public. Evidence acquired in breach of these rules does not automatically render it inadmissible in court and this is one of the areas where many observers think a bill of rights could be most useful. Thus the National Council for Civil Liberties, although hostile to the idea of a bill of rights because it could shift power to the non-elected judiciary, produced in its evidence to the Select Committee a cogent argument for reform in this area because it felt that the Judges' Rules and directives did not constitute adequate safeguards of suspects' rights. Although the Criminal Law Act of 1977 now makes provision for a person held in custody to be able to inform someone of the fact, which gives an opportunity for access to a solicitor, the entitlement is still subject to 'no more delay than is necessary' and was inserted in the Act against the wishes of the Home Office.[17] The frequent delay in putting a suspect in touch with a solicitor arises both because the police are not always enthusiastic about having a lawyer present during questioning and because it is sometimes difficult to find one immediately. Lawyers do not wait around prisons and lower courts as they do in the United States, and it has been suggested that duty solicitors at magistrates' courts are much more needed. As the NCCL emphasized in its evidence to the Select Committee on a Bill of Rights, much greater care needs to be taken to see that convicted prisoners can obtain access to a lawyer if necessary.

The development of public concern about such matters as confessions obtained in police stations and the general powers of the police in relation to the acquisition of evidence has led to a number of special inquiries recently. Thus a departmental committee of the Home Office in 1977 reported in favour of a limited experiment with tape-recording the police interrogation of suspects. Also, the disquiet occasioned by the *Confait* case in which charges were made on the basis of confessions obtained after prolonged questioning, and in which one policeman admitted that he had misunderstood the Judges' Rules, contributed to the decision to establish a Royal Commission on Criminal Procedure to look in more detail at existing practice in relation to the whole area of police questioning.[18] The Royal Commission has not, however, had an easy task before it. There is a clear division of public opinion between those who want to see stricter safeguards for the individual and those who believe, as the Chief Commissioner of the Metropolitan Police argued in his evidence to this Commission, that the police are already impeded in their attempt to secure convictions against known criminals – and the majority are probably on the side of the police rather than the suspect.[19] The difference of opinion among those who wish to maintain civil liberties even when a price has to be paid for them has recently become apparent in the general area of freedom of speech and assembly. The freedom to hold peaceful meetings and to take part in demonstrations is acknowledged in most international and national statements of civil liberties. In Britain, however, the law guarantees no absolute right either to hold a political meeting or to demonstrate; both rights are subject to statutory and common-law restrictions which in effect allow the police and the courts a great deal of discretion in their methods of maintaining public order, as well as a variety of powers to curtail and control public meetings if they decide that to be necessary.

Police discretion and the attitude of the courts about public order have become a subject of controversy in contemporary Britain as a result of the events of the post-1968 period, during which a variety of organizations and causes have sought to spread their message by recourse to direct action. One recent occasion which caused controversy about the extent of the right to demonstrate was the series of clashes which occurred when the National Front's marches and demonstrations were met by groups opposed to the Front's policies, who were determined to prevent the Front from marching at all. Inevitably, such conflicts have led to violence which the police have proved unable to control; they have raised the question of whether it is desirable to place stringent restrictions on marches and meetings which seem likely to produce such disruption.

The law relating to public meetings is somewhat different from the law relating to processions. In theory the only restriction on a public meeting is the absence of a suitable meeting-place: a hall may prove difficult to find if the group involved has a history of violent meetings. But there was strong demand in 1979 for a tightening of the law when riots, in which one man was killed, followed a National Front meeting in Southall. Open-air meetings require the consent of the local authority if its land is to be used and for the special centres of public protest – Hyde Park and Trafalgar Square in London – the consent of the Secretary of State for the Environment is required. As far as processions are concerned the police have additional statutory powers, which are the product of the fascist marches of the 1930s which led to legislation. The Public Order Act of 1936 gave the Home Secretary additional power to regulate processions which seemed likely to produce serious disorder, and gave the chief police officer in each police authority the power to impose conditions on the organizers of marches and demonstrations. Thus if the circumstances of a proposed march warrant such intervention, for example if the National Front propose to march through an immigrant area, the police can prescribe the route which a procession must take. In addition the chief officer of police can, if he thinks the overall situation in an area sufficiently serious, ask for a general ban on all processions in the area for a period not exceeding three months. The application for such a ban has to be made to the appropriate local authority which may then make an order imposing it, providing that the consent of the Home Secretary has been obtained. In London the Metropolitan Police Commissioner himself makes the order if the consent of the Home Secretary is given.

Quite clearly these provisions give the police, the local authorities and the Home Secretary substantial power to control the arrangements governing processions and in the last resort would enable the imposition of a blanket prohibition on certain kinds of marches. The problem from the point of view of the police is to know when to use their powers. Lord Scarman, who was the chairman of a tribunal of inquiry into demonstrations in Red Lion Square in which one student died in 1974, expressed the dilemma in a lecture:[20] 'A policeman is the servant of both sides in a street confrontation.' In other words, it is a delicate question of when to sacrifice one party's right to demonstrate for another's right to try to interfere with its message, and when to sacrifice the right of peaceful protest to the general interest of the public in being free to carry on their business and use the streets without interruption. The problem is particularly sensitive when the groups involved in demonstrations are those, like the National Front, which claim they have only limited access to the normal channels of political communication such as the mass media. As Lord Scarman has emphasized, the task of trying to maintain a balance in this area is made even more difficult by the obscurity of the law, which in his view 'has not adjusted itself to the realities of an industrial society entitled to exercise freedom of speech, protest and assembly not only through representative institutions but directly – by assembly, march and protest in public places'.[21] The principle that any lawful use of the highway is permissible and that a procession is nothing more than a number of people passing along it will not really help either the courts or the police to cope with such phenomena as mass picketing and concerted demonstrations. Indeed, if Lord Scarman's assertion is correct that 'the truth is there is no modern law governing the basic priorities in the use by society of streets and public places', then the traditional approach to civil liberties once more seems deficient. It is deficient, too, in a way which as Lord Scarman suggests places a heavy burden on the police.[22]

A large part of the controversy generated by the National Front's demonstrations in the 1970s stemmed from the fear that they would not merely cause civil disorder but also stimulate racial antagonisms if given wider publicity as a result of their violence. Concern with the promotion of racial harmony in an increasingly plural society has prompted successive British governments to provide specific protections for minority groups which might be vulnerable to discrimination against them. These protections, provided in the Race Relations Acts of 1965, 1968 and 1976, do however have implications for the exercise of civil liberties, for they constitute an additional inroad into the freedom of speech of the rest of society.

The Race Relations Act of 1965 effectively extended the Public Order Act of 1936 by making it an offence to use in any public place or meeting threatening, abusive or insulting words or behaviour or to distribute or display any writing, sign or visible representation with intent to provoke a breach of the peace or whereby a breach of the peace was likely to be occasioned. It created the new offence of incitement to racial hatred, which made it illegal to stir up hatred against any section of the public distinguished by colour, race or ethnic or national origins regardless of whether a breach of the peace was likely to be committed as a result. With this Act the law began to move away from the prohibition of offences because of their contribution to civil disorder and instituted a category of offences which were to be prohibited on grounds of their inherent undesirability. When this category is added to the already formidable range of common-law and statutory offences which bedevil the exercise of the liberty to march, demonstrate and speak freely – riot, affray, rout, unlawful assembly, public nuisance, obstructing the highway and obstructing a police officer in the execution of his duty – it would seem that public protest is likely to become an increasingly hazardous venture.

Freedom of expression in Britain, like freedom of assembly, exists only insofar as it is not restricted by legislation or common law. Thus the extent of that freedom in any period depends very much on the prevailing attitudes among legislators and the judiciary. Those attitudes are not always consistent; after a period of liberalization the United Kingdom may now be experiencing something of a return to less permissive attitudes on such questions as censorship. Nor is the question of freedom of expression one which is affected by formal restraints only; the legal provisions do affect what newspapers and the media say and publish but also, alongside the formal restrictions, there is a range of informal ones which effectively constrain and control the free circulation of ideas. Thus the extent to which control over the mass media is concentrated in the hands of a few and the operation of the internal mechanisms of censorship are as significant as the formal legal controls.

Several branches of the law constrain the free expression of opinion in the United Kingdom. Statements likely to damage an individual's reputation may fall foul of the defamation laws, which in the United Kingdom protect persons in public life on the same basis as private citizens. Certain categories of proceedings, such as verbatim reporting of parliamentary debates and legal proceedings, are protected; this privilege sometimes protects reporters who might be at risk from a libel suit by allowing them simply to repeat allegations made in the context of a court case, for example. Journalists may invoke defences which mitigate the effects of the law, for example the defence of fair comment, but British newspapers are often forced to delay their comments on political scandals either until their evidence is watertight or until foreign newspapers and the underground press have made an item common knowledge. Since not merely the author but also the publisher and vendor of a libel can be sued, journals such as *Private Eye* are frequently sold only by small newsagents and not by big retail chains.

A second restriction on freedom of speech is the law of obscenity and blasphemy. The obscenity laws were liberalized by the Obscene Publications Act of 1959, as amended in 1964; although there were spectacular prosecutions against well-known works of literature to test the law in the early 1960s – both D.H. Lawrence's novel *Lady Chatterley's Lover* and Cleland's *Fanny Hill* were prosecuted – the general climate had so changed by the end of the 1960s that it was difficult to persuade the Director of Public Prosecutions to initiate prosecutions and to obtain convictions from juries. However, occasionally prosecutions do succeed, as happened in 1971 when the so-called 'School-Kids' Issue' of *Oz* produced one of the longest obscenity trials in British legal history and led to the conviction of the three editors Richard Neville, Felix Dennis and Jim Anderson.[23] Not all prosecutions take place under the Obscene Publications Act, however. It is an offence to send obscene literature through the post so that a conviction under the Post Office Act of 1953 may be secured if the police wish to stamp out the distribution of pornography. Similarly, customs officers have the power to seize obscene material under the Customs and Excise Act of 1952 – although Britain's right to regulate such *European* imports occasioned legal controversy.

The courts have also from time to time revived archaic common-law crimes, despite the important objection that a criminal conviction is such a serious matter as to be only acceptable in contemporary society where the offence is clearly defined in advance. Thus in 1961 the House of Lords used the crime of 'conspiracy to corrupt public morals' to secure the conviction of a man called Shaw who published and distributed a directory of prostitutes.[24] More recently, the common-law crime of blasphemous libel was used to secure the prosecution of the editor of *Gay News*. This prosecution occasioned protest not merely because it seemed out of place in an increasingly secular and liberal society but because the law of blasphemous libel had not been invoked since 1921.[25]

Other legal restrictions on freedom of speech stem from the

Race Relations Acts, which make incitement to racial hatred an offence, from the Official Secrets Act of 1911 and from the developing law of confidentiality. The initial caution of the Government in the sphere of race relations was evidenced by the fact that under the 1965 Act no prosecution could be brought without the consent of the Attorney General, and intention to stir up racial hatred had to be proved. While it is difficult to tell how many complaints have been referred to the Attorney General since 1965, there have been very few prosecutions. An early opportunity to test the law occurred in 1967 when Colin Jordan was prosecuted for distributing stickers and pamphlets on behalf of his National Socialist Party; in the same year Michael X, a black-power leader, was prosecuted for using inflammatory language at a meeting of his black-power group.

The problems of securing a conviction under s.6(1) of the 1965 Race Relations Act and the development of opinion in favour of strengthening the legislation in this sphere encouraged the Government to eliminate in the 1976 Race Relations Act the need to prove subjective intention to stir up racial hatred.[26] Section 70 of the Act therefore now makes it a criminal offence to use, publish or distribute threatening words or written matter in circumstances where racial hatred is likely to be stirred up. The penalties for committing this offence are quite severe – six months' imprisonment or a fine of £400 on summary conviction, and a maximum of two years' imprisonment on indictment. However, a prosecution still requires the consent of the Attorney General, and it may be assumed that this law will be used sparingly.[27]

The restrictions on freedom of speech inherent in the Official Secrets Act raises the broader question of the quality and character of British government, which according to many critics has been far too secretive about even the ordinary processes of decision making.[28] A start has recently been made on trying to redress the balance between a desirable openness in government and the natural tendency of politicians to try to conceal the operations of government from inspection. Thus increasingly, consultative papers are published in advance of government's formulation of its own views and, although this provision has been restrictively interpreted, government departments are now supposed to release a wide variety of background material of a factual nature, so that press and public can make their own judgements about the reasoning behind policy decisions. On one front, however – the repeal of the Official Secrets Act – progress has been extremely slow. The document published in response to the strictures of the Fulton Committee on the topic of secrecy, *Information and the Public Interest*, denied that this cornerstone in the edifice of governmental secrecy was really any impediment at all to greater openness in government. However, by 1969 criticism of the Act had become so loud that the Conservative Party manifesto of 1970 committed the Party to reviewing it, and when they came into government in 1970 they duly instituted a committee of inquiry into its operation.

The Official Secrets Act is unpopular partly because of the uncertain way in which it operates; it is also unpopular because as far as liberal critics are concerned it encapsulates a large number of assumptions about what the proper balance between public scrutiny and government confidentiality should be. The 1911 Act was passed to replace earlier legislation, and Parliament, assuming that its purpose was to produce additional legislative power to deal with German espionage, subjected its provisions to very little detailed scrutiny. Thus the broad terms of s.2, which have occasioned most hostility, were not commented upon despite the fact – and this is what makes the Act obnoxious to journalists – that it makes the unauthorized *receipt* as well as the unauthorized communication of information an offence. In practice, government has not used the Act in a consistently repressive manner, but it hangs over the media and the public as a weapon which could be used if government felt sufficiently strongly that certain information should not be published. The sheer unpredictability of a government's attitude towards leaks and disclosures made the operation of the law arbitrary, and on those occasions when it was used against journalists they inevitably became akin to martyrs in the cause of press freedom. It was perhaps ironic that the Conservative Government, shortly after deciding to establish a committee to review the Official Secrets Act, should have used the legislation to prosecute two *Daily Telegraph* journalists who had published a secret assessment of the Nigerian civil war. Both journalists were acquitted, and the judge's comments on the nature and scope of s.2 of the Act were sufficiently hostile to add further strength to the demand for the radical revision of its provisions.[29]

Above all, however, exception to the Act has arisen because it symbolizes the contrast between the British approach to governmental relations with the general public and the approach adopted by some other countries. In the United States and Sweden it is assumed that the public has a right of access to information unless there is some good reason, usually of compelling national security, why such information should not be disclosed. The burden of proof falls on government to justify withholding information, and the goal of open government is embodied in Sweden's Freedom of the Press Act of 1949 and the United States' Freedom of Information Act of 1974. In Britain, on the other hand, no such right is acknowledged in principle, and the timing and speed of government concessions on the release of information is entirely within the hands of the executive. Green papers, background material, greater publicity for civil servants and more frequent examination of government activity before the PCA and before select committees of Parliament – certainly all these have been gains for the proponents of a more democratic and accountable governmental system, even if their modest nature must also be acknowledged. However, while the Report of the Committee to review the Official Secrets Act – the Franks Committee – admitted that s.2 of the Official Secrets Act was 'a mess', it was not prepared to see the defence of disclosure in the public interest introduced; indeed, for many people the committee's proposals suggested a tightening up rather than a liberalization of the law. The Conservative Government which established the Franks Committee did not, it should be noted, introduce any legislation on the basis of its 1973 Report – perhaps because its proposals were too liberal for the Government while too timid for the press critics. The Labour Government announced in 1976 that it intended to legislate to replace s.2 of the Official Secrets Act with a law, usually referred to as an Official Information Act, which would restrict the operation of the criminal law to certain categories of information.

Then, in 1978, the Government published a white paper which discussed the options available to it, although it stated that legislation would not be possible in that parliamentary session.[30] The Conservative Government elected in 1979 announced its intention to introduce legislation to reform s.2.

The question of the secrecy of Cabinet papers had been raised in two dramatic incidents during the 1970s – controversies which perhaps did more than the exhaustive governmental deliberations to extend openness in British administration. The first incident was the publication by Jonathan Cape and *The Sunday Times* of the diaries of the late Richard Crossman, who had been a Cabinet minister from 1964 to 1970. The novelty of the diaries was their detailed recording of Cabinet proceedings, sometimes with quotations from Cabinet papers, and their frank, if not tactless, remarks about colleagues including civil servants. The convention on ministerial memoirs had been understood to require that all material intended for publication should be submitted for approval to the Cabinet Secretary first; however, for Richard Crossman the point of his diaries was to cut through the web of secrecy and hypocrisy which he saw permeating Whitehall. Therefore, although his executors submitted the manuscript to the Cabinet Secretary for comment, they were unwilling to allow his objections to publication to alter their determination to publish the diaries in full.[31] The Attorney General sought an injunction to prevent publication, but Lord Widgery, the Lord Chief Justice, refused to grant one. Two points of interest emerged from his judgment; this turned not on whether there was any statutory bar on publication – the Attorney General was not relying on the Official Secrets Act – but on whether the court had the legal power to restrain the publication of confidential information. Although the court allowed the publication of the Crossman diaries, it asserted that it did have such a power, by analogy with its power to protect confidences given in private relationships such as marriage.[32]

However, whether the court should restrain publication depended upon the circumstances, including for example the nature of the confidential information involved and the degree of time which had elapsed between the actions and the revelations.

Thus the court had not merely expanded the law of confidentiality in a way which might give government a new instrument for protecting its operations but had transferred the question of disclosure in this area from the realm of convention and consensus to the realm of judicial control. The establishment of a Committee of Privy Councillors to examine the whole question of the publication of ministerial memoirs, together with its recommendations, seemed to suggest that there is still substantial faith in the efficacy of informal guidelines rather than precise legal rules, and that the iconoclastic actions of Richard Crossman will prove the exception rather than the norm.[33] The Committee recommended that publication of material affecting national security, international relations and the relations between ministers and their advisers – the frank accounts of the contributions of individual civil servants to the policy-making process had been the cause of a large number of objections to the publication of the diaries – should not occur for fifteen years after the events described. Only time will tell whether this recommendation leads to any further loosening of the rules governing access to papers for scholarly purposes, but it is to be hoped that it will.

The second incident which raised the question of the confidentiality of Cabinet documents was the publication by *New Society* of Cabinet papers relating to the withdrawal of a proposed child benefit. In this case it was clear that either a member of the Government or someone with access to cabinet papers had leaked the documents to the editor of the journal. The disclosure sparked off an internal Cabinet inquiry and a police investigation, both of which proved inconclusive but which raised again the logic of a system which penalized – or might penalize – the supply of material of public interest in such a way.[34]

One further source of legal restrictions on the media ought to be mentioned, although it applies equally to private citizens, and that is the law of contempt. The Attorney General has power to prevent the publication of material which relates to pending legal proceedings, whether they are of a criminal or a civil nature. The justification for this law is that it prevents 'trial by newspaper' which, especially in a criminal trial, would mean that a jury would be exposed to information and allegations that would make an objective assessment of the legal evidence impossible. The reverse of the coin is that a number of cases have arisen in which the law of contempt has been used to restrict comment on matters of public controversy. The *cause célèbre* – which went to the European Court on Human Rights – was the thalidomide controversy of the 1970s previously mentioned, where *The Sunday Times* risked contempt proceedings by commenting on the responsibility of Distillers Ltd, a drug company, for congenital malformations in the children of mothers who took the drug during pregnancy. A committee had been established under Mr Justice Phillimore and its inquiries were proceeding when the case arose. It recommended that proceedings had to be imminent before a writ for contempt could be issued, in other words a date for trial or hearing had to be fixed, and it was not enough for the simple possibility of litigation to exist. The Phillimore Committee also recommended a defence that the matter was one of serious public concern and that discussion of it only 'incidentally and unintentionally created a risk of prejudice to particular proceedings'. However, the Government, in a white paper published in 1978, seemed unwilling to implement the Committee's proposals, and at the time of writing the contempt rules are unchanged.[35]

Apart from these restrictions on what can be said or published, the Theatre Act of 1968 subjects live performances to the same guidelines as those that govern books under the Obscene Publications Act of 1959. (The provisions of the Act have recently been extended to films.) The advisory classification system applied by the British Board of Film Censors, an independent body, allows a certain amount of choice by local authorities, which have the final say in relation to what may be screened within their jurisdiction. Local authorities need not take account of certificates granted by the British Board of Film Censors and may exclude a film from their area altogether, although the system also allows liberal authorities to show films which have not been granted a certificate.[36]

As far as radio and television are concerned both the British Broadcasting Corporation and the Independent Broadcasting Authority have elaborate arrangements for operating internal self-censorship. The British Broadcasting Corporation, although its connection with government is ostensibly greater than that of the Independent Broadcasting Authority, paradoxically may exercise greater latitude in its interpretation of what needs to be censored and what does not. This is because the prestige of the BBC and its very public link with government – the original powers of the Corporation derive from a Royal Charter, but the Minister of Posts and Telecommunications may issue directives to the Corporation while the income of the BBC is derived from licences issued by the Post Office – make it less likely that subtle political pressures will be exerted as threats to the Corporation's position. For the Independent Broadcasting Authority, which sub-contracts programmes to a variety of independent television companies, the possibility of government intervention is much more real, as was evidenced in 1967 when Lord Hill, the chairman of what was then called the Independent Television Authority, announced a rearrangement of the distribution of franchises for the fifteen programme-companies which served the authority. Franchises, it seemed, were conditional on good behaviour, which was defined by the government-appointed chairman and a government-appointed body.[37]

The closeness which marks the relationship between the broadcasting authorities and the state does not affect the press in the same way. Its problems in the 1960s and 1970s have stemmed from rather different sources. First, there has been the problem of concentration of ownership, which in the view of many critics has serious implications for the diversity of opinion to be found at the national and provincial level of the press. Secondly, there is the problem of the general lack of commercial viability – a problem which accounted for the closure of two newspapers, the *Daily Herald* and the *News Chronicle*. Finally, although this is a much more recent problem and one not entirely unconnected with the question of commercial viability, there are the difficulties which arise from internal staffing problems. The print unions are strong and have frequently seemed to prefer to cripple their newspapers rather than moderate their stance on manning, pay or methods of work. This attitude was in large part responsible for a conflict which caused *The Times* to suspend publication in 1978. The refusal of the National Union of Journalists to allow journalists to be exempted from the closed-shop provisions of the Trade Union and Labour Relations Act suggests that those few newspapers which do survive will find it difficult to avoid the uniformity of outlook which stems from a concentration of ownership on the one hand and the homogeneity of practice in such matters as recruitment which springs from a closed shop on the other.[38] It may, alas, be that although Britain will continue to exhibit more diversity in terms of its population, its politics and its social life, the trend of journalism will be in the opposite direction.

12 The Citizen and the Administration II: The Control of Government and the Redress of Grievances

As was seen in the last chapter, constitutional history and political expediency have combined to make the protection of civil liberties in the United Kingdom dependent upon the self-restraint of Parliament and the ordinary processes of the common law. However, as the recent debate about the desirability of introducing a codified bill of rights into the British legal system suggests, opinion is now very much divided about whether a more self-conscious and comprehensive approach to questions of individual rights and freedoms is required. The provisions made for the defence of the classic political freedoms such as freedom of speech and assembly will always be a sensitive matter, since those freedoms lie at the heart of the relationship between the individual and the state. Yet in the context of a society where the activities of government are extensive and where in consequence the individual comes into frequent contact with public authorities, the quality of administration will itself be a matter of central concern to him. The procedures employed by government in assessing a whole range of entitlements and obligations, from welfare benefits to income tax, must be able to command the respect of those who are likely to be affected by them. The last decade has in fact seen increased opportunities for subjecting to scrutiny administrative decisions and the policies on which they are based, so that the individual who finds himself in conflict with an agency of the state is perhaps in a better position to secure a fair resolution of that dispute now than he was ten years ago.

The longstanding view that Parliament should be the primary channel for voicing complaints against government, and the emphasis placed upon the MP's role as the champion of his constituents against executive error, have meant that the devising of remedies for maladministration has lagged far behind the expansion of governmental functions. Alternative procedures to parliamentary ones for reviewing the decisions of public authorities were for a long time weak and ill-developed, and the analysis of the problem of securing justice in the welfare state was frequently ill-informed or antediluvian. Rapid developments in the intellectual climate have now, however, had an impact on the political system; new techniques for obtaining governmental accountability and the redress of grievances have been introduced and adapted to the existing pattern of institutions. And, as these experiments have proved successful, it has become apparent that devices adopted initially to supplement existing administrative and constitutional arrangements have themselves generated further pressures for reform in the administrative and political environment.

Ministerial Responsibility and the Franks Report

Parliament's central position as the instrument whereby accountability could be secured in the United Kingdom was enshrined in the doctrine of ministerial responsibility. In essence this doctrine meant that, although civil servants had to remain anonymous, Parliament could hold ministers answerable for their actions. The distinction between errors made as a result of personal incompetence by civil servants and mistakes occasioned by faulty administrative practices was not significant in this doctrine: a minister was in theory as responsible to Parliament for both categories of maladministration as if he had personally carried out the action complained of. The kind of sanction which Parliament would impose on a minister responsible for a department in which mistakes were discovered naturally varied with the seriousness of the offence and the reasonableness of holding him accountable for it. However, in theory there was no doubt about Parliament's right to impose some sort of sanction, whether it took the form of a critical debate, which would result in a loss of esteem for the minister concerned, or of an enforced resignation. Parliamentary procedures reflected the importance attached to this theory of how the people's representatives might keep control of the executive: Question Time afforded regular opportunities for the quality of a minister's stewardship to be examined, and in the event of a serious allegation of malpractice or incompetence the device of an adjournment debate was always possible.

Although weaknesses were apparent from twentieth-century experience of the doctrine's operation, it took a very long time before parliamentarians would admit to them. Instead subtle shifts occurred in the interpretation of the doctrine, which was frequently modified to take account of political reality. However, while these shifts were able to conceal the fictitious aspects of the doctrine of ministerial responsibility, they did little to reassure critics that the vast apparatus of modern government was subject to effective political scrutiny or that an individual grievance against a decision could be thoroughly investigated. For example, although it was evident that sanctions were in fact rarely imposed on a minister and that Cabinets would usually prefer to support one of their number to admitting an error which might reflect on the competence of the administration as a whole, this tendency could be accommodated by defenders of the traditional doctrines associated with parliamentary control of the administration. It was the potential embarrassment of a pertinent parliamentary question which was the important factor in keeping the administration on its toes, and it was not important that Question Time had been increasingly transformed into an extension of the adversarial badinage between the parties, which marked other aspects of the style of the Commons, rather than a genuine forum for the redress of grievances or the probing of administrative failures. If necessary, it was confidently assumed, the occasion could still be employed for its theoretical purpose and the exposure of maladministration would not be obscured by the ritualistic character of Question Time.

Also, although by the early post-war period it had become increasingly apparent that ministers had little hope of understanding all the complexities of their departments' internal arrangements, much less of controlling them, it was still thought possible that clear organization of responsibilities could produce a chain of command which would permit a minister to identify where and how individual decisions were taken. Few MPs were prepared to concede that while such an aspiration might have been justified in a period where central government's activities were limited, it hardly corresponded to the situation of vastly expanded personnel and functions following the Second World War.

The deficiencies of the doctrine of ministerial responsibility and the need to reappraise the machinery for reviewing administrative actions were highlighted by the so-called 'Crichel Down affair', which jerked the British public, albeit temporarily, out of its complacency about the methods available for citizens to challenge executive activity. Debate continues about the significance of the Crichel Down case but its merit was that it focused attention on a range of issues connected with the quality of the British administrative system, and publicized the flaws in orthodox constitutional assumptions about the relationship between Parliament and the public on the one hand and ministers and officials on the other.[1] In particular, it underlined the extent to which a minister, far from being able to control his civil servants, was their prisoner when it came to the information at his disposal and, through him, available to Parliament; it revealed the effort, resources and sheer luck required to enable an individual to extract a remedy for administrative injustice from the existing machinery.

The facts of the Crichel Down case – which involved the compulsory purchase of land for use as a bombing site and a refusal to return it when it was no longer required for that purpose – were perhaps less important than the general questions which it raised.[2] How widespread was the arrogant and peremptory attitude towards the general public which the civil servants engaged in the decision had displayed? Were ministers regularly as ill-informed or deceived about the true facts of a decision as Sir Thomas Dugdale had been? Were there large numbers of other citizens whose complaints had not been effective because they lacked the skills, persistence and resources of the complainant in the case? And to what extent could the resignation of a minister like Sir Thomas Dugdale really be taken as an effective sanction on government or even as a spur to improved administrative habits? (Sir Thomas Dugdale's resignation, although it represented no real damage to the Government of the day, provides the last major instance of a resignation because of administrative failings within a department; individual ministers have resigned since then on policy grounds but not because of their civil servants' mistakes.) Perhaps the Crichel Down case raised too many fundamental issues for the public criticism which followed it to produce an adequate response from government. Because of general dissatisfaction with the protection afforded the citizen when governmental decisions materially affected his interests, the Government did, however, establish in 1954 the Franks Committee on Administrative Tribunals and Enquiries.[3] It was widely assumed that this Committee would be permitted to undertake the general examination of administrative decision-making processes which Crichel Down indicated was necessary, but in fact the restriction of the Committee's terms of reference to formal tribunals and inquiries excluded the kind of discretionary decisions which had aroused so much criticism in that instance.[4] In other words, the category of decisions outside the ambit of the Franks Committee's deliberations were precisely those where the remedy could only be secured through parliamentary questioning with all the defects exhibited during Crichel Down. It was not until the institution of a Parliamentary Commissioner for Administration was created in 1967 that any reform occurred which involved this area of decision making.

Although the Franks Report was confined to the area where formal machinery for challenging governmental decisions already existed, the Committee's work did bring about significant improvements in that field and stimulated discussion of the machinery of accountability and redress in the United Kingdom. Moreover, it is at least arguable that by defining the characteristics which ought to mark tribunals – the holy trinity of 'openness, fairness and impartiality' – it articulated values which could be applied by others to the administrative process as a whole. Thus even if the range of the Franks Committee's work was a disappointment, it was able to make a not-inconsiderable contribution of its own to the intellectual climate in which administrative procedures are discussed.

The Franks Committee recognized that a large part of the

problem under its consideration was a result of the rapidly changing character of governmental activity and the sheer increase in the number of decisions taken by government which might be open to objection. The need was to 'consider afresh the procedures by which the rights of individual citizens' could be harmonized with 'wider public interests'. It also recognized that, while the administration should be efficient in the sense of being able to secure policy objectives speedily, care must be taken to show that where an individual's interest had to be disturbed in order to promote the general interest, every consideration had been given to the individual's case. If this care was not thoroughly demonstrated, the administrative process would not be able to command the assent of the general public and would be unlikely to be efficient in the long term. The specific recommendations of the Franks Committee were largely directed towards identifying the conditions which would produce that assent.

Although the Committee was limited in its inquiries to the field where statutory machinery already existed for appealing against a governmental decision, there was even within this area a great diversity of institutional structures – as well, of course, as a wide variety of subject matter covered by them. Appeal against a decision might be made to a court, to a specially constituted tribunal or to a minister, who was bound to follow a specific procedure if the matter related to compulsory purchase orders or planning appeals. As the Committee noted in 1957, the heterogeneity of tribunals made even this classification something of a simplification. But since Franks called attention to the amorphous area covered by tribunals, further legislation has extended their scope and number and magnified the complexity of their jurisdiction.

By 1979 the most frequently used kind of tribunal was that which determined entitlement to welfare benefits. However, other types of tribunals dealt with the whole range of industrial disputes, the multiplicity of questions concerning immigration (where a tribunal structure has operated since 1971), the granting of patents, and the assessment of the reasonableness of rents required by private landlords. There is also an extremely important and elaborate series of tribunals to hear appeals against tax assessments. Whereas in the case of entitlement to welfare benefits the parties in the dispute will actually be the individual citizen and a state agency, this is by no means true of all disputes which come before tribunals. Some, such as conflicts between landlord and tenant or employer and employee, are primarily between private individuals, although the conflict is of course regulated by principles laid down in public legislation.[5]

The reasons for using tribunals to decide appeals against government decisions, or to provide some protection to the citizen in the context of such special relationships as that of employer and employee, have been varied. Tribunals were established in connection with the initial legislation on welfare matters passed by the Liberal Governments of 1905–16. The justification for using tribunals rather than the ordinary courts was the lingering suspicion that the judiciary would be hostile to the collectivist philosophy behind the legislation, and that it would be better administered through specialized bodies. Tribunals have also been seen to have the additional advantages of speed, cheapness and informality, and to offer a degree of expertise which the ordinary courts may not be able to match. Like so much else in British government, therefore, they are a pragmatic response to the problems created by the need to administer policies and adjudicate disputes in areas where hitherto government and the formal processes of law have not intervened.

When it surveyed the burgeoning sphere of tribunal activity the Franks Committee isolated one aspect of tribunals which distinguished them from other mechanisms of appeal. The point of Parliament's setting up a structure of tribunals to hear appeals, Franks thought, was that there was then a guarantee of independence in the appeals mechanism. The very existence of a tribunal in a particular area of administration indicated that the issues involved were not so suffused with policy considerations as to render neutral determination impossible. Thus Franks drew a sharp distinction between areas of tribunal jurisdiction and fields where the policy element was so important that even individual cases had to remain subject to ministerial or departmental intervention. The conclusion which the Committee drew from this observation was that the procedure and structure of tribunals ought to be treated as part of the machinery for adjudication rather than as an extension of the machinery of administration. In other words, the principles governing their operations ought to be similar to those applied in the courts, and they ought not to be approached as though they were simply appendages of government departments. By conceptualizing tribunals as instruments of adjudication Franks was able to elaborate the manner in which the characteristics of the judicial process – openness, fairness and impartiality – could be applied to the operation of tribunals. Despite the succinct clarity of the Committee's approach it proved rather more difficult in practice to apply these criteria than it had been to identify them. Improvements have been made since 1957, but the values of openness, fairness and impartiality do not fit the subject matter of every set of tribunals equally well. Openness, for example, might seem a straightforward ideal which could be attained by simply forcing all tribunals to sit in public. Not merely would this be reassuring to the general public but it could have an educative role if proceedings were reported in the local press. However, the fact that many tribunals deal with such personal matters as tax assessments, supplementary benefits and mental health precludes the imposition of a general requirement for open hearings. The Franks Committee could therefore only endorse the principle of public proceedings where appropriate, and had to accept the continuation of a discretion on the part of a tribunal to exclude observers. Thus although many tribunals do sit in public, many of the ones which are most used by the average citizen, for example the General Commissioners of Income Tax and the Supplementary Benefit Appeal Tribunal, sit in private.

The view of tribunals as fair and impartial bodies was enhanced by a number of the Franks Committee's recommendations. Some were admittedly symbolic rather than substantive, as for example the recommendation that tribunals should not hold their proceedings in the offices of government departments but should operate in some neutral territory. This suggestion was designed to dispel any impression on the part of the public that tribunals were adjuncts of government rather than genuinely neutral bodies. A more significant recommendation, perhaps, was the requirement that all tribunals should give reasoned decisions to the appellant. The form of reasoning employed by tribunals is not easy to categorize, and certainly they do not adopt the same approach to precedent and rule-following as that employed in the ordinary courts. Indeed it has been seen as a major advantage of tribunals that these bodies can decide cases on their individual facts and merits rather than rigidly following a corpus of rules of precedents. Nevertheless because there are formulae which tribunals apply it is important that parties to a case, even in the informal circumstances of a tribunal, should know the grounds of a decision, and this practice is now regularly followed. In addition the Franks Committee was of the opinion that while appeals to the courts on points of fact should not be entertained, there ought usually to be the opportunity for an appeal to the courts on points of law. It also thought that there should normally be some appellate tribunal to which general appeals on points of law, fact or merit could go, and such appeals, as a matter of principle, should never be to a minister.

The major institutional innovation which occurred as a direct result of the Franks Committee was the establishment of a general review body for England and Wales. Its task was to supervise generally the workings of all tribunals within that area. The idea was that such a body would keep the general principles enunciated by Franks under consideration and seek ways of applying them to the diversity of tribunal procedures and constitutions. The point that tribunals were part of the machinery of justice was emphasized by the suggestion that the review body, the Council on Tribunals, should report to the Lord Chancellor. The 1958 Tribunals and Inquiries Act implemented these proposals, and its annual reports provide a regular assessment of the whole structure of tribunals.

Perhaps the most important remaining defect in the tribunal system is the ambiguity surrounding the role to be played by those with legal qualifications in the daily operations of these bodies. As has been seen, the rationale of much of the Committee's arguments was that the whole network of tribunals should be regarded as part of the legal system, and it was therefore thought important that tribunals should have legally qualified chairmen who could follow legal arguments. However, there remains a general unwillingness to acknowledge the general right to legal representation before a tribunal in case this should interfere with the informality of the proceedings.

Even where legal representation is permitted there is the additional problem of cost, for although Franks recommended that legal aid should be made available to parties in a tribunal hearing on the same basis as in a court case, no action has been taken on this matter.[6] Moreover, while it is admirable in theory to suggest that tribunals should have legally qualified chairmen, the number of such appointments places a heavy burden on the pool of talent available. Indeed, when an increase in the jurisdiction of industrial tribunals was proposed in early 1970, the Chairman of the Council on Tribunals wrote to the Lord Chancellor – whose office is responsible for the appointment of tribunal members with legal qualifications – warning him that it would become necessary to revise the qualification requirements for their chairmen. The number of people available with the very high qualifications previously demanded was not infinite; whereas it had previously been customary to select chairmen from the ranks of barristers with at least seven years' experience of practice – though solicitors were also eligible for appointment – it would in future, the Chairman of the Council on Tribunals suggested, be necessary to rely more heavily on local solicitors to perform these tasks. At present the requirement of a legally qualified chairman is not applicable to all tribunals: for some, such as industrial tribunals, national insurance commissioners and betting levy appeal tribunals, the qualification is a statutory requirement, while for others, such as rent tribunals and supplementary benefit appeals tribunals, it is not.

The Franks Report was not solely concerned with the operation of tribunals: it also had the task of examining the way inquiries worked. Inquiries are used in a number of situations, but they nearly always involve the use of land; for example, an inquiry might be used in connection with an appeal against a refusal of planning permission or in connection with the proposals for development put forward by a local authority. The Second Report of the Council on Tribunals drew a distinction between tribunals and inquiries by underlining the fact that, whereas tribunals could be seen as part of the machinery for adjudication, inquiries were an integral part of the process of exercising ministerial discretion. Since a minister would be answerable to Parliament for the resolution of any conflict between private and public interests he could not be entirely impartial, though he could – and this was the purpose of an inquiry – ensure that all the evidence relevant to a decision had been heard. Thus although it is important that the inquiry part of the procedure be entirely fair and that opportunities exist for objections to any scheme to be heard, there can be no guarantee that the evidence brought out by an inquiry will carry any weight with the minister concerned. As the Council on Tribunals put it, 'The inquiry is modelled on judicial procedure, but it cannot lead to an equally objective decision. In the last resort the Minister must do what he thinks most expedient.'[7]

Nevertheless the Council on Tribunals took as its mandate the application to inquiries and hearings of standards which would satisfy the average citizen's sense of justice and the observation of the Franks values of openness, fairness and impartiality in this sphere also. Thus when an incident like the Chalk Pit case came to light a change in the rules governing inquiries was secured. (In that case the Minister had rejected the report of an inspector on the basis of fresh evidence which had come to light *after* the inquiry, without offering the objectors any opportunity to challenge the evidence.) The greater political salience of inquiries, compared with tribunals, has entailed rather more controversy surrounding their operation in the last fifteen years, especially with the increase in demands for more extensive participation in the planning process. Thus inquiries do not only have to ensure that procedures are followed which are scrupulously fair to affected individuals; they also have to reckon with the range of pressure groups which may use inquiries as a means of influencing decisions about the general environment and local amenities.

The Skeffington Report of 1969 advocated a much greater association of individuals and pressure groups in the planning function but, as was the case with the Franks criteria, there are limits to the extent to which this ideal can be implemented.[8] Considerations of cost and delay inevitably restrict the processes of examining objections to a planning proposal, as well as the amount of publicity which can be given beforehand to each proposal. Even where, as in the case of the Windscale inquiry, the proceedings are exhaustive, at the end of the day the objectors may still feel that the hearings were window-dressing for a decision which had already been taken by the Minister concerned.[9]

One change occasioned by the altered climate of the 1960s and 1970s relates to structure plans, which are concerned with general land use. Formal inquiries using the adversarial method of cross-examination of witnesses have been replaced when an area's structure plan is being prepared. Instead, a more informal seminar approach is used, and public examinations of the plan take place without the delay and stiffness occasioned by rigid rules of procedure.[10] It is perhaps too early to say how far this experiment has improved the public's appreciation of the planning process, but at least it reveals a willingness to consult with interested groups before final decisions on such plans are taken.

The Parliamentary Commissioner for Administration

If the episode of Crichel Down brought improvements to the procedures employed by tribunals and inquiries, progress was infinitely slower in the area where no formal machinery for review existed. The catalyst for change in this sphere, however, was the British Section of the International Commission of Jurists which in 1958 established a small study group to examine how ombudsmen operated in other countries as a protection against maladministration.[11] A further inquiry followed this initial one, and the result was a recommendation that Britain should establish a modified version of the ombudsman, to be called a Parliamentary Commissioner for Administration. The idea was rejected by the then Conservative Government but was taken up by the Labour Party immediately prior to the 1964 election. The ultimate result of that commitment was the Parliamentary Commissioner Act of 1967 which created the British version of an ombudsman.

Although the House of Commons returned in 1966 contained a large number of new recruits to politics who were sceptical about the relevance of traditional constitutional theories to the conditions of a complex welfare state, there remained some ambiguity about the Parliamentary Commissioner's functions.

The introduction of such an institution threatened to erode one of the most cherished roles of the back-bencher; and even if the proliferation of governmental activities made the MP's role more difficult to perform, such a development was unlikely to be viewed with enthusiasm. Moreover, although MPs and civil servants were becoming increasingly aware of the difficulties of maintaining detailed control within the departmental structure, natural conservatism and inertia – not entirely absent from the British bureaucracy – produced hostility to an innovation which could cause additional work. The nature of the proposal, even in the diluted form proposed by the Labour Government, was of course inherently radical, for it seemed designed to destroy much of the anonymity associated with the civil service and to reveal the inner workings of the governmental machine in ways which could have numerous repercussions. Indeed, it was thought that the development might seriously undermine the principle that advice given by officials to ministers is confidential, and that this in turn would transform the whole character of the relationship between the elected and the permanent elements in government.

In practice, while the Parliamentary Commissioner has stimulated further movements in the direction of a more open style of government, it is probable that his existence has not fundamentally undermined the morale of the Civil Service. Indeed, it could be argued that the institution has improved it by serving as a public witness to the generally high administrative standards of British central government.

The initial fears about how well the Parliamentary Commissioner would fit into British administrative process largely explain the restricted jurisdiction and powers given to him and the style adopted by the first Parliamentary Commissioner, Sir Edmund Compton. Sir Edmund had been Comptroller and Auditor General, and the cautious approach to the office which he adopted reflected a conception of the Parliamentary Commissioner's role which paralleled the internal auditing functions of the Comptroller's Office.[12] Since Sir Edmund Compton, however, the incumbents of the office of Parliamentary Commissioner have gradually modified many of the initial interpretations of the PCA's powers and it is highly probable that the appointment in 1979 of a non-civil servant, Mr C.M.

Clothier, QC, marks a further shift away from the theory of the office as one in which maladministration was to be checked by a specialized corps of civil servants.

The assumption that the Parliamentary Commissioner would operate in a manner analogous to the Comptroller and Auditor General, combined with the need to allay MPs' fears that they would be rendered redundant as far as constituency case-work was concerned if the PCA proved successful, was responsible for the most controversial feature of the British ombudsman. Unlike other ombudsmen, with the exception of the French médiateur, the Parliamentary Commissioner was precluded from receiving complaints from the public directly, and could only consider a case if it had been forwarded to him from an MP. In theory this restriction was designed to locate the responsibility for the redress of grievances very firmly in the House of Commons; in practice it seems clear that it has limited the utility of the PCA and caused some confusion to the public – especially since the local ombudsmen and the PCA himself in his capacity as Health Service Commissioner apply different rules with regard to access. The Health Service Commissioner permits direct access and has broader powers than the PCA; the local commissioners can take complaints from the public, though they would normally be referred through a councillor. The drawbacks of indirect access can be measured by the fact that the United Kingdom's Parliamentary Commissioner investigated only 252 cases in 1974 although Britain had a population of 55 million; in Sweden in the same year 2,368 cases were investigated for a population of only 8 million.[13]

The criticisms directed at the restrictions on access to the Parliamentary Commissioner prompted Sir Idwal Pugh to modify his practice when complaints were sent directly to him. He decided to adopt a policy of taking the initiative in forwarding complaints to MPs which would then be sent back to the PCA, rather than simply returning them to the citizen. This may seem a peculiar device, but at least it prevents a large number of complaints going uninvestigated simply because the rules of access discouraged the complainant at an early stage. In the long run, it is probable that direct access to the Parliamentary Commissioner will occur as MPs realize that his office is no substantial threat to their own relationship with constituents.[14]

THE GOVERNMENT OF THE UNITED KINGDOM

Indirect access to the Parliamentary Commissioner inevitably created complications: it did not take account of the fact that many people who might want to use the mechanism to challenge a governmental decision would probably not be familiar with the intricacies of government. Another obstacle to the Parliamentary Commissioner's provision of a successful source of support for the average citizen in dispute with a government department is even more fundamental: the early style of the office, and the emphasis on its subordination to Parliament, have meant that the work done by the PCA is not as well publicized as it might be. The lack of publicity was partly a reflection of the format of reports and of the process of indirect access, which also meant indirect communication to the press. But in part it was also the corollary of the rather cautious, low-key approach that was initially felt necessary to allow Whitehall to accommodate itself to the innovation. However, more recently the Parliamentary Commissioner has been taking a more aggressive approach to the problem of publicity, and in 1977 he engaged with the Central Office of Information in a concerted campaign to spread details about the operation of the PCA.

The 1967 legislation establishing the institution of Parliamentary Commissioner was viewed as inadequate for reasons other than the difficulties produced by its provisions governing access. Those who hoped that the Parliamentary Commissioner might provide a remedy where no other machinery existed to challenge a governmental decision obviously wanted the range of his potential investigations to be as broad as the sphere of governmental operations. Yet large areas of governmental activity were excluded from his jurisdiction. Moreover, the jurisdiction of the Parliamentary Commissioner was further confined by limiting it to cases of maladministration; this was intended to put the emphasis firmly on procedural irregularities rather than substantive errors of judgement. The experience of the past decade suggests that the ambiguity surrounding the concept of maladministration has meant that, as Parliamentary Commissioners have become bolder, they can expand their jurisdiction by altering their interpretation of that concept. The early interpretation of maladministration relied on the so-called 'Crossman catalogue' of administrative disorders – instances where 'bias, neglect, inattention, delay, incompetence, ineptitude, perversity, turpitude, arbitrariness etc.' enter the decision-making process. Decisions which were simply unjust, unreasonable or oppressive in substance were apparently excluded from investigation so long as they had been made without maladministration. However, with encouragement from the Select Committee the Parliamentary Commissioner has moved towards finding maladministration in decisions which are 'thoroughly bad in quality'. Indeed in 1978 the PCA announced his belief that he already had powers to investigate 'unjust or oppressive' governmental actions, although he combined this with the reservation that it was no part of his function to reconsider decisions taken without maladministration, nor to substitute his decision for a minister's. However, it is perhaps a pity that an institution primarily designed to reassure the individual that bureaucracy and government can be subordinated to standards of fairness should be saddled with such an incoherent notion as maladministration as its guiding principle.

The subject areas which the Parliamentary Commissioner was empowered to investigate are approximately those for which a parliamentary question would be accepted – those covered by the major departments of central government. The 1967 legislation excluded him from local-authority matters, the decisions of health authorities, the nationalized industries, the police, and civil service and personnel matters. Nor could he examine matters where the issue was a commercial or contractual one – an exclusion which underlined the conception of the office as a tool for strengthening Parliament in defence of the citizen, rather than as a method of monitoring governmental standards independently of elected representatives.[15]

The restrictions over subject matter have to a large extent been remedied by subsequent legislation, which has set up specialized institutions covering the fields initially excluded from the Parliamentary Commissioner's jurisdiction. In 1969 a Northern Ireland Complaints Commissioner was established, and because discrimination in employment has been a subject of controversy in the Province his powers now include the right to investigate personnel matters within the Northern Ireland Civil Service.[16] A system of local-government ombudsmen was established in 1974, and following the 1973 reorganization of the National Health Service a Health Service Commissioner was established – an office which the Parliamentary Commissioner in practice occupies, although he issues separate reports in that capacity. Moreover, since the 1967 legislation, as has been seen, provision has been made for an independent element in the machinery for handling complaints against the police.[17]

Each specialized jurisdiction has spawned its own problems, but there seems to be a common tendency for them now to be more willing to contemplate extensions of their functions; thus the Health Services Commissioner has investigated the feasibility of including within his ambit complaints which involve clinical judgements (originally excluded from his powers of review), and the local-government ombudsmen have pressed successfully to be allowed to recommend financial remedies where maladministration is found.[18]

The 1967 legislation confined the PCA's powers to the review of 'action taken in the exercise of administrative functions'. This restriction has been criticized because, although the Government clearly intended to preclude the PCA from intervening in a department's legislative activities, the pre-legislative stages of policy making are very much administrative functions. As one authority has pointed out, the routine processes of consultation with affected interests could well lead to maladministration, and it seems unnecessarily restrictive to prevent the PCA from examining them.[19]

The complaints which the PCA has investigated have ranged from the mundane to the politically contentious. By far the largest number seem to reflect general dissatisfaction with the Inland Revenue and the DHSS – both areas where the volume of work is likely to produce a corresponding number of errors. The top five departments for complaint in 1977 were as follows:

Department of Health and Social Security: 204 (of which 116 were accepted for investigation)
Inland Revenue: 184 (of which 90 were accepted for investigation)
Department of Transport: 74 (of which 57 were accepted for investigation)
Department of the Environment: 69 (of which 32 were accepted for investigation)
Home Office: 30 (of which 19 were accepted for investigation).[20]

The PCA himself has no authority to compel a government department to consider making recompense for cases in which maladministration has been found. However, normally it will be logical for the appropriate department to make amends, whether in the form of an apology or of an *ex gratia* payment. It has been found that the opportunities for parliamentary follow-up are anyway a powerful incentive for government to take action to redress grievances if they are found by the PCA to be justified. Thus in 1977 the PCA was able to report that a taxpayer who was found by him in 1975–6 to have suffered an injustice was ultimately granted restitution from the Inland Revenue, although the Department had initially declined to restore the money lost.

Departments seem fairly willing to make *ex gratia* payments where these seem appropriate. Thus in the third report for the 1976–7 session the PCA showed that such payments had been made in six cases – although the amounts ranged from £17.82, the cost of car hire while a licence was issued, to £500, which represented the cost of the treatment abroad undertaken by the complainant when he was misled by the DHSS into thinking that the Department would finance it. In most cases a formal apology is all that is offered, and perhaps all that is necessary given the nature of the incidents involved.

Some authorities argue that in many respects the negative aspects of the PCA's work – what he does *not* find – are as important as the positive ones. The existence of the office, and the relatively small number of cases in which maladministration is discovered, may serve to reassure the public that the general standards of administration are high and that the small proportion of errors will be swiftly corrected. Moreover, suggestions for improvement have been effected by the PCA in instances where difficulties were likely to arise on a regular basis; thus during the 1976–7 session the PCA investigated two cases in which immigration officers imposed restrictive conditions of entry upon returning residents whose passports did not record the fact that they were entitled to unrestricted abode in the United Kingdom. The PCA suggested that the Home Office might therefore more widely publicize the need to carry adequate documentation when travelling abroad; he also proposed that when a passport expired it should be returned to the owner if it recorded the permission to reside in the United Kingdom. Indeed, it seems that as a result of the PCA's strictures the Home Office decided to issue revised instructions to immigration officers for cases where it was necessary to determine residence qualifications at the port of entry.[21]

Most of the cases for consideration will be ones where a department's officials, not a minister, will have been solely responsible for the decisions taken. However, in a few cases ministerial judgement is involved; here the association of the Select Committee with the work of the Parliamentary Commissioner, as an impartial servant of the House of Commons, is invaluable because it can pursue politically contentious matters in ways which he would find embarrassing. Two such cases which arose in 1975 were the question of the safety of invalid tricycles and the Court Line affair, in which a major travel company went bankrupt although the Government had vouched for its financial viability after Cabinet consideration of the matter. In the case of the tricycles the PCA actually commented that DHSS ministers had been 'less frank than they should have been' in response to parliamentary questions on the subject – a comment on internal parliamentary proceedings which must be unusual for an agent of Parliament. However, in the second case there seemed – as had happened in the Sachsenhausen affair – to be a doubt in the Government's mind: should it seek to return to the pre-1967 doctrines of ministerial responsibility and simply reject the PCA's conclusions and the Select Committee's probings, or did the fact that the PCA had found maladministration mean that his authority had to be accepted and recompense made to the aggrieved persons? The fact that a Cabinet minister was involved naturally made the Government reluctant to accept the latter proposition, but equally any attempt to close the matter was much more difficult with the evidence of the PCA before the House of Commons.

One aspect of the PCA's activities which has since been scrutinized by the Select Committee is the range of documents he can see. The 1967 Act precluded him from viewing Cabinet papers, but the Select Committee has now recommended that he should be able to view all cabinet papers relevant to an inquiry. The effect of a change of this sort would be to bring him much closer to the heart of the political process and to make his relationship with government potentially more inflammatory. Yet the logic of much official thinking on open government, including a willingness to remove cabinet papers from categories to be covered by an Official Information Act, suggests that the PCA should be allowed access to those documents in the few cases where it would be necessary.

What the Court Line affair revealed – as both Sachsenhausen and the invalid tricycles case also revealed – was how an institution introduced to supplement traditional procedures of scrutiny could accelerate trends elsewhere in the system, and lead to the further erosion of traditional ideas about ministerial responsibility and bureaucratic anonymity. In the Sachsenhausen affair George Brown, the Foreign Secretary, had attempted to protect his civil servants after an investigation by the PCA had found maladministration in the execution of an Anglo-German compensation scheme for concentration-camp victims. His argument was that it was not appropriate for the Select Committee to attempt further debate on a matter once the PCA had achieved a reversal of the decision. In particular the Select Committee excited controversy by attempting to interview the civil servants who had made the initial error over the payment of compensation. Ultimately the Attorney General informed the Select Committee that it could interview only the principal officer of a department and not his subordinates. In other words, the doctrine of ministerial responsibility, though flexible enough to accommodate the PCA's inquiries, would, it was thought, be undermined by routine investigations by select committees against the wishes of the Permanent Secretary and the minister. The Select Committee has not forced this issue any further, and it may be taken as a general rule that civil servants do not appear before the Select Committee unless the Permanent Secretary gives his permission.[22] However, the operations of the Select Committee and the inquiries conducted by the Parliamentary Commissioner himself have subjected the actions of civil servants at all stages of the policy process to more effective scrutiny and have, at the very least, enabled a more informed understanding of British administration as well as concrete improvements in the machinery of accountability.

The Courts and the Development of Administrative Law

The central importance of the theory of ministerial responsibility in the British constitution thus partly explains some of the peculiar features of the British ombudsman, features which can still raise difficulties in his relationship with the general public. The central role of Parliament as the primary institution for securing redress may also have been a factor in the relatively slow growth of judicial techniques for controlling and regulating administrative activity. However, just as the number of occasions when individual grievances against discretionary decisions occurred has caused Parliament to reconsider its methods in this sphere, so the multiplication of individual encounters with administrative authority have prompted an increase in the likelihood of judicial intervention in the administrative process and an elaboration of the principles on which that intervention is possible. Thus the past few years have seen the courts struggling to reconcile public and private claims, and openly acknowledging the need to articulate more general principles of administrative justice irrespective of the opportunities for parliamentary control of government. Sometimes their attempts – involving, as they have done, pronouncements in areas which are often unfamiliar to traditional legal exegesis – have forced the courts to be more innovative than they would naturally be and have occasionally incurred the criticism of politicians.

Part of the reason for the relatively undeveloped state of British public law is historical; it has to be traced probably at least to the seventeenth-century alliance of the common lawyers with Parliament against the claims of the monarch, which included the claim that matters affecting the state should be tried in special courts. Dicey gave eloquent if misguided expression to this traditional hostility to special administrative jurisdictions; his attitude appears to have remained part of British legal orthodoxy at least until the 1950s, when academic authorities began pointing out that such specialized jurisdictions as prevailed in France and Germany were as much there to protect the citizen from the arbitrary exercise of governmental power as to support it.

Yet it was not really until the early 1960s that English judges commenced the task of refining the rules and principles which should govern the relationships between public authorities and private persons in the modern welfare state. Obviously the development of the law in this area was somewhat piecemeal and not necessarily consistent, because judges took very different views as to the urgency of the task and action could only be taken when appropriate cases presented themselves.[23] Nevertheless some features of the last few years deserve specific mention. First, the doctrine of natural justice has been developed by the judges, so that it can now be applied to decisions which are administrative as well as those which are deemed to be judicial or quasi-judicial. The distinction between administrative decisions and judicial and quasi-judicial decisions seems to have been injected into British administrative theory in the 1930s when the Donoughmore Committee had considered the remedies necessary to cope with the enormous growth of ministerial powers. The principles of natural justice, it asserted, had to be observed in decisions which were of a judicial or quasi-judicial character, but certain aspects of these principles – particularly the right to know the reasons for a decision – made them inappropriate where the decision was an administrative one. Although the Franks Committee, a quarter of a century later, also underlined the significance of the principles of natural justice in areas where tribunals operated, it was not until 1964 that they were applied to administrative decisions. In 1964 a watch committee's decision to dismiss a Chief Constable was held to be a nullity because he was afforded no opportunity to make representations to the committee before the decision was taken.[24] Thus the watch committee had failed to observe one of the fundamental principles of natural justice, which insists that 'no party ought to be condemned unheard'. One of the judges who decided the case when it reached the House of Lords, Lord Reid, noted in his judgment that the concept of natural justice was vague, but that it did not follow that because a thing could not be cut and dried or nicely measured, it did not exist. Lord Reid and his fellow Law Lords emphasized that the principles of natural justice were inherent in all judicial thinking, even if they now had to be applied to a host of new situations.

The new situations to which these principles of natural justice were to be applied were as varied and as complex as the welfare state in which they had to subsist. Nevertheless, since 1964 the courts have applied these standards to a range of decision-making authorities which have the power to affect the material and spiritual lives of individual citizens. Thus the duty to allow the affected party to make his case heard has been imposed on tax tribunals, on immigration officers, on such bodies as the Monopolies Commission and the Race Relations Board and even on private bodies such as professional organizations and trade unions. Although there is no general right to be represented by counsel, individuals do also in many cases have the right to legal representation and the right to know the basis on which a decision against them was taken.

A second area in which a new determination to subordinate the exercise of public power to juristic principles could be seen was the manner in which questions of ministerial discretion and executive privilege were treated in the courts during the 1960s. One of Dicey's main arguments against a separate system of administrative law in Britain had of course been that the rule of law demanded the absolute equality of parties before the law and the determination of any dispute between them in the ordinary courts. However, as many commentators had pointed out, the idea that there was equality between public authority and private citizen was a fantasy even in Dicey's day, when the doctrine of Crown privilege existed as much as it does today, and when, however undeveloped the pre-1945 state, the extent of ministerial discretion was still wide.[25]

A third area in which the courts exerted their power to review the discretion of the executive concerned the discovery of documents which were needed in a legal suit. In 1942 the House of Lords had laid down that when a minister objected to the production of documents in legal proceedings because they were potentially damaging to the public interest, that objection was conclusive.[26] It was not for the courts thereafter to question the reasonableness of such an assertion. However, the particular case involved had been decided in the middle of the Second World War and related to submarine plans. During the postwar years, therefore, the extent of this doctrine – which meant that many litigants were deprived of documents germane to their case – aroused considerable distaste. Thus in 1968 the House of Lords modified its 1942 ruling, and stated that refusal by a minister to produce documents on the grounds that their production would be contrary to the public interest was not necessarily conclusive.[27] The courts could review a decision, in order to weigh considerations of justice to litigants against considerations of public interest as this was defined by the executive. One authority has called this change the most striking example of judicial activism in administrative law since the war; certainly in broad terms it appears to accord well with the new mood of hostility towards unduly sweeping claims of governmental discretion, and with the growing sensitivity to the need for more openness in the administrative process. Yet the extent of the change's effect is uncertain; the courts still seem willing to give full consideration to executive claims for secrecy where, for example, taxation matters are concerned or issues relating to national security are involved. (One such case arose in 1977 over the decision to deport Mark Hosenball, a journalist, who claimed that the Home Office should have disclosed the case against him on grounds of natural justice; the Court of Appeal, however, found that there was no necessity for the Home Office to disclose any reasons for the decision.)

Unwillingness to tolerate broad claims of executive discretion was also evident in another spectacular case of 1968 – *Padfield v. the Minister of Agriculture, Fisheries and Food*.[28] Generally speaking, although the courts will not review discretionary powers exercised by virtue of the royal prerogative, they will review statutory discretions to see whether discretionary powers have been exercised in accordance with the intention of Parliament. Padfield's case spelled out the legal standards which controlled such powers; in particular it emphasized the importance attached by courts to ensuring that only legally relevant considerations are taken into account when reaching a discretionary decision. In the court's view, the only legally permissible considerations were ones which did not frustrate the purpose of the parent Act. Thus judicial review sought its justification in the doctrine of parliamentary supremacy, rather than in abstract notions of the public interest which might apply in France. In this instance, the minister had refused to establish an investigatory committee to review prices under a statutory milk-marketing scheme, and it emerged that his reason for refusing was that he might be politically embarrassed by the report of such a committee. Although the House of Lords acknowledged that the decision to establish a review committee was a discretionary one, it declared that discretionary powers were not unfettered. They had to be exercised reasonably, and they were not being so exercised if irrelevant considerations were allowed to enter into the decision-making process. The question of political embarrassment was not a relevant consideration and was unlawful because its intrusion tended to frustrate the purpose for which discretion had been given to the minister by Parliament. Moreover, Lords Reid, Hodson, Upjohn and Pearce went further and said that where there was even *prima facie* evidence of irregularity, the courts could infer from a minister's refusal to justify his decision that he had acted unlawfully.

It would be a mistake to see the *Padfield* decision as one which entirely clarifies the law in this area. Administrative law has at its heart the notion that there are peculiar circumstances surrounding decisions in which the state and considerations of national or public policy are involved; the more we move towards a system of administrative or public law, the more we may have to rely on particular courts to weigh the competing considerations and special circumstances. Individual judges, and perhaps courts, vary in their willingness to criticize executive judgements directly – especially since, in the political environment of modern Britain, there is a lingering suspicion that the individualistic approach of the legal system and the middle-class background of the legal profession combine to produce hostility to collectivism and working-class interests. Yet despite the natural tendency of the judiciary to avoid political controversy wherever possible, *Padfield* has been applied, and in circumstances where it might have been thought that the courts would be wary of a confrontation with the Labour Government. Thus in 1976 a Conservative-controlled local authority was supported by the courts in its refusal to accept the direction of the Secretary for Education to introduce plans for comprehensive reorganization of its schools.[29] Also the Home Office incurred judicial criticism for its attitude in a case which was unusual because it had previously been considered by the Parliamentary Commissioner for Administration who had criticized the Home Office's attempt to collect additional sums from persons who had pre-empted a rise in the cost of television licences by buying them early.[30]

The constraints on ministerial discretion and the role of the judiciary became the subject of intense political controversy in 1977 when the Court of Appeal, and Lord Denning in particular, suggested that the Attorney General's discretion had to be exercised in conformity with legal standards of reasonableness, and that unlawfulness might be inferred from a refusal to furnish reasons for a decision.[31] The Attorney General claimed that the exercise of his discretion was subject to parliamentary control rather than control by the courts, and the House of Lords upheld his view of the law. Whether this decision will in fact serve as a warning to activist judges that, in the field of administrative law, they risk political censure if they go too far too fast remains to be seen. Certainly the controversy revealed that judicial intervention was no more acceptable in some political quarters in the 1970s than it had been at the beginning of the twentieth century; it showed that the arguments in favour of a detailed code of administrative fair practice, to which even government itself would be subject, were still alien to parliamentarians.

One limited reform in the field of administrative law which was conceded by the Government in 1977 was a rationalization of the method whereby an individual could seek judicial review of an administrative decision. Until 1977 procedures for doing this were extremely complex, and an application for the wrong remedy could mean that the action would fail altogether. (Review might be sought through the prerogative orders of *certiorari*, which quashes a faulty decision; prohibition, which will restrain the performance of an unlawful action; or *mandamus*, which is sought when an authority is failing to perform a legal duty.) The courts which granted review could not award damages for a defective decision, and it was frequently found that an application for review, even if successful, was of little concrete benefit to the aggrieved citizen. The deficiencies in the procedures for seeking judicial review of administrative activity had been pointed out with great clarity by the British Section of the International Commission of Jurists and by two Law Commission working parties. Indeed, in 1969 a Law Commission working party recommended a Royal Commission with broad terms of reference, and in 1971 it proposed that a general procedure – an application for a review – should replace all the distinct remedies. The 1977 changes, which have been effected not by legislation but by amendment to the Rules of the Supreme Court, replaced applications for existing prerogative orders by applications for judicial review; it also allowed applications for review to be combined with applications for other remedies, including the award of damages. The other apparent change is that a new test of standing seems to have been introduced, so that the court may grant anyone an application for review if it considers that 'the applicant has a sufficient interest in the matter to which the application relates'. It is unclear at the time of writing just how the courts will interpret this provision, but it would seem to afford the courts an opportunity to cut through the complexities of existing rules about standing, and to develop a more comprehensive and flexible approach to the problem.[32]

The position of the individual who wishes to challenge a government decision is thus infinitely better in 1978 than it was in 1958. However, the progress made is to a large extent dependent upon the incumbents of the various offices – ombudsmen at all levels, judges and members of tribunals – to keep the institutions and procedures of accountability supple, and capable of adaptation to new circumstances. The slow extension of jurisdiction by the Parliamentary Commissioner for Administration, reinforced by the support of the Select Committee on the PCA, suggests an optimistic assessment of future trends in this field. If the progress made by the judiciary is neither as even nor as comprehensive, the fault perhaps lies not with the judges but with the politicians in their failure to articulate their interpretation of the role of law in the modern state.

13   The Limits of Independence

Much of the argument of the preceding chapters has tacitly assumed that the government of the United Kingdom is fully autonomous in the decisions that it makes. It is however clear that in reality the situation is a very different one and that the making of policy is powerfully affected by external constraints. In the contemporary world all countries are to some extent in this situation. In Britain's case there are three factors that bulk particularly large. First, there is the legacy of Empire; secondly, there is the country's continuing dependence upon external trade; and finally there is the continuing ambiguous relationship with the European Communities, of which Britain is now a member. These three factors affect not only British policy but also the machinery through which it carries on its external relations.

To illustrate the importance of these constraints, two very different examples may be given. Because of Britain's position as a trading nation, and the particularly important role assumed by invisible exports in compensating for balance of payments which is often adverse where visible trade is concerned, much attention has to be paid to the views of the City of London and to the Bank of England as its spokesman. Secondly, Britain's former reliance on overseas garrisons and on naval power to guard its trade routes meant that it developed a professional army rather than the mass conscript army that became normal among its continental neighbours. Furthermore, except for its duties in Ireland – which is anyway perhaps best treated as the original area of British imperial expansion – the army's role since the seventeenth century has been overwhelmingly an external one. In consequence the army has played no significant role in domestic politics, in striking contrast not only to Britain's principal European partners but also to the other former island empire, Japan.

As for the imperial inheritance itself, the problem of determining the impact upon the British social structure and the British public mind of the rapid withdrawal from Empire over the past three and a half decades remains an intractable one. Quite apart from the demographic contribution of former imperial territories to the population of the United Kingdom some of whose consequences have been referred to already, what other effects have there been on the British themselves? How far were enterprise and the exercise of rule overseas a cause of the frequently noted failure to recruit the best young talents to industry in Britain itself? How far does the cessation of career opportunities abroad help to explain the current malaise referred to in the opening chapter? Where does the typecast 'district officer', or for that matter 'Governor General', find his niche today? Is there resentment at the sense of the country's being diminished in stature, and if so how does it manifest itself? Can one deduce that because the 'European' cause has been an upper- and middle-class rather than a working-class enthusiasm there is some feeling – however obscure – that the creation of a new Europe may provide an alternative field of activity for frustrated imperialists? These are questions that will be answered by future historians.

Traditionally the different geographical areas covered by Britain's external relations were on the whole dealt with separately. The Foreign Office was responsible for the conduct of relations with foreign countries, and the Colonial Office and India Office for relations with areas which were outside the British Isles but inside the area over which the United Kingdom Parliament claimed to have sovereignty. As the original 'dominions' came to exercise autonomy within the system, the Colonial Office seemed an improper vehicle for relations with their governments. The Dominions Office – later the Commonwealth Relations Office – was thus brought into being to handle these relations. With the increasing insubstantiality of the Commonwealth tie, and the granting of independence to the component parts of the Indian Empire and later in turn to all but a few colonies, the situation changed again. The Foreign and Commonwealth Office, backed by a single Diplomatic Service, now conducts all Britain's external affairs, and there are only small differences of nomenclature to betray the existence of the earlier situation; for instance, while Britain maintains an Ambassador at Washington, it is represented by a High Commissioner in Canada.

The Commonwealth today retains hardly any vestiges of a common institutional structure. The British monarch's role as the symbol of the association is a shadowy one of no practical consequence, and in the few Commonwealth countries where the monarch is still Head of State, the title is of no political significance. It was notable that when the Governor General of Australia intervened to solve that country's political crisis in November 1975, it was at once made plain that the monarch herself had not been consulted in any way. However, the very existence of the Commonwealth does involve a number of constraints upon the British Government's actions in the field of external relations, and even in some domestic matters such as the control of immigration. These constraints are in effect the claims made upon Britain by members of the Commonwealth as a result of their previous position of much closer association. It is thus assumed, for instance, that in its international economic policies Britain will pay particular attention to these countries' needs for markets or for aid, and that Commonwealth citizens will be treated preferentially in Britain in matters of immigration, access to educational facilities and so forth. There are also occasionally direct political demands arising out of the process of decolonization; thus Commonwealth members insisted that Britain had special responsibilities to end the 'illegal' regime in Rhodesia, and to force upon the settler community the acceptance of majority rule.

The forum for the expression of such grievances and claims is the Conference of Commonwealth Prime Ministers which is the successor to the former Imperial Conference. Because these conferences are meetings of heads of government of independent states, members have no sanctions against a recalcitrant member other than those generally available in the international community; however, successive British governments have obviously attached great importance to maintaining the

Commonwealth in being, and have thus been susceptible to threats of withdrawal from it. They have in the past gone to some lengths to try to prevent this happening. Yet as regional and other bloc politics have come to dominate the international scene more and more, and as the currents of world trade and investment increasingly follow channels quite different from those followed under the earlier British imperial system, the Commonwealth aspect of British policy has steadily declined in importance. Member governments are now readier to ignore the opinions of other members of the Commonwealth, and to give priority to relationships of a more immediate relevance to their interests.

It is not insignificant that Britain does not receive much assistance, or even sympathy, from most Commonwealth members in international disputes in which Britain is involved. Such disputes often arise from what would once have been considered imperial issues, notably where the population of some dependency prefers the continuation of British rule to national independence or absorption into another sovereignty. The clashes with Spain over Gibraltar, with Argentina over the Falkland Islands and with Guatemala over Belize fall into this category. In such cases most Commonwealth members prefer to view the matter in terms of 'colonialism', which means assuming from the outset that Britain must be in the wrong. Such differences of perspective and of ideology combine to diminish the impact of the legacy of the Westminster style of constitutional government in Commonwealth countries. The changes in the character of the Commonwealth make its perpetuation as an organization a matter of dwindling significance to most of the British electorate. Yet because all the ties that the member states have developed run through Britain, a Commonwealth without Britain, as was at one time mooted, would be almost meaningless. The perpetuation of the Commonwealth would thus in the long run appear most improbable. Instead it is likely that Britain will still retain particularly close links with certain individual Commonwealth countries where economic ties are reinforced by those of history, race and culture – although post-war immigration from the New Commonwealth has extended those links beyond the white dominions of Canada, Australia and New Zealand.

From the point of view of British domestic government the most important survival from the imperial past is the anomalous relationship with the Irish Republic. The Irish Republic, though a completely independent country and by its own choice not a member of the Commonwealth, has been allowed to enjoy important privileges. Some, such as freedom of travel without passports between the two countries, are reciprocal. Others are not; for example Irish citizens are free to settle at will in Britain and to enjoy equality of treatment with British citizens, including, as has been seen, the right to vote. In addition, the Irish Republic has been recognized by successive governments as having a valid claim to a consultative voice in settling a British domestic problem, that of determining the future political system of Northern Ireland.

Direct relations with other foreign countries, or indirect relations through international organizations of the United Nations type, impose upon British governments constraints which are no different from those experienced by many other states. In general the degree to which such constraints are felt by a particular state depends upon that state's own strength. As a permanent member of the UN Security Council with a veto, Britain has some advantages over many other states, though it is bound by valid resolutions of that body, for instance in the matter of sanctions.

The most striking feature of the international scene in the period since the Second World War has been the increasing regulation of the economic relations between countries by treaty. The tariff policies of any government, including Britain's, are governed by the provisions of the GATT, the General Agreement on Tariffs and Trade. Even more important is the influence of international monetary institutions, which can directly control the domestic policies of individual governments if they have severe balance of payments problems. During the economic crisis in the second half of 1976, the British Government sought help from the International Monetary Fund. Before receiving help, it was necessary to give officials of the IMF much information about the country's economic situation and to enter into formal undertakings about its policies on public expenditure and the money supply. The existence of such external constraints upon British policy undermines the plausibility of assertions about Britain's ability to deal with economic problems on its own.[1] A very significant degree of commitment by Britain is also involved in its memership of the North Atlantic Treaty Organization. The direction of Britain's defence effort, and to a considerable extent its size, depend upon agreements reached within that Organization.

Even before Britain became a member of the European Communities – the most important single source of constraints upon Britain's independence of action – the machinery of British government was in all its aspects showing the impact of the growing international dimension in Britain's affairs. Departments that were previously considered wholly domestic now have to take into account many factors outside their national jurisdiction. The representation of British interests abroad and in international conferences cannot be left entirely to professional diplomats, nor can the framing of policy be left wholly to the Foreign and Commonwealth Office. Delegations to the major international organizations, and the staffs of embassies and high commissions, have to include specialists on many topics who will work closely with their relevant home departments, from which they have probably been seconded. The Washington embassy, for example, is a sort of Whitehall in miniature. International conferences of a specialized kind, some of them meeting over very long periods of time, claim much of the energies of home-based civil servants.[2]

The proposals of the Central Policy Review Staff mentioned earlier advocated going further than this and replacing the Diplomatic Service itself with a 'foreign policy group' within a unified Civil Service. They also recommended downgrading the Foreign and Commonwealth Office from its role as the main co-ordinator of external policy.[3] These proposals were subject to severe criticism in a number of quarters;[4] in all except comparatively minor respects they were ultimately rejected by the Government.[5] It must be assumed, therefore, that although greater opportunities for interchange between the home departments and the Diplomatic Service will be actively encouraged, the basic structure of overseas representation will not be fundamentally altered in the near future.

International obligations are not confined to the economic sphere. As has been seen, by adherence to the European Convention on Human Rights, Britain laid itself open to the investigative and judicial functions of the European Commission on Human Rights and the European Court of Human Rights. This situation has enabled the Irish Government to bring proceedings against the British Government over the alleged ill-treatment of members of the IRA in Northern Ireland. It is true the decisions of the European Court of Human Rights are not binding in British courts, but it is difficult for government to ignore them, while if the Court were to declare a piece of British legislation to be in conflict with the Convention, Britain would be in breach of her international obligations if it was not consequently amended.

British membership of the European Communities – the Coal and Steel Community, Euratom, and above all the Common Market, or European Economic Community set up by the Treaty of Rome – raises a new and potentially more far-reaching set of issues. The problems posed by membership arise in part from the ambiguity inherent in the concept of the EEC itself. From one point of view, it can be regarded simply as a further tier of inter-governmental activity not essentially different from what goes on in other international organizations. The countries concerned have agreed by treaty to certain derogations from their own autonomy, principally in the fields of commercial policy and the control of the market in agricultural products. They have also accepted, as part of the machinery for carrying through these common policies, a role for the executive of the Communities – the European Commission – which although more extensive than that customarily allocated to the secretariats of international organizations is not so distinct from them as to be unrecognizable. The main powers of decision have in fact come to rest with the national governments, who possess the ultimate right of veto. However, there is another point of view. For in addition to the powers about which the Treaties are explicit, there are aspects of the Communities which suggest a very different result from their creation, namely the establishment in some form of a 'United States of Europe'. The unease that all member governments feel from time to time when confronted with the demands made upon them by the Communities is caused by an an awareness of this fundamental duality of character. In the British case, where the issue of membership has been argued on pragmatic rather than on ideological grounds and where attachment to the country's own constitutional arrangements including the sovereignty of Parliament has remained very much alive, this ambiguity is particularly difficult to accept.

One can summarize the objections to membership of the Communities – even with their present veto-limited powers – of those who continue to believe in the desirability of independent national action. To begin with, the Communities have legislative powers in the spheres of economic activity that they regulate. As already noted this means that whereas for British courts an Act of Parliament has hitherto been the supreme source of law on a particular topic, they now have to take into consideration another body of law. This law is derived from the Treaties themselves or consists of legislation made under their provisions by the Communities. Some of it consists of regulations which have the immediate force of law in the countries concerned; the remainder consists of directives which oblige the member states to alter their domestic legislation to conform with them. Ultimate decisions about the interpretation of the Treaty, and about any conflict between Community law and the domestic laws of member states, are made by the European Court. In other words, we face for the first time the possibility of a British Act of Parliament being adjudged subordinate to other legislation, because Parliament's right to override earlier legislation when it passes new Acts does not hold good for the Treaties or general Community legislation. It is unnecessary to discuss whether Parliament could repeal the European Communities Act itself. The Treaty of Rome contains no provision for member states to withdraw. However, it is certainly possible to endorse what one of the main partisans of Britain's entry said at the time Britain became a member, namely that we have 'for the first time in part and covering a relatively narrow field, a written constitution in the shape of the treaties'.[6]

Also, the techniques of statutory interpretation would seem to require some revision. For instance in 1978 the very active House of Lords Select Committee on the European Communities devoted a report to the subject of the use by the EEC of article 100 of the Rome Treaty, under which directives can be issued to member governments to ensure that their laws on certain subjects are 'approximated'. The Committee pointed out that this article should be interpreted under article 2 of the Treaty, which sets out the objectives of the EEC in economic terms; economic goals are accordingly to be attained by the establishment of a common market and the progressive approximation of the economic policies of the member states. The Committee proceeded to argue that therefore directives under article 100 are not valid if the areas they affect lie outside this essential framework.[7] While this argument has some resemblance to the way in which delegated legislation may be challenged on *ultra vires* grounds, the broad scope of the matters involved makes the debate much more akin to the constitutional jurisdiction of the US Supreme Court. Thus aspects of British law are likely in the long run to be affected by European Community law. Lord Denning's prediction in 1974 that the effect of the change would be like that of an incoming tide, flowing into the estuaries and up the rivers, was held to be an exaggeration; four years later it could be regarded by a expert observer as an understatement.[8]

Membership of the Communities is also objected to because of its impact upon the legislative process at home. It has been argued from the beginning of the debates over British membership that Parliament must be able to have its say before the Council enacts European legislation. The problem is a dual one: how is Parliament to get to know what is being proposed by the Commission before it goes for approval to the Council; and how, supposing it has the information, can it influence Britain's representative at the Council – a minister – to express and maintain a specifically British point of view when it is probable that the proposed regulations or directives will have been drafted to take into account national desiderata urged upon the Commission earlier? Proposals by the Commission will thus represent a bargain, perhaps involving more than one area of policy, that may be difficult to take apart.

After some experiment and debate, the instrument chosen by the House of Commons to handle these questions has since May 1974 been the Committee on European Secondary Legislation etc. which is entitled to receive draft legislation emanating from the Commission within two weeks of the relevant documents' arrival in Whitehall. Its main task is to decide which of the thirty or forty documents that have to be dealt with weekly are so important that they should be given further consideration; they are then referred to a standing committee – which can only 'take note', a procedure infrequently used – or to the House as a whole. Most documents recommended for debate are in fact debated. However there has been disquiet about the limited time available, and the refusal of ministers to accept the view that no action should be taken until the House has had its say.[9]

The twenty-three-member Select Committee on the European Communities of the House of Lords, which has wider terms of reference and which normally works through seven subject subcommittees, covers much of the same ground with the aid of of specialist advisers and provides another instrument for scrutiny. The two Committees cooperate, and receive evidence from ministers and civil servants; thus the risk of anything of very serious concern slipping through unnoticed is minimal.

However, the matter is not simply one of alerting Parliament; there is also the question of what Parliament can do if it objects to a piece of Community legislation to which government has already agreed. As has been seen, there is no way in which Parliament can force a minister to alter his policy, except by withdrawing support from government as a whole. The unlikelihood of such an eventuality has already been made plain.

A further development, the effects of which will be felt in the future, is that the EEC is acquiring from the common tariff and in other ways revenues of its own. In this way it is developing attributes that are sharply different from those of conventional international organizations, which are dependent upon contributions from member states. This distinction is similar to the contrast between the United States under the Articles of Confederation and the United States under the Federal Constitution. The EEC is thus in a position to have its own positive policies of economic and social intervention. The resultant problem of transfers of financial resources between states can be resolved in two possible ways: either the British Government, as the government of one of the poorer member countries, could try to limit the growth of the EEC budget and its own indirect contributions to it, or it could concentrate on channelling as much as possible of the money available to the benefit of Britain's disadvantaged areas or industries. Perhaps because the battle lines on this issue are not yet clearly drawn, more attention has been paid to another new feature of the situation; this is the advent of a European Parliament which is directly elected instead of being, as hitherto, merely a nominated assembly of national delegations of parliamentarians. Although the British commitment to direct elections was implicit in its membership of the Communities, the issue played little part in the national referendum campaign and was indeed deliberately muted by the pro-Europeans to prevent alarm.[10] However, because new legislation to provide for direct elections was necessary it provided an issue for a last-ditch struggle by the anti-Europeans from 1975 to 1978. The issue was further highlighted by the argument over devolution for Scotland and Wales which was going on at the same time, since it was clear that whatever the mode of election to the European Parliament, Scotland and Wales's share of the UK's total representation would be settled by the size of their populations and would therefore be much inferior to England's share. It was provided that each country could use any system it chose for the first direct elections only, pending agreement on a common system which would have to be introduced before the second round; nevertheless the choice of method was a burning issue in Britain because of the parallel discussions over the Scottish and Welsh Assemblies, and the feeling that proportional representation in this context might create a precedent for electoral reform affecting the House of Commons itself.

In 1975 a Select Committee was appointed to look into the question; it reported that it would be possible to hold the elections in 1978, the EEC's target date, and suggested that a single-member constituency system of the ordinary first-past-the-post kind should be adopted. Only Jeremy Thorpe, the representative of the minor parties on the Committee, disagreed with this recommendation. The Government was in no hurry to legislate, which is understandable because the Labour Party Conference in September endorsed the opposition of the NEC to the whole idea of direct elections. The Government's bill was published only in 1977. As part of the pact with the Liberals, the bill provided for a form of proportional representation but allowed the House of Commons to strike this out, on a free vote, if it so chose. The bill got its second reading towards the end of the session. In the new session it was reintroduced and again received a second reading, but when it came to voting on the proposed electoral system, the choice was for the single-member constituency system in preference to proportional representation by a majority of 321 votes to 224. The majority consisted of 115 Labour MPs, 198 Conservatives and 8 Ulster Unionists.

The time required to demarcate the eighty-one new European constituencies and to make other necessary arrangements made it impossible for elections to take place in 1978. In August 1978 it was announced that the date for these elections had been set for 7 June 1979. The legislation left it open whether there was to be a dual mandate – that is to say whether membership of the European Parliament should now become incompatible with membership of the House of Commons. The Labour Party, however, decided to bar the dual mandate for itself, so that Labour nominations to the European Parliament could not be sought by those wishing to remain in or enter the House of Commons. The Conservative Party took no formal decision, although it was made clear that Conservative leadership would not take kindly to the idea of a dual mandate, which might make the whips' task harder in assembling members for divisions, since there would be no Labour members with whom to pair their own men. It looked as though a very few Conservative MPs would nevertheless put themselves forward. There would also of course be a few peers of either party who might secure election.

What was now in question was the nature of the future links between the European Parliament and the Parliament of the United Kingdom. Various methods of dealing with the problem were canvassed, including *ex officio* non-voting membership of the House of Lords for all Britain's European MPs, the establishment of some new committee structure and so forth.[11] Formal links might, however, matter less than informal ones between ideologically sympathetic parties across national boundaries. For British parties, the non-elected European Assembly had already shown the difficulties. The Labour representatives, coming as they did from a party which is officially anti-European, found it hard to discover common ground with the European social democrats who are in the main very strongly pro-European. The Liberal Party does cooperate with continental Liberals, but its own views on many issues are a good deal further to the left than are theirs. The biggest difficulty is that facing the Conservatives. The Christian Democratic parties are still too close to their clerical origins for British Conservatives to feel wholly at ease with them. President Giscard d'Estaing's Independent Republicans are more acceptable as partners, but also in France there is the problem of the British Conservatives' relations with the Gaullist Party, which likes to think of itself as straddling the left–right divide. What would best suit the British Conservatives would be an all-embracing European anti-socialist bloc, but this ideal may prove unattainable.

The committees in the European Parliament will probably be manned like those in the existing European Assembly on the basis of party groupings. A party which has no allies across the national frontiers is thus likely to suffer. In the long run the situation may change and the party structure in Europe may become determined by actual European issues, such as whether to confer more or less power on the European Commission. For the British, what was more worrying was the possibility that the European Parliament would try to remove further powers from Westminster at a time when the British Parliament might have delegated powers downwards to the Scottish, and perhaps the Welsh, Assemblies. The result could have been too many tiers of elected governments for comfort, with a strong need for government by consensus but with greater difficulties in the way of its achievement.[12]

Enough has been said to show that in Britain – as indeed elsewhere in Western Europe – the tasks of government and the manner in which they are performed can no longer be assessed solely by reference to the framework of national politics of domestic institutions. Much of the traditional language of political analysis is therefore difficult to use with conviction.[13] Moreover, such a development does not result merely from membership of the EEC; rather, it is changing circumstances that have brought about both the creation of the EEC and Britain's decision to join. For many centuries it seemed that the way forward in European politics was towards the creation of self-contained nation states, organizing their affairs and making their decisions, guided only by their own conceptions of the national interest. A clear distinction was made between international relations and domestic matters. In the twentieth century this process has gone into reverse. At both the formal and the informal levels of government and politics, we have to take account of institutions and allegiances that transcend national frontiers. Despite the apparent continuities in the substance and form of British institutions, there are now real differences from the situation of the nineteenth century from which we derive our classical definitions of British constitutional practices. Of these differences, by no means the least is the now very qualified sense in which Britain can be regarded as a wholly independent state.

Appendix I
General Election Results, 1918–79

	Total Votes	MPs Elected	Candidates	Un-opposed Returns	% Share of Total Vote	Average % Vote per Opposed Candidate	% Share of Seats
	Coalition 1918. Sat., 14 Dec.						
Coalition Unionist	3,504,198	335	374	42	32.6		47.38
Coalition Liberal	1,455,640	133	158	27	13.5		18.81
Coalition Labour	161,521	10	18	—	1.5		1.41
(Coalition)	(5,121,359)	(478)	(550)	(69)	(47.6)		(67.61)
Conservative	370,375	23	37	—	3.4		3.25
Irish Unionist	292,722	25	38	—	2.7		3.54
Liberal	1,298,808	28	253	—	12.1		3.96
Labour	2,385,472	63	388	12	22.2		8.91
Irish Nationalist	238,477	7	60	1	2.2		.99
Sinn Fein	486,867	73	102	25	4.5		10.33
Others	572,503	10	197	—	5.3		1.41
Elec. 21,392,322 Turnout 58.9%	10,766,583	707	1,625	107	100.0		100.00
	Conservative (Maj) 1922. Wed., 15 Nov.						
Conservative	5,500,382	345	483	42	38.2	48.6	56.10
National Liberal	1,673,240	62	162	5	11.6	39.3	10.08
Liberal	2,516,287	54	328	5	17.5	30.9	8.78
Labour	4,241,383	142	411	4	29.5	40.0	23.09
Others	462,340	12	59	1	3.2	28.3	1.95
Elec. 21,127,663 Turnout 71.3%	14,393,632	615	1,443	57	100.0	—	100.00

	Total Votes	MPs Elected	Candi- dates	Un- opposed Returns	% Share of Total Vote	Average % Vote per Opposed Candidate	% Share of Seats
Labour (Min) 1923. Thu., 6 Dec.							
Conservative	5,538,824	258	540	35	38.1	42.6	41.95
Liberal	4,311,147	159	453	11	29.6	37.8	25.85
Labour	4,438,508	191	422	3	30.5	41.0	31.06
Others	260,042	7	31	1	1.8	27.6	1.14
Elec. 21,281,232 Turnout 70.8%	14,548,521	615	1,446	50	100.0	—	100.00
Conservative (Maj) 1924. Wed., 29 Oct.							
Conservative	8,039,598	419	552	16	48.3	51.9	68.13
Liberal	2,928,747	40	340	6	17.6	30.9	6.50
Labour	5,489,077	151	512	9	33.0	38.2	24.56
Communist	55,346	1	8	—	0.3	25.0	.16
Others	126,511	4	16	1	0.8	29.1	.65
Elec. 21,731,320 Turnout 76.6%	16,639,279	615	1,428	32	100.0	—	100.00
Labour (Min) 1929. Thu., 30 May							
Conservative	8,656,473	260	590	4	38.2	39.4	42.28
Liberal	5,308,510	59	513	—	23.4	27.7	9.59
Labour	8,389,512	288	571	—	37.1	39.3	46.83
Communist	50,614	—	25	—	0.3	5.3	—
Others	243,266	8	31	3	1.0	21.2	1.30
Elec. 28,850,870 Turnout 76.1%	22,648,375	615	1,730	7	100.0	—	100.00

	Total Votes	MPs Elected	Candidates	Un-opposed Returns	% Share of Total Vote	Average % Vote per Opposed Candidate	% Share of Seats
Coalition 1931. Tue., 27 Oct.							
Conservative	11,987,745	473	523	56	55.2 ⎫		76.91
National Labour	341,370	13	20	—	1.6 ⎬ 62.9		2.11
Liberal National	809,302	35	41	—	3.7 ⎭		5.69
Liberal	1,403,102	33	112	5	6.5	28.8	5.37
(National Government)	(14,532,519)	(554)	(696)	(61)	(67.0)	—	(90.08)
Independent Liberal	106,106	4	7	—	0.5	35.8	6.5
Labour	6,649,630	52	515	6	30.6	33.0	8.46
Communist	74,824	—	26	—	0.3	7.5	—
New Party	36,377	—	24	—	0.2	3.9	—
Others	256,917	5	24	—	1.2	21.9	.81
Elec. 29,960,071 Turnout 76.3%	21,656,373	615	1,292	67	100.0	—	100.00
Nat. Govt (Con) 1935. Thu., 14 Nov.							
Conservative	11,810,158	437	585	26	53.7	54.8	70.09
Liberal	1,422,116	21	161	—	6.4	23.9	3.41
Labour	8,325,491	154	552	13	37.9	40.3	25.04
Independent Labour Party	139,577	4	17	—	0.7	22.2	0.65
Communist	27,117	1	2	—	0.1	38.0	8.16
Others	272,595	4	31	1	1.2	21.3	0.65
Elec. 31,379,050 Turnout 71.2%	21,997,054	615	1,348	40	100.0	—	100.00
Labour (Maj) 1945. Thu., 5 July							
Conservative	9,988,306	213	624	1	39.8	40.1	33.28
Liberal	2,248,226	12	306	—	9.0	18.6	1.88
Labour	11,995,152	393	604	2	47.8	50.4	61.41
Communist	102,780	2	21	—	0.4	12.7	0.31
Common Wealth	110,634	1	23	—	0.4	12.6	0.15
Others	640,880	19	104	—	2.0	15.4	2.97
Elec. 33,240,391 Turnout 72.7%	26,085,978	640	1,682	3	100.0	—	100.00

	Total Votes	MPs Elected	Candi- dates	Un- opposed Returns	% Share of Total Vote	Average % Vote per Opposed Candidate	% Share of Seats
Labour (Maj) 1950. Thu., 23 Feb.							
Conservative	12,502,567	298	620	2	43.5	43.7	47.68
Liberal	2,621,548	9	475	—	9.1	11.8	1.44
Labour	13,266,592	315	617	—	46.1	46.7	50.40
Communist	91,746	—	100	—	0.3	2.0	—
Others	290,218	3	56	—	1.0	12.6	0.48
Elec. 33,269,770 Turnout 84.0%	28,772,671	625	1,868	2	100.0	—	100.00
Conservative (Maj) 1951. Thu., 25 Oct.							
Conservative	13,717,538	321	617	4	48.0	48.6	51.36
Liberal	730,556	6	109	—	2.5	14.7	0.96
Labour	13,948,605	295	617	—	48.8	49.2	47.20
Communist	21,640	—	10	—	0.1	4.4	—
Others	177,329	3	23	—	0.6	16.8	0.48
Elec. 34,645,573 Turnout 82.5%	28,595,668	625	1,376	4	100.0	—	100.00
Conservative (Maj) 1955. Thu., 26 May							
Conservative	13,286,569	344	623	—	49.7	50.2	54.60
Liberal	722,405	6	110	—	2.7	15.1	0.95
Labour	12,404,970	277	620	—	46.4	47.3	43.97
Communist	33,144	—	17	—	0.1	4.2	—
Others	313,410	3	39	—	1.1	20.8	0.48
Elec. 34,858,263 Turnout 76.7%	26,760,498	630	1,409	—	100.0	—	100.00
Conservative (Maj) 1959. Thu., 8 Oct.							
Conservative	13,749,830	365	625	—	49.4	49.6	57.94
Liberal	1,638,571	6	216	—	5.9	16.9	0.95
Labour	12,215,538	258	621	—	43.8	44.5	40.95
Communist	30,897	—	18	—	0.1	4.1	—
Plaid Cymru	77,571	—	20	—	0.3	9.0	—
Scottish Nat. P.	21,738	—	5	—	0.1	11.4	—
Others	12,464	1	31	—	0.4	11.0	0.16
Elec. 35,397,080 Turnout 78.8%	27,859,241	630	1,536	—	100.0	—	100.00

	Total Votes	MPs Elected	Candidates	Unopposed Returns	% Share of Total Vote	Average % Vote per Opposed Candidate	% Share of Seats
Labour (Maj) 1964. Thu., 15 Oct.							
Conservative	12,001,396	304	630	—	43.4	43.4	48.25
Liberal	3,092,878	9	365	—	11.2	18.5	1.43
Labour	12,205,814	317	628	—	44.1	44.1	50.32
Communist	45,932	—	36	—	0.2	3.4	—
Plaid Cymru	69,507	—	23	—	0.3	8.4	—
Scottish Nat. P.	64,044	—	15	—	0.2	10.7	—
Others	168,422	—	60	—	0.6	6.4	—
Elec. 35,892,572 Turnout 77.1%	27,655,374	630	1,757	—	100.0	—	100.00
Labour (Maj) 1966. Thu., 31 Mar.							
Conservative	11,418,433	253	629	—	41.9	41.8	40.16
Liberal	2,327,533	12	311	—	8.5	16.1	1.90
Labour	13,064,951	363	621	—	47.9	48.7	57.62
Communist	62,112	—	57	—	0.2	3.0	—
Plaid Cymru	61,071	—	20	—	0.2	8.7	—
Scottish Nat. P.	128,474	—	20	—	0.2	14.1	—
Others	170,569	2	31	—	0.6	8.6	0.32
Elec. 35,964,684 Turnout 75.8%	27,263,606	630	1,707	—	100.0	—	100.00
Conservative (Maj) 1970. Thu., 18 June							
Conservative	13,145,123	330	628	—	46.4	46.5	52.38
Liberal	2,117,035	6	332	—	7.5	13.5	0.95
Labour	12,179,341	287	624	—	43.0	43.5	45.56
Communist	37,970	—	58	—	0.1	1.1	—
Plaid Cymru	175,016	—	36	—	0.6	11.5	—
Scottish Nat. P.	306,802	1	65	—	1.1	12.2	0.16
Others	383,511	6	94	—	1.4	9.1	0.95
Elec. 39,342,013 Turnout 72.0%	28,344,798	630	1,837	—	100.0	—	100.00

391

	Total Votes	MPs Elected	Candidates	Un-opposed Returns	% Share of Total Vote	Average % Vote per Opposed Candidate	% Share of Seats
Labour (Min) 1974. Thu., 28 Feb.							
Conservative	11,868,906	297	623	—	37.9	38.8	46.77
Liberal	6,063,470	14	517	—	19.3	23.6	2.20
Labour	11,639,243	301	623	—	37.1	38.0	47.40
Communist	32,741	—	44	—	0.1	1.7	—
Plaid Cymru	171,364	2	36	—	0.6	10.7	0.32
Scottish Nat. P.	632,032	7	70	—	2.0	21.9	1.10
National Front	76,865	—	54	—	0.3	3.2	—
Others (G.B.)	131,059	2	120	—	0.4	2.2	0.32
Others (N.I.)[1]	717,986	12	48	—	2.3	25.0	1.89
Elec. 39,798,899 Turnout 78.7%	31,333,226	635	2,135	—	100.0	—	100.00
Labour (Maj) 1974. Thu., 10 Oct.							
Conservative	10,464,817	277	623	—	35.8	36.7	43.62
Liberal	5,346,754	13	619	—	18.3	18.9	2.05
Labour	11,457,079	319	623	—	39.2	40.2	50.24
Communist	17,426	—	29	—	0.1	1.5	—
Plaid Cymru	166,321	3	36	—	0.6	10.8	0.47
Scottish Nat. P.	839,617	11	71	—	2.9	30.4	1.73
National Front	113,843	—	90	—	0.4	2.9	—
Others (G.B.)	81,227	—	118	—	0.3	1.5	—
Others (N.I.)[1]	702,094	12	43	—	2.4	27.9	1.89
Elec. 40,072,971 Turnout 72.8%	29,189,178	635	2,252	—	100.0	—	100.00

	Total Votes	MPs Elected	Candi-dates	Un-opposed Returns	% Share of Total Vote	Average % Vote per Opposed Candidate	% Share of Seats
Conservative (Maj) 1979. Thu., 3 May							
Conservative	13,697,690	339	622	—	43.9	44.9	53.39
Liberal	4,313,811	11	577	—	13.8	14.9	1.73
Labour	11,532,148	269	623	—	36.9	37.8	42.36
Communist	15,938	—	38	—	0.1	0.9	—
Plaid Cymru	132,544	2	36	—	0.4	8.1	0.31
Scottish Nat. P.	504,259	2	71	—	1.6	17.3	0.31
National Front	190,747	—	303	—	0.6	1.3	—
Ecology	35,116	—	53	—	0.1	2.0	—
Workers' Rev. P.	13,535	—	60	—	0.1	0.5	—
Others (G.B.)	85,338	—	129	—	0.3	1.3	—
Others (N.I.)[1]	695,889	12	64	—	2.2	18.8	1.90
Elec. 41,093,264 Turnout 76.0%	31,217,015	635	2,576	—	100.0	—	100.00

Source: Butler and Sloman, *British Political Facts 1900–1979*.

[1] For the 1974 and 1979 elections, no candidates in Northern Ireland are included in the major party totals although it might be argued that some independent Unionists should be classed with the Conservatives and that Northern Labour candidates should be classed with Labour.

Appendix II
The European Election
Results, 1979

The first direct elections to the European Assembly (Parliament) were held in Britain on 7 June 1979. In Great Britain itself the elections were run on the customary first past the post system with the country divided into 78 constituencies. The turnout was barely 31% compared with 76% in the general election a month earlier and 65% in the referendum on Europe in 1975.

The results were as follows:

	Votes cast	Percentage of those voting	Seats
Conservatives	6,504,481	50.6	60
Labour	4,253,210	33.0	17
Liberals	1,690,600	13.1	0
Others	421,533	3.3	1 (Scottish Nat. P.)

In Northern Ireland the whole Province was treated as a single constituency electing three members by the single transferable vote system. This produced one Democratic Unionist (the Rev. Ian Paisley), one SDLP member and one Official Unionist.

Of the Conservatives elected, four had been elected to the new House of Commons. In the European Parliament with a handful of continental colleagues they formed the European Democratic Group.

Appendix III
Prime Ministers in the Twentieth Century

Arthur Balfour	(Conservative)	12 July 1902
Sir Henry Campbell Bannerman	(Liberal)	5 December 1905
Herbert Henry Asquith	(Liberal)	7 April 1908
	(Coalition)	25 May 1915
David Lloyd George	(Coalition)	7 December 1916
Andrew Bonar Law	(Conservative)	23 October 1922
Stanley Baldwin	(Conservative)	22 May 1923
J. Ramsay MacDonald	(Labour)	22 January 1924
Stanley Baldwin	(Conservative)	4 November 1924
J. Ramsay MacDonald	(Labour)	5 June 1929
	(National)	24 August 1931
Stanley Baldwin	(National)	21 January 1936
Neville Chamberlain	(National)	28 May 1937
Winston Churchill	(Coalition)	10 May 1940
	(Conservative)	23 May 1945
Clement Attlee	(Labour)	26 July 1945
Winston Churchill	(Conservative)	26 October 1951
Sir Anthony Eden	(Conservative)	6 April 1955
Harold Macmillan	(Conservative)	10 January 1957
Sir Alec Douglas-Home	(Conservative)	19 October 1963
Harold Wilson	(Labour)	16 October 1964
Edward Heath	(Conservative)	19 June 1970
Harold Wilson	(Labour)	4 March 1974
James Callaghan	(Labour)	5 April 1976
Margaret Thatcher	(Conservative)	4 May 1979

Notes

Introduction

1 The figures are those given by the Runnymede Trust. On a mid-year estimate of population they reckoned the proportion of the population of New Commonwealth or Pakistani descent to be 3.4%. We have taken their mid-year figures and compared them with the official population figures for 1977.

2 These opinion polls were conducted by Marplan for News International Ltd and primarily published in the *Sun*. We have taken the surveys referred to in the Introduction from the collection of such polls gathered together and published under the title *The Public View* in 1977.

3 *Ibid.*

4 The EEC is used in this book to connote the European Communities, although this usage is not altogether accurate. The first of the European Communities to be established was the Coal and Steel Community set up by the Treaty of Paris of 18 April 1951. The Treaties of Rome of 25 March 1957 established the European Economic Community (the 'Common Market' or EEC) and the European Atomic Energy Community. At the same time it was agreed that the institutions of the Coal and Steel Community, the High Authority (its executive), the Council of Ministers, the Assembly and the Court would be fused with those of the two new Communities – the Commissions (the executive), Council of Ministers, Assembly and Court. The United

Kingdom's 'entry into the Common Market' involved participation in all three Communities and their common institutions. For this reason, 'the EEC', which should strictly refer only to the Economic Community, is used for all three.

Chapter 1

1 *The Attorney General* v. *Times Newspapers Ltd* (1975) 2 Q.B.
2 See *Dr Bonham's* case (1610) 8 Co. Rep.
3 See *Edinburgh & Dalkeith Railway* v. *Wauchope* (1842) 8 Cl. & F. 710.
4 See *Marbury* v. *Madison* (1803) 1 Cranch 103.
5 See for example the writings and speeches of Lord Hailsham including *The Dilemma of Democracy* (London, 1978). See also Lord Scarman, *English Law – The New Dimension* (London, 1974).
6 A.V. Dicey, *Introduction to the Study of the Law of the Constitution*, 10th ed. (London, 1959).
7 *Vauxhall Estates Ltd* v. *Liverpool Corporation* (1932) 1 K.B. 733; *Ellen Street Estates* v. *The Minister of Health* (1934) 1 K.B. 590.
8 *MacCormick* v. *The Lord Advocate* (1953) S.C. 396; *Gibson* v. *The Lord Advocate* (1975) S.L.T. 134.
9 *Blackburn* v. *The Attorney General* (1971) 1 W.L.R.
10 See *Bulmer* v. *Bollinger* (1973) 2 CMLR 114 (C.A.) (1974) Ch. 40.
11 See R. Clutterbuck, *Britain in Agony* (London, 1978).
12 Formerly the Socialist Labour League.
13 Quoted from M. Hatfield, *The House the Left Built* (London, 1978).
14 H. Wilson, *The Governance of Britain* (London, 1975).
15 See for example P. Norton, *Conservative Dissidents 1970–1974* (London, 1978).
16 The phrase 'adversary politics' is explained in S.E. Finer (ed.), *Adversary Politics and Electoral Reform* (London, 1975).

Chapter 2

1 See *The Civil Service: Government Observations on the Eleventh Report from Expenditure Committee*, H.C. 535 (1978).
2 See J. Bruce-Gardyne and N. Lawson, *The Power Game: an examination of decision-making procedures in government* (London, 1976).
3 See M. Shanks, *Planning and Politics* (London, 1977). See also relevant essays in A.H. Hanson (ed.), *Planning and the Politicians* (London, 1969).
4 On physical planning see L.J. Sharpe, 'Innovation and change in British land-use planning', J. Hayward and M. Watson (eds), *Planning, Politics and Public Policy* (Cambridge, 1975).
5 See *The Times*, 7 March, 1978; H.C. Deb., 15 May 1978.
6 See Jean Floud, *The Governmental Impact on Research*, a paper presented at the Conference of the International Council on the Future of the University (Toronto, 1977).
7 Central Policy Review Staff, *Review of Overseas Representation* (1977). See also M. Beloff, 'The Think Tank and Foreign Affairs', *Public Administration*, 55 (1977).
8 *The United Kingdom's Overseas Representation*, Cmd. 7308.

Chapter 3

1 See M. Stewart, *The Jekyll and Hyde Years* (London, 1977).
2 See Norman St John-Stevas (ed.), introduction to Walter Bagehot, *The English Constitution*, in *Collected Works of Walter Bagehot, Vol. 5* (London, 1974).
3 See St John-Stevas (ed.), *Collected Works*.
4 Ministry of Reconstruction, *Report of the Committee on the Machinery of Government*, Cd. 9230.
5 See F.M.G. Willson, 'Coping with Administrative Growth: Super-Departments and the Ministerial Cadre', D.E. Butler and A.H. Halsey (eds), *Policy and Politics* (London, 1978).
6 See *First Report of the Select Committee on Procedure* (1977–8), chapt. 7, para. 6.

7 *Report of the Select Committee on the Parliamentary Commissioner for Administration* (1977–8).
8 For a pre-war example see A. E. Booth, 'Administrative Experiment in Unemployment Policy in the Thirties', *Public Administration*, 56 (1978).
9 See R.S. Goldston, 'Patronage in British Government', *Parliamentary Affairs*, XXX (1977). See also Alan Doig, 'Public Bodies and Ministerial Patronage', *Parliamentary Affairs*, XXXI (1978); and P. Holland and M. Fallon, *Public Bodies and Ministerial Patronage* (London, 1978).
10 For a personal view, by an exceptionally self-conscious minister, of what this relationship entails see R.H.S. Crossman, *The Diaries of a Cabinet Minister, Vol. I* (London, 1975).
11 See Christopher Pollitt, 'The Central Policy Review Staff 1970–4', *Public Administration*, 52 (1974). See also Lord Rothschild, 'The Government's Think-Tank and the Nation's Business', a lecture delivered in 1974, reprinted in *Meditations of a Broomstick* (London, 1974).
12 *The Reorganization of Central Government*, Cmnd. 4506.

Chapter 4

1 See David Butler and Uwe Kitzinger, *The 1975 Referendum* (London, 1976).
2 See *Specialist Committees in the British Parliament; the experience of a decade*, P.E.P. (1976); S.A. Walkland and Michael Ryle (eds), *The Commons in the Seventies* (London, 1977); and *First Report of the Select Committee on Procedure* (1977–8).
3 Ivor Burton and Gavin Drewry, 'Public Legislation; a survey of the sessions 1975–6; 1976–7', in *Parliamentary Affairs*, XXXI (1978).
4 J.P. Morgan, *The House of Lords and the Labour Government 1964–70* (Oxford, 1975).
5 Nora Beloff, *Freedom Under Foot* (London, 1976).
6 See S.E. Finer (ed.), *Adversary Politics and Electoral Reform* (London, 1976).
7 *The Preparation of Legislation* (Renton), Cmnd. 6053 (1975).
8 See memorandum by members of the Study of Parliament

Group published in the *First Report of the Select Committee on Procedure* (1977–8), III.

9 See J.A.G. Griffith, *Parliamentary Scrutiny of Government Bills* (London, 1974).

10 See S.A. de Smith, *Constitutional and Administrative Law*, 3rd ed. (London, 1977), chapt. 15.

11 See *First Report of the Select Committee on Procedure* (1977–8), chapt. 3.

12 See Terence Higgins, 'Parliamentary Control of Public Expenditure – A Back Bench Revolt?', *National Westminster Bank Quarterly* (August 1978).

13 See *The Economist*, 22 October 1977.

Chapter 5

1 See Walter Bagehot, 'Why has the "Settlement" of 1832 so easily melted away', N. St. John Stevas (ed.), *The Collected Works of Walter Bagehot*, vol. 6 (London, 1974).

2 A general history of the electoral system in the twentieth century is given by D.E. Butler, *The British Electoral System Since 1918*, 2nd ed. (Oxford, 1963).

3 Cmnd. 3342 (1967).

4 See D.E. Butler, 'Modifying Electoral Arrangements', D.E.Butler and A.H. Halsey (eds), *Policy and Politics: Essays in Honour of Norman Chester* (London, 1978).

5 See Daniel Lawrence, 'Race, Elections and Politics', Ivor Crewe (ed.), *British Political Sociology Yearbook, Vol. 2: The Politics of Race* (London, 1975).

6 Cmnd. 6601 (1976).

7 Anthony Wedgwood Benn was Lord Stansgate until 1963. Lord Home of the Hirsel was 14th Earl of Home until 1963; Sir Alec Douglas-Home 1963–74; and created Lord Home of the Hirsel 1974.

8 Representation of the People Act 1949 s.4 (3), as amended by the Mental Health Act, 1959.

9 On the general question of the disfranchisement of mental patients see L. Gostin, 'A Mental Patient's Right to Vote', *Poly Law Review* 2: 1 (1976).

10 On the elimination of corrupt practices see C. O'Leary, *The Elimination of Corrupt Practices in England* (Oxford, 1960).

11 On Lord Salisbury's attitude to the extension of the franchise and his ideas generally see M. Pinto-Duschinsky, *The Political Thought of Lord Salisbury* (London, 1967). On corruption generally see *Report of the Royal Commission on Standards of Conduct in Public Life* (Salmon), Cmnd. 6524.

12 See R.B. McCallum and A. Readman, *The British General Election of 1945* (Oxford, 1947).

13 These figures are taken from the *Report of the Hansard Commission on Electoral Reform* (1976).

14 *Hammersmith Borough Council v. Boundary Commission for England, The Times,* 15 December 1954; *Harper v. Home Secretary* (1955) Ch 238.

15 D.E. Butler, 'Modifying Electoral Arrangements', Butler and Halsey (eds), *Policy and Politics: Essays in Honour of Norman Chester* (London, 1978).

16 Representation of the People Act, 1978.

17 *Grieve v. Douglas-Home* (1965) Scotland 251.

18 See *The Sunday Times,* 20 August 1978.

19 See D.E. Butler and D. Kavanagh, *The British General Election of October 1974* (London, 1975). See also J. Whale, *The Politics of the Mass Media* (London, 1977). For a comparative perspective see Anthony Smith (ed.), *Television and Political Life: Studies in Six European Countries* (London, 1979).

20 On the background to direct elections see C. Cook and Mary Francis (eds), *The First European Elections: A Handbook and Guide* (London, 1979).

21 See *Draft Regulations for the Conduct of European Assembly Elections in Great Britain* (London, 1978).

22 See C. Cook and M. Francis, *op. cit.*

23 See for example S.E. Finer (ed.), *Adversary Politics and Electoral Reform* (London, 1975). See also N. Johnson, *In Search of the Constitution* (Oxford, 1977). For a discussion of the impact of the party and electoral systems on economic policy see M. Stewart, *The Jekyll and Hyde Years* (London, 1977).

Chapter 6

1 See N. Gash, 'From the Origins to Sir Robert Peel', Lord Butler (ed.), *The Conservatives* (London, 1977).
2 The discussion of general themes in British party politics can be found in slightly different form in W. L. Miller, *Electoral Dynamics in Britain Since 1918* (London, 1977). See also S. E. Finer, 'The Changing British Party System', *Report to the European Consortium on Political Research on the Party Systems of Western Europe* (Washington D.C., 1978).
3 For the Conservative policy on law and order see the 1979 manifesto.
4 On the early twentieth-century history of the Conservative Party see J. Ramsden, *The Age of Balfour and Baldwin* (London, 1978).
5 See Z. Layton-Henry, 'Race, Electoral Strategy and the Major Parties', *Parliamentary Affairs*, XXXI, 3 (1978).
6 These figures are quoted from T. Forrester, *The Labour Party and the Working Class* (London, 1976).
7 Labour Party constitution, 1918. Quoted in G. Le May (ed.), *British Government: Select Documents* (London, 1955).
8 See D. Steel, 'Nationalisation and Public Ownership', J. Ramsden and C. Cook (eds), *Trends in British Politics Since 1945* (London, 1978).
9 'Let Us Work Together' (February 1974) and 'Britain Will Win With Labour' (October 1974), F. W. S. Craig (ed.), *British General Election Manifestos* (London, 1975).
10 See for example B. Donoghue and G. Jones, *Herbert Morrison: Portrait of a Politician* (London, 1973).
11 See I. McLean, 'Labour Since 1945', J. Ramsden and C. Cook (eds), *Trends in British Politics Since 1945* (London, 1978).
12 See R. Taylor, *The Fifth Estate* (London, 1977). See also T. May, *Trade Unions and Pressure Group Politics* (London, 1975).
13 See John Vincent, *The Formation of the Liberal Party* (London, 1966).
14 See C. Cook, *A Short History of the Liberal Party* (London, 1976). See also J. Rasmussen, *The Liberal Party* (London, 1964).

15 See I. Crewe, J. Alt and B. Sarlvik, 'Angels in Plastic: The Liberal Surge in 1974', *Political Studies*, XXV, 3 (1977). See also P.H. Lemieux, 'Political Issues and Liberal Support in the February 1974 British General Election', *Political Studies*, XXV, 3 (1977).

16 D.E. Butler, *Coalitions in British Politics* (London, 1978).

17 See A. Michie and S. Hoggart, *The Pact: The Inside Story of the Lib–Lab Government 1977–78* (London, 1978).

18 See H. Pelling, *The British Communist Party: A Historical Profile*, 2nd ed. (London, 1975).

19 These figures are taken from *Comment: 35th National Congress Report*, parts 1 and 2.

20 See D.E. Butler and A. Sloman (eds), *British Political Facts 1900–1974* (London, 1975).

21 See R. Taylor, *The Fifth Estate* (London, 1977).

22 *Ibid.*

23 *Ibid.*

24 See H. Pelling, *The British Communist Party: A Historical Profile* (London, 1975).

25 Communist Party of Great Britain, *The British Road to Socialism* (London, 1977).

26 M. Walker, *The National Front* (London, 1977).

27 On this theme of race see Z. Layton-Henry, 'Race, Electoral Strategy and the Major Parties', *Parliamentary Affairs*, XXXI, 3 (1978).

28 See M. Steed, 'The National Front Vote', *Parliamentary Affairs*, XXXI, 3 (1978).

29 See I. McAllister, *The Northern Ireland Social and Democratic Labour Party: Political Opposition in a Divided Society* (London, 1977).

30 *Ibid.*

31 See Richard Rose, *Northern Ireland: A Time for Choice* (London, 1976), and I. MacAllister and Sarah Nelson, 'Developments in the Northern Ireland Party System', *Parliamentary Affairs*, XXXII, 3 (1979).

32 *Ibid.*

33 For an excellent recent discussion of types of party system see G. Sartori, *Parties and Party Systems: A Framework for Analysis* (Cambridge, 1976). I have slightly modified his conditions for a two-party system.

Chapter 7

1 R.T. McKenzie, *British Political Parties* (London, 1964).
2 See for example S.E. Finer (ed.), *Adversary Politics and Electoral Reform* (London, 1975).
3 See N. Fisher, *The Tory Leaders* (London, 1977).
4 See Philip Norton, *Dissension in the House of Commons 1945–1974* (London, 1975).
5 See C. Mellors, *The British MP* (London, 1978).
6 *Ibid.*
7 See Richard Rose, 'Parties, Factions and Tendencies in Britain', *Political Studies* XII (1964), 33–46.
8 See Philip Norton, *Conservative Dissidents* (London, 1978).
9 These figures are taken from 'Guide to the Bow Group 1979–80'.
10 For a recent discussion of Tory politics which pays particular attention to the Tory Reform Group see T. Russel, *The Tory Party* (London, 1978).
11 See Norton, *Dissension in the House of Commons, op. cit.*
12 *Ibid.*
13 For the impact of the 1922 Committee see Philip Goodhart, *The 1922* (London, 1973).
14 See Fisher, *The Tory Leaders, op. cit.*
15 See Martin Burch, 'Leadership Styles in Opposition: Edward Heath and Margaret Thatcher', unpublished paper presented to the SSRC Conference on the Conservative Party, Nuffield College Oxford, 1978.
16 National Union of Conservative and Unionist Associations, *The Selection of Parliamentary Candidates* (London, 1971).
17 See D.E. Butler and Dennis Kavanagh, *The British General Election of October 1974* (London, 1975).
18 See R. Punnett, *Front Bench Opposition* (London, 1973).
19 See Mellors, *The British MP, op. cit.*
20 On this process and the role of Conference generally see Lewis Minkin, *The Labour Party Conference* (London, 1978).
21 See *Labour Party Annual Conference Report*, 1978.
22 See Minkin, *The Labour Party Conference, op. cit.*
23 *Ibid.*
24 See *Labour Party Report to Conference, 1978.*
25 *Ibid.*

26 *Report of the Committee of Inquiry on Financial Aid to Political Parties* (Houghton), Cmnd. 6601.
27 *Ibid.*
28 *Ibid.*
29 *Ibid.*
30 See D. E. Butler and D. Stokes, *Political Change in Britain*, 2nd ed. (London, 1974).
31 See *Labour Party Annual Conference Report*, 1977.

Chapter 8

1 For a general review of elites in British society see P. Stanworth and A. Giddens (eds), *Elites and Power in British Society* (Cambridge, 1974).
2 See D. E. Butler and D. Stokes, *Political Change in Britain*, 2nd ed. (London, 1974).
3 See *The Civil Service, Vol. 1: Report of the Committee* (Fulton), Cmnd. 3638; there are four further volumes of evidence and surveys. See also *Eleventh Report of the Expenditure Committee (1977–8)* (1977), with three volumes of evidence and memoranda; and *The Civil Service: Government Observations on the Eleventh Report from the Expenditure Committee* (1978).
4 See *Eleventh Report of the Expenditure Committee*, appendices 1171–3.
5 See for example G. K. Fry, *Statesmen in Disguise: The Changing Role of the Administrative Class of the British Home Civil Service, 1853–1966* (London, 1969).
6 See H. Roseveare, *The Treasury* (London, 1969) 246 *et seq.*
7 M. Beloff, 'Examining the Working of Whitehall', *The Times*, 19 June 1968, reprinted in *The Intellectual in Politics* (London, 1970). The article refers to the powerful arguments put forward by his distinguished predecessor as Gladstone Professor, Sir Arthur (later Lord) Salter in his book *The Slave of the Lamp* (London, 1967).
8 See *Eleventh Report of the Expenditure Committee*, appendices 1090–112.
9 Sir James Dunnett, 'The Civil Service after Fulton', *Public Administration*, 54 (1976).

10 See R. N. Heaton and Sir Leslie Williams, *Civil Service Training* (London, 1974).

11 Dunnett, *The Civil Service after Fulton, loc. cit.*

12 For a discussion of the *grands corps* see J. Hayward, *The One and Indivisible French Republic* (London, 1973).

13 *Eleventh Report of the Expenditure Committee*, appendices 1097.

14 Civil Service Department, *A Directory of Paid Public Appointments made by Ministers* (1976).

15 H.C. Deb, written answers, 28, 29 June 1978.

16 See Ronald Butt, in *The Times*, 20 July 1978.

17 See P. Holland and M. Fallon, *Public Bodies and Ministerial Patronage*.

18 See *The Times*, 2 August 1978. For a general discussion of the issues see Alan Doig, 'Public Bodies and Ministerial Patronage', *Parliamentary Affairs*, XXXI (1978).

19 See *The Times*, 17 June 1978.

20 See Joan E. Mitchell, 'Special Advisers: a Personal View', *Public Administration*, 56 (1978); see also *The Times*, 13 June 1978.

21 See *The Times*, 2 August 1978.

22 See *The Times*, 31 May 1978.

23 Further proposals for dealing with this problem came in the *Fourteenth Report of the Expenditure Committee (1977–8)*.

24 See *Eleventh Report of the Expenditure Committee*.

25 See *Report of the Committee of Inquiry on Industrial Democracy (Bullock Report)* (1977).

26 *Eleventh Report of the Expenditure Committee*, lxxviii–lxxxiii.

27 Central Policy Review Staff, *Review of Overseas Representation* (1977).

28 *Report of the Review Committee on Overseas Representation* (Duncan), Cmnd. 4107.

29 W. Grant and D. Marsh, *The CBI* (London, 1977).

30 For the political role of trade unions see R. Taylor, *The Fifth Estate* (London, 1977) and Eric Wigham, *Strikes and the Government* (London, 1976).

Chapter 9

1 These figures are taken from *Local Government Finance*, Cmnd. 6813.
2 *Ibid.*
3 See J. Garner, 'The Ultra Vires Rule', Local Government Studies, 1 : 2 (1973).
4 On the question of conflicting values in local government see L.J. Sharpe, 'Theories and Values of Local Government', *Political Studies*, XVIII, 2 (1970).
5 See J.G. Griffith, *Central Departments and Local Authorities* (London, 1966).
6 *Report of the Committee of Inquiry into Local Government Finance* (Layfield), Cmnd. 6543.
7 For some indication of the line of government thinking in relation to organic change see Cmnd. 7457.
8 See G.W. Jones, 'Central–Local Relations', D.E. Butler and A.H. Halsey (eds), *Policy and Politics* (London, 1978).
9 See B. Keith Lucas and P. Richards, *A History of Local Government in the Twentieth Century* (London, 1978).
10 S.E. Finer, *Edwin Chadwick* (London, 1954), p. 17.
11 W.A. Robson, *The Development of Local Government* (London, 1931).
12 On London's local government see G. Rhodes and S.K. Ruck, *The Government of Greater London* (London, 1970).
13 See R.H.S. Crossman, *The Diaries of a Cabinet Minister, Vol. 1, 1964–6* (London, 1975).
14 *Report of Royal Commission on Local Government in England* (Redcliffe-Maud) 1966–9, Cmnd. 4040; *Report of Royal Commission on Local Government in Scotland* (Wheatley) 1966–9, Cmnd. 4150.
15 See C. Jones, *Immigration and Social Policy in Britain* (London, 1977).
16 See *Report of the Committee on Local Authority and Allied Social Services*, Cmnd. 1968.
17 *Local Government Boundary Commission for England: Reports Nos 3, 5 and 6*, and S.I.s Nos 1110, 1973 and 1939 all deal with the question of successor parish status.
18 *Local Government Boundary Commission for England: Report No. 6* covers the Commission programme of review up to 1978;

the Commission review programme up to 1983 is set out in Department of Environment circulars 121/77 and 33/78.

19 *Report of Committee on Management of Local Government* (Maud) (1967); *Report of Committee on Staffing in Local Government* (Mallaby) (1967); *New Local Authorities. Management and Structure (The Bains Report)* (1972).

20 See Wyn Grant, *Independent Local Politics in England and Wales* (London, 1977).

21 See C. Mellors, *The British MP* (London, 1978).

22 Department of the Environment, *Report of the Committee of Inquiry into the System of Remuneration of Members of Local Authorities* (1977).

23 See *Ibid.*, Vol. *11: Survey of Councillors and Local Authorities*.

24 *Report of the Royal Commission on Standards of Conduct in Public Life*, Cmnd. 6524.

25 On the work of the Commissions see N. Lewis and B. Gateshill, *The Commission for Local Administration: A Preliminary Appraisal* (London, 1978).

26 See Local Government Act, 1978.

27 On the general question of central–local relationships see Central Policy Review Staff, *Relations between Central Government and Local Authorities* (London, 1977).

28 See *The Secretary of State for Education and Science* v. *Tameside Metropolitan Borough Council* (1976) 3 W.L.R.

29 See *The Attorney General* v. *Fulham Corporation* (1921) 1 Ch. 440.

30 See *Roberts* v. *Hopwood* (1925) A.C. 578

31 *Asher* v. *Lacey* (1973) 3 A.E.R. 1008.

32 Though the legislation did not relieve the disqualification.

33 See M. Kogan, *The Politics of Educational Change* (London, 1978).

34 For an excellent introduction to the whole topic of local-government finance see N. Hepworth, *The Finance of Local Government*, rev. 4th ed. (London, 1978).

35 See Cmnd. 6813.

36 See for example G. W. Jones's comments in D. E. Butler and A. H. Halsey (eds), *Policy and Politics* (London, 1978).

Chapter 10

1 See for example R. Clutterbuck, *Britain in Agony: The Growth of Political Violence* (London, 1978).
2 The phrase is used by D. Harkness, *The Restless Dominion* (London, 1969).
3 See Conor Cruise O'Brien, *States of Ireland* (London, 1972).
4 See Clutterbuck, *Britain in Agony, op. cit.*
5 *The Northern Ireland Constitution*, Cmnd. 5675.
6 The phrase is C.E. Lindblom's.
7 *Statistics of Education in Wales No. 3*, 1978. Quoted in *The Economist*, 7 October 1978.
8 See Alan Butt Phillip, *The Welsh Question* (London, 1975).
9 See Erskine May, *Parliamentary Practice*, 19th ed. (1976).
10 *Report of the Royal Commission on Scottish Affairs* (Balfour), Cmd. 9212.
11 Central Office of Information, *Scotland* (1974).
12 *Ibid.*
13 *Report of the Royal Commission on the Constitution* (Kilbrandon), Cmnd. 5460–11.
14 Cmnd. 5460–1.
15 *Democracy and Devolution: Proposals for Scotland and Wales*, Cmnd. 5732 (1974).
16 *Our Changing Democracy*, Cmd. 6348 (1975).
17 *Devolution to Scotland and Wales – Supplementary Statement*, Cmnd. 6585 (1976).

Chapter 11

1 The Royal Commission on Legal Services (Benson) reported in October 1979 (Cmnd. 7468).
2 Administration of Justice Act, 1969.
3 Courts Act, 1971.
4 For a personal account see Lord Denning, *The Discipline of Law* (London, 1979).
5 O'Connell's Case (1844) 11 C.L. & F. 155. For a discussion see L. Blom Cooper and G. Drewry, *Final Appeal* (Oxford, 1972).
6 The rule was formalized in *London Tramways* v. *London County Council* (1898) A.C. 375.

7 See the Practice Statement, 26 July 1966, 1 W.L.R. 1234.

8 The basis of the present system is the Justices of the Peace Act, 1949 which followed a Royal Commission on Justices of the Peace (1946–8).

9 See Royal Commission on Quarter Sessions and Assizes (Beeching), Cmnd. 415.

10 For the background to the merger see *Report of the Interdepartmental Committee on the Court of Criminal Appeal* (Donovan), Cmnd. 2755.

11 On references to the European Court see *Bulmer* v. *Bollinger* (1973) 2 CMLR 114 (C.A.) (1974) Ch. 40 and *McCarthy's Ltd* v. *Smith* (1979) 3 CMLR 44 (C.A.).

12 A good starting point for an appreciation of the merits of this approach to the judiciary is J.G. Griffith, *The Politics of the Judiciary* (London, 1977).

13 Gallup Survey, May 1976. We are grateful to Mr Bob Wybrow for drawing our attention to it.

14 Lord Scarman, *English Law: The New Dimension* (London, 1974). See also Lord Hailsham, *Elective Dictatorship* (London, 1976) and *The Dilemma of Democracy* (London, 1978).

15 *Report of the Select Committee on a Bill of Rights* H.L. 176 (1978). See also Minutes of evidence H.L. Sessions 1976–7 and 1977–8.

16 *R.* v. *Chief Immigration Officer, Heathrow Airport ex parte Salamat Bibi* (1976) 3 A.E.R. 843.

17 Criminal Law Act, 1977, s.62. See also H.C. Debs 935 cols 496 *et seq.* and 936 col. 721 *et seq.*

18 The *Confait* case was the subject of a special inquiry by Sir Henry Fisher (H.C.P. 90, 1977–8). See also *Modern Law Review* (1978) 455. The Royal Commission on Criminal Procedure was established in February 1978 under the chairmanship of Sir Cyril Philips.

19 See Part I of the written evidence of Sir David McNee (1978). See also *The Times*, 3 August 1978.

20 Lord Scarman's Frank Newsom Memorial Lecture was delivered to the Police College, Bramshill, in July 1978. We are indebted to Lord Scarman for a text of this lecture.

21 *Ibid.*

22 *Ibid.*

23 On the *Oz* trial see T. Palmer, *The Trials of Oz* (London,

1971). For a general survey of the law in this area see G. Robertson, *Obscenity* (London, 1979).
24 *Shaw* v. DPP (1962) A.C. 220 and *Knuller* v. DPP (1973) A.C. 435.
25 *R.* v. *Lemon, The Times*, 18 March 1978.
26 On the development of the offence of incitement to stir up racial hatred see P.M. Leopold, 'Incitement to Hatred – The History of a Controversial Criminal Offence', *Public Law* (Winter, 1977).
27 See New Society, *Guide to the Race Act* (London, 1976).
28 See R. Wraith, *Open Government* (London, 1977).
29 See J. Aitken, *Officially Secret* (London, 1971), and the discussion on the 'A.B.C.' trial in 1979.
30 *Reform of s.2 of the Official Secrets Act*, Cmnd. 7285.
31 See Hugo Young, *The Crossman Affair* (London, 1976).
32 *Attorney General* v. *Times Newspapers Ltd* (1973) 1 A.E.R.
33 *Report of the Committee of Privy Councillors on Ministerial Memoirs* (Radcliffe), Cmnd. 6386.
34 The discussions were published in *New Society*, 17 and 24 June 1976. On the policy implications of the benefit see A. Ogus and E. Barendt, *The Law of Social Security* (London, 1978) 447–52.
35 The Phillimore Committee, *Report on Contempt of Court* (1974), Cmnd. 5794; *The Attorney-General* v. *Times Newspapers Ltd* (1973) 1 A.E.R. 815 and *Contempt of Court: A Discussion Paper*, Cmnd. 7145; and *Law Quarterly Review*, XCV (1979), p. 348.
36 On film censorship generally see *Screen Violence and Film Censorship*, Home Office Research Study No. 40 (London, 1977).
37 See John Whale, *The Politics of the Media* (London, 1977). See also A. Smith (ed.), *Television and Political Life* (London, 1979).
38 See N. Beloff, *Freedom Under Foot* (London, 1976), and Michael Beloff, 'Closed Shop and Press Freedom', *The Observer*, 2 March 1975.

Chapter 12

1 For a discussion of Crichel Down see K.C. Wheare, 'Crichel Down Revisited', *Political Studies*, XXIII (1975).

2 K.C. Wheare, *loc. cit.*, has a succinct statement of the facts of Crichel Down. See also R. Douglas Brown, *The Battle of Crichel Down* (London, 1955).

3 See Cmnd. 218.

4 See K.C. Wheare, *loc. cit.*

5 For a general survey of the range of tribunals in Britain see R.E. Wraith and P.G. Hutchesson, *Administrative Tribunals* (London, 1973).

6 For the general question of representation before tribunals see A. Frost and Coral Howard, *Representation and Administrative Tribunals* (London, 1977).

7 *Second Report of the Council on Tribunals* (London, 1961).

8 On the topic of inquiries see R.E. Wraith and G.B. Lamb, *Public Inquiries as Instruments of Government* (London, 1971); *Report of the Committee on Participation and Planning* (Skeffington) (1969); and the Benson Report (Cmnd. 7468).

9 On the background to Windscale see I. Breach, *Windscale Fallout* (London, 1978).

10 Town and Country Planning Act, 1971.

11 The history of the Parliamentary Commissioner for Administration and admirable discussions of the institution can be found in F. Stacey, *The British Ombudsman* (Oxford, 1971) and R. Gregory and P. Hutchesson, *The Parliamentary Ombudsman* (London, 1975). A comparative perspective is taken in F. Stacey, *Ombudsmen Compared* (Oxford, 1978).

12 On this point see F. Stacey, *Ombudsmen Compared* (Oxford, 1978).

13 These figures are taken from Justice, *Our Fettered Ombudsman* (London, 1977).

14 See *Annual Report of the Parliamentary Commissioner for Administration* (1977).

15 The Royal Commission on Standards of Conduct in Public Life recommended that Orders in Council be made to enable existing ombudsmen to consider complaints relating to commercial or contractual transactions.

16 Parliamentary Commissioner Act (Northern Ireland), 1969.

17 Police Act, 1976.

18 On the work of the local ombudsmen see F. Stacey, *Ombudsmen Compared* (Oxford, 1978) and N. Lewis and B.

Gateshill, *The Commission for Local Administration: A Preliminary Appraisal* (London, 1978).

19 Geoffrey Marshall, 'Parliament and the Redress of Grievances', S. Walkland and M. Ryle (eds), *The Commons in the 70s* (London, 1977).

20 These figures are taken from the *Annual Report of the Parliamentary Commissioner for Administration* (1977).

21 *Ibid.*

22 See F. Stacey, *Ombudsmen Compared* (Oxford, 1978).

23 On the general topic of judicial scrutiny of the administration see the classic work by S.A. de Smith, *Judicial Review of Administrative Action* (London, 1973).

24 *Ridge* v. *Baldwin* (1964) A.C. 40.

25 See Michael Beloff, 'The Silkin Squeeze', *New Society*, 10 February 1977 for a useful summary.

26 See *Duncan* v. *Cammell Laird* (1942) A.C. 624.

27 *Conway* v. *Rimmer* (1968) A.C. 910.

28 *Padfield* v. *The Minister of Agriculture, Fisheries and Food* (1968) A.C. 997.

29 *The Secretary of State for Education and Science* v. *The Tameside Metropolitan Borough Council* (1976) 3 W.L.R.

30 *Congreve* v. *The Home Office* (1976) Q.B. 629. See also *Special Report of the Parliamentary Commissioner for Administration* (1975) H.C. 680.

31 *Gouriet* v. *Union of Post Office Workers* (1977) 2 W.L.R. See also 3 W.L.R. 300. For Lord Denning's views see also his book, *The Discipline of Law* (London, 1979).

32 See Rules of the Supreme Court (Amendment No. 3) Order, 1977. For comment see editorial in *Public Law* (Spring, 1978).

Chapter 13

1 On the 1976 crisis and its sequel see Samuel Brittan, *The Economic Consequences of Democracy* (London, 1977), chapt. 12.

2 On the earlier phases in this process see M. Beloff, *New Dimensions in Foreign Policy: a Study of British Administrative Experience* (London, 1961). See also *Report of the Committee*

on *Representational Services Overseas* (Plowden), Cmnd. 2276; *Report of the Review Committee on Overseas Representation* (Duncan), Cmnd. 4107; R. Boardman and A.J. Groom, *The Management of Britain's External Relations* (London, 1973); and W. Wallace, *The Foreign Policy Process in Britain* (London, 1975).

3 Central Policy Review Staff, *Review of Overseas Representation* (1977).

4 See J. Mackintosh, 'The Think Tank should have remembered what Foreign Policy is for', *The Times*, 22 August 1977; M. Beloff, 'The Think Tank and Foreign Affairs', *Public Administration* 55 (1977); and *Fourth Report of the Expenditure Committee (1977–8)* (1978).

5 See *The United Kingdom's Overseas Representation*, Cmnd. 7308; and *Interchange between the Home Civil Service and the Diplomatic Service: Report of a Working Group* (London, 1978).

6 Sir Con O'Neill, *Our European Future* (London, 1972).

7 *Twenty-Second Report of the Select Committee on the European Communities* (1977–8) H.L. 131 (1978).

8 See Marcel Berlins, 'Britain in Europe: Impact of Community Law', *The Times*, 2 February 1977. On the European aspects of one branch of English law see A.I. Ogus and E.M. Barendt, *The Law of Social Security* (London, 1978) 663–5 and 668–83.

9 *First Report of the Select Committee on Procedure (1977–8)* H.C. chapt. 4.

10 D.E. Butler and U. Kitzinger, *The 1975 Referendum* (London, 1975) 172.

11 House of Lords Select Committee on the European Communities, *Relations between the United Kingdom Parliament and the European Parliament after Direct Elections* H.L. 256–1 (1978).

12 See the lecture given on 19 January 1978 by the then head of the Civil Service, Sir Douglas Allen, now Lord Croham, *National Westminster Bank Review*, August 1978.

13 See for an early expression of this point of view M. Beloff, 'The Frontiers of Political Analysis', *The Cambridge Journal*, IV (1951), reprinted in M. Beloff, *The Great Powers* (London, 1959).

Further Reading

The literature on British government is vast and what follows is a select bibliography of some of the most important works of recent years as well as of a few classic treatments of British government where they may still be relevant. Government papers are referred to in the footnotes but not listed here. For basic statistics etc. reference should be made to the current editions of *Britain: an official Handbook* (London, H.M.S.O.) and the *Ulster Year Book* (Belfast, H.M.S.O.)

General

Walter Bagehot's *The English Constitution* gives useful insight into the operation of British government on the eve of the Second Reform Act of 1867. It should be compared with J.S. Mill's *Representative Government* (1861). Bagehot's work inspired R.H.S. Crossman to develop the thesis of prime-ministerial government in his introduction to the Fontana edition of *The English Constitution* (London, 1963) and the whole debate is summarized with judicious commentary in N. St J.-Stevas (ed.), *The Collected Works of Walter Bagehot* 5 (London, *The Economist*, 1974).

The classic doctrines of the rule of law and parliamentary sovereignty are to be found in A.V. Dicey, *An Introduction to the Study of the Law of the Constitution*, 10th ed. (London, Macmillan, 1959).

For some different perspectives on the constitution and British government as they appeared to writers in the 1950s see

Harold Laski, *Reflections on the Constitution* (Manchester U.P., 1951) and L.S. Amery, *Thoughts on the Constitution* (London, O.U.P., 1953). Herbert Morrison's *Government and Parliament*, 3rd ed. (London, O.U.P., 1964) is still of use; and the works of Sir Ivor Jennings contain a standard treatment of several major themes in British politics. Of particular relevance are his *Cabinet Government*, 3rd ed. (C.U.P., 1969) and *Parliament* (C.U.P., 1957). The three-volume work *Party Politics* (C.U.P., 1960–2) is also useful as a guide to thinking in the 1950s about the role of parties in the constitutional system. A classical study of the subject by an American authority is S.H. Beer, *Modern British Politics* (London, Faber, 1965).

Recent Periodicals and Collections

Parliamentary Affairs, Public Law and *Public Administration* are the most useful periodicals for following British constitutional and political developments.

The Economist is a useful source of contemporary information; *New Society* deals more specifically with social policy. K. Macdonald's *Essex Reference Index* (London, Macmillan, 1975) is an invaluable guide to articles in British political and sociological journals up to that date.

Recent collections of essays are a useful corrective to the standard treatments of British government. Of particular use from a sociological perspective is R. Rose (ed.), *Studies in British Politics*, 3rd ed. (London, Macmillan, 1976) which also contains a useful bibliography of articles. D.E. Butler and A.H. Halsey (eds.), *Policy and Politics: Essays Presented to Norman Chester* (London, Macmillan, 1978) contains a number of useful if rather brief essays on subjects in the general area of public administration. C. Cook and J. Ramsden (eds), *Trends in British Politics Since 1945* (London, Macmillan, 1978) contains a number of essays on British politics and British parties. D. Kavanagh and Richard Rose (eds), *New Trends in British Politics: Issues for Research* (London, Sage, 1977) contains some useful chapters on different problems with special reference to the way in which recent developments may have altered the concepts which are applicable to British political behaviour.

The Constitution

The best theoretical introduction to the issues and problems of the British constitution is Geoffrey Marshall's *Constitutional Theory* (Oxford, Clarendon Press, 1971) which contains helpful American and Commonwealth comparisons. N. Johnson, *In Search of the Constitution* (Oxford, Pergamon, 1977) is a stimulating personal critique of British constitutional conventions and practices. The best legal surveys are to be found in S.A. de Smith, *Constitutional and Administrative Law*, 3rd ed. (London, Penguin, 1977) and E.C.S. Wade and G. Phillips, *Constitutional and Administrative Law*, 9th ed. (London, Longman, 1977). K.C. Wheare, *Government by Committee: an Essay on the British Constitution* (Oxford, Clarendon Press, 1955) offers an original interpretation of the constitution.

The Functions of Government in the British Welfare State

Useful historical introductions to the evolution of the contemporary welfare state can be found in B.B. Gilbert, *British Social Policy, 1914–1939* (London, Batsford, 1970) and D. Fraser, *The Evolution of the British Welfare State* (London, Macmillan, 1963). T. Marshall, *Social Policy*, 4th ed. (London, Hutchinson, 1975) is also a useful historical review. Two guides to current social-service payments can be found in P. Willmott, *Consumer's Guide to the British Social Services* (London, Penguin, 1971) and the Family Welfare Association's *Guide to the Social Services* (London, Macdonald & Evans, 1978). R. Titmuss's works provide an interesting perspective on the goals of the welfare state and how far it remains defective: *Essays on the Welfare State*, 3rd ed. (London, Allen & Unwin, 1976), *Commitment to Welfare*, 2nd ed. (London, Allen & Unwin, 1976), and *Social Policy* (London, Allen & Unwin, 1974) are all worth reading. Catherine Jones, *Immigration and Social Policy in Britain* (London, Tavistock Publications, 1977) is an excellent introduction to the impact which immigrants have had on British social services and the deficiencies which have been revealed in the structure of social administration.

The Executive

The role of the British Cabinet is covered in J. Mackintosh, *The British Cabinet*, 3rd ed. (London, Stevens, 1977) and in Patrick Gordon Walker's much shorter work, *The Cabinet*, rev. ed. (London, Collins, 1972). Hans Daalder, *Cabinet Reform in Britain* (London, Stanford U.P., 1964) is a more specialized study and B. Headey, *British Cabinet Ministers* (London, Allen & Unwin, 1974) is helpful. Personal insights are provided by R.H.S. Crossman, *Diaries of a Cabinet Minister*, 3 vols. (London, Hamilton, 1975–7) and by Harold Wilson, *The Labour Government 1964–70: a Personal Record* (London, Michael Joseph/ Weidenfeld & Nicolson, 1971). Harold Wilson, *The Governance of Britain* (London, Michael Joseph, 1976) has interesting information on the problem of collective responsibility. D.N. Chester and F. Willson, *The Organization of British Central Government 1914–1964*, 2nd ed. (London, Allen & Unwin, 1968) may be supplemented by F. Willson's essay in D.E. Butler and A.H. Halsey (eds), *Policy and Politics*. H. Heclo and A. Wildavsky, *The Private Government of Public Money* (London, Macmillan, 1974) is informative and amusing on the budgetary process. N. Lawson and J. Bruce Gardyne, *The Power Game* (London, Macmillan, 1976) has revealing studies of the decision-making process viewed through several case studies. Anthony King (ed.), *The Prime Minister* (London, Macmillan, 1969) is still very relevant to discussions of the office as is the two-volume *British Prime Ministers* edited by John Mackintosh (London, Weidenfeld & Nicolson, 1977–8).

Parliament

The development of opinion on parliamentary reform can be traced by comparing two collections of essays – A.H. Hanson and B. Crick, *The Commons in Transition* (London, Fontana, 1970) and S. Walkland and M. Ryle, *The Commons in the 70s* (London, Fontana, 1977). For a detailed study of the legislative process, there is little to compare with J.A.G. Griffith, *Parliamentary Scrutiny of Government Bills* (London, Allen & Unwin, 1974). On financial procedure D. Coombes (ed.), *The Power of the Purse* (London, Allen & Unwin, 1976) has the merit of putting British procedure in comparative perspective. Ann Robinson discusses the work of the Expenditure Committee between 1970 and 1976 in *Parliament and Public Spending* (London, Heinemann, 1978). D. Coombes, *The Member of Parliament and the Administration* (London, Allen & Unwin, 1966), though slightly dated, is still useful. D.N. Chester and N. Bowring, *Questions in Parliament* (O.U.P., 1962) is the standard work but needs supplementing with D.N. Chester, 'Questions in the House', S. Walkland and M. Ryle, *op. cit.* On back-benchers' roles see P.G. Richards, *The Backbenchers* (London, Faber & Faber, 1972). R. Barker and M. Rush, *The Member of Parliament and his Information* (London, Allen & Unwin, 1970) is invaluable, as is the later work M. Rush and M. Shaw (ed.), *The House of Commons: Services and Facilities* (London, Allen & Unwin, 1974). R. Punnett, *Front Bench Opposition* (London, Heinemann, 1973) gives an excellent, comprehensive coverage of the functioning of opposition in Britain. A. Morris (ed.), *The Growth of Parliamentary Scrutiny by Committee* (Oxford, Pergamon Press, 1970) contains some interesting individual essays on the way committees might develop. The House of Lords is covered until 1970 by J.P. Morgan, *The House of Lords and the Labour Government 1964–1970* (Oxford, Clarendon Press, 1975).

The Electoral System

The authoritative introduction is D.E. Butler, *The Electoral System in Britain Since 1918*, 2nd ed. (Oxford, Clarendon Press, 1963). Peter Pulzer, *Political Representation and Elections in Britain*, 3rd ed. (London, Allen & Unwin, 1975) is a useful introduction. The debate about electoral reform is brought up-to-date by the collection of essays edited by S.E. Finer, *Adversary Politics and Electoral Reform* (London, Anthony Wigram, 1975) which also contains chapters on the operation of various alternative electoral systems. *The Report of the Hansard Society's Commission on Electoral Reform* (London, Hansard Society, 1976) summarizes the arguments for reform and the status quo.

The Political Parties

The standard modern work on the role of parties in the British system of government is R. Rose, *The Problem of Party Government* (London, Penguin, 1976).

On the history of individual parties see R. Blake, *The Conservative Party from Peel to Churchill* (London, Fontana, 1972). Lord Butler (ed.), *The Conservatives* (London, Allen & Unwin, 1977) is also worthwhile, although it concentrates very much on 'high politics' rather than the history of the Party as such. A major history of the Conservative Party is being written but so far only two volumes have appeared. The volume most relevant to the contemporary Conservative Party has yet to appear but J. Ramsden, *The Age of Balfour and Baldwin* (London, Longman, 1978) is excellent on the inter-war period.

On the Labour Party, Henry Pelling has produced two excellent studies – *A Short History of the Labour Party*, 6th ed. (London, Macmillan, 1978) and *The Origins of the Labour Party*, 2nd ed. (O.U.P., 1965). On the ideology of the party see F. Bealey (ed.), *The Social and Political Thought of the Labour Party* (London, Weidenfeld & Nicolson, 1970). On the role of trade unions in the party see M. Harrison, *Trade Unions and the Labour Party since 1945* (London, Allen & Unwin, 1960) though the picture he gives is now of course somewhat dated. More up to date are R. Taylor *The Fifth Estate* (London, Routledge & Kegan Paul, 1978) and Lewis Minkin, *The Labour Party Conference* (London, Allen Lane, 1978). The constituency parties are covered in E. Janosik, *Constituency Labour Parties in Britain* (London, Pall Mall, 1968). A recent study of the unions and their role in policy making is T. May, *Trade Unions and Pressure Group Politics* (London, Saxon House, 1975).

Detailed examination of the policy-making process inside the Labour Party can also be found in M. Hatfield, *The House the Left Built* (London, Gollancz, 1978).

On the Liberal Party, C. Cook, *A Short History of the Liberal Party* (London, Macmillan, 1976) is reliable. More detailed studies of different aspects of Liberal Party history and politics include J. Vincent, *The Formation of the Liberal Party 1857–1868* (London, Hutchinson, 1966), T. Wilson, *The Downfall of the Liberal Party 1914–35* (London, Collins/Fontana, 1968) and A. Cyr, *Liberal Party Politics in Britain* (London, Calder, 1977).

Martin Walker, *The National Front* (London, Fontana, 1977) is the only serious study of the movement. D. Schoen, *Powell and the Powellites* (London, Macmillan, 1977) is a useful supplement to this work on the impact of race on British political life. The Communist Party is covered in H. Pelling, *The British Communist Party* (London, A. & C. Black, 1975) and in K. Newton, *The Sociology of British Communism* (London, Allen Lane, 1969).

There are as yet no full-scale histories of either the Scottish National Party or Plaid Cymru but much material about these two parties can be found in general works on Scottish and Welsh nationalism.

Northern Irish parties are also rather sparsely covered but the Ulster Unionists have been accorded scholarly treatment in J. F. Harbinson, *The Ulster Unionist Party 1882–1973* (Belfast, Blackstaff, 1974); and Ian McAllister, *The Northern Ireland Social Democratic and Labour Party* (London, Macmillan, 1977) is a judicious study of the Province's major Catholic party.

On voting behaviour and party choice there is an enormous wealth of material but D. E. Butler and Donald Stokes, *Political Change in Britain*, 2nd ed. (London, Macmillan, 1977) is the most comprehensive treatment of the subject. Shorter studies include J. Blondel, *Voters, Parties and Leaders* (London, Penguin, 1974).

The problem of working-class Conservatism is treated in R. T. McKenzie and A. Silver, *Angels in Marble* (London, Heinemann, 1968) and Eric Nordlinger, *The Working Class Tories* (London, MacGibbon & Kee, 1967). More general works on the relationship between class structure and political behaviour are F. Parkin, *Class Inequality and Political Order* (London, Panther, 1972) and Tom Forester, *The Labour Party and the Working Class* (London, Heinemann, 1976). The thesis of the affluent worker is examined in J. Goldthorpe *et al.*, *The Affluent Worker, Vol. 2: Political Attitudes and Behaviour* (C.U.P., 1968). W. E. Miller, *Electoral Dynamics* (London, Macmillan, 1977) is an excellent study of the factors affecting voting behaviour.

The Nuffield General Election Studies provide competent

summaries of the issues raised in individual general elections and contemporary analysis of the factors shaping the results. J. Ramsden and C. Cook, *By-Elections in British Politics* (London, Macmillan, 1973) is the only available study on the incidence and political impact of by-elections in the system. D. E. Butler and U. Kitzinger, *The British Referendum of 1975* (London, Macmillan, 1976) is a detailed study of the background to the referendum on British membership of the European Communities.

Influence and Bureaucracy in Modern Britain

The subject of Britain's political elites is covered in a collection of essays edited by P. Stanworth and A. Giddens, *Elites and Power in British Society* (C.U.P., 1974). The older work by W. Guttsman, *The British Political Elite* (London, MacGibbon & Kee, 1964) remains useful. Anthony Sampson's *The New Anatomy of Britain* (London, Hodder & Stoughton, 1971) is a journalist's look at the interconnections between some important groups in British society. Colin Mellors, *The British MP* (London, Gower, 1978) deals sociologically with Members of Parliament. An earlier work is P. W. Buck, *Amateurs and Professionals in British Politics* (Chicago U.P., 1963). The changes in the Civil Service over the last decade have not received a definitive study and apart from the official publications referred to in the footnotes, the student is best off with the articles in *Public Administration*. Of older works G. K. Fry, *Statesmen in Disguise* (London, Macmillan, 1969) and Henry Roseveare, *The Treasury* (London, Allen Lane, 1969) remain useful.

Pressure groups have received extensive study. The standard work is still S. E. Finer, *Anonymous Empire*, 2nd ed. (London, Pall Mall, 1966). For trade unions, apart from the works already noted see also Eric Wigham, *Strikes and the Government* (London, Macmillan, 1976). W. Grant and D. Marsh, *The CBI* (London, Hodder, 1977) surveys the literature on the business side. G. K. Wilson, *Special Interests and Policy Making* (London, John Wiley & Sons, 1977) deals with the agricultural interest on a comparative basis and supplements Peter Self and H.J. Storing, *The State and the Farmer* (London, Allen & Unwin,

1962). William Wallace in his *The Foreign Policy Process in Britain* (London, Allen & Unwin, 1977) deals very fully with their impact on foreign policy. One could also consult R.J. Shepherd, *Public Opinion and European Integration* (London, Saxon House, 1975).

Local Government

The excellent New Local Government Series of which Peter Richards is editor and Allen & Unwin the publisher has a number of important studies and provides comprehensive coverage of the new local government structure in England and Wales. Of particular interest are Bryan Keith-Lucas and P.G. Richards, *A History of Local Government in the Twentieth Century* (London, Allen & Unwin, 1978) and Noel Hepworth, *The Finance of Local Government*, rev. 4th ed. (London, Allen & Unwin, 1978).

Central government's relationships with local authorities are covered in J.A.G. Griffith, *Central Departments and Local Authorities* (London, Allen & Unwin, 1966).

The Diversity of the United Kingdom

A short introduction to the question of devolution is A.H. Birch, *Political Integration and Disintegration in the British Isles* (London, Allen & Unwin, 1977). Tam Dalyell, *Devolution – The End of Britain?* (London, Cape, 1977), though written from a distinctly hostile perspective, contains much interesting information and is a forceful presentation of the argument against constitutional change. The best general discussion is that by Vernon Bogdanor in his *Devolution* (O.U.P., 1979).

Ireland

The best introductions to modern Irish politics are F.S.L. Lyons, *Ireland Since the Famine*, 2nd ed. (London, Collins/Fontana, 1973) and Richard Rose, *Governing Without Consensus*

(London, Faber, 1971). Richard Rose, *Northern Ireland: a Time for Choice* (London, Macmillan, 1976) covers the period between 1970 and 1975. The impact of the strike on Ulster politics is the subject of R. Fisk's study, *The Point of No Return* (London, Deutsch, 1975).

The constitution of Northern Ireland prior to the suspension of Stormont can be found in H. Calvert, *Constitutional Law in Northern Ireland* (London, Stevens, 1968). Relations between Church and state in Ireland receive comprehensive treatment in J.H. Whyte, *Church and State in Modern Ireland 1923–1970* (London, Macmillan, 1971).

The role of the Irish Republican Army is covered in J. Bowyer Bell, *The Secret Army* (London, Blond, 1970) and the period after 1970 is partially covered in G. Styles, *Bombs Have No Pity* (London, Luscombe, 1975). On the campaign on the mainland see Brian Gibson, *The Birmingham Bombs* (London, Rose, 1976).

Scotland

J. Kellas, *The Scottish Political System*, 2nd ed. (C.U.P., 1975) is a stimulating introduction to Scottish government and politics which takes into account the distinctive features of Scottish institutions and does not regard them as a pale imitation of English institutions.

D. Walker, *The Scottish Legal System*, 4th ed. (Edinburgh, Green, 1976) is useful.

Wales

The best historical introduction is D. Williams, *A History of Modern Wales*, 2nd ed. (London, John Murray, 1977). Ken Morgan, *Wales in British Politics*, rev. ed. (Cardiff, University of Wales Press, 1970) is also extremely useful. A. Butt Phillip, *The Welsh Question* (Cardiff, University of Wales Press, 1975) provides a comprehensive examination of Welsh nationalism since 1945.

The Legal Order and Civil Liberties

The structure of the English and Welsh legal system is described in R. M. Jackson, *The Machinery of Justice in England*, 7th ed. (C.U.P., 1977). Also of use as a competent and straightforward introduction is R.J. Walker and M.G. Walker, 4th ed. *The English Legal System* (London, Butterworth, 1976). B. Abel-Smith and Robert Stevens, *Lawyers and the Courts* (London, Heinemann, 1970) puts the law in historical and social perspective. Studies of individual courts can be found in L. Blom Cooper and G. Drewry, *Final Appeal* (O.U.P., 1972).

A critical appraisal of the current organization of legal services can be found in M. Zander, *Lawyers and the Public Interest* (London, Weidenfeld & Nicolson, 1968).

The machinery of law enforcement and the penal system is covered in R. M. Jackson, *Enforcing the Law* (London, Penguin, 1972), which may be supplemented by N. Walker, *Sentencing in a Rational Society* (London, Allen Lane, 1969). Very little of political interest has been written on the contemporary British police force. Jenifer Hart, *The British Police* (London, Allen & Unwin, 1951) provides a useful survey and G. Marshall, *Police and Government* (London, Methuen, 1965) raises some questions about accountability which remain relevant.

The impact of immigration and the police handling of race relations is treated in J. Lambert, *Crime, Police and Race Relations* (O.U.P., 1970) and in rather different vein in D. Humphrey, *Police Power and Black People* (London, Panther, 1972). Also of interest are M. E. Cain, *Society and the Policeman's Role* (London, Routledge & Kegan Paul, 1973) and T. Bunyon, *The History and Practice of the Political Police in Britain* (London, Friedmann, 1976).

Two works dealing with different aspects of the growth of violence in Britain are R. Clutterbuck, *Britain in Agony* (London, Faber, 1978) and Stuart Hall *et al.*, *Policing the Crisis* (London, Macmillan, 1978).

Civil liberties are discussed in H. Street, *Freedom, the Individual and the Law*, 4th ed. (London, Penguin, 1977) and in the National Council for Civil Liberties, *Civil Liberty: The NCCL Guide to Your Rights*, 3rd ed. (London, Penguin, 1978).

The interconnection between the legal and political systems

is explored in G. Drewry, *Law, Justice and Politics* (London, Longman, 1975) and in T.C. Hartley and J.G. Griffith, *Government and Law* (London, Weidenfeld & Nicolson, 1975). J.G. Griffith, *The Politics of the Judiciary* (London, Fontana, 1977) is a controversial account of the personnel of the bench.

On the question of whether or not Britain should introduce a bill of rights see F. Stacey, *A New Bill of Rights for Britain* (London, David & Charles, 1973). On the Official Secrets Acts see D. Williams, *Not in the Public Interest* (London, Hutchinson, 1965). On the theory of open government and the extent to which it has been implemented see G. Wraith, *Open Government* (London, RIPA, 1977).

The Control of Government and the Redress of Grievances

On the ombudsman or Parliamentary Commissioner the most comprehensive work is R. Gregory and P.G. Hutchesson, *The Parliamentary Ombudsman* (London, Allen & Unwin, 1975). B. Schwartz and H.W.R. Wade, *Legal Control of Government* (O.U.P., 1972) puts the subject in comparative Anglo-American perspective. The most detailed work on judicial review is S.A. de Smith, *Judicial Review of Administrative Action*, 3rd ed. (London, Stevens, 1973).

Tribunals and inquiries are covered in two useful publications by the Royal Institute of Public Administration – R.E. Wraith and P.G. Hutchesson, *Administrative Tribunals* (London, Allen & Unwin, 1973) and R.E. Wraith and G.B. Lamb, *Public Inquiries as Instruments of Government* (London, Allen & Unwin, 1971). Also of interest is J. Farmer, *Tribunals and Government* (London, Weidenfeld & Nicolson, 1974).

A general survey of the possible methods of redress is to be found in K.C. Wheare, *Maladministration and its Remedies* (London, Stevens, 1973).

The Limits of Independence

Apart from the important work by William Wallace, already referred to, there has been little of consequence written on the management of British foreign policy since M. Beloff, *New Dimensions in Foreign Policy* (London, Allen & Unwin, 1961). Useful, however, is R. Boardman and A.J.R. Groom (eds), *The Management of Britain's External Relations* (London, Macmillan, 1973). Much of interest can be found in the journal *International Affairs* and in the other publications of the Royal Institute of International Affairs.

Index

428

)